FORGED THROUGH FIRE

Forged
Through
Fire

War, Peace, and the
Democratic Bargain

JOHN FEREJOHN

and

FRANCES McCALL ROSENBLUTH

LIVERIGHT PUBLISHING CORPORATION
A Division of W. W. Norton & Company
Independent Publishers Since 1923
New York | London

For information about permission to reproduce selections from this book,
write to Permissions, Liveright Publishing Corporation, a division of
W. W. Norton & Company, Inc., 500 Fifth Avenue, New York, NY 10110

For information about special discounts for bulk purchases, please contact
W. W. Norton Special Sales at specialsales@wwnorton.com or 800-233-4830

Manufacturing by Quad Graphics
Book design by Dana Sloan
Production managers: Julia Druskin and Anna Oler

ISBN: 978-1-63149-160-3

Liveright Publishing Corporation
500 Fifth Avenue, New York, N.Y. 10110
www.wwnorton.com

W. W. Norton & Company Ltd.
15 Carlisle Street, London W1D 3BS

1 2 3 4 5 6 7 8 9 0

We dedicate this book to the next generation,
for whom we hope there will be
more democracy and less war
(Penelope, Simon, Finnie, Moe, Alistair, Ben, John, and William . . .)

CONTENTS

LIST OF ILLUSTRATIONS

FORGED THROUGH FIRE

INTRODUCTION

H UMANS HAVE INFLICTED untold horrors on each other through wars of aggression and preemptive defense. While the death tolls from history's ten deadliest wars add up to over 300 million people, it is impossible to count the shattered lives of survivors, the obliterated civilizations, the destroyed economies. But from the ashes and rubble new kinds of civilizations and economies have emerged, ones that are sometimes more advanced than what came before. What kind of alchemy of iron and blood, then, accounts for the fact that wars have also been responsible for some of the biggest franchise expansions in human history?[1] For example, the historian Alexander Keyssar traces the growth of voting rights in the United States from the Revolution through subsequent wars.[2] Göran Therborn notes that national wartime mobilization seems to have hastened suffrage expansions in Denmark in 1849, Germany in 1871, Norway in 1898, Finland against the tsar in 1906, and Austria in 1907, and that World War I prodded the extension of the franchise in Italy, Canada, Belgium, and Britain.[3]

The short answer to the question of how war can promote the cause of democracy is simple: during wartime, when governments are desperate for manpower to help them fight more effectively, they may be forced to pay more attention to the common man.

The contemporary form of democracy with which we are so familiar—representative democracy that combines universal suffrage with property protection—emerged only recently, in the nineteenth and twentieth centuries, and in very specific historical circumstances. The Industrial Revolution

gave rise to the working class, whose combined power terrified not only conservative landowners but also antimonarchical liberals in the explosions of
labor unrest in the 1830s and 1840s. Were it not for the Napoleonic Wars,
which stoked genuine bottom-up nationalism, these splintered societies
might have remained mired in internal discord. Crucially for the creation
of modern democracy, nationalism was potent enough to mobilize mass
support for war, but not so intoxicating as to enable war-fighting capacity
without franchise concessions to the common man. In this sense, nationalist
mobilization had to build upon class cleavages to produce large, well-funded
armies that outcompeted their rivals.

Given the all-out effort needed to fight and win wars, it is no coincidence
that some of the most successful military powers in the world today embody
the compromise adopted between the working poor and the economic elite:
legal and political checks against at-will redistribution of wealth by electoral
majorities. Legislatures, one step removed from the masses who vote them
into office, have created laws and fostered norms that protect property rights.
The modern democracies that took shape in the United States, the United
Kingdom, and France in the nineteenth century gave property holders various ways to control democratic impulses, principally through representation
that allowed for lobbying behind closed doors, and de facto control of suffrage by making it hard or expensive for the poor to vote.[4]

Today the preponderance of world military power—over 60 percent
of military budgets in 2014—belongs to modern democracies that have in
one way or another bridged the natural animosity between the elite and the
masses. In the twentieth century Hitler and Stalin demonstrated not only
that coercion and jingoism can mobilize without making democratic concessions but that national solidarity based on fear alone is harder to maintain in
peacetime. Authoritarian regimes of various stripes routinely pay democracy
unintended homage by calling themselves democratic, representative, and "of
the people" and by sponsoring elections on a wide franchise with large turn-
outs. Universal obeisance to international norms of self-governance requires
parading elements of democracy and masking repression.[5] Warfare appears
to have been instrumental in brokering the modern democratic compromise
between wealth and manpower, and although democracies tend not to fight
other democracies, they have tended to win the wars they do engage in.[6]

Like the fantasy of science fiction writers that intergalactic threats will someday unite all peoples of the world into harmonious cooperation against a common enemy, perhaps democracy would have emerged everywhere on earth if interstate competition had been over some threshold of inefficiency-eliminating ferocity. Earthly wars have been more haphazard and uneven than that apocalyptic scenario conjures up. Interstate competition in successive maelstroms of war was fierce enough to create the nation-state, but not so fierce as to advance the interests of the general public in many countries by eliminating every inefficient form of statehood in the world. Militarily inefficient nondemocracies can sometimes survive with other strategies, ranging from accommodation to bluster on the international front and from feel-good nationalism to repression at home.[7] As proof, twenty-first-century governments come in a cornucopia of garden varieties, from saber-rattling dictatorships of every size and shape to armed democracies and neutral democracies.

In addition to seeing that wars do not necessarily increase popular representation, we must also recognize that there are other paths to democracy besides wars. This is particularly relevant in today's world, when the wizardry of military technology can eclipse rank-and-file soldiery. When armies no longer need flesh and blood, what can take their place to stabilize democracy? To the degree that the modern democratic form evolved in an environment of manpower-intensive fighting that no longer characterizes warfare today, democratic populations should be alert to a slackening of pressure on governments to be accountable to the citizenry. Some unsettling corollaries follow from this line of reasoning: Might modern democracy no longer be best suited to winning wars? If a case can be made that democracy is not optimal for war fighting but is nevertheless desirable for the sake of protecting the greatest good of the greatest number, how might citizens adapt and adjust their political institutions to ensure that wars and threats of wars do not erode political accountability?

By almost any measure we can agree on today, elections are a better way to hold governments accountable than sit-down strikes on the battlefield. For one thing, the war-democracy link has historically valorized manly power and courage rather than the whole range of human concerns of which women are a full complement. Athens' all-male assembly included the fisherfolk and farmers who rowed the warships while excluding the wives, mothers, and sisters of even the richest men. After the first year of Athens' long war with

Sparta, Pericles sought to comfort the families of the war dead by remind-
ing them of the Athenian principle that "the noblest citizens are enlisted in
the service of the state," a principle that excluded women from establishing
public virtue.[8] The recent divorce between warfare and democracy affords
a welcome opportunity to consider whether current democratic institutions
are sufficient for the job and to devise necessary supplements to monitor and
motivate political representatives.

We also take note that war can simultaneously push in the opposite
direction, when fearful populations cede to their governments extraordinary
powers to act against their enemies even at the cost of civil liberties. The British and American governments during wartime have often ridden roughshod on the habeas corpus right against illegal imprisonment and the right
to a speedy and fair trial, and the U.S. population continues to debate the
boundaries of appropriate authority that Congress ceded to the executive in
the USA Patriot Act of 2001. Democracy's fragility in wartime is the canary
in the coal mine, warning us not to rely on the ancient vice of human aggression to protect the rights and liberties that all citizens of modern democracy
have come to take for granted.

The ancient Greeks were right: designing a constitution to promote the
common good is tricky business. They recognized that the rich and powerful in any society—the aristocrats—have a chance to protect their privileges
if they can prevent anyone among themselves from currying favor with the
masses. Members of the general public, outside the charmed circle, want
more money and power for themselves and would follow any political leader
who would cater to that wish.[9] Like any cartel, an aristocracy's rules that
protect the status quo by disallowing pandering to the masses are vulnerable
to cheating. An ambitious leader can catapult himself to power by punching
through competition-limiting rules, buying himself a big following in
exchange for giving away a cut of the aristocracy's wealth and power. If he
really follows through, this might produce democracy; if he manages to
manipulate the population into gratitude and submission, he might be able
to install himself as dictator instead.

Plato (428 or 424 to 348 BC) noted that every form of government of
the "one, the few, and the many" had a pure and a corrupt form. Being
a purist at heart, he favored the improbable solution of a dictatorship by
public-spirited and wise philosophers. The more empirically minded Aris-

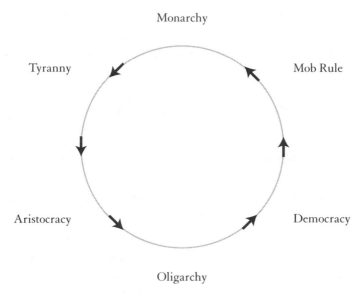

Monarchy

Tyranny

Mob Rule

Aristocracy

Democracy

Oligarchy

Anacyclosis: Polybius' cyclical theory of constitutional forms.

totle (384–22 BC) recommended government by the middle class, which was likely to have the most moderate interests; but failing that, he advised a "mixed government" that would combine the best elements of the various parts of society to counterbalance the corrupt forms that any one of those might take on its own.[10]

Polybius (200–118 BC), a Greek aristocrat held hostage in Rome to ensure Greek treaty compliance, is commonly credited with a cyclical theory of constitutional forms (anacyclosis)[11] that fused elements of Plato's and Aristotle's thought with observations of his own about the Roman Republic. Monarchy, Polybius reasoned, was vulnerable to tyranny. Aristocrats would then overthrow the tyrant, after which time the aristocracy would degrade into an oligarchy. Democrats would in turn overthrow the oligarchy, but democracy would itself devolve into mob rule.

With echoes of Aristotle, Polybius suggested getting off the cycle altogether by mixing elements of the one, the few, and the many. Extolling the virtues of Republican Rome to a Greek audience, Polybius wrote in *The Histories*, "The best and most useful aim of my work is to explain to my readers by what means and by virtue of what political institutions almost the whole world fell under the rule of one power, that of Rome, an event that is absolutely without parallel in earlier history."[12] Polybius describes how executive officials such as the consuls were elected by wealth-weighted classes of voters and were held in check by the aristocratic Senate and popularly elected tribune.[13]

Since Polybius' time, the long history of warfare in the Western world has effectively ranked constitutional forms by their ability to mobilize for war. Democracy heads the ranking in a form that Polybius would have called mixed government: modern representative democracy enshrines the dual principle of universal franchise, which empowers the general public, and property rights, which protect the rich from easy expropriation by political majorities.

But Polybius did not get everything right: he failed to predict that autocracies would historically surpass aristocracies in military strength. Since aristocracies bypass employing the manpower of the masses for military purposes in order to avoid making concessions to them, they can survive only in weakly competitive military environments. While states must develop the administrative capacity to tax, mobilize, train, and protect, having that capacity, as the distinction between democracies and autocracies shows, is not the same thing as having a political monopoly. Monarchies are militarily more effective than aristocracies only when they use their political monopoly to counteract the predatory behavior of economic elites. Kings were able to field armies of healthier and more grateful peasants if they

A hierarchy of constitutions by military capacity.

could get the nobility to give up the institution of serfdom that bound peasants in servitude.

Vulnerability to external threat puts pressure on governments to make constitutional deals with those who might be able to protect them. For example, farmers have from earliest times been likely to contract with autocrats for defense of their valuable livelihood against marauders.[14] Less vulnerable populations who enjoy the natural protections of mountains and water have enjoyed self-rule as long as they have not needed to trade away freedoms for security.[15] The "mountain republics" (or island republics) that the historian Fernand Braudel noticed in the Mediterranean world bear resemblance to the communities living outside state control in the "Zomia" hill country documented by the political scientist James Scott in Southeast Asia.[16] People living in the mountainous areas of southern China and northern Burma and Thailand have been able to evade political control for centuries. In mountains like those, "the heavens are high and the emperor is far away" as the Chinese have always said.[17]

But such freedom is tentative. Technological advances in transportation and engineering have sometimes lowered topographical barriers to invasion, bringing previously free peoples into subjugation. Technology is important to politics in a second sense as well. Once military technologies shift to those that favor manpower over money, the mass mobilization of manpower can upend the political privileges of the wealthy. Gun-toting armies spelled the end of aristocrats on horseback who had ruled feudal Europe. Although technology by itself never solely determines outcomes, it is an ever-changing dimension of warfare with consequences that are sometimes both large and surprising.

The relatively small number of modern states fighting wars at any given time makes it notoriously hard to generate and defend empirical claims about international politics with confidence. Expanding the number of cases by exploring large swaths of history helps, but our inquiry requires understanding the historical specifics of military threat: the types of players who make up the state, the ones that are potentially available to fight, and their level of vulnerability given their terrain and the military technologies available to them with which to fend off their enemies. Low levels of threat have produced relatively low levels of political centralization, ranging from democracy to some form of "mixed government" in which the aristocracy retained a political role. Greater vulnerability undermined aristocracies in favor of autocracy.

Autocracies, in their turn, often fell in direct contests against democracies in which both money and manpower were more fully mobilized.

For admirers of democracy, the most sobering lesson from history is that there is no linear and assured process toward an ever-more perfect system of government. As Tolstoy might have said, everything has to line up just right to get a healthy democracy started, but there are many ways for democracy to fail.[18] Athens was much smaller than Macedonia, which overran it with bigger armies. Democracies can also collapse from within, once the pressure to mobilize recedes: the Dutch Republic ended its brief fling with democracy in the sixteenth century after the public helped throw off the Habsburg overlords, and seventeenth-century Sweden retreated into economic and political elitism when it failed to expand southward during the Thirty Years' War. A democracy that rests on military capability is not a secure democracy.

That's the theory, and it can also be witnessed in the Greeks' cycle of constitutions rolling through an evolutionary gauntlet that rewards the fittest. As with species on earth, some governments have settled into niches that keep them off the front lines of competition. But just as the evolution of the species is not linear in any predictable way, neither is the evolution of the state. If states can change the environment in which they compete for survival, the nature of the state itself faces new evolutionary pressures. Humans may be just as capable of creating a toxic environment for constitutional evolution as they are of destroying the physical environment of the earth through runaway greenhouse emissions.

Chapter One

THE TWENTY-FIRST-CENTURY WARS

WITHOUT CITIZEN ARMIES

There Is No Indispensable Man

Sometime when you're feeling important;
Sometime when your ego's in bloom
Sometime when you take it for granted
You're the best qualified in the room,
Sometime when you feel that your going
Would leave an unfillable hole,
Just follow these simple instructions
And see how they humble your soul;
Take a bucket and fill it with water,
Put your hand in it up to the wrist,
Pull it out and the hole that's remaining
Is a measure of how you will be missed.

—SAXON N. WHITE KESSINGER, 1959

WHEN SANDRA DAY O'CONNOR stepped down from the Supreme Court in 2006, she used this poem to deflect exclamations of her indispensability.[1] In its folksy way, it captures a deep truth about impermanence. It is worth asking, for example: What becomes of Afghanistan and Iraq when U.S. forces pull out? This chapter addresses questions even closer to home. What becomes of democracy when warfare replaces manpower with money? Do mechanized militaries make worse decisions once the public has less at stake? If drones are to the twenty-first century what cavalry was to the Middle Ages, does the place of the common man in politics inevitably weaken? What does society need to do to ensure democracy's survival in a capital-intensive age?

Recent American wars in Vietnam and in Afghanistan/Iraq are alike in that the United States did not achieve its intended goals of democratization, prosperity, and peace in the respective regions. At least in the short run, however, one perceptible difference between the two was that President George W. Bush managed to stay in power after the Iraq War turned sour, whereas the Vietnam War so damaged President Lyndon B. Johnson by 1968 that he did not even run for his party's nomination for a second term.

Vietnam cost far more American lives.[2] After a roaring start, the United States did not end the Iraq War in a matter of weeks as promised, let alone the Afghanistan War. But the 900 American servicemen who had died in Iraq by November 2004 were far fewer than the 3,000 American civilians who died when terrorists crashed airliners into the Twin Towers and the Pentagon on September 11, 2001, and far fewer still than the 58,000 American servicemen who died in Vietnam. Moreover, although the United States paid more for the Afghanistan and Iraq wars than it did for Vietnam, counted in 2016 dollars, it paid for Iraq with increases in government debt, which took out the financial sting at least temporarily.[3]

If Iraq was a diversionary tactic to buoy the president's sagging popularity, it had only the fleeting effect that is typical in American politics.[4] The American public rallied around the flag at the war's onset but had settled into a kind of mild repugnance by election time. By then Bush's popularity was down to 45 or 50 percent, unimpressive but enough to get him over the finish line.[5]

As the Bush-Johnson comparison illustrates, voters are less intent on stopping wars in which their own kin do not die, however much destruction may be wrought and how many lives lost in foreign lands. Not only is this terrifying for non-Americans who may be at the other end of these operations,[6] it also leads to bad foreign policy bets that American voters eventually pay for. Congressman Charles Rangel (D-NY), writing after the 9/11 attacks set the United States on the warpath, captured this insight when he advocated bringing back the military draft. "I believe," he said, "that if those calling for war knew that their children were likely to be required to serve—and to be placed in harm's way—there would be more caution and a greater willingness to work with the international community in dealing with Iraq. A renewed draft will help bring a greater appreciation of the consequences of decisions to go to war."[7]

Understandably, the draft is not a popular institution. Who wants to put their husbands, children, and brothers in harm's way? But the fact that citizens hold their lives dear, and that they get to decide which wars to fight, probably makes democracies potent war machines. Democracies have won three out of every four wars they have fought since 1815.[8] The reason is likely rooted in political accountability: democratically elected leaders are more careful to choose wars they can win because costly and unpopular wars will get them thrown out of office.

Johnson paying with his political career for Vietnam fits this rule of democratic accountability; Bush escaping culpability for Iraq does not.[9] Increased military mechanization (as measured by the number of men for every armored vehicle) raises the odds of military defeat against insurgency groups, since counterinsurgency rests on winning over local populations more than on inflicting physical destruction.[10] If American voters relax their foreign policy vigilance when their own blood is not on the line, is America bound for failed military adventurism when machines substitute for men?

In addition to an increased potential for bad foreign policy decisions, a second concern is the erosion of civil liberties at home. Habeas corpus, the right to challenge unlawful detention, has regularly been suspended during wartime and reinstated afterward in the United Kingdom and the United States.[11] Other rights, including free speech, are also routinely limited during mass conflicts. In 1919 Justice Oliver Wendell Holmes Jr. echoed English common law in response to antiwar protests during World War I: "When a nation is at war, many things that might be said in time of peace are such a hindrance to its effort that their utterance will not be endured so long as men fight and . . . no Court should regard them as protected by any constitutional right."[12] While not a new problem, the capping of civil protections for long periods compared to short wars could be more damaging to democratic habits of mind.[13] If America's "War on Terror" becomes perennial, will the desire for security place a permanent tax on freedom? Moreover, if the "War on Terror" entails finding and crushing the terrorists who may be living among us incognito, will our judicial attitudes begin to lean toward harshness?

The concern about the militarization of American values is real and not yet fully measured, but it is important to take regular stock of the facts.[14] A majority of citizens polled since the "War on Terror" began in 2001 consistently remain repulsed by the use of torture (electric shock, waterboarding, sexual humiliation, forced nudity, exposure to extreme heat and cold, punching, and kicking) even under extreme threat conditions, although majority opinion is more accepting of some "enhanced" interrogation techniques such as sleep deprivation, stress positions, and noise bombs.[15]

In the United States, the fact that elite opinion is unhappier than the general public about judicial and administrative shortcuts to keep out and deter terrorists may hint at bigger problems with unequal access to education and accurate information than the ability of the general public to express its views through the democratic process.[16] Gleaning information principally from media sources, the American public may not have gathered that most *military* officials polled believe that torture is *never* justified, given the poor quality of information that can be obtained that way, the hatred that it generates, and the PTSD that it causes for the soldiers performing it, to name just a few reasons.[17]

A third worry, the flip side of the fear of bad foreign policy decisions, is that machine-based warfare could fail to support the political power of the common man. Although civil liberties historically have languished during wars, the franchise has often expanded when governments desperately needed men to fight with vigor. In the almost infinite variations of warfare through human history, military threats are more conducive to democratic governance when geography provides natural protection from invasion (reducing the public's sense of vulnerability and of a need for central authority) and when military technology relies heavily on manpower (increasing the military value of the ordinary citizen). How different will a world of mercenary-fought, drone-assisted, debt-funded wars be from the one we have known thus far? Can modern democracy, a creature whose "environment of evolutionary adaptation" was incessant warfare, remain strong or, more optimistically, even become stronger under alien conditions of peace?

✦ ✦ ✦

Immanuel Kant's 1795 recipe for "Perpetual Peace" called, above all, for ridding the world of dictatorships. A dictator would be prone to military adventurism because he could grab the benefits of victory while foisting the costs of defeat onto his powerless subjects. As the despicable Lord Farquaad intoned to his soldiers in the 2001 movie *Shrek,* "Many of you will lose your lives in this war, but that is a price I am willing to pay." A democratic population making its own decisions about war and peace may also choose to fight if it expects to come out ahead from the war, but at least its collective decision will be based on the expected costs and benefits of fighting.

Even dictatorships fear overthrow by internal rivals who can mobilize the aggrieved. Not surprisingly, governments have typically preferred mercenary to conscript armies, if they could afford them, to avoid incurring blood debts to their subjects.[18] In the absence of such resources, governments faced a choice: mobilize a citizens' army even if it meant granting new political concessions (as King Gustavus Adolphus did in Sweden during the Thirty Years' War), or use coercion to require subjects to fight (as France and Spain did in their sixteenth-century wars of conquest and as many of the world's governments of the twentieth and twenty-first centuries continue to do).

At the end of the fifteenth century in Florence, Machiavelli built a citizens' militia to fight Pisa and defend the city against the Spanish and Imperial armies, even though mobilizing citizens to fight could be dangerous to the Florentine oligarchy.[19] He had some sense, though the view was not widely shared, that Florence's survival against powerful enemies with national armies, such as those of France and Spain, would require not only a local militia but also an expanded franchise to embolden and empower it.[20] Machiavelli's experiment, if that is what he had in mind, was never tried on the pan-Italian scale that would have been needed to defend against the enormous French and Spanish armies.

The citizens of many modern democracies also seem content to hire volunteer and mercenary armies to avoid paying the blood costs of national security. Even better, machines can do much of the work of soldiers and armies. In response to a hypothetical question involving attacking a terrorist stronghold, the average American citizen prefers the use of air strikes to the use of ground troops.[21] If all went well, voters could, through their political representatives, direct military commanders and their armies and weaponry in all matters of war and death. Unfortunately, popular sovereignty loses some traction in these long chains of command and accountability. If voting publics no longer bear the costs of war, measured painfully in blood and taxes, their representatives feel less urgency in second-guessing their generals' recommendations. However differently autocrats and democracies come by their paid soldiers, the results could be more similar than we would like to think: a drift toward military incaution.

Democracies can, of course, abandon the draft as a way to reduce the costs of war to their citizens, and many democratic countries did just that in the twentieth century, as the Cold War wound down. Aside from Germany and Japan, which were forcibly demobilized following World War II, Canada quickly dropped the draft in 1945. Britain held on to a pared-down National Service until 1960 to protect the empire.[22] Australia and New Zealand sent troops to Vietnam but ended the draft during the domestic uproar over the war in 1972.[23] The United States modified the Selective Service in 1968 in response to public outrage over the Vietnam War and ended conscription altogether in 1973.[24] Still others—France, Italy, Spain, Belgium, and the Netherlands—ended national mandatory conscription after the Berlin Wall came down, and most of Europe anchored itself to a new security system centered on NATO. In 1997 Spain's Partido Popular won an absolute legislative majority on an election campaign to end conscription.[25] Eastern European countries that embraced electoral democracy also abandoned the draft and sought NATO membership in the 1990s and 2000s. Sweden ended its national conscription in 2010 while Denmark and Norway continued to debate whether to retain their systems of national conscription armies within the NATO framework. Whereas during the twentieth-century wars of full mobilization, the draft had supplied the manpower to match large opposing armies, the post–Cold War world was pockmarked with insurgencies, better handled with smaller, more professionalized, and more flexible forces. As the military commands of many countries saw the problem, the costs of mass conscription, including uproars over lives lost and questions raised about ends and means, were not worth paying.[26]

A few western European democracies—Austria, Finland, and Switzerland—maintained a stance of "militarized nonalignment" through the Cold War, protected only by their own national conscription armies in which all males of military age participate as members of a national reserve that can be called up swiftly if necessary. Switzerland, for example, has a reserve force thirteen times the size of its active-duty military.[27]

As we would expect, the number of men in uniform per capita is discernibly lower in countries without the draft. France has 6.4 servicemen for every thousand citizens, Britain 6.3, Germany 4, Italy 5.8, Sweden 5.5, Spain 4.7, and the United States 7.9.[28] Compare this to democracies with national conscription: Denmark has 14.6 servicemen for every thousand citizens, Norway 14.9, Finland 74, Switzerland 26.5, Israel 79.2, South Korea 103.6, and Taiwan 85.5. Austria, a more or less demilitarized country with a latent conscription system, looks more like a country with a voluntary army, with 6.5 servicemen for every thousand citizens. Of course strategic factors are at play as well.[29] Countries with insurgencies and with militarized neighbors tend to have disproportionately large conscription armies.[30]

It is impossible to think about twenty-first-century democratic warfare without acknowledging the vast place taken by the United States in all things military. U.S. government spending on national defense, after the twentieth-century peaks of 20 percent of GDP during World War I and 40 percent during World War II, has waned to 5–6 percent in the twenty-first century.[31] Because of the enormous size of the U.S. economy, that modest-sounding number as a proportion of GDP amounts to about 40 percent of the world's military expenditures. European countries, taken together, account for 20

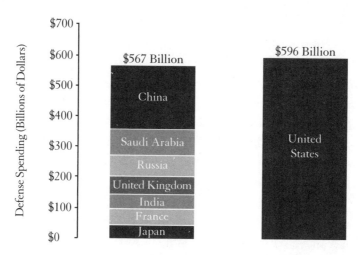

The United States spends more on defense than the next seven countries combined.

percent; China and Russia each spend about 10 or 11 percent of the world's total. All of the rest of the world—Africa, Asia, the Middle East, and the Americas—account for the remaining one-quarter or so of global spending on national security.

Of total U.S. defense spending, technology has increased its share relative to manpower. A pillar of President Dwight D. Eisenhower's commitment to getting "more bang for the buck" was the Defense Advanced Research Projects Agency (DARPA), which he established in 1958. Eisenhower amalgamated Roosevelt's smaller National Defense Research Council and the Office of Science Research and Development under the DARPA tent to harness scientific innovation for national security.[32] In the consultant-speak of McKinsey & Co., the military can "streamline logistics [with] the wholesale reconfiguration of facilities and processes, which typically reduces the number of echelons and facilities and increases industrial involvement."[33] The more colorful language of Secretary of Defense Robert Gates in 2011—"health care costs are eating the Defense Department alive"—alludes to the ongoing budgetary pressure to shift from men to machines and from regular employees to subcontractors.[34]

Since the end of the draft, the United States has increased expenditures on equipment relative to personnel.[35] One striking example of the substitution of equipment for men is the use of unmanned aerial vehicles (drones) in Afghanistan, Iraq, and Pakistan, up from 25,000 flight-hours in 2002 to 625,000 in 2011.[36]

Another way to reduce the reliance on citizen-soldiers is to hire civilian contractors, including foreign personnel. The portion of the defense budget allocated to subcontractors—for everything from research and development in the high-tech defense sector to personnel safeguarding and equipment maintenance in combat locations—rivals the portions spent on official military personnel and on equipment.[37] Much of the Defense Department's subcontracting is to firms in the United States for research, base support services, and equipment development and manufacture. One megacontractor, Science Applications International Corporation (SAIC), established in 1969 in McLean, Virginia, had 44,000 workers in 2013 courtesy of government contracts amounting to $13.6 billion. The attractions to the government are obvious: because SAIC employees are not government employees, the company can hire and fire them depending on the flow of contracts from the

Department of Defense, the Department of Homeland Security, and other government agencies.[38]

Military contractors, in staggering numbers, also provide a wide array of services for U.S. government operations abroad. Between 2002 and 2011, the government spent $192 billion in contracts and grants in support of operations in Afghanistan and Iraq.[39] The vast majority of the contracted services were performed by foreign employees: in 2010 in Afghanistan and Iraq alone, the U.S. government had more than 260,000 contractor employees, over 80 percent of whom were citizens of Iraq or Afghanistan.[40]

The Geneva Conventions of the International Committee of the Red Cross of 1949, as periodically revised, bar the employment of private actors in combat positions in efforts to hold combatant countries accountable for the actions and treatment of individual soldiers.[41] The United States, though not a signatory to the subsequent agreements about mercenaries, unofficially bars civilians from serving in explicitly combat roles.[42] In practice, however, some supporting roles make virtual soldiers out of civilian employees: gathering military intelligence, building and guarding infrastructure, transporting fuel and equipment, de-mining and destroying explosives, and training and supporting police.[43] Private security companies now typically guard U.S. diplomats and embassies, including the diplomatic post in Benghazi that militants attacked on September 11, 2012.[44]

Although most private contractors perform their jobs valorously and without incident, a few have dramatically drawn attention to questionable accountability. A number of the interrogators, interpreters, and guards involved in the torture of Abu Ghraib prisoners were not soldiers but civilians and therefore were excluded from the purview of the Geneva Conventions governing the conduct of war.[45] In response to public outrage against assorted failures including Abu Ghraib, a congressional study recommended discontinuing some kinds of high-security, high-risk guard services.[46] Meanwhile the Justice Department leveled a criminal charge against a Blackwater Security contractor who killed seventeen people while protecting a diplomatic convoy in a traffic jam in Nisour Square, Baghdad.[47]

Subcontracting to private companies, at least in the short run, economizes on two kinds of costs for the government: financial and political. Private contract workers are paid less on average because most are foreign nationals with lower-than-U.S. wages; the rest are contract workers without the employment protections and benefits of full-time government employees. Domestic political costs are also lower, because the deaths of private citizens, particularly of foreign nationals, are less likely to galvanize domestic political opposition to war. The American public recoils episodically at gratuitous violence, as in the uproar over Abu Ghraib or civilian casualties in drone strikes, but otherwise tunes out to the steady stockpiling of anti-American grievances in the countries where the country is engaged.

It is no mystery, then, that democracies may be reluctant to undertake unpopular wars, especially with citizen armies, and when they do get into unpopular wars, they resort wherever possible to mechanized and mercenary forces to reduce the burdens on their own populations. The United States and other democracies have struggled with how best to respond to perceived threats from the Middle East in the twenty-first century.

The 2001 U.S.-led NATO operation in Afghanistan had wind at its back, politically speaking. With worldwide support for the United States at an all-time high after the terrorist attacks on September 11, 2001, allies rallied to reclaim Afghanistan from the Taliban and the Al Qaeda groups to whom they provided refuge.[48] On October 7, the U.S.-led coalition targeted Al Qaeda training camps and military installations with air strikes and cruise missiles. A ground operation led by the Afghani Northern Alliance of ethnic minority groups and Hazara Shiites in subsequent months forced the Taliban and Al Qaeda to retreat to mountainous hideouts along the Pakistani border and in the Pashtun heartland in southern Afghanistan, from where they continued to fight as insurgents.[49]

Eighteen months later U.S. allies were less enthusiastic about invading Iraq, a mission ostensibly to obliterate Saddam Hussein's never-found "weapons of mass destruction."[50] The U.S. government, keen to appear multilateral for both domestic and diplomatic reasons, had spent busy months prior to April 2003 trying to build a "Coalition of the Willing," but Germany and France refused to participate without a UN Security Council mandate, which never materialized.[51] Václav Havel of the Czech Republic had a dilemma: he wanted to stay in the European orbit, but he felt obligated to support the United States in repayment for U.S. sponsorship for the Czech Republic's joining NATO in 1999. With a bare parliamentary majority and a skeptical public, he swung in favor of joining the Coalition of the Willing— but with only volunteer troops.[52]

Some observers began to call it the "Coalition of the Billing," as the United States spent millions on favors of various kinds to cajole allies into participating. It used every kind of carrot and stick: providing aid to Angola, Guinea, and the Philippines; concluding military training and arms deals with Bahrain, Qatar, Hungary, Poland, Kuwait, and the UAE; undertaking construction projects in Iraq to Bulgaria; opening markets to Cameroon, Chile, and Costa Rica; dropping hints about NATO membership for Estonia, Latvia, Lithuania, Macedonia, Romania, Slovakia, and Slovenia; supplying aid to Israel and Jordan; finalizing trade, trafficking, and immigration deals with Mexico; and offering debt forgiveness to Pakistan as well as aid and anti-insurgency help for the Philippines.[53] Of the countries that contributed troops to the initial invasion—the United States (150,000), United Kingdom (46,000), Australia (2,000), and Poland (200)—only Poland had a conscription army at the time, but new Polish legislation allowed only volunteers to participate in the invasion.[54] The additional thirty-seven countries in the coalition provided some troops in the ensuing months, entreated with gifts or threatened with American disfavor. Norway, a country with mandatory conscription, sent radars and other equipment in deference to domestic opposition to committing Norwegian soldiers.

Few conscripted soldiers from any country fought in Iraq, but even countries with voluntary forces began to withdraw in droves when "shock and awe" turned into shocking and awful.[55] Making good on his campaign promises to have nothing more to do with the war, Spain's Socialist prime minister José Zapatero pulled his country's contingent of 1,300 as soon as he was elected in March 2004;[56] many others followed suit.[57] By August 2009, at the end of the "surge," all coalition members aside from the United States and Britain had left Iraq. Still on the ground were 16,263 employees of private security companies, a number that swelled to 28,000 by 2010.

Sweden, which retained its national conscription system until 2010, did not participate in the war in Iraq at all, even after the center-right government came into office in October 2006. We know from WikiLeaks that the new prime minister Fredrik Reinfeldt explained to the U.S. ambassador Michael Wood that the Swedish people felt that the war in Iraq was "not working" but that Sweden would continue to help train local forces prepare for self-governance in Afghanistan.[58] Sweden ramped up its participation in the NATO-led International Security Assistance Force (ISAF) in Afghanistan in 2010, by no coincidence the same year Sweden abandoned national conscription.[59]

By 2014, over 3,500 soldiers had been killed in Afghanistan (of whom about 2,500 were Americans and nearly 500 were British) and about 5,000 in Iraq (of whom about 4,500 were Americans and 200 were British).[60] In addition, 1,500 contractors were killed in Iraq and 900 in Afghanistan.[61] Those contractors serving as armed guards and security personnel were 1.5 to 4.8 times more likely to be killed in Iraq or Afghanistan (respectively) than were U.S. uniformed soldiers.[62] Civilian contractors undertaking infrastructural work also came into the line of fire. One of the most tragic deaths was that of Nicholas Berg, a twenty-six-year-old small-time businessman from Pennsylvania who was kidnapped in Fallujah in May 2004, where he had gone in search of contracts to fix communications antennas. Five masked men filmed his execution, claiming revenge for American cruelty at Abu Ghraib. The video shows them pushing Berg, screaming, to the floor and decapitating him.[63]

The greatest costs of the war, however, were borne by the civilian populations of Afghanistan, Iraq, and Pakistan. According to Brown University's Costs of War project, over 20,000 civilians died in Afghanistan and 134,000 civilians died in Iraq following the American-led invasions of those countries.[64] Over a decade later, despite billions of dollars spent on infrastructure and rebuilding in both countries, access to food, clean water, education, and health care remained a challenge.[65]

The War on Terror rode roughshod on habeas corpus for noncitizens in the United States.[66] The War on Terror was no different from other wars in this respect, even those waged by democracies.[67] The Supreme Court historically has allowed the executive branch to detain suspects in time of war, within some limits: Congress must provide specific legislative authorization for each war, and Congress must offer an adequate substitute to habeas corpus that offers prisoners a meaningful opportunity to demonstrate that they are held pursuant to an erroneous application or interpretation of relevant law.[68] The Court's rulings have unleashed new rounds of legal wrangling about what constitutes "adequate substitutes" for trials in the civilian judicial system.[69]

Not surprisingly perhaps, habeas corpus is one of the first rights to go in wartime, especially when it comes to potential enemies in our midst. Democracies are not known for their generosity to unpopular minorities, and no one is less popular than possible terrorists. Apart from the moral unattractiveness of xenophobia, wiretapping and record-keeping raise the further question of how far democratic publics are willing to impinge on their *own* rights out of fear of foreigners under conditions of war, especially terrorist wars. If the twenty-first-century insurgency wars constitute a new evolutionary environment for the modern state, will xenophobia subvert domestic rights more broadly? Events are too recent to be a reliable guide, and evidence is mixed. Americans seem to have somewhat higher but still limited tolerance for government spying on American citizens.[70] If American citizens were currently fighting overseas in large numbers, one wonders if the Supreme Court in 2013 would have rejected Section 5 of the 1965 Voting Rights Act on grounds that civil rights are no longer precarious in the United States.[71] The abolition of the draft is a blessing we wished upon ourselves in 1972, but its disappearance could also mean that the rights of American citizens remain imperfectly and asymmetrically secured.

✦ ✦ ✦

Counted in American lives, the operations in Afghanistan and Iraq together cost 15 percent of those of Vietnam. The reputational cost was far more equal: within two years of 9/11, the outpouring of sympathy and support for the United States had evaporated. Public opinion toward the United States, especially in Muslim countries, was in free fall. Even among America's allies, the percentage of the population favorably disposed toward it slumped from 78 to 60 percent in Germany, from 83 to 75 percent in Britain, and from 79 to 50 percent in Poland. Obama's election was a public relations windfall for the United States, but the overwhelming view around the world was that the country had squandered its goodwill on high-cost, low-return conflicts in Afghanistan and Iraq.[72] World opinion goes so far as to blame the rise of ISIS, the Islamic State of Iraq and Syria, on American destabilization of the region's admittedly repugnant authoritarian regimes.

Apart from potential long-term damage to international reputation from bloody invasions, the shift to counterinsurgency wars cries out for scrutiny because of its domestic consequences. In centuries past, the temporary erosion of civil rights during wartime—including free speech and freedom from detention without trial—was often counterbalanced by extensions of the franchise to fighting men (and sometimes to the women who supported them). The manpower needs of warfare gave democracies a kind of built-in correction from the grassroots. Contrast this with the small number of cyberwarriors, volunteers all, who fight the counterinsurgency wars of today. No one wishes a return to wars of existential threat that require mass conscription and widespread death. But it is important to recognize that technological and geopolitical changes have removed a democratic check on government. Depending on how deeply accountability has eroded, democracies may consider reinstituting it through other means such as, for example, the requirement of a superlegislative majority before a government could set out on any warpath or dilute personal rights and protections. Short of that, Rangel may have been right to argue for bringing back the draft.

Part I

FROM
ANTIQUITY TO
MEDIEVAL TIMES

Chapter Two

WAR AND DEMOCRACY IN

CLASSICAL ATHENS

To UNDERSTAND WHEN WARFARE pushed in a democratizing direction and when it led instead to repression and central control, Athens in the fifth century BC is a good place to begin. The Greek notion of a cycle of constitutional forms, which Polybius had gleaned from Plato and Aristotle, captured something important about politics: that every conceivable system of government traded off some strengths for other weaknesses. Polybius' crystal ball seems to make out, in rough outlines, that democracies forged through centuries of war would tend to be big (at some cost to local autonomy) and indirectly democratic through representation (at some cost to individual engagement with politics).

Although the classical democracy of Athens in the fifth century BC with which we begin was by no means the world's first democracy—ancient self-governing tribes and villages long predated Athens—the strains of warfare shaped Athenian institutions in discernible ways that establish a benchmark against which to measure subsequent constitutional forms.

◆ ◆ ◆

"I shall stop you fornicating with the sea. She is mine!"[1] For Athens, this taunt from the Spartan admiral Callicratidas at the Battle of Arginusae in 406 BC, toward the end of the Peloponnesian War, was a wrenching reminder of how far Athens had fallen from its naval hegemony of the fifth century. It was not just a matter of wounded pride. Having reconfigured its economy from rural subsistence to trading entrepot, Athens was substantially dependent on food imports from lands along the Aegean, the Black Sea, and the Mediterranean.[2] Even with its rural hinterland in Attica, its ability to control sea-lanes through the Bosporus and through island narrows was of existential importance.

Prosperous and democratic, Athens had been the pearl of the Aegean. Its great port at Piraeus dominated trade and finance of the entire region. Its assembly of all male citizens, twenty years and older, presided over policy decisions, civil and military. Two decades of war against oligarchic Sparta, however, had left the city in a much-weakened state.

This Battle of Arginusae came on the heels of a series of calamities for Athens. After catastrophic losses to Sparta and its allies in 415 BC, when thousands of captured Athenian soldiers died of sunstroke and thirst in open mine pits in Sicily, the city struggled to reestablish its livelihood on trade; sea-lane control was still its principal foreign policy goal. The effort was made even more difficult without the tribute from erstwhile allies who had been willing to help fund the Athenian navy when Athenian hegemony had seemed unassailable. Athenian sailors had to supplement their income by selling their services as manual laborers while in port or by pillaging.

In one telling example, the Athenian general Alcibiades—proud, rich, and not entirely reliable—had been dispatched on a mission to protect trade through the Bosporus but without sufficient funds from public coffers to pay his men. His response was to go with most of his sailors to earn or take what they could along the coast of Asia Minor near Ephesus, leaving a fleet of triremes moored in a sheltered cove under the command of his steersman Antiochus. When a Spartan fleet passing by destroyed twenty-two of the docked Athenian ships, Alcibiades left with only one ship to a stronghold in the Sea of Marmara at the mouth of the Bosporus rather than return to Athens, where he knew he would have to face the wrath of the Athenian Assembly.[3]

Athens' greatest military challenge was to stop Sparta from destroying its naval power. Just before the Battle of Arginusae, the Athenian Assembly had elected the veteran admiral Conon to command a fleet of seventy triremes to intercept Spartan ships heading for the Bosporus and the Ionian coast. As it turned out, however, Sparta, with help from Persia as well as other allies, had

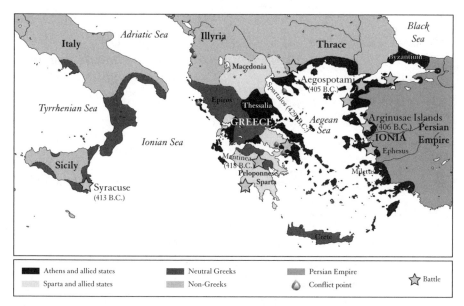

Naval battles in the Peloponnesian War.

mobilized a fleet twice that size. After getting trapped in the port of Mytilene, on the Aegean island of Lesbos, the Athenians prepared to fight for their lives. To amass a force capable of breaking the siege, the Athenian Assembly quickly took the extraordinary step of voting to extend citizenship to resident aliens and slaves who were willing to serve in the navy. Although Athenians had closely guarded their citizenship, they were desperate to compensate for the tens of thousands of Athenians who had died in the naval and land battles in the Peloponnesian War. The Assembly voted to melt down sacred images and other treasures into coins to pay for new ships, and it accepted gifts of timber from the kingdom of Macedonia that, with expansionist designs, had its own reasons for wanting to see Athens and Sparta at odds.[4]

Now with eighty additional ships under the command of eight elected generals, the Athenians prepared to challenge Sparta at sea near Mytilene with overwhelming force. Keeping close to the Arginusae islands, off the coast of today's Turkey, to make the best use of their inexperienced crews, the Athenians lured the Spartans into close combat in which they killed Callicratidas, the Spartan general who had taunted them. His death broke the morale of Sparta's allies, and in the ensuing rout, the Athenians lost 25 of their 150 ships against nine of Sparta's ten (only ten!) ships and more than 60 ships of Sparta's allies.[5] Arginusae was a spectacular win for Athens.

What followed the Athenian victory was one of the most bizarre sequences of events in recorded history. The Athenian generals—who by this time had valiantly broken through the blockade at Mytilene on their own—received urgent word from Athens to return home to explain why they had allowed so many sailors to perish at sea. A storm had impeded efforts to rescue shipwrecked sailors or (we don't know how many of the sailors were still alive) to pick up the war dead from the sea and beaches for proper burial at home.[6]

Six of the eight generals obeyed the summons to return to Athens; the other two, afraid of what the summons could mean, fled for their lives.[7] The generals defended themselves before the Council of Five Hundred, the Assembly's executive body, which was made up of fifty men from each of the ten tribes, and then before the Assembly, explaining their roles in the battle and describing the problems caused by the storm.

One of the generals' fiercest public critics was Theramenes, a ship commander at the Arginusae battle. He had been a leader of the 411 BC coup against Athenian democracy until he parted company with the narrowest oligarchs and was subsequently restored to citizenship when the Assembly reestablished popular rule. When Theramenes spoke out against the Arginusae generals, the generals declared that they had assigned the rescue operations to him and another ship commander, Thrasybulus. The Assembly heard arguments on both sides, but stunningly, at least from our vantage point today, it tried and *executed* the six generals for taking too lightly their responsibility to the Athenian citizens who were their sailors, alive or dead.[8]

The execution of Athens' most experienced generals set the stage, many historians argue, for the catastrophic defeat of its navy just months later by the Spartans at Aegospotami in 405 BC.[9] To be fair to Athens, much of Sparta's advantage came from Persian support, putting the city in an impossible situation. But observers throughout the ages have seized upon Assembly decisions such as this, which appeared rash in hindsight even to the Assembly itself, to disparage the very foundations of Athenian democracy. Apart from the damage it inflicted on individual lives, the Assembly's rashness possibly instilled in Athenian generals perverse incentives to take unreasonable risks with disastrous results, as when some years earlier, according to Thucydides,[10] the Athenian general Nicias refused to stage a strategic retreat upon defeat by Spartan forces in Sicily in 415.

The reason to begin an exploration of Athenian politics with the calamity of Arginusae in 406 BC, so late in the history of war and democracy in Athens, is that it throws into high relief our two central themes: the effects of the Athenian institutions of governance on the quality of decisions about warfare and everything else; and conversely, the way Athens' naval warfare shaped the political institutions themselves. Because the verdict against Athenian democracy is blind to the weaknesses of nondemocracies like Persia or Sparta, an evaluation of alternative decision-making structures is only fair. The Athenians' own experimentation in institutional design, sometimes in response to military threats, provides much grist for this analysis.

Holding periodic public meetings in the central square had been a common practice in Greek polities from Homeric times. At a minimum, fighting-age men were expected to gather for military mobilization when the city-state came under threat. Even Sparta had a popular assembly, although it was an echo chamber for the kings and elders who had the right to overturn "crooked" decisions.[11] Athens was not unusual in having an assembly, but its assembly became unusually powerful.

Athenian democracy was preceded by pan-Hellenic clashes between the landed elite and the poor farmers who worked the land. Although precise information is scant, the great Athenian military and political leader Solon appears to have responded to peasant upheavals in 594 BC by eliminating indentured servitude and reopening public lands. He lowered the penalty for theft from death to double the value of the item stolen if it was recovered, ten times if it was not. He also introduced limited elections: wealth-qualified male citizens in each of four tribes would elect ten candidates for executive office, and from these forty, nine executives would be drawn by lot. Solonic reforms were far-going in their day, but some scholars have wondered if the Solonic debt reforms made it harder for the peasants to get credit, for there were new revolts in subsequent years and a coup by the populist dictator Peisistratus, who ruled Athens for thirty-one years.[12] The anonymous antidemocratic historian sometimes known as the "Old Oligarch" or "pseudo Xenophon," who wrote the *Athenaion Politeia* in the fifth century BC, claimed that the public supported Peisistratus in those predemocracy days because he took the side of poor farmers against the rich. This suggests that a deep class divide continued to fester after Solon's time.[13]

The full-fledged democracy that made Athens famous was born when

Cleisthenes, the scion of an exiled aristocratic family, transformed elite rivalry into patriotic self-defense. It all started, the Old Oligarch suggests, because the sons of Peisistratus (who had died in about 527 BC) had forged an alliance with the city of Argos, on the Peloponnesian peninsula, that threatened Sparta, the peninsula's dominant city. Cleomenes, king of Sparta, marched into Attica with a hoplite force, defeated the Peisistratus dynasty, and restored Athens to aristocratic rule in 510 BC. But the rivalrous aristocratic families of Athens could not settle on a power-sharing arrangement among themselves, and when one aristocratic Athenian family invited Sparta back to Athens two years later to help defeat another, the losing side played its strongest card: populism. Cleisthenes, of the Alcmeonid family, promised to turn political power over to the Athenian public in exchange for their help in repelling Spartan intervention. The people of Athens—one pictures them equipped with ordinary farm implements—besieged the Spartans and their Athenian allies in the Acropolis for two days and were poised to win. On the third day, when the Spartans sued for peace, the Athenian peasant army agreed to let them leave, along with the Athenian aristocrats who had holed up with them.[14]

Cleisthenes, now the leader of a newly mobilized Athenian public, made good on his side of the bargain.[15] A public assembly, in which all male citizens over the age of twenty could participate, would now be the principal governing body of Athens. The Assembly met at least forty times a year to debate matters of public concern and to pass decrees on specific policy issues.[16] Anyone who attended the Assembly was permitted to speak, although speaking to a body of 5,000 to 8,000 assembled citizens was not for the faint-hearted.[17] During the fifth century BC, it is likely that there were 30,000 to 40,000 adult male citizens in a resident population of 300,000 to 350,000.[18] Because Athens was a long walk from the far reaches of Attica, only one in five citizens might have turned out to participate in the Assembly on any given day.[19]

Establishing a citizens' army was one of the first orders of business for Cleisthenes, who owed his ascendency to popular support. He created ten "tribes" in the place of Solon's four and ensured that each of the tribes was a microcosm of the whole of Attica rather than reflecting subgroups with natural affinities arising from class, kinship, geographic location, or occupation. He apportioned Attica so that each of the ten tribes included three kinds of territories: an area in and around the city of Athens, an area along the coast, and an inland area. The tribes were ten roughly equal population units from which to form army regiments. Each tribe elected one general to serve in the Athenian military for a one-year term but without term limits.[20]

Tribes also constituted the units from which to recruit civilian government officials. Apart from the elected generals, virtually all public officers were chosen by lot. Although the use of lot predated Cleisthenes for at least some positions, allowing every male citizen of eligible age to rule and be ruled in turn significantly extended the principle of political equality.[21] The citizens of Athens paid salaries to hundreds of public officials chosen by lot to manage the affairs of the city on their collective behalf: diplomats, law clerks, financial administrators, tax collectors, customs officials, directors of religious festivals, and policemen, as well as jailors, executioners, and janitors.

To supervise the public administrators and to preside over the business of the Assembly, fifty men drawn by lot from each tribe each year formed the Council of Five Hundred. As a result, as many as two-thirds of Athenian citizens might have served, at some point in their lives, on the council.[22] The council heard reports of officials, deliberated the Assembly's agenda, and prepared motions for the Assembly's consideration. A steering committee of fifty men, five from each tribe, led the council. Each tribal delegation took the helm for about a month at a time, and each day in that month one man was selected by lot from the leading tribal delegation to head the steering committee. It was probably in this role, as tribal representative on the steering committee, that Socrates had tried in vain to save the Arginusae generals from a speedy group trial. The Athenians were keen, it is clear, to diffuse executive power as a way to inhibit the dangerously ambitious.

Reforms introduced in 462 BC changed the way that members were selected for the Areopagus, a vestige of predemocratic Athenian government in which a council of wise men had ruled the polity. Despite its elite origins, the Areopagus sometimes played a substantial role, especially when other institutions broke down. Capital crimes continued to be prosecuted in the Areopagus even after democratic reforms stripped it of its other jurisdictions, but its other roles waxed and waned with events, as we shall see.

Ruling and being ruled in turn diffused power among many citizens, breaking up the elite's old monopoly of political authority. In addition, the

Athenians devised a variety of procedures to minimize the danger of personal aggrandizement. First, officials chosen by lot were subjected to a review of their personal record before being commissioned.[23] Second, anyone could bring charges of treasonable activities against someone about to step into public office.[24] Charges of major public offenses were brought before the council and referred to a court or to the Assembly.[25] Third, to deter corruption, officials were subjected to a review upon leaving office.[26] A designated group of public inspectors were chosen by lot to receive, review, and turn over to courts of law complaints about outgoing officials. Lot-selected administrators who handled money were subjected to even closer scrutiny, including a monthly audit by inspectors chosen by lot. Following their examination, auditors placed the officials' accounts before a court of the people for acceptance or rejection.[27]

Public courts of law were, by today's lights, major public assemblies themselves.[28] Each court was composed of citizen-judges chosen just before daybreak on the day of the trial, ranging from 500 to 1,500 in number depending on the perceived seriousness of the case.[29] With courts this size, the Athenians reasoned, it would be impossible to bribe a majority. Like most other public officials, citizen-judges were chosen by lot, though the judge/jurors, unlike Assembly-goers, had to be at least thirty years old and were required to pledge the Helliastic Oath: "I will cast my vote in consonance with the laws and decrees passed by the Assembly and by the council, but, if there is no law, in consonance with my sense of what is most just, without favor or enmity. I will vote only on the matters raised in the charge, and I will listen impartially to the accusers and defenders alike." The courts were tasked with hearing, debating, and deciding a case in a single day. Only the magistrates or those who were selected to prosecute or defend cases made speeches, and the juries voted their decisions by secret ballot. The Old Oligarch spoke for many well-to-do Athenians when he disparaged the citizen courts for drawing disproportionately from Athens' elderly and poor.

The historian Herodotus held the unflattering view that democracy inevitably becomes corrupt, which in turn incites oligarchical intrigue.[30] But he also believed that democracy was unparalleled in at least one respect: it motivated its citizens to fight for their polity. He credited Athens' democracy for its unexpected military victories over Boeotia and Chalcis in 506 BC, close on the heels of Cleisthenes' reforms, when Athens wreaked revenge on these neighbors for taking sides with Sparta.[31]

✦ ✦ ✦

Athens' conflict with Sparta long predated the Peloponnesian War (431–404 BC), which was perhaps inevitable given both their physical proximity and Athens' new military prowess after 506 BC. Notwithstanding that rivalry, the looming threat of Persia to the east periodically threw Athens back into provisional alliances with nondemocratic neighbors including Sparta, giving rise to a nascent notion of "Greece" alongside city-state loyalties. In 499 BC, after making one failed attempt through Thrace and Macedonia, King Darius of Persia prepared to invade Greece from the Aegean. He mobilized a large army: according to the educated guesses of historians who must deflate national myth, his host consisted of some 25,000 light armored soldiers accompanied by 10,000 cavalry who marched across a magnificently engineered pontoon bridge over the Hellespont from Asia Minor into Thrace toward Athens.

An Athenian force of about 10,000 armored soldiers—unaided by a Sparta that was preoccupied with religious celebrations but with help from

Battle of Marathon.

an additional 1,000 soldiers from neighboring Plataea—defeated the much larger Persian force at the epic Battle of Marathon in 490 BC. Ten generals elected by the Athenian Assembly shared command, and although Miltiades was found to be the strategic genius among them—he convinced the other generals to break with conventional phalanx tactics and instead run into the Persian army at full speed—the Assembly was adamant that he share the credit with the other generals and with their men.

According to Plutarch,[32] when Miltiades asked the Assembly to reward him with a crown of olives, Sophanes of Decelea, "rising up from the middle of the Assembly," objected: "Let Miltiades ask for such an honor for himself when he has conquered the barbarian single handed." The Assembly sided with Sophanes.[33]

Ever vigilant to keep its leaders accountable, the Athenian Assembly fined Miltiades an enormous sum the following year, when it learned that he had used an Athenian fleet to attack and loot the city of Paros for slandering him.[34] According to the Old Oligarch, it was also about this time that the Assembly passed a law institutionalizing ostracism, the practice of expelling people who it deemed, by a plurality, posed a danger to the democracy.[35] Writing names on pottery shards used for this purpose, the Assembly banished scores of people, from powerful aristocrats to men of lower birth with a smell of ambition.

Persia's King Darius died in 486 BC but not before passing along to his son and successor, Xerxes I, his determination to vanquish Greece. Sensing this, Athenian general Themistocles persuaded the Athenian Assembly to direct the windfall from the Laureion silver mines in Attica to build a much bigger Athenian navy.[36] When in 480 BC Xerxes led the second invasion of Greece with a force even more massive than the one his father assembled, the Athenians were still David to the Persian Goliath, but at least they were not caught off guard. At first the Persians seemed poised to succeed, defeating the combined Greek land forces (led by Athens and Sparta) at the Battle of Thermopylae (480 BC), where three hundred brave Spartans in the rear guard made their last stand. At sea, however, the Athenians were in their element. Themistocles, the great Athenian politician and general, had the idea of luring the Persians into the narrows at Salamis, off the coast of Attica, where the nimble and well-coordinated Athenian fleet rammed hundreds of Persian ships that were packed in too tightly to maneuver or escape.[37] The following year the Greeks finally defeated the Persian army at the Battle of Plataea, disrupting its supply lines and feigning retreat after refusing to be lured into a field where the Persian cavalry would have had the advantage. Xerxes gave up on conquering Greece head-on and went home to craft a new strategy that would take advantage of the rivalry between Athens against Sparta.

With the Persian threat gone for the time being, Themistocles and his successors transformed Athens' navy from a ragtag corps of volunteers into a standing fleet manned by thousands of professional soldiers, who were paid out of state coffers to train regularly and stay at sea for months at a time on patrolling missions. With 200 men in each trireme,[38] a fleet of 100 ships would require 20,000 men—more than double the 9,000 Athenian hoplites who had fought at Marathon a decade earlier. Athenian rowers, training together for months or years, became masters of collective maneuver and knew how to turn a trireme into a deadly ramming machine. Triremes were no longer transport vessels for hoplites but were themselves precision instruments of war.[39]

In addition to Athens' large navy, an estimated fifteen thousand state employees worked in the Piraeus dockyards building and repairing ships.[40]

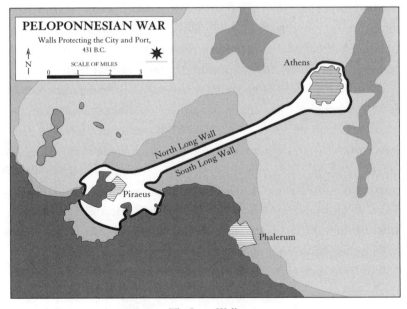

The Long Walls.

In the mid-450s BC the Assembly voted to build the Long Walls, which would stretch all seven-and-a-half miles between Athens and Piraeus and be wide enough to accommodate chariots passing in opposite directions. The walls gave Athens protected access to the sea, on which it depended for food imports even more than it relied on Attican farms. When the Spartans invaded Attica in 431 BC, burning grapevines and olive groves, many citizens from the surrounding countryside were able to take refuge within the city without starving, although epidemics took many lives, including that of Athens' great leader Pericles.[41]

Athens' regional naval supremacy in the fifth century BC brought not only prosperity from trade but also riches in the form of tribute that other Greek city-states paid, ostensibly in appreciation for Athens' keeping the sea-lanes kept free of pirates and enemy ships.[42] The Delian League, an Athenian-led alliance system that convened on the island of Delos in preparation for the war against Persia, became the Second Athenian League in the 460s or 450s, against which the Spartans formed the Peloponnesian League.[43] Athens used its prosperity and the dues from its alliance to finance its vast public sector. Between 800 and 300 BC, per capita consumption in Athens increased by 50 percent despite a tenfold increase in population.[44] The acknowledgment of the common man's role in supporting Athenian power gave rise to the phrase "to give the people their own," including pay for serving the city in public roles.[45] Plutarch tells us that about 479 BC Aristeides, an Athenian general who played prominent roles in the cities of Salamis and Plataea, convinced many Athenians to leave their farms and live in the city, where they could work as public employees, some as soldiers, others as jurors or administrators of various kinds. According to Plutarch, more than twenty thousand Athenian men were supported from taxes and tribute.[46]

Seen in retrospect, decades after the Persian Wars, the battles of Marathon in 490 BC and Salamis in 480 BC carried vastly different political significance. Salamis was a naval (mass public) victory that overtook the hoplite (middle class and up) triumph at Marathon. For Thucydides, writing in the late fifth century BC, Athens' shift toward a naval strategy after Salamis set the stage for Athenian greatness that only some democratic leaders were wily enough to manage.[47] The Athenian philosopher Plato, writing in the fourth century, was unequivocal that politics took a turn for the worse. In *The Laws,* Plato puts his views in the mouth of the "Athenian Stranger":

> **Cleinas:** *[W]e Cretans are in the habit of saying that the battle of Salamis was the salvation of Greece.*
>
> **Athenian Stranger.** *Why, yes; and that is an opinion which is widely spread both among Greeks and barbarians. But Megillus and I say rather, that the battle of Marathon was the beginning, and the battle of Plataea the completion, of the great deliverance, and that these battles by land made the Greeks better; whereas the sea-fights of Salamis and Artemisium . . . made them no better, if I may say so without offence about the battles which helped to save us. And in estimating the goodness of a state, we regard both the situation of the country and the order of the laws, considering that the mere preservation and continuance of life is not the most honorable thing for men, as the vulgar think, but the continuance of the best life, while we live.*[48]

For Plato, Athenian naval policy was a source of moral corruption. Sailors, Plato claimed, would flee when given a chance rather than fight to the death the way hoplites would.[49]

Whether they liked it or not, Athens' wealthy and conservative citizens seem to have understood that the city's survival rested in the hands of thousands of commoners who rowed the triremes, rather than solely in the hoplite armies of the well-to-do who fought land battles. The mass public had a claim on politics as their own. Unhappy masses could refuse to row when it most mattered to Athenian security, and politically ambitious men seeking election as generals required their favor. Reflecting as it did the whole population and not just the privileged, Athenian democracy was often a source of consternation for Athens' rich. At the symbolic level, the mere fact that the poor and uneducated were taking turns governing the state caused umbrage.

As a practical matter, the Assembly had at its disposal several instruments of wealth redistribution. Rich citizens were required to make contributions to the life of the city, including sponsoring religious festivals, athletic competitions, and drama contests and even outfitting ships.[50] Many ship commanders were rich young men willing to pay considerable sums from their own fortunes to build and staff a ship in exchange for a commission, presumably to increase their chances of being elected general in the future.[51] These voluntary contributions could, of course, cut both ways, since generous provisioning could win followers and create patronage networks.[52] By the fourth century, liturgies had become regularized, resembling a tax more

than a voluntary show of goodwill. In emergencies, the Assembly sometimes resorted to an emergency levy from which the poor were exempt. For
rich citizens found guilty of corruption, fines could be enormous, amounting to dispossession.[53] Court records are full of professions—many of them
far-fetched—of abject poverty, in the attempt, one imagines, to win the
sympathy of poor jurors.[54]

Although rich and poor often clashed in Athenian politics, it is impossible to draw a political map along class lines alone; competition was as
likely to erupt around clan loyalties and personal rivalries. While many
of Athens' rich supported democracy and became some of its most distinguished leaders, others looked for opportunities to bring democracy
to its knees. Before two oligarchic coups succeeded, in 411 BC and in 404
BC following military defeats at the hands of Sparta, multiple assaults
on Athenian democracy met with various levels of success. Cimon, a
pro-Spartan aristocrat and prominent political leader, took advantage
of the general public's irritation at Themistocles' pride for Salamis and
organized his ostracism from Athens in 471–70 BC.[55] Cimon moved
Athenian foreign policy in a pro-Spartan direction, leading a brigade
of Athenian hoplites to help Sparta put down a revolt of the serfs who
worked the land in Sparta.[56]

Ephialtes, an Athenian champion of popular rule, used Cimon's sojourn
to Sparta to put a bill before the Assembly powers stripping the Areopagus of its residual, predemocratic powers as the "guardian of the constitution." Ephialtes sought to free the Assembly from aristocratic oversight
and urged it to seize more complete power. At the same time, Ephialtes
may have made all male citizens eligible to be chosen by lot to the Council of Five Hundred and the subset chosen by lot to serve on the council's steering committee. This was significant. Even with lesser powers,
it remained a symbol of traditional authority.[57] Ephialtes also replaced
Solonian appeals courts with courts of the people, open to all citizens
and filled by lot.

Had Cimon and his hoplites been in Athens at the time of the Assembly vote on these reforms, it is impossible to know for certain if he could
have blocked the vote. But when he returned in 461 and tried to reverse the
Assembly's decision, it was his turn to be ostracized. Ephialtes was murdered shortly thereafter, but a pro-democracy group led by the extraordi-

narily eloquent Pericles came to dominate Athenian politics for many years to come, and Ephialtes' reforms were not again assaulted until 411.[58] Pericles was of aristocratic birth, but his sympathies lay with the people, and it was he who made it possible for the working poor to participate in the council, Assembly, and juries by providing daily wages for the people who undertook these jobs.[59] He also promoted a citizenship law in 451–50 outlawing marriage with foreigners, an aristocratic custom that common people regarded as undermining of Athenian solidarity.[60]

In 415–413 BC, however, the death of thousands of Athenian soldiers in the Sicilian Expedition of the Peloponnesian War once again left Athenian democracy vulnerable to the machinations of those who wanted to get rid of it. The composition of the Assembly was vastly different with so many of the rowing men missing.[61] The leading modern scholar of the era, Mogens Hansen, calculates there were 60,000 adult male citizens living in Attica at the outbreak of hostilities with Sparta in 431, about 43,620 of whom (over two-thirds) were mobilized for active service. The massive fleet drew in the majority of citizens who were too poor to be hoplites. Resident aliens, slaves, and allies, all took part, but most seem to have been Athenian citizens from the lower classes.

Seeing their opportunity, a group of naval officers stationed on the Athenian base at Samos returned to Athens in 411 to encourage the aristocratic clubs to join forces with them against democracy.[62] They proposed that a Committee of Ten be chosen and given full powers to draw up proposals for government reform for ratification. In the most cynical move of their gambit, they held the Assembly in a narrow place at Colonus about a mile out of the city, where far fewer than the usual four to five thousand Assembly-goers could fit. There a self-appointed Committee of Ten proposed that any Athenian should be allowed to make suggestions with impunity, to circumvent Athenian vigilance against unconstitutional proposals. The oligarchic leader Pisander rose to argue that a constitutional change would placate the Persians, making it possible to win the otherwise hopeless war against Sparta.[63] Pisander went on to propose that the present constitution should end; five men would be elected as presidents, each of whom would choose one hundred men, who in turn would choose three more. "We need a more integrated form of government with the power in fewer hands so that the King [of Persia] may trust us. At the moment what we have to think about is our survival, not the form of our constitution." They could always change it later, he blandished.[64]

The Four Hundred, as they were called, were to replace the Council of Five Hundred. The Four Hundred could rule as they pleased, or they could convene a new assembly of the Five Thousand, composed of the hoplite class but excluding the lowest census class that made up the bulk of the navy.[65] The sitting Assembly ratified the proposals with no word spoken in opposition, allowing itself to be dissolved.[66] On the appointed day for the new government to take the reins, the Four Hundred appeared, each carrying a concealed dagger and accompanied by 120 burly "Hellenic youths" as bodyguards. Entering the council chamber, they told the sitting councilmen chosen by lot to take their pay and leave.[67]

In the ensuing months, some citizens were put to death, while others were imprisoned or sent into exile, but for the most part the citizens of Athens kept quiet and out of trouble. With most of the navy either killed or on the naval base at Samos, the poorest citizens known to be the staunchest supporters of direct democracy were not present to defend the system. Meanwhile in Samos, the island playing host to Athens' largest overseas naval base, the democracy came under threat as well. With the help of Athenian soldiers, local Samian democrats defeated the coup attempt. The Athenian democratic leaders in Samos included the trireme captain Thrasybulus and the hoplite Thrasyllus. When some three hundred sympathizers of oligarchy attacked, Athenian sailors came to the rescue and executed thirty of them, exiled three others, and allowed the rest to disperse.[68] Thrasyllus' name is familiar because we have encountered him already—he was one of the generals at Arginusae, to be executed in 406, five years thence, on orders of the Athenian Assembly.[69]

By the summer of 410, the government of the Four Hundred had fallen apart at the seams between the "moderate" oligarchs who wanted a larger role for the Five Thousand (still excluding the commoners) and the "conservative" oligarchs who favored a narrower base. The first order of business of the newly restored, full-franchise Assembly was to pass a decree against the overthrow of democracy.[70] Democracy in Athens again reigned supreme.

This brings us to where we began our narrative, with Arginusae in 406 BC. Theramenes—a ship commander in the victorious fleet who then led the prosecution against the Arginusae generals whom he served—had been one of the "moderate" oligarchs of 411. Whether he intended it or not, the execution of six Athenian generals deprived the city of several of its democratic leaders. Some scholars speculate that the conservative Theramenes manipulated the public mood, taking advantage of a public festival for the dead to stoke fury at the generals' supposed disregard for the shipwrecked, dead or alive.[71] But along with the departure of these generals went valuable expertise. The profound tragedy of the generals' execution was revealed only later, when it became clear that Athens could not do without the generals' political savvy or military acumen.

Callicratidas, who had mocked the Athenians for losing their mastery of the sea, had died that very day at Arginusae in 406 BC, but another Spartan commander, Lysander, faced down an Athenian fleet bereft of its skilled generals a year later at Aegospotami. Now with a stronger navy than Athens', Sparta's blockade was as tight as a cork in a bottle. Athens held out against Sparta for about six more months, but without food imports and having already forgone their countryside farms, the Athenians were starved into submission in April 404 BC. Sparta lost no time tearing down the Long Walls to Piraeus that had been Athens' lifeline to the sea, as Xenophon tells it, "amidst scenes of great joy and to the music of flute girls."[72]

A pro-Spartan group of aristocrats within Athens installed a narrowly based government called "the Thirty," which set about dismantling Athenian liberties at a rapid clip. Only 3,000 Athenians—fewer even than the 5,000 in 411—were granted some political rights and the right to carry weapons or receive a jury trial; citizen courts were bypassed altogether for most trials.[73] The Thirty did not at first abolish the Council of Five Hundred, but they handpicked its members, as the oligarchs had done in 411.[74] The Thirty restored the Areopagus, the predemocratic council of city elders, to pre-Ephialtes status and function, although the membership of the Areopagus had become quite reflective of the citizenry as a whole, on account of Ephialtes' reforms, which selected the council's steering committee by lot.[75] The Thirty nevertheless hunted down democratic leaders in Athens, executed hundreds, and forced thousands more into exile.

As in 411 BC, however, the oligarchs began to turn on each other. Some Athenian democrats living in exile took the Thirty's execution of Theramenes in 404 BC as a sign that the new antidemocratic government had become a fractious and narrow tyranny, unlikely to enjoy support from

Athens' intimidated but quiescent citizenry. In the winter of 404–2 BC, Thrasybulus—once a soldier at the Athenian naval base in Samos who, with Thrasyllus (later one of the executed generals), had helped Samian democrats block the oligarchic coup there in 411—set out from his refuge in Thebes with seventy men and landed at a mountain refuge in Phyle, Attica. There, with a force augmented by the many Athenians who flocked to join him, Thrasybulus' surprise tactics defeated a force of Athenian cavalry and Spartan hoplites.

With Athenian democrats poised to retake their city, Sparta's King Pausanias led an army of the Peloponnesian League to Piraeus, where it stopped the Athenian rebels in their tracks.[76] But in negotiations following his victory, Pausanias accepted the restoration of Athenian democracy, with only the proviso that the small town of Eleusis, 11 miles west of Athens, be set aside as a safe haven for the Thirty and their partisans. Pausanias himself was sent into exile for being soft on the Athenians, reflecting internal differences about the wisdom of Spartan empire building.[77]

With the Spartans gone and the Thirty exiled, Athenians set about rebuilding institutions and practices to protect against further coups—one can imagine, intending to guard against their own propensity to make hasty judgments in the Assembly that they later came to regret.[78] Possibly with the input of the Areopagus, which was made up principally of lot-selected city leaders from pre-Thirty days, the Athenians restored old institutions and designed new ones aimed at constitutional stability and legal continuity. From sometime around 415 BC, any citizen had the right to challenge in criminal court the appropriateness of a proposal brought before the Assembly.[79] But to elevate the importance of laws with constitutional significance, the Athenians created two legislative boards, one elected by the Council of Five Hundred and the other selected by lot from the tribes in their tribal assemblies. The group elected by the council compiled the canon of existing laws; the second (the so-called *nomothetai*) held hearings on the appropriateness of the laws and to ratify those deemed worthy of Athenian democracy.[80] At the same time that the Assembly voted to add a legislative board to compile the legal canon, it also rejected a proposal to institute a property requirement for full citizenship that would have meant a return to the Solonic constitution and made it unconstitutional to propose that the Assembly abolish democracy (an early rejection of the Weimar German legislature's self-dissolution at Hitler's insistence in 1933). Thus did the Athenians erect institutional barricades around their system of government.

As with other courts, the Athenian legislative boards were chosen by lot from the same pool as were the public court juries: men over thirty who had sworn the Helliastic Oath. On a given day, the boards would be composed of at least 501 men for routine issues but of 1,001 or 1,501 for more important matters. They met several times a year to pass or reject laws and to deal with challenges to laws in an adversarial procedure similar to that used in the courts. The Athenians established another process to challenge decrees and still another to challenge laws of constitutional status.[81] For a sense of comparison between decrees and laws: the Assembly passed several hundred decrees in 403–2 BC, while the legislative board ratified only seven laws that same year.[82] Institutional experimentation did not stop there. Many decades later, in 330 BC, the procedure of allowing courts to deal with conflicting laws was superseded by the Inspection Law, which required a new body of auditors to inspect the laws annually.[83] They announced any conflicts they discovered to the Assembly, which in turn would refer them to the legislative board to decide which laws were valid.[84]

Athenian democracy still stands in the dock of world historical opinion. Generations of historians and theorists, beginning with some of the greatest thinkers of all time, have pronounced their condemnation. Socrates (469–399 BC), whom we know principally through his dialogues recorded by Plato, fought with distinction as an Athenian foot soldier alongside his fellow citizens in several battles against Peloponnesian armies.[85] We know little of his views of Athenian democracy, given his greater preoccupation with the life of the mind and soul. As chance would have it, at least according to some sources, Socrates had been chosen by lot to represent his tribe to head the steering committee of the Council of Five Hundred the day the Arginusae generals were tried by the Assembly in 406.[86] What happened next illustrates the power of the Assembly relative to the steering committee's executive authority. Socrates argued before the Assembly that being tried as a group violated the Athenian law that required a separate trial for every defendant in a capital crime. In the face of an emotionally aroused and angry Assembly, he and a colleague were outnumbered in standing for the law of individual trial. A man named Euryptolemus, a relative of Pericles and friend of the general Diomedon, initially received Assembly support for making a motion for separate trials, but a procedural maneuver by the generals' detractors forced an up-or-down vote on the generals' fate first, and the Assembly voted to execute them.

An Athenian court's order in 399 BC that Socrates himself be executed for the capital crime of religious impiety (*asebeia*) is taken as additional proof of the monumental foolishness of Athenian democracy. Socrates argued before the jury that, if he corrupted the young, he did so unwillingly; and if unwillingly, he should be instructed rather than eliminated.[87] He also criticized the Athenian legal code that allowed a person to be tried for a capital crime in one day—a flaw he had noted in the prosecution and execution of the generals of Arginusae.[88] When the jury nevertheless found him guilty—in the one day of proceedings prescribed by Athenian law—Socrates refused his legal right to go into exile in the place of execution, and he took the fatal dose of hemlock oil that the Eleven, the prison officials chosen by lot that day, administered in the name of Athenian democracy.

Plato, Socrates' most famous student and forty-two years old when his master died, openly despised Athenian democracy. In mocking tones, he describes a democracy as a people drunk on excessive quantities of undiluted freedom.

> *"I suppose that when a democratic city, once it's thirsted for freedom, gets bad winebearers as its leaders and gets more drunk than it should on this unmixed draught, then, unless the rulers are very gentle and provide a great deal of freedom, it punishes them, charging them with being polluted and oligarchs."*
>
> *"Yes," he said, "that's what they do."*
>
> *"And it spatters with mud those who are obedient, alleging that they are willing slaves of the rulers and nothings," I said, "while it praises and honors—both in private and in public—the rulers who are like the ruled and the ruled who are like the rulers. Isn't it necessary in such a city that freedom spread to everything?"*[89]

Plato thought that demagogues could easily manipulate people, robbing the rich of money with which to pander to the poor and pad their own pockets.[90] The theater aspect of Assembly rule elevated rhetoric over reason, and the selection of government officials by lot put power in the hands of people unfit to rule. A sick polity, Plato thought, was the inevitable result. Plato expressed only contempt for Athens' chronic legislative tinkering, sham reforming, and innovation. By contrast, he ranked the Spartan government second after his own ideal state because the magistrates, the military, and the breadwinners (serfs among the subjugated population, called helots) held complementary roles that cultivated excellence in each.[91]

Aristotle, forty-three years old when Plato died in 347 BC, shared his teacher's low opinion of Athenian democracy. But unlike Plato's unworldly vision of society governed by philosopher-kings, his politics were grounded in the empirical world around him: a perfect constitution—a benevolent monarchy, a goodly aristocracy, or a wise democracy of the well fed—was unachievable given income inequality and human greed. Like Plato, Aristotle thought that the Athenian practice of paying jurors and Assembly-goers gave the poor a disproportionate incentive to participate in government whether or not they were qualified, while also making them dependent on political leaders who manipulated crowds in service of their own ambition. By its own intemperance, the Assembly provoked oligarchic conspiracy. An Assembly dominated by the poor was prone to making petulant decisions, often at the behest of professional politicians who profited from attacking the rich.

Aristotle thought that "when the unpropertied class with the support of a middle class gets on top by weight of numbers, things go badly and they soon come to grief." In his view, societies could instead construct a "middle type of constitution" in one of two ways: by limiting the franchise to the propertied classes,[92] or by mixing the attributes of three pure "types" of constitution—of the rule of the one, of the few, and of the many—to create balance across the orders. Either mechanism could create reasonable conditions for approximating the common good, because the desires of the public would be moderate to start with or at least moderated by those with competing interests and power. The Athenian Assembly, in contrast, was composed of a poor majority that could change any law at will, making Athens a deviant constitution on both counts.[93]

Aristotle's harsh appraisal of Athenian democracy worked its way into the genetic material out of which modern democratic republics have been fashioned. Of Aristotle's two mechanisms for achieving the common good in politics—to limit the franchise to those with means or to create institutional checks on a majority constituted by poor people—the latter has become received wisdom. Later thinkers, starting with Polybius—who was a Greek expatriate living in Rome two centuries after Aristotle—argued that any unchecked majority, whatever its demographic composition, would be a functional tyranny because of its power to overturn any law at will. Polybius historicized Aristotle's three constitutional categories when he argued that each pure form degenerates over time into its respective corrupt form of tyranny, oligarchy, or mob rule.[94]

Although the connection between ideas and their political adoption is by no means straightforward, the lineage of political theorists and practicing politicians who have reached back to Aristotle's recommendation of mixed government over pure majority rule is striking.[95] James Madison in 1788 wrote in *Federalist* 55, "Had every Athenian citizen been a Socrates, every Athenian Assembly would still have been a mob." A few years later in Germany, Immanuel Kant, who championed republican government for the cause of world peace, also equated direct democracy Athenian style with despotism, in words that echo Aristotle's: "Of the three forms of the state, that of democracy is, properly speaking, necessarily a despotism, because it establishes an executive power in which 'all' decide for or even against one who does not agree; that is, 'all,' who are not quite all, decide, and this is a contradiction of the general will with itself and with freedom."[96] For Madison and Kant, direct democracy was an inadvisable instrument, producing predictably selfish but fickle majorities.

The indictment of Athenian democracy rests in part on mischaracterizations of the Athenians' decision-making processes but not entirely. Assembly meetings, attended by upward of six thousand male citizens, must have been a difficult venue in which to have a reasoned debate. Without secret ballots, only the brave would vote against their patrons or elders. And as we know from the study of human psychology (although Socrates had figured this out for himself), crowd moods can be contagious in a way that can play into the hands of the persuasive, particularly if a decision has to be made in one sitting. More heads are better than one, but a setting such as the Athenian Assembly may often have reduced the number of heads at work.

The Athenian Assembly's tendency toward mobbishness notwithstanding, criticisms of Athenian democracy have conflated two very different things: who participated in politics, and how effectively they expressed their views. Plato, Aristotle, and the aristocratically inclined thought the wrong kind of Athenian was making decisions. An alternative diagnosis, that mass politics produces defective decisions, suggests the possibility of rescue by institutional adjustment. Jean-Jacques Rousseau, for example, advised against deliberation among voters or legislators. But first we set aside prescriptive positions to investigate *why* the Athenians adopted democratic decision-making procedures, and why they adjusted them when they did.

The demise of Athenian democracy in 320 BC was caused not by institutional disintegration or other internal challenges but by external conquest. Philip of Macedon had built a land force, based on his military innovation of the phalanx, for which a restored Athenian navy of the fourth century was no match. Demosthenes, Athens' central political leader in the 330s BC, is known to us principally from his "Philippics"—his passionate speeches to shore up Athenian opposition to the expansionist Macedonians. Philip and his successor Alexander the Great both died before conquering Greece, but their successor, Antipater, made it a condition of peace to rid the Greek city-states of opponents of Macedon. Demosthenes fled Athens with his friends and, when caught by exile hunters, killed himself with poison. Athens collapsed as an independent entity.

Its tragic end notwithstanding, Athens left a legacy that if anything has gained luster with time. The Athenians were the first to institutionalize a wide male franchise without regard to property qualifications and to experiment self-consciously and on record with various decision-making rules, and they gave democracy its name. But how did war shape those experiments with democratic decision-making, and how well did they serve Athens? Answering those questions requires, of course, specifying the goals against which effectiveness is measured. The two that the Athenians themselves cared most about remain paramount in theorizing about democracy today: the compatibility of democracy with an effective foreign policy, and good governance.

Athens depended, as we have seen, on secure sea-lanes for its sustenance, not to mention for its prosperity and growth. In maintaining them, Athens was spectacularly successful against heavy odds. Thucydides reports the "Corinthian assessment" of Athens' military prowess in 432 BC, just before the Peloponnesian War: the Athenians were agile in putting technical innovation to military need, they were ambitious, and the citizens acted self-sacrificially for the good of all.[97] They adapted the trireme to their advantage by creating an attack vessel that relied more on coordination than on armored warriors, and they allowed brilliant upstarts like Themistocles to improvise their maneuvers as they went along. Athenian ramming and oar-jamming tactics, used to lethal effect against an array of enemy fleets, required high levels of training made possible in part by public provisioning of the navy and its sailors. This public provisioning, as well as the political pressure on the wealthy to supplement public shipbuilding and operating expenditures, rested in turn on popular support for the navy and for its role in the defense of Athens.[98]

Athens was a stunningly successful military power for nearly two centuries, despite its defeats at the hands of Sparta in 404 BC and Macedonia in 322 BC, and it would be a mistake to pin those or its other defeats on the pathologies of democratic decision making. As Thucydides pointed out, Assembly-elected generals might have worried too much about how their campaigns would be viewed by the public since rival leaders were likely to levy charges of criminal negligence when a battle was lost.[99] But fear of botching a military expedition is also likely to have spurred generals to do their best. In 425 BC, when Nicias and Cleon were rival generals, "the more that Cleon tried to get out of sailing to Pylos . . . the more [the Assembly] encouraged Nicias to hand over his command." So Cleon took command— and managed against all odds to bring the Spartans to heel.[100] It is hard to argue that public pressure produced more bad decisions than good overall. For every Sicilian disaster, there was a Salamis triumph, and the ledgers do not stack against democracy on the question of war-fighting capacity.

No one, however, claims that Athenian democracy was a paragon of good governance. Politically elected generals might or might not have, on balance, strived harder than their technocratic or appointee counterparts in nondemocracies. But the ostracism, fines, and in extreme cases execution of leaders who fell afoul even temporarily of public mood were not just tragic for the individuals in question; one could say that political leaders knowingly bore a risk and that it was a reasonable cost of motivating the rest to behave. Ostracism, which excluded men from politics for ten years, was the clumsy tool to prevent charismatic men, adept at manipulating emotions in the Assembly, from trying to become tyrants. Thucydides himself was exiled on the implausible charges of accepting bribes to let the Spartans capture the city of Amphipolis.[101] More important, the Athenians themselves came to regret petulant decisions they had made in the heat of debate, often in the crosshairs of political rivalries that bore only indirect connection to key concerns of public interest.[102] In 427 BC the Assembly voted with Cleon to kill every man, woman, and child in Mytilene for revolting against the Athenian alliance, only to vote with his rival Diodotus the next day to reverse the decision. Fortunately for the Mytileneans—as well as, most likely, for the Athenians, who had a reputation for decency to maintain with other allies—a second trireme on its mercy mission rowed fast enough to overtake the first trireme that had been dispatched for slaughter.[103]

Even discounting for the antidemocratic bias in the thinking of men like Thucydides, Xenophon, and Plato (who minimize worse behavior on the antidemocratic side, such as the political assassinations of Ephialtes in 462–1 BC and of Androcles in 411 BC, each in his time the most influential of the popular leaders), the Athenian Assembly could blow hot or cold on a question depending on the persuasiveness of particular speakers before it.[104] Athens' own democratic leader and orator Demosthenes, as he languished in exile at the end of his life, asked Athens' patron goddess Athena why she favored such a rabble as the Athenian public. Having served Athens for thirty years as a public figure and politician, sixty-year-old Demosthenes was condemned by an Athenian court in 323 BC for taking bribes from Harpalus, the late treasurer of Alexander the Great. Fined fifty talents and then imprisoned when he couldn't pay, Demosthenes escaped and went into voluntary exile in Aegina or Troezen. In the colorful language of Sir Thomas North's 1579 translation of Plutarch's *Life of Demosthenes,* the great Athenian orator cried out as he gazed upon his native city, "O Lady Minerva (Athena), lady patroness of this city, why dost thou delight in three so mischievous beastes: the owl, the dragon, and the demos?"[105]

While Athenian direct democracy might have produced many bad decisions, as a system of government it was nevertheless remarkably resilient. In the face of disgruntled elites who were vocal in their opposition to direct democracy, the franchise shrank only twice over the entire period, for some months in 411 and 404 BC. The Assembly responded to these and other constitutional challenges by successive rounds of institutional tinkering, the first of which expanded the pool of administrators and jurors in the 460s BC onward by increasing the number of jobs that came with a public stipend, thereby underpinning Athens' trireme democracy. A subsequent set of constitutional reforms, following the ouster of the Thirty in 403 BC, sought to place larger hurdles in the way of would-be tyrants who might try again to intimidate the Assembly into voting against democracy. By creating a legislative board to review and ratify laws, anyone putting a proposal before the Assembly to change Athenian institutions would be subject to a trial-like procedure before a body charged with protecting democracy. In 336 BC, after a terrible military defeat at Chaeronea, the loss of men and public confidence once again put Athenian democracy under extreme strain; the legislative review board passed the antityranny decree, forbidding any legislative body to consider proposals made by a tyrant, and ensured automatic amnesty for whoever killed the tyrant.[106]

Contrary to the view of the democracy-skeptics of the day, impetuous decisions were less the result of who ruled Athens than of how they made decisions. The Assembly recognized the potential problem of its own fickle majorities and made the remarkable decision to check itself. In instituting the legislative review board, it did not put decision-making authority in the hands of a different social stratum of society, as some philosophers and elite groups urged, although of course eligible members had to be over thirty rather than twenty years old. They aimed rather to slow the decision-making process and to thereby subject their own political choices to more intense scrutiny.

Ingenious institutional engineering protected Athenian democracy for many years, solidifying the link between mass political participation and mass mobilization for war. But the loyalty of Athenian elites to the city—and to the democracy in particular—was ever questionable. Clan, class, and even a sense of adventure sometimes trumped allegiance to Athens, as evidenced by the extreme opportunism of men like Cimon and Alcibiades and Xenophon, who thought nothing of fighting with the Spartans or the Persians. It is impossible to know, in retrospect, if an alternative set of institutions that reserved privileges for their interests would have generated greater mobilizational capacity for war and defense, in part because Greek city-states were too small to fight empires. Complete mobilization of Athenian manpower was simply no longer enough for self-defense in a world of increasing military scale.

✦ ✦ ✦

With the generous help of centuries of hindsight, the verdict should be clear: Athens was at times a hotheaded democracy, but it was no more foolish and was often more successful than its monarchical or oligarchical rivals. The Athenian elite complained about the Assembly's impetuous and ill-informed choices. As in modern times, much of the information available to the Assembly was generated by competition among elites. The philosophers of the day worried that the poor were ill prepared to judge arguments, generating instead an undignified game of pandering and patronage. But compared to what? The elite tried to narrow the franchise on multiple occasions, but there is no reason to believe that had they succeeded, decisions would have been superior in any way.

The Athenian aristocrat Alcibiades was a case study in poor leadership, talking Athens into launching the calamitous Sicilian expedition and then betraying Athens to Sparta or Persia at various times. It was the Assembly, when all was said and done, that reshaped Athenian institutions to reduce the role of excitement or arbitrary will. The right of any citizen to subject an Assembly proposal to a kind of constitutional review is a stunning milestone in the history of self-governance. Not only did the legislative review board likely deter further assaults on Athenian democracy, but it also gave the Assembly time to review arguments and to make more considered judgments about a multitude of issues. Without abandoning the principles of majority rule and wide franchise, Athens figured out how to inject caution into its decision-making process.

Our second concern, to understand how war shaped Athenian institutions, has also come into focus: mobilization for war underpinned and sustained Athens' broad franchise. There is nothing deterministic about how things turned out; Athens could have been just another Greek city-state with a modest capacity for self-defense, pulled into the orbit of one or another greater power. The connection between war mobilization and the mass franchise is a contingent one that rests on factors such as the ability of a man-powered navy to protect Athens, given island geography and the military technology of the day. Athens' form of self-rule—a direct, unicameral democracy also could not have happened without relatively small territorial size and without the failure of the elite to form a cartel against the poor rather than compete with one another for popular support.

While Athens governed itself for nearly two centuries as a direct democracy, Rome was also being transformed by war but along different lines. On a continuum of forms of self-rule with straightforward majoritarian rule on one end and multiple veto points on the other, Athens stands at the majoritarian end: the triumph of the lower social stratum was remarkable and nearly complete. Rome, by contrast, is close to the other end of the continuum. It is to Rome that we turn in the next chapter, because it is important for modern citizens to understand the consequences of various forms of popular rule for military capacity as well as for the quality of democracy.

While the importance of the Roman army to its war-fighting capacity anchored the lower classes' political voice in the Roman Republic, the upper classes never relinquished their financial dominance and political independence through the Senate. And though war pushed Rome, too, into making more concessions to those whose manpower was needed to fight, the Roman Republic remained, with its multiple chambers, an institutionalized struggle of the orders.

Early modern state builders in Europe and America preferred the Roman model to the Athenian one, reflecting the power of wealth to shape the compromise with manpower even during times of war. One wonders if Greek history might have turned out differently had the aristocratic classes been more motivated, within the construct of a republic giving them legal and property protections, to defend against outsiders. But of course the Roman Republic, though stable for several centuries, also fell under the weight of interelite rivalry and tyrannical reaction. If history tells one tale clearly, it is that no human arrangements are perfect. Institutional engineering, often in response to the need for self-defense, is a human answer to societal entropy. And because all social arrangements known to man entail giving up some desirable properties for the sake of gaining other desirable properties, the tinkering continues. We forget history's lessons about these trade-offs at our peril.

Chapter Three

THE GLORY THAT WAS ROME

I F ATHENIAN DEMOCRACY IS MADE KNOWN TO US by its critics, the Roman Republic is memorialized by its admirers. Polybius, a Greek cavalry officer and military hostage brought to Rome in the 160s BC, credited the stability of the Republic and its military prowess to the struggle between the nobles and the commoners. To Polybius, the consuls, the Senate, and the voting assemblies looked like Aristotle's ideal "mixed constitution," which Polybius believed was superior to any of the "pure" forms of monarchy, aristocracy, or democracy. What he thought was unique to Rome, however, was the successful embodiment of class conflicts in Roman political institutions: the aristocrats dominated the Senate and filled the important offices, while the popular assemblies chose which aristocrats were to hold office.

The legendary orator and public prosecutor Marcus Tullius Cicero, who wrote a century later during the Republic's death throes, was an ardent admirer of the "good old days" of Polybius when the lower classes "knew their place."[1] For Cicero, the republic's fatal flaw was the aristocratic class's inability in later years to stand firmly against popular leaders such as Catiline, Clodius, and Julius Caesar who, as Cicero saw it, pursued personal glory by pandering to the masses. Cicero wrote reams condemning the self-aggrandizing miscreants and pleading with the senatorial class to repair its moral decay. In Cicero's view, the introduction of the secret ballot and subsidies for imported grain for the urban poor were ploys for personal popularity by office-seeking aristocrats that upset Rome's "harmony of the classes" (*concordia ordinum*).

53

Many centuries later still, in the late 1400s, Machiavelli championed Polybius' more optimistic view that the tension between the aristocracy and the masses could be managed. In fact, Machiavelli argued, Rome owed its greatness to the inclusion of the masses in Rome's assemblies and armies. He excavated from Livy's *Histories of Rome* and from Polybius' writings an appealing model of "people power" for how a Roman-style republic might confer on his native Florence the political vitality and military might with which to repel French and Spanish invaders. Eschewing on the one hand the model of Athens' impetuous democracy and haphazard empire (or so Athens' critics had warned) and on the other hand Cicero's gloomy retrospective, Machiavelli attributed the glory of Rome to the perfection of its institutions.

The Roman Republic that Polybius, Cicero, and Machiavelli loved existed in an earlier period, in the fourth to second centuries BC, when the popular assemblies were dominated by middle-class yeoman farmer-soldiers. As Polybius had noted, these farmers had won political rights for themselves

The Expansion of the Roman Republic (201 BC–AD 117)

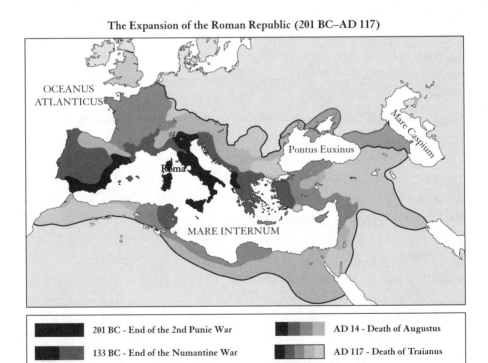

201 BC - End of the 2nd Punic War		AD 14 - Death of Augustus	
133 BC - End of the Numantine War		AD 117 - Death of Traianus	
44 BC - Assassination of Julius Caesar		Colchis	Roman Protectorates in AD 117

by insisting on a political voice in exchange for fighting for Rome. As the empire expanded across the Mediterranean world and beyond after the long wars with Carthage, however, essential parts of the Polybian equation began to change. For one thing, Rome's soldiers, often stationed in distant corners of the empire, became a more or less professional class. No longer farmers returning home at seedtime and harvest, they instead owed their livelihood to war booty and continuous military campaigning. For another thing, Rome expanded the franchise to include residents of the vast empire, cutting the links between fighting for Rome and showing up to vote. The irony is that Rome "purchased" an empire by diluting its citizenship to the point that citizens could no longer play the role that Polybius attributed to them in 150 BC.

Rome's military success, which lasted nearly five centuries and controlled 1.2 million square miles by the time of Caesar's assassination in 44 BC, was bookended by the aristocracy's elimination of powerful leaders: Tarquinius Superbus in 509 BC and Brutus' regicide half a millennium later. The Roman rich believed that the twin evils of dictatorship and mob-led chaos were the inevitable offspring of runaway elite ambition. Cicero expressed this conviction the most clearly in his defense of Titus Annius Milo, a candidate for consulship who had killed Clodius, a competing candidate for praetorship, in a street fight in 52 BC. Cicero stressed the need to restrain the ambitions of powerful men like Clodius: "It occurred to [Clodius] that his praetorship would be crippled and powerless if Milo was consul; . . . He betook himself to his competitors but in such a manner that he alone managed the whole election, even against their will."[2]

The checks and balances of the Roman Republic were designed to limit the powers of ambitious aristocrats and of the magistrates to whom they delegated public authority. To the extent that the checks worked, they protected the status quo for those who benefited from it most. A coalition of aristocrats in the Senate consistently stood in the way of deep land reform and wealth redistribution to commoners and veterans and sought to block anyone from acting like a king. But in the end, their rules were no match for the public clamor for a bigger share of Rome's riches and the generous promises of ambitious leaders.

"As he was valiant, I honor him: but, as he was ambitious, I slew him." With these words in Act 3, Scene 2 of *Julius Caesar,* Shakespeare's Brutus sought public approval in the Roman Forum for his murder of the popular consul who had led Roman armies in far-flung conquests. Although Marcus Junius Brutus might or might not have been as silver-tongued as this (he was in fact a famed orator), Shakespeare's words well capture the Roman senatorial class's ferocious determination to hold in check Rome's popular elements and the demagogues who could stir them up.

When Brutus and his collaborators killed Caesar in 44 BC, the Senate was no longer in a position to save the Republic with arguments, let alone an assassination. By then, field generals, not the republic or its politicians, commanded the loyalty of Rome's massive armies. Stationed semipermanently in far-flung provinces and augmented in large measure by foreign-born citizens who might never have set foot in Rome itself, the armies of Rome were no longer "the people of Rome" as they once had been. Shakespeare depicts Mark Antony deftly turning the crowd against Brutus and Cassius, describing them as vicious murderers and Caesar as an unsuspecting victim and kindly patriot: "For Brutus, as you know, was Caesar's angel: / Judge, O you gods, how dearly Caesar loved him! / This was the most unkindest cut of all; / For when the noble Caesar saw him stab, / Ingratitude, more strong than traitors' arms, / Quite vanquish'd him: then burst his mighty heart."

To Brutus' astonishment, the public did not hail him as the savior of the republic but instead rushed past Caesar's corpse, figuratively speaking, to anoint populists like Mark Antony to save them from Brutus and the aristocracy.

Much had changed since the fourth century BC, when Rome's farmer-soldiers formed the backbone of the Roman Republic.[3] Their centrality to Roman security and glory might have given them the nerve to demand an effective political voice and the clout to back it up, but by Caesar's time at the turn of the millennium, the growth of the empire had disproportionately enriched the aristocrats who amassed lands that they tilled with imported slave labor, undermining the agrarian economy of small farms that had been the backbone of the Republic. Professional soldiers, often foreign-born, deployed for years on end in far-flung provinces—their wages paid and armor supplied from the largesse of Roman generals—replaced the iconic Roman farmer and ex-consul like Lucius Quinctius Cincinnatus, who legendarily dropped his plow midfurrow and donned his panoply in order to save his country in time of crisis in 458 BC,[4] then returned to his old farm to pick up the plow where he had left it.[5]

The connection between Rome's soldiers and the Republic thus attenuated, the balance between the aristocrats and the ordinary citizens fell askew. Roman glory, over the centuries, proved to be iron-brittle.

Rome did not have a particularly auspicious beginning. Whoever the Romans were at the end of the sixth century BC, Rome and Athens exhibited many striking similarities. Both were medium-size city-states situated slightly inland from the sea and surrounded by hostile neighbors. Both Athens and Rome had been ruled by kings who managed to keep powerful aristocrats in check by pursuing policies that were popular in the city.[6] In both cases, these aristocrats had at least some constitutional presence in the form of an advisory council, but they failed to make common purpose with one another. As their monarchies collapsed, both cities suffered intervention and threats from neighboring powers.

From ancient times, in both Athens and Rome, it had been taken for granted that men with sufficient incomes to supply their own panoply of armor would defend their homelands. This was presaged by the twelfth-century-BC discovery of iron—a material cheaper than bronze—that undermined Bronze Age cultures throughout the Aegean and Anatolia.[7] Warfare based on iron-armed infantry, known as hoplites in Greece, passed from Greece to Rome through the Etruscans, who occupied Italy prior to the Republic.[8] Athens had moved on to an even more inclusive military structure based on peasant-pulled triremes, while Rome remained rooted to land-based armored infantry. All Athens' men, regardless of income, were eligible to serve in the navy. In Rome, urban wage earners without land of their own were traditionally excluded from military service.

Rome too, in time, would eventually look to commoners to fill its infantry ranks. In 216 BC Hannibal of Carthage in northern Africa brought his invading army through Spain and down into Italy across the Alps, although with few surviving elephants. Against a larger Roman force at Cannae, Hannibal's men killed an estimated seventy thousand Romans in an encircling maneuver. Shocked at the unprecedented loss, the Roman state then began in a limited way to recruit the rural and urban poor, along with Italian allies, who had previously not been allowed in the army.[9] From that point on, the history of the Republic was the history of a widening franchise.

In effect, Rome's upper classes gave poor soldiers the right to vote, but they income-weighted the voting to keep their political voice in check. Roman

men between the ages of seventeen and sixty were liable for muster. Polybius, in the second century BC, described the basic Roman panoply for the
youngest soldiers (*velites*) as consisting of an iron thrusting sword, iron-rein-
forced javelins, a shield three feet in diameter, a helmet, and greaves.[10] Older
soldiers carried a bigger shield two and a half feet wide and four feet long
with a thickness at the rim a palm's breadth. It was made of two planks
glued together, the outer surface of which was covered first with canvas and
then with calfskin. Iron edging bolstered its upper and lower rims, and an
iron boss strengthened its center. An older soldier would also wield two iron-
reinforced spears, hang a short iron thrusting sword on his right thigh, wear
a brass breastplate called the heart-protector or a coat of chain mail, and top
it all off with a feather-ornamented bronze helmet.[11]

While their armor was distinct, the Romans borrowed weaponry and
tactics from their enemies and vice versa, so that phalanx-formations of
sword-bearing infantry became the standard form of fighting. With spears
pointing forward and shields tightly locked, they pushed into the enemy
while stabbing their short swords between the shields. In response to an
ever-growing variety of enemies as Rome expanded, the Romans abandoned
the solid phalanx in favor of modular units (*maniples*, literally "handfuls")
that could move more freely to where they were needed during the fight.
The youngest fighters, manning the front row, threw spears to break an
opposing army and then rushed in with their swords. Veteran fighters in the
second and third rows would wade into the fight where needed.[12] Practice
and harsh discipline enabled the Roman infantry to move quickly or to stand
against the terrifying massed charges of the Gauls and Iberian Celts.[13]

At home, and away from the battlefield, almost constant warfare shaped
the Republic's "constitution," the evolving set of rules and practices that
reflected the deals that the aristocracy needed to make with those whose
manpower it needed to protect it from hostile neighbors. In contrast to wars
in the modern world, with its states, large armies, and secure borders, wars
in the ancient world could mean all or nothing. As the French historian
Claude Nicolet puts it, "In Roman eyes a citizen and a soldier were the same
thing."[14] It did not start out that way. By legend, the fighting men of Rome
seized a place for themselves in the politics of the city in 494 BC, when they
threatened to secede unless they were granted a public assembly.[15] Rome's
principal popular assembly—the *comitia centuriata*, literally "the assembly of

the centuries"—elected the most important magistrates. The assembly organized the citizens of Rome into the same five wealth classes that composed the military, but unlike the hundred-man centuries in the army, the centuries in the assembly varied greatly in size, with the largest ones relegated to the lower wealth classes. As a result, the highest two classes, the senatorial class and the knights, controlled a majority of assembly votes. At the bottom of the wealth scale were the poor proletarians who had been included in the army and politics after Cannae but were all but disenfranchised by being lumped into a single and sequentially last voting group. The enormous wealth premium in politics magnified the wealth distinctions in the military.

We know much about Rome's complicated checks and balances, but its tumultuous history of wars and rebellions layered institutions on top of one another without a master plan. From the third century BC, a majority of votes of the plebeian assembly became binding on everyone as Roman law. Because consuls of the military-based assembly and tribunes of the plebeian assembly had to stand for election if they wanted to ascend the ladder of offices, they and all other elected officials had to compete for popular favor. De jure, the people had a degree of influence over the content of law, while the elected members of the aristocracy controlled day-to-day policies. Although ordinary citizens could stand for office, it took so much money to run a successful campaign that high office was in practice limited to the old, well-connected aristocratic families or to wealthy plebeians. One could doubt how well this juridical bargain described political reality. On the one hand, the aristocrats were generally well armed and often found ways to coopt or terrify the people and their tribunes to get the results they wanted. On the other hand, competition among aristocrats might have restrained these efforts to a degree. Rome was well governed only insofar as the constitution permitted it to channel endemic and irremediable social conflicts into relatively peaceful constitutional struggles.

Polybius became a great admirer of Rome's system of countervailing vetoes in the hands of contending classes, the rich and the poor,[16] although, as historian John North argues, "the assemblies were convoked, presided over, addressed, and dismissed by elite members in their roles as magistrates, and they were conducted according to voting systems privileging the well off and inhibiting the poor from conducting any kind of conflict with the well off."[17] The senatorial class continually sought to keep in check the common soldiers who formed the backbone of Roman power and who strove openly in publicly sanctioned forums for a greater share of Rome's riches.[18]

Polybius thought Rome's "struggle of the orders" in centuries past had by his time produced a healthy constitutional equipoise, but he worried about its stability. He believed that his crystal ball—his theory of political disequilibrium (anacyclosis) and inevitable cycle among the good and bad monarchical, elitist, and popular elements of any constitution—foretold inevitable wobble and decay of the Roman order, even if Rome's "mixed government" would decay more slowly than the pure forms.[19] Because Rome mixed elements of monarchical, aristocratic, and democratic governance, Polybius did not venture to guess exactly *how* Roman institutions would degenerate.

None of Rome's laws or practices fixed the wealth-biased malapportionment of the public assemblies. Rome remained securely aristocratic until Polybius' time. This began to change soon afterward as reform-minded tribunes of the people, elected by somewhat less malapportioned assemblies, began pushing land reform laws that threatened tribal rule. From the early fifth century the tribunes, armed with the power to block actions of the Senate and its magistrates, had been elected in public assemblies organized by tribes rather than centuries.[20] The Polybian constitution provided the aristocracy with no protection from these new populist leaders. The patricians tried to ensure that at least one of the tribunes was sympathetic to their side of things. Cicero joked darkly that the tribunate was an office born in sedition designed to create more sedition.[21] But the consular office was just as dangerous. By the end of the second century, Marius, elected consul five times, began providing arms and armor to the poor to fight in his African campaigns, permitting him to build a loyal following of veterans. Athens' naval-based military strategy gave commoners political status as full and equal citizens, whether or not they owned property and paid taxes; the panoplied Roman army created an opening for money in politics that both senators and populists amplified.

With the advantage of hindsight, we can see Rome's constitutional vulnerabilities. Its aristocrats tried to stave off "mob rule" by killing anyone who appealed directly to the people and by using term limits and other rules to block the ambitious among their own ranks. While decrying the practice, leaders also bribed voters to get their own men elected.[22] What the aristocracy preferred to avoid, if at all possible, was addressing the problem that fueled demands for change in the first place: growing wealth inequality.[23]

Rome's vast expansion undermined the traditional farmer-soldier economy. Annual military campaigns were consistent with thriving Roman agriculture as long as families had able-bodied men to plant and harvest when the seasons required it. Scholars estimate that not only did 70,000 soldiers die at Cannae in 216 BC, but over 300,000 Roman and Italian soldiers died in the wars against Carthage (264–146 BC), more than a third of those mobilized.[24] Although military mortality was favorable to the poor in the short run because it created a shortage of labor with which they could extract a premium, a subsequent population boom produced rural poverty and vast migrations to the cities.[25] Prospectors bought up enormous tracts of land on which they replaced small-scale subsistence farming by a free population with an ancient variant of serfdom.[26]

To keep up its fighting machine, given these new demographics, Rome lowered the minimum property requirement for military service for the first time, provisioning their panoplies from the Senate's store of taxes. The government of Rome bought slaves to fight in the military and freed prisoners in exchange for fighting for Rome.[27] Plutarch tells us that Tiberius Gracchus became passionate about land reform when, on his way to Numantia in 137 BC, he passed through Etruria, a land of large estates tilled by slaves rather than by free farmers.[28] When he became tribune in 133 BC, Gracchus proposed to redistribute land to free farmers to right the sinking ship of state.[29]

Rather than conceding benefits to the poor recently incorporated into the Roman army, senators tried to safeguard their own control. The Senate, many of whose members grew enormously rich from imperial investments and conquests, combatted the redistributive policies of Tiberius Gracchus and his younger brother Gaius by inventing a new edict, the *senatus consultum ultimum*, that authorized consuls to do whatever was necessary to defend the Republic.[30] Not surprisingly, these edicts stoked further popular fury against the senatorial class. Alarmed by the rising tide of violent populism, the Roman aristocracy armed itself for action. A posse of senators and their private militia beat Tiberius and his followers to death and threw them into the Tiber in 133 BC. In 121 BC Gaius was attacked by a larger force by order of a *senatus consultum ultimum* led by the consul Lucius Opimius.

Gaius committed suicide before they reached him, but hundreds of his followers were hunted down and massacred.[31]

The Roman aristocracy failed to see that its good fortune could be its
undoing. By the time Rome defeated Carthage in 146 BC, the Roman state
had become a very different institution: armies were more or less in permanent service, often in distant lands. Their professionalization made them
more loyal to generals than to Rome and allowed them only an episodic and
attenuated connection to the public assemblies in the capital.[32] In 101 BC
the consul Marius, faced with a chronic shortage of soldiers to fight overseas, breached standard practice to recruit proletarians into military service
and at the same time reformed the traditional class-based army structure to
make better use of the lower quality of the recruits.[33] Marius himself was
of humble origins, born in Arpinum outside Rome, like Cicero some years
later. Marius, in effect, turned the army into a more or less professional force
since volunteers had to be incentivized to reenlist for long and hard service in
Africa or Gaul. While Rome still occasionally used traditional conscription
in the first century BC, it increasingly relied on professional soldiers who
hoped to gain through wars and who would be loyal to a commander who
could make their service profitable.

Other constitutional controls of the military also decayed after the wars
against Carthage. Romans, for the first time, created "improvised dictatorships" when they named private people to lead armies in times of extreme
threat.[34] Scipio Africanus, the Roman general who defeated Hannibal, had
already ended his consulship when he was given the command against Hannibal, despite the fact that both consuls wanted it; the Senate must have
thought that he was the best man for the job even if it flew in the face of
constitutional protocol. This was to be the path to power and glory of two of
Rome's later famous generals, Pompey and Caesar. The Senate handed them
control of important military campaigns over the heads of elected consuls.[35]

The departures from traditional republican practice had the effect
of breaking the deep linkage between the army and the citizenry. By the
middle of the first century BC, many of the legionnaires were professionals
and were neither Roman nor Italian. They were also outside the traditional
wealth classification and under the command of generals who were often
commissioned but not elected magistrates. These generals had the support
of veterans loyal to them and could raise legions independently if need be,

rather than consuls and praetors who figured in the older constitutional practices. The long-term consequences of these changes were profound.

The Roman aristocracy's constitutional concessions to the "public" during the struggles between the senatorial class and the plebeians, including the powers of the tribunes to veto actions of the magistrates or the Senate, rested on the ability of citizen soldiers to refuse to fight at critical moments. The constitution took its shape from popular force or the threat of it. As the army became increasingly professionalized following the defeat of Carthage in 146 BC and the overseas expansion of the empire, the constitutional prerogatives of the classes lost vital military anchorage. At the same time, however, the threat that armies would invade the sacred limits of Rome grew ever more real in the last century of the Republic.

Roman expansion also weakened the Republic by inadvertently diminishing the meaning and function of citizenship. Rome had initially granted partial citizenship to the neighboring Latin and Italian cities it had conquered, in order to build military strength in a way that was more or less acceptable to them.[36] These cities enjoying partial citizenship were liable for certain taxes and a quota of soldiers, without necessarily gaining the right to vote.[37] Rome also established colonies for various purposes and granted citizens in certain colonies special arrangements; certain people were exempt from service in the legions, for example.

The value of full Roman citizenship became much more significant by the end of the second century BC, with the enactment of new agrarian laws of Tiberius and Gaius Gracchus. Other populist leaders used public money to subsidize the cost of grain to Roman citizens and established the rights of veteran soldiers returning from foreign wars to settle or colonize newly confiscated lands. These new privileges were often at the direct expense of the Italian cities or their citizens. In response, Italian cities began to demand full citizenship and, faced with Roman resistance, eventually fought the costly and dreadful Social War (90–89 BC) that was not settled until the Romans agreed to concede full citizenship rights.[38] Soon after citizenship was divorced from proximity to Rome, the Romans adopted a policy of extending full citizenship rights well outside central Italy and eventually throughout the Roman Empire.

However, because the Romans had not developed a system of political representation that would allow for political participation from a distance, democratic concessions to the population outside Rome diluted the political power of the people in Rome itself, and the connection between military participation and politics in the capital was attenuated beyond recognition. In other words, citizenship, once divorced from proximity to Rome, reduced dramatically the proportion of citizens who could participate regularly in elections and assemblies.

Those who fought for Rome received political concessions in return, but the elites never ceased to struggle to retain the upper hand. By the first century BC, aristocrats were desperately trying to hold together their collective privileges in the face of great personal temptations to become exalted leaders by appealing to the greater populations' unfulfilled hopes for a greater voice and more economic equality. Aristocratic glue seems to have thinned with Rome's geographic spread, for some of the most ambitious men came from outside Rome itself: Marius and Cicero from Arpinum, Pompey from Picenum, and Octavius from Velletri.

Consuls on military expeditions abroad held the fates of their men in their hands and often became their champions for booty and land. This was the sense in which a populist dictatorship could be more inclusive than an aristocratic republic, even if populist leaders were accountable to the people in ways too tenuous to call democratic. The soaring popularity of one charismatic consul after another who ventured down this path threatened the normal functioning of the Republic since a popular general with loyal veterans could swamp the voting pens to secure election.[39] Sometimes the rich ruled, and sometimes the poorer elements dominated, according to chance events. Either way it was hard to see the city as well governed, even before it degenerated into decades of civil war.

Conservatives did everything they could to stop political leaders from exploiting their popularity to punch through constitutional barriers that favored the aristocracy. When Sulla made himself dictator in 82 BC, he tried to reverse these trends by enlarging the Senate, reducing the legislative power of the tribunes, restoring ancient senatorial veto power over legislation, and while he was at it, killing anyone he thought an enemy of himself or the Republic. Most of his reforms lasted barely a decade.[40]

Cicero, whose rise to prominence as a prosecutor of corrupt officials won him popular acclaim, turned his oratory and political acumen to protecting Rome's aristocratic tilt when he became consul in 63 BC.[41] As a "new man" who came from outside Rome and won election as consul, Cicero tended to hold views more meritocratic than those of the older patricians, but he did not think that the general public was competent to make good laws. He had little patience with direct popular legislation since it could not have been carefully formulated in the deliberative way that grounded advice from the Senate. The tribunes could serve useful legal functions in ensuring that legal procedures were followed and that executive powers were not abused. As long as the people were not corrupted by demagogues and were able to hear advice from the best men, he thought, the most talented and public-spirited men would tend to win elections to high office and thereafter would serve in the Senate, as advisers to each newly elected crop of magistrates.

Cicero was convinced that the Rome he lived in had been seriously corrupted.[42] His vision of the Republic and its laws, not to mention his advice to future magistrates, was couched in an idyllic setting that looked back to the period in which Polybius wrote, before populist demagogues began undermining the old constitution. The plebeian tribune Tiberius Gracchus who favored land redistribution "caused the existing form of government to totter to some extent." Tiberius' younger brother and also a champion of the poor, Gaius, was a "dangerous character" for disturbing the existing state of affairs.[43] Both men were killed by the Senate's henchmen.

Cicero Denouncing Catiline in the Senate, *by Cesare Maccari, 1889.*

The populists eventually reversed the effects of the Sullan regime, and Cicero worried that some details of the "Gracchan constitution" had been restored.[44] He went after the men of his day who, in his view, took advantage of the gullibility of ordinary people to catapult themselves to power at the expense of republican norms and institutions.[45] Cicero publicly excoriated his fellow senator, the patrician Catiline, for advocating debt cancellation and land redistribution. Cicero then accused Catiline of plotting to defeat the Senate with an insurgency army, which turned out to be true. Shortly afterward Catiline fled the Senate and died fighting with his insurgents against Roman legions in northern Italy, while his associates in Rome were executed with the Senate's approval but without a public trial.

Melodrama reached soap-operatic proportions in the Republic's final decades. In 58 BC Caesar and Pompey permitted the populist patrician Publius Clodius Pulcher to become a plebeian, which in turn allowed Clodius to be elected tribune. Tribune Clodius lost no time in exiling Cicero for his part in executing without trial Catiline's five co-conspirators. Cicero in turn sought to prosecute Clodius for corruption.[46] When Cicero failed to convince the jury, which voted 31 to 25 for Clodius' acquittal, Cicero had more choice words for Clodius: "Twenty-five of them trusted me, but thirty-one gave you no credit for they got their money in advance."[47]

Caesar then made a great show of saving Cicero from Clodius, permitting Cicero to return from exile, so that Cicero would not unite with Pompey against Caesar. Meanwhile Marcus Cato, a staunch republican aristocrat opposed to Caesar's populist tactics, collaborated with Gabinius, a protégé of Pompey whom Cicero wanted to prosecute for corruption, to prevent an alliance between Pompey and Cicero.[48] Following Caesar's defeat of Pompey's forces at Pharsalus in 48 BC, however, Cicero found himself sidelined by the populist tide in Roman politics that he was powerless to turn back, and he became a despairing chronicler of Rome's demise. A native of Laodicea told Cicero he had come to Rome to ask Caesar for the liberty of his state. Cicero replied, "If you happen to find it, act as envoy for us also."[49]

Our story comes back full circle to the events that opened this chapter. After Brutus led a group of senators to kill Caesar in 44 BC, Cicero once again roused himself to oratorical brilliance in Rome, against the advice of his old friend Atticus, in hopes that the Senate would reverse once and for all the assaults on republican government.[50] Cicero's speeches in the Senate, along with those of Cato and others, were demonstrations of public courage in standing up to Mark Antony, who sought to seize Caesar's fallen mantle.[51] Cicero and his colleagues failed, notwithstanding bold speeches and bloody assassinations, to restore the aristocratic cartel of olden times that could block men from appealing over the heads of the Senate to the broader public.[52]

◆ ◆ ◆

Roman history documents that wars and how they were fought profoundly shaped the Roman state. The aristocracy, which supplanted the old Etruscan monarchy at about the same time that Athens became a full-blown democracy, grudgingly granted commoners a political voice in exchange for fighting, first to defend Rome against aggressive neighbors, then to grab more lands to share among themselves. Unlike the naval-based Athenian Empire, which was supported by commoners in triremes, the Roman Empire was won by ironclad infantry on foot. The iron revolution, which had put the panoply within reach of prosperous farmers, had created a symbiosis between home defense and Rome's military power based on an extensive mustering of men. We need not believe that soldiers literally engaged in a sit-down strike in 494 BC (the so-called *secessio*) in order to win a political voice in the Roman state, but it is easy to see that Roman military accomplishments rested on wide manpower mobilization rewarded by citizenship and political voice.

Rome remained, from beginning to end, an aristocracy that was never able to come to terms with its popular elements. Iron-based infantry warfare gave political staying power to farmer-soldiers who could afford the panoply. Until the middle of the second century, this formula was successful in maintaining social peace. But in time the state was forced to supply arms to the lower orders, and to foreign allies, in order to maintain and expand its empire, eroding the prestige of the yeoman farmer. Few noticed that the growing empire was destroying the small-farm economy of the panoplied infantryman and, along with it, the political voice of the farmer-soldier who had once controlled the military fate of Rome. Those who did see the rot, like the Gracchi, were hunted and killed for it. No amount of republican institutional engineering or appeal to the common good could block ambitious politicians, populist or aristocratic, who sought to outbid one another with bread and circuses for the loyalty and votes of a rootless and landless populace. The collapse of the Republic was a collapse not of democracy but of aristocracy and the institutions and ethos that sustained it.

To get to the next chapter on decentralized European aristocracy in feudal times, we skip over the five hundred years of the Roman Principate with its predictable combination of repression and pandering. European feudalism, windshield-shattered compared to the centralized rule of imperial Rome, was also set of aristocratic cartels that degenerated along paths recognizable from the elite decay that we have just witnessed in Republican Rome.

Chapter Four

A MILLENNIUM OF

LANDED ARISTOCRACY

O N AUGUST 9, AD 378, in sweltering late summer heat at the Roman garrison city of Adrianopolis—just west of Istanbul in today's Turkey—an
avalanche of Gothic warriors, tens of thousands strong, led by their leader
Fritigern, charged down a hill. The Roman cavalry who opposed them
were quickly sent skittering into flight, only to plow into the left flank of the
Roman infantry line.[1] According to the vivid accounts of Roman historian
Ammianus Marcellinus, "The barbarians poured on in huge columns, tram-
pling down horse and man and crushing our ranks so as to make orderly
retreat impossible. . . . A cloud of dust hid the sky, which rang with fearful
shouting." The Roman emperor at the time, Valens, was killed by an arrow
or later in a house in which he had taken refuge.[2]

Ten thousand Roman soldiers died that day, a slaughter comparable to
Hannibal's crushing victory at Cannae in 216 BC.[3] While Rome's defeat at
Adrianopolis did not destroy the empire in a single day, it exposed a deep and
irreparable crack in Roman power: Rome's military strategy, which relied
principally on disciplined and well-armed infantry, was no longer supreme.
Three decades later, in AD 410, the Goths burned down Rome itself.

Various tribes tried to resurrect the western empire, without lasting
success. When Charlemagne's empire collapsed in the waning years of the
ninth century, aristocratic domains littered Europe like a field of boulders
left behind receding glaciers. In broad strokes, this period "in the middle"

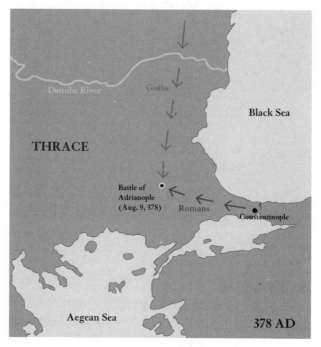

Battle of Adrianople.

illustrates the impact of warfare on politics in a particularly dramatic way. In the place of powerful states that could field large armies, those warriors and aristocrats who could afford to field heavy cavalry forces ruled western Europe. Politics had become radically decentralized.

To understand the deep roots of the Middle Ages, it is necessary to go back several centuries before the Germanic invasion at Adrianople. During that time, for as long as anyone could remember, fear of the Gauls (*metus Gallicus*) had been a driving force of Rome's foreign policy.[4] Much of it stemmed from 390 BC, when a Gallic tribe had invaded the peninsula, overwhelming Roman defenders. The triumphant Gauls then marched on to Rome and sacked the city. They agreed to leave only after being paid a thousand pounds of gold.[5] Although this bribe persuaded the Gallic invaders to leave Rome, many of them settled in Liguria and the plains south of the Alps.

That was too close for Roman comfort, as the Gauls who remained in the peninsula often sided with Rome's enemies during the wars of territorial consolidation during the third century BC. New generations of Gauls crossed the Alps in the 230s and 220s, striking terror into the very heart of

Rome; and although the Republic eventually won these wars, they kept the memories fresh in lore and history lessons.[6]

At the heavily garrisoned northern frontiers of the Roman Empire, the Romans had been forced to give cavalry a larger role, as early as the second security BC, to fight mounted Gallic warriors.[7] During the Republic the "equestrian class" (*equites*) referred both to those who served Rome in the cavalry and to those who were qualified by their wealth to do so. But for the most part Rome "rented" its cavalry, bringing over to its side entire units of once-hostile tribesmen willing to fight for Rome on horseback, while the Romans continued to fight on foot.[8]

The Senate feared not only Gallic invasions but also the dilution of senatorial control should the new allies and military recruits demand more political voice and economic spoils than was convenient to share. Roman policy, instead, aimed to limit the flow of settlers into its territories, while weakening indigenous leadership by cooptation, assassination, or dispersion.[9]

When the Greek commercial city of Massilia (present-day Marseille) requested Roman help to fend off fresh invasions from the north, Rome sent one of its consuls for 125 BC, Fulvius Flaccus, who defeated several Gallic tribes attempting to cross the Druentia (today's Durance) River into Massilia's hinterlands.[10] Thus began Rome's northward expansion into Gaul.

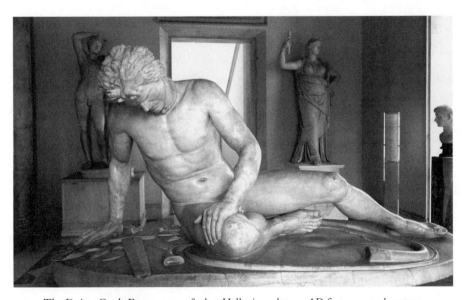

The Dying Gaul, *Roman copy of a lost Hellenic sculpture, AD first or second century.*

The Gallic tribes' disinclination to work together repeatedly played to Rome's advantage, and in 121 BC Consul Fabius Maximus defeated the Arverni by taking advantage of their border disputes with two other tribes. Julius Caesar, his own chronicler of wars in Gaul and Britain in 58–50 BC, deftly shifted his allegiances from one Gallic tribe to another, dividing what could have been a formidable collective opponent. He conquered the Helvetii, who were attempting to migrate west from what is now Switzerland.[11] Vercingetorix, a very charismatic leader of the Gauls, planned to rout Caesar's troops in 52 BC but was foiled when the Gallic cavalry defected to the Roman side in the heat of battle. Julius Caesar captured Vercingetorix, whom he had admired for military genius and "iron discipline," and imprisoned him in Rome until 46 BC, when the captive was publicly beheaded as part of Caesar's triumph.

During Caesar's first attempt to invade the British Isles in 55–54 BC, British warriors and charioteers occasionally outfought Roman legions and auxiliary Gallic cavalry. Then when Rome landed in AD 43, its overwhelming force of perhaps forty thousand men finally vanquished them. Rome secured its occupation by playing favorites among the British tribes and tribal leaders.[12] Britain's largest tribe, the Brigantes, was ruled by Queen Cartimandua, about whom Tacitus wrote disapprovingly for divorcing her husband in favor of his armor bearer and for her "cunning stratagems" of various kinds.[13] She capitulated to the Romans rather than persisting in a war of attrition against powerful and disciplined Roman legions.

Occupying territories far from home is, however, very expensive both in gold and in the allegiances of soldiers and colonists alike. Rome's capacity to finance extensive fortified and garrisoned frontiers began to unravel in around AD 100, when it lost control of one rich province after another to hostile tribes. Increasing tax resistance from Rome's own landowners and peasants made matters worse.[14] As a result, Rome found it increasingly useful, even necessary, to employ indigenous tribesmen and their military units to man Roman garrisons and to campaign against their own tribes. The result was a "barbarianized" Roman army with mixed loyalties and limited commitment to the empire.

This almost brings us to the moment of Adrianople. The importance of cavalry in Rome's military strategy had grown with the need for greater

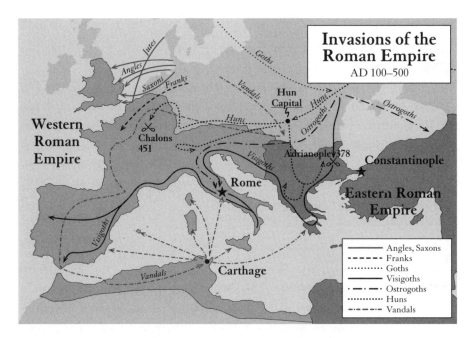

speed and maneuverability over ever-larger expanses of territory. Both to augment his cavalry and to buy off the Gothic tribes that constantly raided eastern lands and waterways, Emperor Constantine in AD 332 contracted for the services of forty thousand Tervingi soldiers who lived north of the Danube to fight for the empire.[15] While this tactic may have worked for a while, it was no answer for the tsunami of tribes arriving at the frontiers in the 370s in flight from the Huns. Following their herds westward, perhaps with the desertification of the Gobi,[16] the Huns drove out the tribes in their path or assimilated them into their "hordes." Like a multicar pile-up, one tribe pushed into another until in 376 BC the Gothic tribes that had once been satisfied to stay on the north of the Danube requested Roman permission to cross the river into Roman territory.[17]

In addition to the warriors, there were many more thousands of women and children in the six to eight thousand wagons spread over nine miles, "a whole people on the move."[18] Emperor Valens granted their requests for asylum but seems to have panicked at the swarms of newcomers. Contrary to his initial promise to provide the Goths with lands sufficient for their livelihood in exchange for loyal service, Valens restricted them to refugee camps that soon deteriorated into squalor and destitution. A revolt broke out among the Gothic warriors over their raw deal, and the group gathered strength through several battles until they demolished Roman defenses at Adrianople in 378.[19] It was a defeat from which Rome never completely recovered.

As the Roman Empire crumbled, a succession of foreign invasions and occupations began: the Ostrogoths in Italy, the Visigoths in southern Gaul, the Burgundians in today's Rhineland and Swiss lowlands. Each of these new states struggled to provide security against the others and against new invaders. The most successful of the invaders were the Franks, from their homeland along the Rhine. Led by their warrior king Clovis, the Franks defeated the forces of Syagrius, the ruler of vestigial Roman Gaul, at Soissons in AD 486.[20]

In earlier times of agrarian settlement, the Celtic tribes of Germany, of which the Franks were one, worshiped fertility gods and goddesses. In his youth Clovis, like many warriors, had worshipped Odin, the god of war, a practice that glorified political and military domination. Clovis, more ambitious than pious, soon converted to Catholicism in order to secure the support of the Catholic Church and wealthy Catholic landowners.[21]

Clovis' alliance with the Catholic Church put him on a collision path with the Visigoths who had settled in Aquitaine about a century earlier. The Visigoths, on their long trek from Scandinavia to the Black Sea region and back after Adrianople, had acquired diverse religious and cultural habits.[22] The Catholic Church viewed the Visigothic king Alaric as a heretic and cheered as Clovis defeated his armies.[23]

By the time of his death in 511, Clovis had amassed vast lands, spanning much of today's France, western Germany, and the Low Countries. At the time of his death, the Merovingian kingdom, as Clovis' dynasty was called, sat astride a cosmopolitan array of peoples. About 150,000 to 200,000 Frankish transplants from east of the Rhine lived among six or seven million Gallo-Romans.[24] But without an external threat to motivate a broad defensive coalition, Clovis' descendants began murdering one another, leaving their subordinate counts, bishops, and warlords with more power by default.[25] Rival Frankish heirs grabbed lands from one another and gave them out to allies for the sake of increasing the size of their horseback hosts; risky gambits and treacherous alliances could turn the tables in a single battle. For commoners trying to eke out a living on lands claimed by battlefield victors, a good day was one of no raping, pillaging, or burning of crops by marauders. With paltry means for self-defense, commoners had to pay a portion of their crops in exchange for protection from the nearest warlord. Sometimes they had to pay more than that.

While Clovis' dynasty was consumed with infighting, a family of warlords in the service of the Merovingian court rose to prominence. In 710–11 large armies of the Umayyad Caliphate based in Syria crossed from North Africa into the Iberian Peninsula, conquering the Visigoths and threatening lands north of the Pyrenees. The Merovingians turned to warrior-in-chief Pippin II and his illegitimate son, Charles Martel, to defend the realm.[26] In 732 Charles Martel rallied the combined forces of local lords to stop the Umayyads in open fields outside the town of Poitiers.

No one knows exactly how large the opposing armies at Poitiers were, but we know they were big. Frankish lore gives the Umayyad forces a large numerical advantage—80,000 invaders to 30,000 defending Franks—but the combatants may have been roughly even at about 30,000 men on each side.[27] The Frankish foot soldiers broke repeated Umayyad cavalry charges by standing firm in infantry phalanx, shield to shield. The Umayyads, mean-

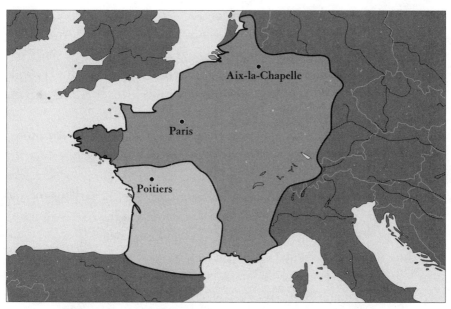

The French kingdom at the beginning of the reign of Pippin the Short, 751

Conquests of Pippin the Short

The Kingdom of France at the Death of Charles Martel, 741.

while, worried about their wives and children (and captured booty) in the caravans to their rear and rushed to protect them as soon as rumors spread that the Aquitainian cavalry had begun to attack the caravans.[28]

Charles Martel's victory over the Umayyads not only saved the Frankish kingdom but also secured his lineage. To his sons, Carloman and Pippin (the Short), he passed on parts of Germany and the Low Countries. From this base, Martel's grandson, Charlemagne, went on to build a Europe-wide empire in a stunning succession of military victories.

Charlemagne had himself crowned the first "Holy Roman emperor" in 800 and nominally ruled over vast territories, from the Atlantic across today's Germany. But he never achieved the taxation or administrative capacity of Chinese or Roman emperors with which to raise and supply massive armies of peasants.[29] But then his dynasty barely outlasted his lifetime; it scarcely had time for the subtler administrative arts. In land-abundant, labor-scarce Europe, Charlemagne was above all a warlord, "first among equals," who depended on his own lands and hired professional warriors to anchor his forces. For larger expeditions, he formed coalitions with other men of means that were easier to finance and organize than a larger infantry would have been.[30] He imposed duties on landholders and "free" men to provide retinues in proportion to their resources by keeping them in his debt.[31] And he followed the Merovingian practice of giving lands in exchange for military service: sometimes in advance of war to make it possible for a vassal to provide a retinue of men on horseback, sometimes after war as a reward for service. He also sometimes awarded his men "borrowed" church lands.[32]

Under Charlemagne, the political and economic center of gravity shifted northward, thanks to the invention of the heavy plow, capable of producing more grain per acre from the deep, wet soils in northern Europe, where agricultural productivity could support more horses per acre.[33] Charlemagne and his allies first vanquished the Saxon tribes in Bavaria in the 780s, beheading as many as eight thousand Saxon warriors in one particularly bloody day. The disorganized Saxon foot soldiers were easy pickings for Charlemagne's relatively disciplined armored fighters.[34] In the 790s his forces all but obliterated the Avars, nomadic warriors from central Asia who had settled in the Danube valley south of the Carpathian Mountains.[35] When Danish Vikings ravaged the coasts of France, Charlemagne and his allies set them to flight.

After Charlemagne's death, Viking rampages continued for another

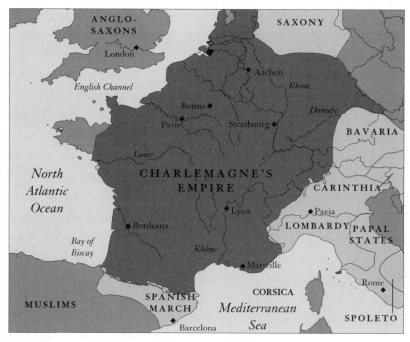

The Empire of Charlemagne in the ninth century.

century, until 918. In 911 Charlemagne's great-great-grandson, Charles "the Simple" granted today's Normandy to them in exchange for their service as warriors defending against further Viking raids. The bribe worked, more or less. Handsomely situated in rich farmlands, the Normans became Christian Frenchmen and supplied warriors to princes throughout Europe, from Scotland to Sicily. But like Aquitaine, Burgundy, and Flanders, Normandy also became a powerful duchy independent enough to resist further incorporation into anyone's centralized realm, either French or English.

The feudal logic of cavalry-based warfare worked continually against territorial size. Bigger armies could win more battles, it was true, but one way to raise that kind of manpower was to give away lands to vassals in exchange for their support and allegiance. When Charlemagne's influence receded, glacierlike, it left in its path local lord-owned estates large enough to provision the same cavalry units that they had once been obligated to provide to the emperor or king. These landed warriors were called dukes, counts, or barons, depending on their rank. They, alongside the bishops who administered Church lands, laid claim to rights over nested and overlapping vassalages of bewildering complexity. Untitled warriors who were able to raise fortresses did the same, claiming status as lords even without any relation to the collapsing empire. As estates were divided and transferred over the years, it was not uncommon for two people to be each other's vassals in respect to different pieces of property.[36]

Landed aristocracy as a constitutional form, even in the guise of the Carolingian Empire, rested on unfree agriculture for its sustenance. Serfs, who were tied to lord and manor, produced food and raised livestock in exchange for protection and subsistence. Crucial for its survival as a constitutional form was the suppression of commoners into a subordinate military role. Like other aristocracies, this one was vulnerable to "democratic" systems that mobilized commoners more fully. But mobilizing peasants was to be avoided at all costs, because in exchange for demanding from commoners a more central role in fighting, the lords would have to give away benefits of elite status. The trade-off was simply too costly. Moreover, because kings depended on vassals for military service, rights were often unclear and contracts to provide service were continually being renegotiated, sometimes in the midst of battles. Feudalism, for all its worship of things military, could never mobilize large armies and remained a militarily weak form of government.

In the ninth and tenth centuries, new threats from Vikings in the north and west, Muslims in the south, and Hungarians in the east required the dispersion of military forces and fortifications to the border regions.[37] Local lords began building separate castles to house their warriors and to protect their livelihoods drawn from the surrounding fields. This weakened the bargaining position of the crown because the king had to rely on far-flung knights, counts, and bishops whose castles proved as effective against the crown as against invaders. Granting fiefs for military service across the realm gave the recipients enormous incentives and opportunities to turn these lands into heritable property, a process that undoubtedly occurred in much of France and northern Italy and elsewhere. To the east, the Vikings ranged through the extensive river systems down to Constantinople. It did not help that the Carolingian rulers after Charlemagne and Louis the Pious fought with one another instead of consolidating a single lineage.[38]

The relative weakening of the Carolingian Empire undermined royal claims to properties that had been granted in fief or as a part of an office. Counts and other vassals who were increasingly providing protection in localities had corresponding opportunities to claim hereditary (allodial) rights over their holdings. The practice, which we might call embezzlement today, was then regarded as fair pay for dangerous service. Imperial and royal law courts that had been, in principle, open to free men of all statuses were increasingly displaced by the local courts run by counts, barons, or bishops, and the justice they dispensed tended to reflect the interests of the local lord when such was at stake.

Counts, as agents of the monarch, got a head start in castle building since kings required them to fortify against raiding Vikings and Hungarians. But lesser warriors could sometimes build castles of their own and claim lordly status. Men who had gained de facto jurisdictional authority over some piece of territory were, as possessors of the "ban," called "banal lords." The process was brutal, particularly at the boundaries.[39] Lords built new domains by offering military protection in exchange for service. Tenants and serfs were driven to commend themselves and any property they might have owned to the most powerful lord in the area.[40] Bishoprics and monasteries were by no means excluded from this process: if they wanted to retain their lands, they had to maintain warriors ready to fight for them against encroaching barons.

The Stellinga (old Saxon for "comrades") rebellion of 841–45 provides a glimpse into the process by which landed aristocrats established themselves at the expense of peasants. Saxon society in the ninth century was stratified into castes that could not intermarry, but the peasants had retained representation in a council that controlled, among other things, the power to make war. Early in his reign between 772 and 804, Charlemagne had incorporated southern Saxony in a series of bloody battles. In 782, in Verden near the Aller River, he slaughtered 4,500 captured Saxons who had rebelled against his lordship. By the end of these decades, Charlemagne and his men had enticed and intimidated his way to lordship of the Saxon elite, sealing the deal with fiefdoms, oaths of fidelity, and mass baptisms.[41]

While the Saxon upper classes accepted Charlemagne's rule on these terms, the lower groups in society, who were expected to continue to work the land as before but now without their voice in council, responded with understandable rage. Taking advantage of a visible crack in Carolingian lordship when Charlemagne's grandsons Lothar and Louis plunged Germany into civil war, the Stellinga rebels revolted against their lowered status, only to be crushed by Saxon nobles themselves.[42]

Peasant revolts in the Saxon lands and elsewhere suggest a reason for heavy cavalry besides military strategy. The loss of status by the lower castes seems a plausible motive for sporadic outbreaks of violence against the symbols of Frankish rule. The Saxon elite probably welcomed the assistance of well-armed and well-fed Frankish knights in repressing resistance to policies that inured to their benefit. Heavy cavalry forces assembled in a military campaign could be useful to whichever king or duke was leading it but also to the knights in that cavalry, who could become a freestanding source of political authority, independent of kings and bishops. The local courts they created transformed local customary property rights, and they often managed to transform their fiefs into owned and heritable property. Heavy cavalry may not have been the most effective form of military organization against a genuine outside threat, but it was a useful way of impressing the lower orders.[43]

Periodically, the peasants at the bottom of the medieval food chain mustered spirited opposition, as had the Stellinga. The Jacquerie of 1358 reveals the plight of peasants during the worst period of French feudalism and shows how the external threat from England began to strengthen the French monarchy in the face of military mobilization. The Jacquerie was so named because the French aristocrats poked fun at peasants for their rough

Defeat of the Jacquerie, *as described in Froissart's* Chronicles, *fourteenth century.*

tunic called a *jacque*. "Jacques Bonhomme" was their general nickname and what they called the uprising's leader, Guillaume Cale. Twenty years into the Hundred Years' War (1337–1453), the French monarch was hemmed in by strong lords but was gathering strength as a leader against the English threat. As chronicled by various contemporaries, some sympathetic and some not, the peasants in St. Leu and neighboring villages in northern France went on a furious rampage against the nobility for a long train of abuses, including allowing the peasantry to bear the brunt of the English assault and failing to protect the king from capture at the Battle of Poitiers in 1356, while forcing the peasants to defend the châteaux of the area.

If the king were in his throne instead of locked up in an English prison, the peasants insisted, things would go better for them. It could have, perhaps, but the nobility had responded to the labor scarcity that followed the Black Death epidemic of the 1340s by even harsher suppression of peasant unrest.[44] The nobility who came from far and wide to help the local Coucy lords suppress the revolt acted with a viciousness that betrays fear and aim to terrify. The fourteenth-century aristocrat Jean Froissart wrote that when the group of peasants reached the city of Meaux "all the noblemen issued out . . . and beat them down by heaps and slew them like beasts and chased them all out of the town, and slew so many that they were weary, and made many of them by heaps to fly into the river. Briefly, that day they slew of them more than seven thousand, and none had scaped, if they would a followed the chase any farther."[45] Charles of Navarre reportedly beheaded the Jacquerie leader Guillaume Cale after the cruel mockery of placing a crown of red-hot iron on his head.[46] In the ensuing weeks, the nobility hunted down the surviving rebels and slaughtered them.[47]

✦ ✦ ✦

On the other side of the English strait, the final withdrawal of Roman legions after 408 left behind a patchwork of chieftancies that gradually amalgamated into larger domains capable of resisting Viking raids. In response to renewed Danish attacks from the late tenth century, the English created a system of national land taxation, the first in western Europe since the fall of the Roman Empire.[48] Landholders were willing to pay the tax—a bribe, really—that went directly to the Danes in exchange for not pillaging their lands.[49] From these early origins in common defense, the English developed a centralized monarchy surrounded by an assembly of tax-paying lords.

An English infantry shield wall against Norman cavalry at the
Battle of Hastings, from the eleventh-century Bayeux Tapestry.

The last "Viking" invasion of England came in 1066 when the Normans, who had been enticed by the French to settle in Normandy rather than plunder along the Seine, decided they wanted more. William the Bastard claimed that he had been promised the English throne by Edward the Confessor and mounted an invasion to seize it from Harold Godwinson. The Norman victory was not a sure thing: the English infantry defense was solid against Norman cavalry attacking uphill but apparently failed when the Normans lured them downhill in feigned retreat.

William's conquest permitted him to redistribute large swaths of already-occupied lands among the Norman conquerors, creating a new Norman aristocracy in England. Orderic Vitalis, a Benedictine monk who lived through these times, wrote that King William "made tribunes and centurions from the lowest followers of the Normans," bestowing upon them property in exchange for loyalty.[50] Someone like Roger Bigod, a man of modest means in Normandy, could become a magnate in East Anglia, a multimillionaire by today's standards.[51]

In time, the Norman warrior economy of land-for-military-service softened under the conditions of island protection. For one thing, vassals were not contractually required to do service overseas, and many landowners paid their way out of military service by way of a substitution tax called the scutage, with which the king could hire mercenary knights.[52] The king's wars, including the Hundred Years' grab for the French crown, were his own expeditions, for which it was hard to extract either military service or scutage without giving extravagant concessions in return. The nobles, for their part, had difficulty extracting more effort from peasants to pay for the king's ambitions.[53] In 1381 an English commoner named Walter "Wat" Tyler (so called because of his profession as a roof tiler) led a peasant revolt against landholders. Tyler was killed while trying to negotiate, and his followers met with no kinder treatment than Guillaume Cale's had, but serfdom withered more quickly on the English vine than on the French.[54]

Labor scarcity after the Black Death and the growing commercial prosperity of these islands drew more peasants into urban centers, where they were often poor but free.[55] The dark side of land surplus, for peasants, was the incentive of lords to hold farmers forcibly.[56] The growing markets for produce, the cities' demand for labor, and the rising value of labor more generally after the Black Death eroded nobles' ability to enforce peasants' unfree status on both sides of the Channel. One big difference was the continued preponderance of mail-clad men in France on account of wars on home territory.[57] As always, heavy cavalry was even more useful against restive peasants than against heavily armed invaders.

✦　✦　✦

In the eastern lands of Charlemagne's old empire, a landed elite of Frankish, Swabian, and Bavarian tribes sat atop a considerable body of freemen who cultivated their own farms.[58] Germany was harassed in this period by Vikings from the north and by Magyar (Hungarian) raids from the east. In the eastern lands, Otto I's crushing defeat of the Magyars at Lechfeld (south of Augsburg) in 955, with about eight thousand European knights against a larger Magyar force, gave him the momentum to consolidate his power over a wide area of central Europe, reaching down into Italy. Gaining the title of Holy Roman emperor in 962, Otto attempted to resurrect Charlemagne's authority over both secular and clerical nobility until the Investiture Controversy ended in stalemate between church and empire in 1122. With neither church nor state able to establish supremacy over the other, local lords carved up much of the contested lands.

Born in 1122, at the end of the Investiture struggle, the Holy Roman emperor Frederick Barbarossa (literally "Red Beard," so called by the Italians he sought to rule) inadvertently strengthened the power of local lords in his German homeland, undermining possibilities for centralized rule. Barbarossa established a streamlined hierarchy of vassals, at the bottom of which were freemen who fell into serfdom if they could not feed and arm a retinue of men for military service.[59] Reestablished in this way, the German agrarian elite lasted longer than that of France and England, where the rise of commercial wealth simultaneously supported the rise of strong kings and sapped the nobility's monopoly of peasant employment.[60] Castles sprouted over Germany like mushrooms after a rain. German families vying for control of the Holy Roman Empire were no less ambitious than the Capetian kings of France, but they did not have the benefit of wealthy cities in their lands that provided the French monarchy with a source of wealth independent of the agrarian nobility from which to build monarchical strength.[61]

Meanwhile, east of the Elbe River, what would become Poland and part of Prussia was beyond the reach of Charlemagne's legacy. There the agrarian elite had not been beholden to the Holy Roman emperor in the first place. The military entrepreneurs and colonists from the West who established themselves as lords, and religious orders such as the Teutonic Knights, were intent on holding farmers to the land precisely because land abundance made peasant labor valuable.[62] Labor scarcity resembled that of England, but the difference was the ferocity of the landed elite. Serfdom was harsh and exploitative precisely where labor was scarce and where lords could use heavy cavalry to suppress peasants. Some historians doubt that manorial lords in eastern Europe were often able to impose serfdom as strictly as they claimed on the books. But this is exactly what we would expect: punishments are fiercest where the state is in the weakest position to enforce them.[63] During the fifteenth and sixteenth centuries, land abundance and peasant enserfment went together as Prussia quadrupled its size and the Austrian Habsburg family grabbed land in Bohemia, Hungary, Croatia, and Transylvania.[64]

Even though feudalism is a relatively weak form of political organization for warfare, the nobility of Russia, Prussia, Poland, and Austria/Hungary resisted enlisting the serfs into great national armies.[65] The agrarian lords seem to have understood that their power depended on the weakness of peasants, which was not to be tampered with even for the sake of wartime mobilization. To keep their peasants subservient and without escape or recourse, nobles not only refused to arm the serfs but also actively undermined cities within their territories with antiurban policies.[66] Not until the Thirty Years' War (1618–48) did large monarchically organized armies manage to defeat feudal hosts in the east on the basis of superior mobilizational capacity.

✦ ✦ ✦

In China, a succession of imperial dynasties from the third century BC onward fended off the same horseback invaders of Central Asia, not with cavalry of their own but with great armies of peasants and a Great Wall.

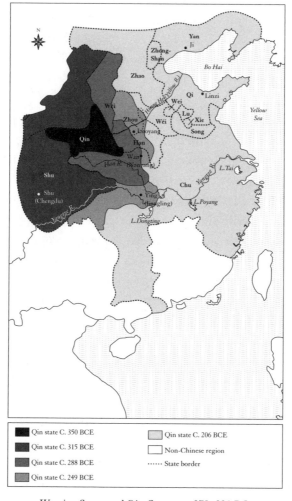

Warring States and Qin Conquest, 278–221 BC.

China was a precocious unifier, creating a large administrative state out of a cluster of warring states.[67] Neither the Warring States period (from 475 to 221 BC) nor the so-called "Chinese middle ages" (from AD 220 to 618) of political fragmentation were "feudal" in the sense of politics dominated by a local landed elite.[68] Polybius would have been curious as to why the monarchical form predominated in China for so many centuries while the rest of the world was prey to rural elites. The threat of war offers part of the answer. By AD 200, China's physically vulnerable Huai valley of wheat and rice farms, bounded by the Yangtze and Yellow rivers, was home to 58 million people and a human reservoir of manpower and taxes. Easily expropriated by their own rulers when not under attack from the horseback invaders, they agreed to supply China's vast armies. When the Mongols ruled China from 1229 to 1368 and the Manchus (Tatars) from 1644 to 1912, they too followed this Chinese system of large infantry armies.[69] China's geographical vulnerability was compelling even to men raised and bred in the saddle.

At the farthest end of Eurasia from the British Isles lay Japan, similarly separated by water from continental warfare. Japan's "feudal" period lasted for several hundred years between two autocracies. Warfare in Japan was not against external enemies, for Kublai Khan's two attempts at invasion with thousands of ships in 1274 and 1281 had failed: fortuitous storms (*kamikaze*) intervened both times to sink the vast fleets.[70] The fighting in feudal Japan was, instead, among renegade imperial officials-turned-warlords seeking to expand their domains at one another's expense.[71] For centuries peasants, helpless to protect themselves and their crops against the armored elite, were drawn into war as taxpayers, as foot soldiers, and if they were talented, as military leaders. The Japanese historian Kan'ichi Asakawa notes that as early as the tenth century, an estate owner would sometimes transfer partial title to a warrior who "would be as efficient for its security as he would be dangerous . . . as a marauder."[72] It was a period in Japan in which "the world turned upside down."[73]

As much as the vying warlords and their retinues cultivated the support of their subjects, they did not go so far as to include the peasantry in the political franchise.[74] There were a few exceptions, for a while. In the mountains of Iga and Koga, and on the swampy delta where the Ibi, Kiso, and Nagara rivers converge at the border of Owari and Ise, for example, communities of farmers and warrior monks held out against warlord conquest for several decades with the help of terrain and stealth.[75]

The rebels were increasingly vulnerable as a growing commercial economy created new funds of wealth that could be used to create and arm centralizing armies. As in Europe, whoever could protect and tax larger areas and trade routes could raise and finance bigger armies that could in turn grab more territory. Gunpowder accelerated Japan's territorial consolidation by making every battle lethal, but also as in Europe, it was the taxes on merchant wealth that paid for the biggest gun-toting armies.[76]

Japan's "unifiers" locked in their triumph by disarming the nation. Hideyoshi Toyotomi, a leading warrior-general generally known as the second of the three unifiers of Japan, famously forbade anyone but samurai to own

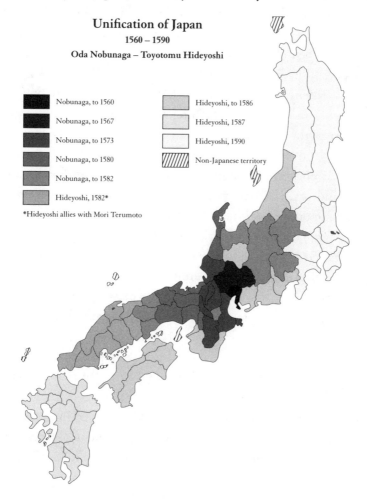

Unification of Japan
1560 – 1590
Oda Nobunaga – Toyotomu Hideyoshi

Nobunaga, to 1560
Nobunaga, to 1567
Nobunaga, to 1573
Nobunaga, to 1580
Nobunaga, to 1582
Hideyoshi, 1582*

Hideyoshi, to 1586
Hideyoshi, 1587
Hideyoshi, 1590
Non-Japanese territory

*Hideyoshi allies with Mori Terumoto

weapons in 1588, and his successors established a monopoly on gun manufacture and procurement. The Tokugawa shogunate, after vanquishing its
enemies in 1600, took the policy of national disarmament even farther by
closing the country to foreign trade in 1635. "Pax Tokugawa" ushered in an
era of peace and stability at home by freezing the military status quo at the
cost of political competition and economic development.

✦ ✦ ✦

In Europe, for nearly a millennium after the fall of Rome, men on horseback
gripped much of the continent in their mailed hands, while the parallels to
medieval Japan's militarized agrarianism reveal broader forces at play. The
system we know as feudalism for short was a protection racket by which the
peasantry, virtually the only part of society creating value at that time, paid
lords not only to protect them from other lords but also not to destroy them
themselves. As the Robin Hood tales attest, the protection was not only inad-
equate but often shaded into predation. As we would expect, feudalism was
principally a system of government for fertile lands that were both vulnerable to predation and that had something worth protecting. As peasants periodically learned the hard way, physical vulnerability translated into political
subordination and abuse.

Except for pockets of peasants in places like the high mountain valleys
of Switzerland or Iga Japan, power was in the hands of men who could
wreak havoc upon everyone else. Feudalism appears to have been looser in
England, where people lived in relative safety, once the Vikings had settled,
and peasants had less reason to give up all they had for protection from local
lords. At the other extreme, had Europe been attacked by more formidable
enemies in these centuries, the military weaknesses of heavy cavalry might
have forced lords to rely more extensively on peasant soldiers, in exchange
for which they might have given peasants back certain representative rights.
Some of these lords, bored with the calm in Europe, went off to take the
Holy Land between 1095 and 1291, where they killed many thousands of
people.

Political power in Europe was at its most fragmented in the twelfth century, until some military entrepreneurs began to make use of new sources of
income with which to outmaneuver rivals and raise even bigger armies: the

taxation of commerce in exchange for protecting urban centers of wealth, and New World plunder. But as the Italian city-states discovered, money alone was insufficient to play a good game of geopolitics. As we explore in the next chapter, states in urbanizing Europe began to grow, not to the extent of the loose-knit Roman or Carolingian empires, but more tightly administered and defended within the borders of the modern nation-state in France and Spain.

Part II

MONARCHY
AND OTHER
EXPERIMENTS

Chapter Five

THE EMERGENCE OF MONARCHY

IN FRANCE AND SPAIN

A S THE SAYING GOES, victors get to write history. A good example of this adage is the House of Toulouse, a once-thriving feudal duchy in Charlemagne's empire. Early French histories describe one of the scions of the house, Count Raymond IV of Toulouse (1052–1105), as a selfish, ill-tempered and superstitious old man who botched the First Crusade (1096–99) by failing to cooperate with other crusaders.[1] Some of Raymond's heirs were vilified as well, including Count Raymond VI (1156–1222), who was excommunicated by the church more than once. To top things off, 1271, the same year the monarchy quelled Toulouse's bid for independence, is celebrated as the year the entire region of Languedoc was "*re*united" with the French crown.[2]

We need look no further than the Albigensian Crusade (1209–29) for a clue as to Toulouse's rogue designation: the French crown joined the church in targeting Raymond VII (1197–1249) and others for tolerating the Cathar heresy in his domains. The Cathars, sometimes called the Albigensians because they were concentrated in villages around Albi, held to a "dualist" belief that accorded Satan more powers than official church doctrine allowed.

Capitalizing on the genocidal attack on the Cathars for their unorthodox beliefs, the Capetian monarchy attacked the proud House of Toulouse to seize its rich lands.[3] Raymond VII played cat and mouse with royal forces for over a decade but by 1242 was outnumbered and outmaneuvered. After enduring the humiliation of a public beating, Raymond submitted to the

93

Cathars being expelled from Carcassonne.

crown and agreed that his lands would be ceded to the king upon the death of his son.[4] The troubadour Guilhem de Tudela paid the rebels the only compliment officially allowed: they were exceptional knights, but unfortunately "they supported the heretics and so they caused their own destruction and their own deaths with dishonor."[5]

We citizens of later centuries take the hexagonal shape of France for granted. As the example of Toulouse shows, however, French nation building was anything but peaceful. The same was true elsewhere: wars of conquest, not voluntary association, created the modern nation-state as we know it. Across much of Europe, in the seventeenth and eighteenth centuries, territorially large and politically centralized monarchies replaced the decentralized rule of the Middle Ages.

Two new ingredients upset the precarious equilibrium of feudal rule in late medieval Europe. The first was the rise of commercial wealth as a source of tax revenues. For a millennium, domain lords had competed with one another for territory, fueling a constant desire for more men-at-arms. As at Poitiers in 732, cavalry forces were not decisive against large infantry armies. Still, the Carolingians kept on investing in heavy cavalry, offering land in exchange for knight service, which again undermined centralized control over large territories.

A new element in the seventeenth and eighteenth centuries was that merchants—having grown rich from manufacturing and trade—acquired an interest in extensive and powerful states that could protect trading routes from disruptive raids. The rise of commercial economies generated revenues—taxes in exchange for protection of commercial wealth—that dramatically raised the ceiling on the size of armies.

The second factor was military technology. From the fourteenth century, heavy cavalry had proved vulnerable to missile fire—crossbows and longbows. Gunpowder, introduced from China in the late fourteenth century, began to shift the advantage still further from heavy cavalry. Because early guns were inaccurate and slow, they were required in larger numbers to be effective; but guns were increasingly lethal against not only horses and their armored mounts but also the medieval fortress. The combat advantage increasingly went to those lords who could afford to buy more and better guns and recruit bigger armies to use them. The territories of lords grew larger, like snowballs rolling downhill: as gun-equipped lords overran or absorbed their feudal rivals, they raised ever more resources from new populations in exchange for protection.[6] By the beginning of the sixteenth century, the kings of France and Spain had not only established territorial sovereignty over their own realms but had also overrun the rich cities of northern Italy.

Even with the technological shift to handheld guns starting in the sixteenth century, the creation of mass armies sometimes produced a wider franchise. These expansions, however, lasted only briefly or in isolated pockets: the mountain cantons of Switzerland during the years of Austrian assault; the kingdom of Sweden during the Thirty Years' War; Dutch city councils during the height of the Dutch Revolt; a few mountain redoubts resisting territorial consolidation in Japan; and only a whiff during the English Civil War. Universal male franchise, which, after classical Athens and Rome, had virtually disappeared from the face of the earth until the American and French Revolutions, did not become a core principle of modern constitutionalism until the great wars of the nineteenth and twentieth centuries.

Centralized monarchy replaced decentralized feudalism in the territorial states of France and Spain, although not without spirited challenges from the other nobility. The Capetian monarchy (987–1328) used strong-arm tactics to push the English out of western France and—as we saw in the seizure of Toulouse during the Albigensian Crusade—formed an opportunistic

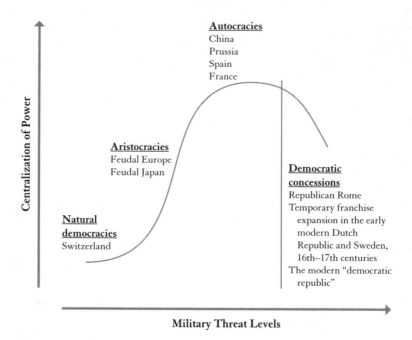

The strongest monarchies emerged in France and Spain,
where geography made subjects vulnerable to invasion and where
monarchs raised money in ways that avoided national taxation.

alliance with the church to consolidate territorial control.[7] In the early centuries of the succeeding House of Valois (1328–1589), commercial taxation left the French monarchy substantially at the mercy of local elites and their cavalry forces for the prosecution of the Hundred Years' War with England (1337–1453).[8] French nobles feuded among themselves over disputed lands, and some, such as the Duke of Burgundy, even sided with the English when the war seemed to be going their way.[9] Joan of Arc was burned at the stake, in fact, only after the Burgundians captured her and sold her to the English. Although a succession of French kings convened assemblies of lords—later known as the Estates General—to ask for money with which to fight the English during the Hundred Years' War, each region of France determined what form of tax to use in paying its share.[10] But after the war was won, successive kings saw little point to calling the Estates. The effect of the war, if anything, was to strengthen the role of regional and subregional estates that met to discuss, negotiate, and apportion the burden of taxation rather than to empower a representative institution to bargain with the king.[11]

Eventually the French monarchy denominated royal taxation in cur rency rather than in the contribution of feudal levies.[12] Towns and cities paid a growing share, bypassing and weakening the idea that taxes were in exchange for feudal lands. Royal emissaries negotiated town by town, province by province, with more success in some parts of France than in others. During the Hundred Years' War, the communities that suffered English scorch-and-burn tactics (*chevauchée*), not to mention the ravages of unemployed French military men between conflicts, were willing to pay more for defense, including taxes to strengthen their own city walls as in Toulouse. On the other hand, the mountain district of Briançon, on the Alpine watershed between France and Italy, often avoided paying taxes altogether.[13]

During this period nobles were exempt from land taxes on grounds that they provided feudal levies in "time of need," which was an inherently vague concept, putting the onus on the king to demonstrate common purpose. Instead, the French monarchy sought to raise money in other ways, by selling venal offices, by taxing church and peasant lands, and by borrowing money from merchants. France was mostly at peace after the Hundred Years' War, and the crown avoided calling the troublesome and dangerous nobility into session from 1484 to 1560 when religious crisis was spreading throughout the country.

The monarchy convened the Estates General (comprising the clergy, nobility, and commercial classes) in 1560, 1561, 1576, 1588, 1593, and 1614. Thereafter, with the religious disputes apparently quieted, Louis XIII refused to call the Estates, inaugurating a period of "personal rule" that lasted 180 years. Personal rule ended, finally and fatally, in 1789, when Louis XVI called the Estates because the country had been bankrupted and was desperate for new revenues. In retrospect, this was a desperate move with little chance of success.

Over the whole period, moreover, the government raised more money on average in the years that the Estates were not in session through various means that avoided bargaining with the nobility as a group.[14] One of the most lucrative tax schemes was the short-run expedient of selling of noble ranks in exchange for future tax exemption. Government coffers temporarily swelled from the sales of venal offices to rich merchants, but because these offices came with tax exemption, the government lost the annual flow of taxes from the men in those offices. A judgeship in the mid-sixteenth century, for example, sold for roughly ten times the annual salary from such a job.[15] The number of venal offices for sale expanded tenfold over a century and a half, from 4,000 in 1515 to 45,000 in 1665.[16] Records of the 1614 Estates General suggest that nobles were anxious about what the political rise of merchants meant for themselves but, unwilling to pay regular taxes, were in no position to convince the crown to suppress the "insolence" of the rising third estate.[17]

Unlike kings in Germany, Scandinavia, and England, French kings did not need to become Protestant in order to grab church lands to solve their fiscal problems. For one thing, French kings had already placed their protégés in many ecclesiastical offices and began to levy on parishes an annual tax of several "tenths" without papal consent. Between 1563 and 1589, the proportion of land owned by the church declined by half because so many parishes and bishoprics had to sell lands for which they could not afford the taxes. The resulting transfer of property from the church to the government in France was comparable to that in Protestant England.[18]

For some of the nobility, Protestantism was more alluring. Several great noble houses rallied together under the banner of Protestantism, especially in the south, where regions relished their tradition of independence.[19] Though it was not as strong in the north of France, Protestant nobility outnumbered Catholics in the Estates General.[20] Between 1562 and 1598, the monarchy embarked on a systematic effort to stamp out Protestantism among the noble houses in a series of military campaigns known as the French Wars of Religion.[21] It began with the premature death of Francis II in 1560, which brought to the throne Charles IX, son of devoutly Catholic Catherine de' Medici. Her Catholic allies in the nobility, led by the Guise family of Lorraine, waged war on Protestant nobles. Hundreds of Protestant nobles were slaughtered in the St. Bartholomew Massacre of 1572, which began, ironically, in an effort to forge religious peace. A wedding celebration was to be held for the marriage of the protestant Henry of Navarre to the king's sister, and the blessed occasion brought the flower of the French nobility to the city. The Duke of Guise, however, took advantage of the occasion to assassinate the Huguenot leader, Admiral Coligny, and a Parisian mob soon took up the slaughter. The Protestants lost more than their majority in the Estates General. In any event, Charles died soon afterward.

Truth is sometimes stranger than fiction. Charles's successor, Henry III, was assassinated in 1589 and left no heir, and under Frankish (sometimes known as Salic) law, the Protestant lord Henry of Navarre was entitled to the throne. Despite strong Catholic and Spanish opposition, he was finally recognized as king in 1594, when he converted to the Catholic faith, allegedly announcing that "Paris is worth a mass."[22]

Henry ended the crown's attack on Protestantism with the Edict of Nantes in 1598, but following his own assassination in 1610, the conflict between crown and nobility continued to roil the country for several more decades, with and without the help of religion. In 1632 the royal army defeated the (Catholic) noble and governor of Languedoc Henry de Montmorency over a conflict over taxes, and executed him in his own town hall courtyard in Toulouse.

The sale of venal offices took off with Henry IV's strategy in the 1590s to build an administrative class loyal to the king that did not rely on traditional nobility. Henry's heirs Louis XIII and Henry XIV appointed a succession of royal financial officials—Richelieu, Mazarin, and Colbert—to bypass the landed nobility by state-sanctioned tax farming (the *Ferme générale*). Although tax farming was not always profitable, many tax farmers became rich enough to buy themselves into higher nobility and tax-exempt status— the venal offices. Until the mid-seventeenth century, the crown sold tax farms to the highest bidders. When rebellion, plague, and economic downturns drove many small, regionally concentrated tax farmers into bankruptcy, Colbert created a consolidated General Tax Farm with a diversified tax base in 1681. Because the Colbert government motivated tax farmers to do their best by giving them a percentage of their collections, the system became terribly oppressive and corrupt.[23]

The fortunes amassed by some tax farmers and their sometimes-brutal methods of collection made them targets of popular fury. Montesquieu wrote in the 1740s, "When the lucrative profession of a farmer of the revenue becomes a post of honor, the state is ruined."[24] Another contemporary observer, Darigrand, was more picturesque: "The poisonous breath exhaled from the depths of the Hotel des Fermes spreads throughout all of France and infects everything."[25] In *Ferragus, Chief of the Devorants,* the nineteenth-century novelist Honoré de Balzac describes the deserted neighborhood of Île Saint-Louis as the "ghost of fermiers-généraux," full of abandoned houses of people unable to pay taxes. Large numbers of peasants were forced to sell their lands for which they could not afford taxes.[26] In southwestern France alone, more than 450 peasant revolts erupted between 1550 and 1700. The

price of bread, the imposition of new taxes, the methods by which tax farmers collected them, and the depredations of self-provisioning armies were
among the objects of rage.[27]

During the seventeenth century the entire judiciary and the accounting
offices (*chambres de compte*) consisted of venal officials who not only contributed to national coffers by paying for their offices but were also easy targets
for forced loans when the king needed additional money. The king's efforts
to squeeze money out of the venal officials eventually produced a tax revolt
that spiraled into a civil war between competing groups of nobles, between
1648 and 1653, known as the Fronde.[28]

The French nobility was too divided to curtail the king's taxation powers,
and therein lay France's weakness. While England's parliamentary controls
gave the English government a stronger credit rating, especially after the
Glorious Revolution of 1688, the French monarchy could only bully, cajole,
and cheat.[29] France's Seven Years' War (1756–63) proved disastrous when the
General Tax Farm's receipts from the tobacco monopoly dropped by 22 percent due to the decline in shipments from America.[30] French success in the
American Revolutionary War proved even more costly, forcing the government to default on loans in 1788 that amounted to a staggering 60 percent of
tax revenues in that year.[31] Although the French crown had been gradually
moving toward more efficient surveillance and monitoring of its tax farmers, the monarch and his minions had been operating not only on borrowed
money but also on borrowed time. They were ushered to the guillotine before
they had devised a politically sustainable fiscal system in support of war.

In Spain, war did even less to deepen the monarchy's negotiations with
its population because Spanish glory, spanning just two hundred years from
the late fifteenth to the seventeenth century, was subsidized by resources
grabbed from the retreating Arabs, by New World plunder, and by taxes
paid by the Spanish Netherlands. In the 1520s about one-fifth of state revenues came from New World riches alone.[32] When stolen treasures from the
new lands and colonies were spent, the Spanish monarchy fell back upon its
dependence on rebellious lords, who had only been bypassed, unconquered,
during the monarchy's flush years. Spanish territorial consolidation and
expansion, which rested heavily on borrowed foundations, did not survive
the collapse of this temporary funding scheme.

The Spanish monarchy emerged out of the violent turmoil of successive invasions. The Visigoths, who had taken the Iberian Peninsula during the "Great Migrations" of the fifth century, were in turn conquered in 711 by the Umayyads from the Arab world. Charles Martel would repel these Arab conquerors from France at Poitiers in 732, but they remained lords of Iberia. From a mountainous redoubt along the northern coast of Spain, a Visigothic remnant established the Kingdom of Asturias that they later expanded into the Kingdom of León, the cradle of the Spanish monarchy.[33]

For the landed elite, jealous of their local autonomy, the incipient Spanish monarchy was a potential threat. But the prospect of grabbing vast domains and treasures from the Arabs in the name of Christianity—in the Reconquista—was irresistible, and the fracturing of the caliphate in 1031 into competing dominions (*taifa*) paved the way.[34] The Kingdom of León in the northwest, and later its dynastic union with Castile in 1037, pushed Muslim armies steadily southward. As in France, the Castilian monarchy exempted the landed elite from taxation on grounds that its service to the crown was military mobilization in times of need.

From the 1300s the conquering Castilians repopulated the high mesas of central Spain with merino sheep from North Africa whose wool, coveted throughout Europe, brought prosperity to this barren, rocky land and untold riches to the magnates who owned it. The great aristocratic dynasties of the Gúzman, the Enríquez, and the Mendoza were founded in these years, and one family, the Albuquerque, was said to have owned so much land that they could travel the breadth of Castile, from Aragon to Portugal, without having to set foot out of their own estates.[35] Later, with the rise of towns, a class of wool merchants gained political representation in local estates in exchange for paying taxes.[36]

It is hard to take seriously the religious piety implied by the Christian sloganeering around the Reconquista, because wars against the Arab domains had not been a consistent policy. Fearing the expansion of the neighboring Kingdom of Aragon, kings of Castile had periodically given aid to the defending Arabs against Aragon.[37] Only as the Arab domains foundered did the kingdoms increasingly join hands, so as not to find themselves on the losing side. In 1469 Castile and Aragon sealed their pact, trumpeting its religious significance while downplaying the geopolitical, in the marriage of Isabella of Castile and Ferdinand of Aragon.

On the coast to the east of Aragon, the commercially wealthy kingdom

of Catalonia resisted amalgamation with its neighbors. In a strange config-
uration that made sense only in the patchwork politics of medieval Europe,
a Castilian dynasty ruled Catalonia from 1412 from an opulent palace in
Naples, while Castile itself gave the Genoese and not the Catalonians control
of the Castilian wool trade from its southern ports.[38] Catalonian merchants
were rich, independent, and disaffected from Castile. Meanwhile Catalonian
peasants unhappy with their Catalonian landlords appealed in 1455 to their
(Castilian) king in a series of petitions known as the *remences* for relief from
oppressive conditions of tenancy. The result was a civil war, from 1462 to
1472, that unleashed massive score settling among factions and families in
the guise of a battle between aristocratic rights and monarchical populism.[39]
Taking full advantage of the nobility's moment of weakness, Isabella and
Ferdinand seized control, declared peasants free of landed servitude, and
instituted a lottery system for public office in Barcelona.[40] Although Catalonia was brought into the expanding kingdom of Spain, its great families
remained strong enough to retain fiscal autonomy from the crown.[41]

Isabella and Ferdinand continued to move against the aristocracy

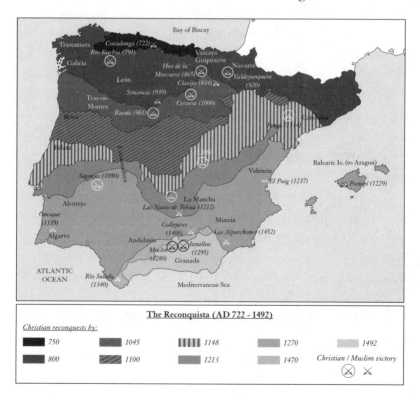

The Reconquista (AD 722 - 1492)

throughout their domains.[42] Still, the monarchs had to play a balancing act: they needed the aristocracy to complete the Reconquista.[43] They appointed prominent magnates to lead the military campaigns, limited the powers of the towns in the Cortes, and continued to grant tax exemptions to the lay and ecclesiastical nobility, conceding aristocratic control over the wool economy. Catholicism and xenophobic patriotism provided the background music.

Although Castile had gained enormous wealth from taking Arab lands, the conquest of the magnificently defended Granada in 1492 came at great cost, depleting the crown's treasury. The expulsion of the Jews, under pressure from the Spanish Inquisition unleashed by the Reconquista, weakened Spain's economic foundations by dislocating the wool market.[44]

The dynastic union between the Spanish crown and the Habsburg empire in 1504 placed a more powerful composite player onto the world stage than either Spain or the Austrian Habsburgs would have been separately. The marriage of Joanna (Isabella and Ferdinand's daughter) to Philip I of Burgundy gave the Habsburgs access to well-trained Spanish armies for their own purposes. After Philip died, his son Charles became heir to the Castilian throne, and in 1516 (when Ferdinand, the Aragonese king, died without an heir) he became Charles I, the first king of Spain as a unified nation. Three years later he was elected Holy Roman emperor, as Charles V, ruler of an immense Habsburg-controlled empire.

Spain's new glory was a poison pill. The French worried about encirclement by the Habsburgs, who were now in every direction: in Spain, Germany, and Italy as well as in the Low Countries. German princes worried that Spanish armies would soon appear on the Habsburg side and upset the constitutional balance within the empire. The Dutch increasingly worried that Charles's loyalty and interest would shift resources from the Netherlands to Spain. They were all right to worry. Charles saw his mission as protector of Catholic Europe against Islam; when the Reformation began, just as he was elected Holy Roman emperor, he became the principal bulwark against Protestantism as well, notwithstanding his fraught relationship with various Italian popes.

Charles V's signature policy, to protect Catholic Europe against both Islam and the Reformation, was an expensive proposition. Spanish armies were built around the *tercio*, sometimes called the Spanish Square, comprising three thousand highly trained infantry soldiers armed with pikes, swords, and handheld firearms. The *tercio* was an invention of Charles's Italian campaigns, crafted to counter the heavy cavalry of the French. These new units pushed the French out of Italy and overran the rich cities of the Italian peninsula.[45]

Spanish cities, already alienated by Isabella's concessions to the landed nobility in the 1490s, were incensed by Charles's imperial ambitions and his spending to match.[46] Charles bypassed their traditional fiscal role by choosing magistrates from outside the municipality and by selling tax farms in competition with their own taxes. With his revenues, he embarked, among other things, on a very costly campaign to succeed his grandfather, Maximilian I, as Holy Roman emperor, managing to outbribe Francis I of France for the privilege. He then left for Germany, leaving behind his Burgundian court and a request that the Cortes pay the bills. The Cortes refused, to which he responded by dissolving the Cortes. A civil war (the *Comunero* revolt) ensued in 1520, led by the cities historically represented in the Cortes.

During the course of the war, Charles agreed to return to Spain, but he also made strategic tax concessions to the landed nobility with which he convinced them to switch to his side. They agreed and suppressed the *Comunero* uprising with brutal swiftness.[47] Following the rebellion he also made some concessions to the cities, restoring some measure of urban fiscal autonomy. None of this changed the fact that he remained in a fiscal bind. He resorted, then, to the sale of religious orders, taxing church property, raising taxes on Dutch subjects, and drawing down the stores of wealth from the New World.[48]

Spanish glory sputtered to an end in the Eighty Years' War—the Spanish effort to put down the Dutch Revolt that lasted from 1568 to 1648. Following Charles's abdication in favor of his son, Philip II, in 1556, the Protestant Dutch provinces, already suffering from high taxes, reacted strongly against the prospect of rule by an even more Catholic monarch. Facing the powerful Army of Flanders, the Dutch armies waged a war of maneuver and siege, successfully avoiding set piece battles and stretching Spanish forces. Deprived of Dutch revenues and plagued by Dutch privateers looting New World silver shipments, the Spanish treasury shriveled just as the Thirty Years' War (1618–48) required new outlays. Deep-pocketed Dutch financiers financed Protestant armies against Habsburg forces. The Spanish agreed to long truces in the hope that their fortunes would change but they never did. By 1648 Dutch independence had become a foregone conclusion.

Spanish territorial consolidation and expansion, which rested heavily on borrowed foundations, did not survive the collapse of its temporary funding scheme of New World treasure and Dutch loans, and Spain tumbled from the pinnacle of world power.[49] The peasants, whose lowly status the monarchy had temporarily boosted as ballast against the landed elite, faded once again into the margins of society. As the rise and fall of the Spanish monarchy shows, the progression through constitutional forms was neither linear nor inevitable: some monarchies simply failed to stay in the big leagues.

From contentious local aristocracies, France and Spain became large centralized monarchies, but only while the king's riches lasted. French kings exchanged crown privileges for merchant wealth, giving them two more centuries of royal splendor than Spain's had. Relations between crown and parliament were always under negotiation but not moving in any particular direction, and both kingdoms were dismantled to the ground floor before they were reconstructed centuries later as democratic republics.

Wars drew in vast armies of men in the sixteenth and seventeenth centuries, but as long as monarchies could buy armies with money, blood did not buy voting rights, as it had in Athens and Rome. The history of early modern Europe underscores two factors that shaped state development: the size of military threats, and who had the resources with which to meet the threats. Rulers conceded as much as necessary but as little as possible and in this period, most governments were able to buy armies with plunder or, where necessary, through exchanges of favors with merchants that were less destabilizing than the bargains they would otherwise have had to strike with the poor.

Subjects were not asked, of course, to which realm they wished to belong, but regions exhausted by the comings and goings of marauding armies were often the first to become attached to expanding powers. To paraphrase Thomas Hobbes, the one, the few, or the many can construct a Leviathan to stand against mayhem; the important thing is that a government so constructed possesses the undivided authority to protect citizens from harm.

Thomas Hobbes focused on one part of the story: strong government can make the difference between life and death. Our concern is with the nature of that government: who controls the state determines the quality of life. The rise of European monarchies provides a window into the conditions under which war forced kings to share decision-making power with the owners of wealth and, in more extreme cases, with the men supplying their labor.

Eventually, but not for several centuries more, all-out interstate war would favor governments in Europe that offered both property rights, securing a steady stream of money, and a wide franchise, underpinning the full mobilization of manpower. But the cauldron of the sixteenth- and seventeenth-century wars was not yet hot enough to melt the ironclad social structures still in the way of universal suffrage.

Not everywhere, even in the sixteenth and seventeenth centuries, did wars produce absolutist monarchy. The combination of geography and resources sometimes favored other responses. The English nobility, comfortably on the other side of the English Channel, refused to provision the king's wars without consultation. The nobility's indifference to royal dynastic wars built the foundation of parliament's robust development. In the Netherlands, at least during the seventeenth-century war to oust the Habsburg overlords, power sharing went even further. The merchant elite shared decision-making power with the working-class rabble who helped them fight. Sweden too went so far as to create a fourth estate—a place at the decision-making table for the peasantry—during its years of full wartime mobilization. The more dramatic periods of political devolution in the Netherlands and Sweden, however, were short-lived. War sometimes required concessions so costly that the aristocracy preferred inglorious peace to warlike democracy.

Chapter Six

WAR AND REPRESENTATION

IN ENGLAND, THE NETHERLANDS,

AND SWEDEN

O N JUNE 15, 1215, on a great meadow called Runnymede about twenty miles west of today's London, a decade-long standoff ended. King John of England, who had sat on the throne since 1199, finally relented and agreed that his barons should have a role in assessing taxes, the right to trial by jury, and—should they be displeased with the king's compliance with these and other provisions—the right "to seize castles, lands, and possessions until amends have been made."[1]

King John might have had no intention of honoring their demands, but at the time he was not in a position to refuse. The Magna Carta balanced a lawyer's wig on the point of a soldier's sword.[2]

King John, the fifth son of Henry II and Eleanor of Aquitaine, had attempted to make good on dynastic claims in Normandy but had been driven out in 1204 by King Philip of France. When he tried to raise revenues for another French campaign, a group of scions of great Anglo-Norman families refused to accept the terms of his lordship. Many of the baronial families were from the northern counties between England and Scotland—much of the land of which Richard the Lionheart, John's older brother and predecessor, had sold to the King of Scotland for ten thousand crowns before sailing off to the Crusades. Not only was the lordship of these lands disputed;

Magna Carta.

many of the barons were in tax arrears to the king as well as to "the Jews" who had advanced loans with which to pay the king's dues.[3] Although the Magna Carta was in large part a debt-restructuring plan, its constitutional significance was far greater: successive generations of English subjects have found in its language foundational principles of representative government. Struggles between the nobility and king, smoothed over but by no means settled by the Magna Carta, illustrate the strong bargaining position of England's landed elite vis-à-vis the crown. This leverage was the impetus for the strong English tradition of parliamentary consultation.

In King John's case, England's barons could push him around because he was trying to stake a foreign claim, not defend England. The Strait of Dover normally deterred invasion without the necessity of a great consolidated effort for common defense, which led Englishmen to doubt the need for foreign adventures. Kings of England, who ruled their ancestral homeland Normandy and much of the rest of western France, nevertheless periodically ran afoul of their vassals, unsure exactly how much was safe to ask of them.

One might have thought that King John's son, Henry III, would have learned his lesson from his father's humiliation at Runnymede; instead, he launched his own French invasions in 1230 and 1242 and attempted to take the Sicilian throne for his second son Edmund in 1256. As a result, the Sixth Earl of Leicester Simon de Montfort (whose father had led the French knights on the Crusade against the Albigensians half a century earlier), and brother-in-law to the king, led the opposition in seeking to place "constitutional limits" on what the king could demand from his subjects for foreign adventures. The barons convened in Oxford, together with merchants from English towns, in what has become known as the "Mad Parliament" of 1258. Some historians wonder if "insane parliamentum" was a typo for *insigne parliamentum* in the earliest list of baronial documents that give the parliament its name, but from the standpoint of the English monarchy, the challenge to monarchical power was unequivocally crazy.[4] In this first-ever meeting of knights and merchants to oppose royal taxation, the assembly placed the crown under the receivership of a council of barons, limited the taxes he could demand, and required him to convene parliaments regularly.

Dissatisfied with the king's lukewarm compliance with the Oxford Provisions, de Montfort then launched the Second Barons' War (1264–67) during which baronial forces managed to capture Henry and his oldest son Edward (later Edward I, "Longshanks") at the Battle of Lewes in 1264 and hold them prisoner for months. Edward somehow escaped to raise an army. A year later, at the Battle of Evesham, Prince Edward, now with a much larger force that dwarfed the barons', annihilated the rebels and killed the combatants rather than accept surrender. Not satisfied to slay Simon de Montfort, Prince Edward had his body mutilated.

The struggle with the barons nevertheless left its mark on the English constitution. While de Montfort and the others were condemned and their heirs dispossessed of titles and property, King Henry III and his son, as Edward I, accepted in principle the Provisions of Oxford as the basis for royal accountability to Parliament.[5]

Compared to their French and Spanish counterparts, English kings had more difficulty concocting a shared sense of national threat large enough to produce tax payments without something in return. England's parliamentary tradition rests on a deep suspicion that kings, with their dynastic claims to continental territories, could cause more trouble than they were likely to solve, if entrusted with large amounts of revenue.[6] A king's right to tax never became automatic; instead, it became customary to require a king to ask parliamentary permission to tax for specific projects. In return, he had to agree to provide legislation to resolve "grievances before subsidies" were given.[7] From the late thirteenth century, parliaments comprised representatives of shires and towns as well as nobles and clergy. A hundred years later the House of Lords, and eventually the House of Commons, customarily submitted lists of grievances to be handled in implicit exchange for taxation. Parliament respected the feudal obligation to give the king what he needed in war, but it wrangled over when, how much, and on what terms.

When English kings sought to recover their French lands during the Hundred Years' War (1337–1453), they had to coax the nobles to lend their forces, as John I had tried to do long before. Individual English kings, of course, varied greatly in the political adroitness with which they played their constitutional roles. Following Edward III's successful French invasions, his grandson Richard II (ruled 1377–99) so alienated the baronage, through extravagance on himself and his favorites, that he was eventually deposed and imprisoned by Henry Bolingbroke (Henry IV). Henry V (ruled 1413–1422) then was able to excite the English nobility with prospects of booty and new lands, enabling him to manage parliament without having to pack its benches.[8] Henry VI (ruled 1422–61, 1470–71), who was to inherit the French throne, was infirm of body and mind for much of his reign and was no match for the French Charles VII, who drove the English back across the Channel. The differences are endless, but every king struggled with limits imposed by subjects who did not fear invasion from the continent.[9] Some members of parliament favored limiting the king's spending to what he could fund from the proceeds of his own domain at war's end, but in the end the nobles agreed to carry the debt in exchange for the right to haggle over what the king could do with money that was not his own.[10]

Henry VIII (ruled 1509–47) temporarily financed expensive military ambitions in Ireland and on the continent by money he grabbed from the church, but this windfall was short-lived. So much land did he and his heir Elizabeth (ruled 1558–1603) give away to their supporters that the English peerage grew from 54 families in 1529 to 121 in 1641, and the gentry from 5,000 to 15,000.[11] Spending so quickly the windfall from seizing church lands meant that the powerful Tudor monarchs were soon forced to grapple with parliament's powers of the purse.[12] Queen Elizabeth's response was to avoid war and parliaments alike. To the extent possible, she lived within the crown's resources—which included booty captured at sea by Sir Walter Raleigh—and mostly governed by decree through her privy council. So great was Elizabeth I's reluctance to spend money on war that in 1588, were it not for the intervention of a lucky storm, England's navy rather than Philip II's Spanish Armada might have been the one to be destroyed.[13]

By the sixteenth century the English king remained by any standards an exalted ruler: politically powerful, financially rich, and protected from dissent by stiff prison sentences.[14] But authority was increasingly shared with Parliament—now differentiated into Lords and Commons. In the early seventeenth century the Stuarts attempted to advance a version of royal absolutism in England that defined acceptable religious practice, thereby increasing the extent and intensity of religious dissent. James I (ruled 1603–25), early in his reign, was agile enough politically to skate through these issues. But his less agile son alienated Parliament so thoroughly that he attempted to rule without it, as his brother-in-law, Louis XIII, was doing in France. Charles I (ruled 1625–49) did not grasp that the brutality of the French religious wars had strengthened absolutist claims in France, whereas religious conflict in England had the opposite effect, culminating in the Glorious Revolution.

It is important to see how Parliament's checks on the English king produced, paradoxically, a stronger government than in France. Although the French king labored to keep his nobility on his side, Burgundy occasionally sided with England in the Hundred Years' War. In England a more unified nobility forced kings to accept correction in the institutional form of Parliament-constrained monarchy. As a result, the wars that the king undertook were generally wars that the nobles, and increasingly the commoners, had agreed to fund and support. As scholars have pointed out, the combined resources of king and Parliament were a kind of force multiplier for English armies in continental wars. But they had to pick their fights carefully.[15]

This is not to say that English kings liked it this way or that they did not probe the limits of Parliament's tolerance. At the beginning of the seventeenth century James I, like his continental counterparts, proclaimed that all laws derived their force and all justice its function through the king, and that the king was accountable only to God for his acts.[16] When Parliament balked at supporting his Scottish retinue and his wife Anna of Denmark in the style they required, however, he could only rail at "the house of hell."[17] In 1610 James's chancellor attempted to work out with Parliament a "Great Contract," by which James would surrender his feudal dues in exchange for a budget for life. The deal foundered on the collision between the king's belief in royal prerogative and Parliament's insistence that the king's purse was its business.[18] James was forced to come back to Parliament hat in hand after 1618, when he sought money to intervene in the Thirty Years' War over religion and territorial control on the continent. Like his father, Charles I claimed absolutist authority and was suspected, moreover, of Catholicism. Whether or not he was a Catholic in fact, the accusations were not without some basis. His wife Henrietta, the sister of Louis XIII of France, brought her confessors to court to celebrate masses and instruct the children. Charles I was as unsuccessful in securing parliamentary support as he was unwilling to submit to its assertions. The three parliaments that Charles I convened between 1625 and 1629 to request funds for the war exacted so many concessions in exchange for military supplies that he finally quit the war and simply stopped calling parliaments altogether.

Beginning in 1629, rather than wrangle with an uncooperative body, Charles sent the members of Parliament home and tried to rule alone. During this period of "personal rule," in 1633, Charles stoked fears of religious intolerance when he appointed as archbishop of Canterbury William Laud, a man of "high church" and Arminian leanings known for his hostility to Puritanism. The king began to insist on his prerogative to take "ship money" to protect the realm, characterizing it a kind of fee for services rather than a tax, avoiding the need for parliamentary assent. In 1639 he attempted to levy an additional tax, to pay for a failed military assault on the Presbyterian Scots for not adopting his new-and-improved Anglican Book of Common Prayer. The grumbling grew to dangerous levels as Scottish Covenanters took up arms against the imposition.[19]

In April 1640 Charles called Parliament into session because he needed still more "ship money" to fight the Scottish Covenanters. After three weeks of wrangling, Parliament refused him money for this cause, so Charles again dissolved it in May 1640.

Although Charles sued the Scots for peace, he nevertheless felt compelled some months later to call a new Parliament to replenish the royal coffers depleted by the Scottish war. Certainly he would have preferred to limp along in poverty had he known that Commons would seize the opportunity to impeach several of his key advisers and put the crown itself on notice. Impeachment, a process by which Parliament exercises criminal jurisdiction over ministers and other public officials, dates to the reign of Edward III (1328–77), when barons punished royal advisers who overstepped the understood limits on the crown's power.[20] In December 1640 Parliament went after Archbishop Laud for antagonizing the Scots in the first place. Accusing Laud of treason, it imprisoned him to await trial.[21]

More urgent, Parliament decided, was to decapitate Thomas Wentworth, Earl of Strafford, who had advised Charles to prosecute the Scottish war without parliamentary support.[22] Parliament impeached the earl for treason on the charge of violating the kingdom's fundamental laws. Londoners crowded the wharf at Westminster every morning to catch a glimpse of the shackled Strafford, arriving by barge from his cell in the Tower, but it was the king for whom the trial had great personal meaning. Recognizing that his own stature was in the dock, Charles attended Strafford's month-long trial every day.[23] The Whig historian Thomas Babington Macaulay, writing two centuries later, captured the prosecution's case against Strafford: his "object was to do in England all, and more than all, that Richelieu was doing in France: to make Charles a monarch as absolute as any on the continent."[24] In the end, the impeachment failed. Strafford could not be convicted of treason for doing what the king asked of him. Charles must have felt a frisson of terror when Commons nevertheless reached the guilty verdict against Strafford's spirited and meticulously argued self-defense, showing that he was simply carrying out the king's commands.[25] When the legal grounds for impeachment crumbled upon close scrutiny (how had Strafford undermined the king?), Commons simply shifted its accusation from impeachment to "attainder"—a right in English common law, dating from the mists of medieval times, to remove a threat to the state with or without evidence of treason per se. While impeachment had to be established on the basis of existing law, attainder allowed Parliament to declare an act to be criminal after the fact.[26]

On April 20, 1641, with only 263 of the nearly 500 members of Parliament present, John Pym, who led the prosecution, locked the doors of the Commons to prevent anyone from leaving. In a vote of 204 to 59, Commons sentenced Strafford to death by beheading.[27] On May 5 the Lords, many of whom by this time feared impeachment themselves, voted 26–19 to convict: "We are of the opinion upon all that your lordships have voted to be proved: that the Earl of Strafford doth deserve to undergo the pains and forfeitures of high treason by law."[28] In the cruelest twist of all, the king himself signed the bill, in hopes of deflecting the wrath of Commons from himself.[29] Strafford was beheaded on May 12.

If anything, Commons was emboldened by its success against the king's minister. Parliament passed the Triennial Act, to which the king readily granted assent, requiring that Parliament be summoned at least once every three years. The king was not to raise money for war without Parliament's consent, through forced loans or other means.

Instead of quelling conflict, however, Parliament's resurgence unleashed a civil war. Triggered initially by bloodshed in Ireland between Catholics and Protestants on opposite sides of the constitutional conflict, forces for and against Parliament began to mobilize in England as well. On January 4, 1642, several hundred of the king's soldiers "pounded on the stout wood" of Parliament's doors demanding entry to arrest five members of Commons, including Pym, who had led the charge against Strafford, for plotting against the king.[30] "I see the birds have flown," said Charles, upon being granted entry. But the two sides had hardened and took to arms.

The armed forces that Parliament arrayed against the king's men began as a haphazard collection of Scottish allies, London's militia, the personal retinues of prominent members of Parliament, and local brigades raised by county commissioners. With unclear lines of command perpetuated by infighting between and within Commons and Lords, early battles with the king's forces were poorly orchestrated and indecisive. The tide turned only in February 1645, after Parliament created the New Model Army, a professional force of some 22,000 conscripted men and full-time volunteers. On the "rebel" side, the Roundheads (so named because many had the haircuts of London apprentices) were principally men on foot—pike men and musketeers—complemented by cavalry and the men and equipment needed

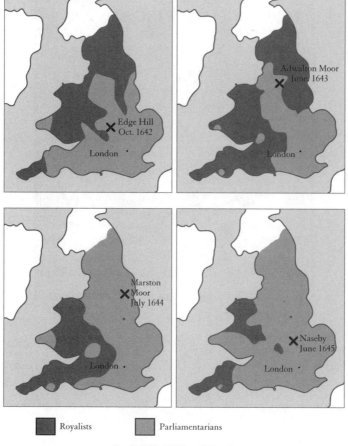

Royalists   Parliamentarians

English Civil War, 1642–45.

for siege warfare. The king's men, Cavaliers, were on horse in greater percentages but also contained Irish Catholic infantry.[31]

Failing to recover ground following a devastating defeat at Naseby in June 1645, Charles I surrendered to the Scots. A second brief round of fighting ensued after Charles escaped to the Isle of Wight, but the New Model Army trounced his forces at Preston, and Charles was captured once again. An ascendant army purged the hundred or so members of Parliament who sought to negotiate a settlement with Charles, leaving only some eighty members to try him for treason. In January 1649, finding him guilty, the Rump Parliament (termed "regicides" later, following the 1680 restoration) beheaded the king.[32]

The 1647 Putney Debates.

From a constitutional perspective, one of the most intriguing aspects of the English Civil War was the failed attempt by a faction in the New Model Army to expand the franchise.[33] Known as Levellers in reference to commoners fighting enclosures in 1607, soldiers from society's lower rungs were temporarily elevated by the desperate needs of war, and they seized the moment to seek inclusion in the electorate.[34] In the fall of 1647, at a series of meetings of the Army Council held at Putney church, John Lilburne, Thomas Rainsborough, and other officers representing the commoner men-at-arms made impassioned speeches for widening the voters' rolls. Rainsborough's assertion that "the poorest he that is in England hath a life to live, as the greatest he," became a rallying cry.[35] In and out of prison, Lilburne challenged Cromwell, Ireton, and the other anti-Leveller officers on behalf of "freeborn Englishmen" in harshly worded pamphlets: "I will not serve you (stoop or submit unto you) nor worship your Idoll or golden Image that you have set up (your Arbitrary power and unlimited greatness)."[36] Lilburne's ally John Wildman, in his "Putney Projects" and "Agreement of the People," laid out the basis for a new constitution in which all men over the age of twenty-one (excepting servants, beggars, and royalists) would have the right to vote for representatives in Parliament.[37]

The commoners' hand was strongest when the outcome of the Civil War was at its most uncertain: when the officers needed them, as with the Roman secessions many hundreds of years earlier. Once the royalists were defeated and Charles had been killed, momentum for an expanded franchise came to a dead halt; the rabble-rousers were rounded up or forced into silence. Executing the king, some historians suggest, might have saved British aristocratic rule by releasing pressure for more drastic constitutional changes, including suffrage expansion.[38] Cromwell and his Puritan associates, assisted at least in principle by a handpicked Barebones Parliament, ruled for a short time with more self-aggrandized executive powers than the Stuarts had ever managed to accumulate.[39] Many moderate members of Parliament had tolerated the rabid anti-Catholicism of the nonconformist religious movement as long as it assisted in wartime mobilization. Both armies saw themselves as Christian, but so strongly did religion infuse the New Model Army that some rank and file murdered captains whom they suspected of being Catholic.[40] Eventually Cromwell's sectarian dictatorship became so unpopular that, when he died in 1658 and his less charismatic son-in-law Richard Ireton was forced to resign the next year, the traditional landed elite easily regained control of Parliament and restored the monarchy in 1660. A vengeful Charles II and his allies exhumed Cromwell and Ireton and executed them posthumously in 1661, along with many others who had had the misfortune of surviving.

Charles II reigned as king for the remainder of his life, until 1685. But when his Catholic brother James II replaced him, Parliament once again took royal succession into its own hands. In 1688 it offered the English crown to William of Orange (a foreign Protestant monarch) and Queen Mary (the Protestant older sister of the deposed monarch James II). This so-called Glorious Revolution of 1688 made explicit Parliament's check on royal spending. Parliament asserted, in an institutionally protected way, the centuries-long role that it had struggled to maintain in checking royal spending and that kings, at least back to Henry III, had accepted. This time the assertion was backed by more than a king's promise that could be and had been broken many times. Institutional mechanisms shifted the bargaining power in the direction of Parliament and especially the House of Commons, whose members represented not only the gentry but also the rich merchants and traders of the new United Kingdom. A newly vocal judiciary, liberated by more secure tenure on the bench, would help enforce the new arrangements and create new ones as well.

This Glorious Revolution was also an important step in the direction of securing the property rights of lenders. As recent scholars have argued, the crown's ability to borrow money on the open market expanded dramatically as investors, many of whom were members of Parliament, laid aside their fears that the king might unilaterally renege on his commitments to repay the loans.[41] With its stronger fiscal capacity, the English government was able to pay for a large military that would come to dominate world politics and a large bureaucracy with which to govern at home.[42] It helped with public relations that the well-financed military tended to win its wars and to extend British rule throughout the world.

More secure property rights, however, were not accompanied by an expansion of the franchise. The battle that Parliament had fought on behalf of its resources was not the battle of the Levellers. Universal male franchise would have to wait two centuries more, when Britain's imperial navies needed more manpower and when the propertied classes and the politicians representing them came to realize, through incremental franchise expansions, that they had less to fear from the popular vote than they had thought. In 1887, campaigning on a ticket of British imperialism that appealed to nationalism and xenophobia, Conservative Benjamin Disraeli won the first election on a vastly increased male franchise in a landslide, while "every beggar in London complained about 'our rebellious subjects.' "[43]

Opposition to the monarchy during the Civil War had, however, spawned an old but increasingly vigorous and popular English debate about the dangers of a standing army. The English were well aware of the huge continental armies that had ranged through Germany during the Thirty Years' War, and they worried that the Stuarts (James I, Charles I and II, and James II) meant to build such a force on the island. In 1656 James Harrington had pointed out, in his *Commonwealth of Oceana*, that an army was "a beast with a large belly that had to be fed," most likely by the nobility that had the means to feed it.[44] The Earl of Shaftesbury, John Locke's patron and an opponent of absolute monarchy, defended the powers of the peerage in 1675 on precisely these grounds, arguing that a strong landed nobility was the best deterrent to a standing army and a tyrannical king.[45] Algernon Sidney, also from the landed gentry, espoused a system of local militia of property owners who would bear arms when necessary in defense of the realm.[46] In these sentiments one hears echoes of Machiavelli, from more than a century before.

The Whig party in Parliament, representing commercial wealth and smaller gentry, also favored a militia of property owners with their "firelocks kept in every parish." In a 1697 pamphlet the Whig firebrand John Trenchard wrote, "If we look through the world, we shall find in no country, liberty and an army stand together; so that to know whether a people are free or slaves, it is necessary only to ask, whether there is an army kept amongst them?" Naval power, Trenchard insisted, was safer because it operated offshore and could not easily be used to oppress the people it was supposed to defend.[47]

Why did English kings cede ground to Parliament rather than, like French kings, sell noble offices to merchants as a way of buying independence at least for a time? Surely English monarchs were not more farsighted. John I and Henry III lost battles with their nobility and were forced to concede constitutional ground to more powerful forces. Richard II was deposed, as was Richard III. Henry VII only barely attained office, in alliance with noble factions, after the War of Roses. Charles I was tried and executed; James II was chased off the throne and defeated in battle. Interspersed among these dramatic events, monarchs sometimes recovered some powers, often by fighting popular wars, but always by deft political maneuvering.

For their gradual adoption of parliamentarism, the English can again thank their small island nation. By the late seventeenth century, because land was limited and trade was booming, the English Parliament had become substantially aligned with commercial interests, and its willing cooperation had become extremely valuable to the king. The landed aristocracy, in many cases, had invested in commercial ventures that gave them interests in common with the merchants, exposing fewer divisions for the crown to manipulate. The monarchy vastly expanded its capacity to raise money for wars and to promote commerce and empire, precisely because the king's power to renege on loans was checked by those holding the debt.

❖ ❖ ❖

Compared to England's Cromwellian interlude, the Netherlands went even farther toward democratizing its politics when it needed to mobilize its male citizens. But after the struggle subsided, it returned to aristocratic rule. For more than eighty years, from 1566 to 1648, the Dutch fought to free themselves of Habsburg control. Occupying a tenuous geopolitical niche created by swamps and the French-Spanish rivalry, the landed aristocracy of the Low Countries maintained a wary peace in which its members exchanged taxes and nominal subordination to Habsburg Spain for substantial autonomy. By 1594 the Dutch "inner line of military and water defenses was so nearly impregnable as to give them virtually an island position," as historian Engel Sluiter puts it.[48] It also helped that England and France were at war with Spain at the same time. But peace was shattered by Dutch commoners' hostility toward Spain's Catholic rule, which had been building since the ascension of Philip II to the Spanish throne. The weapon-wielding commoners' centrality to the success of the Dutch Revolt gave them a place in politics, at least during the most violent phases of the struggle for independence. Fired and united by Protestant religious fervor, the ranks of makeshift rebel armies were filled with clergymen, shopkeepers, craftsmen, fisherfolk, and peasants.

Animosity toward the insistent Catholicism of the Spanish overlords had smoldered for years in predominantly Protestant areas, but a precipitating event, like the first of many dominoes, was "the Breaking of the Images." In western Flanders, during August 1566, Protestant mobs (interspersed with opportunists along for the loot) went on a rampage, demolishing the crosses and images that had been set up along the roads in preparation for the festival of the Ascension of the Virgin Mary. According to Gerard Brandt, a historian writing a century later but purporting to rely on eyewitness accounts, "The consecrated chalices they filled with the wine they found in the churches, and drank to one another's health. They smeared their shoes with the holy oil, defiled the church vestments with ordure, and daubing the books with butter, threw them into the fire." Others "went on plundering and defaced the royal coat of arms. . . . The madness of the people spread like wild-fire, appearing here sooner, there later."[49] Over the following year vast numbers of imitators launched similar attacks on Catholic and Spanish targets in surrounding towns, overwhelming the efforts of Dutch burghers who sought to maintain order. Unlike the commoners, wealthy merchants generally favored the status quo in Holland, including accommodation with Habsburg overlords.[50]

It is not that merchants were peace-loving men by disposition: they often acted as state-sanctioned pirates wherever their ships would take them, seiz-

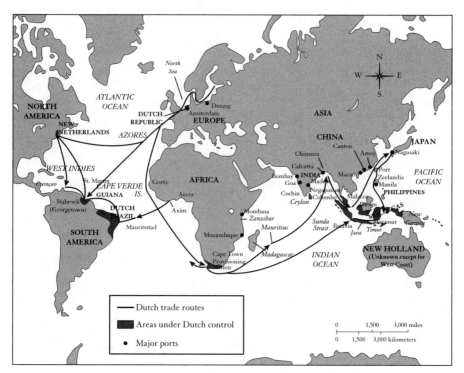

*Dutch East India Company: trade routes and areas of
Dutch control at its peak in the late eighteenth century.*

ing raw materials and human slaves with brutal force. For most of the seventeenth and eighteenth centuries, Dutch merchants were active slavers the
world over. The States General exhorted the Dutch East India Company
(1602–1799) to fight Portuguese influence in East Asia, to meet fire with fire,
and to replace Catholic with Calvinist missions. The Dutch seized Portuguese settlements along the eastern coast of India and sent captured slaves
to work on Dutch plantations in Indonesia. In the Atlantic, the war with
the Spanish Habsburgs gave Dutch merchant marines cover to raid Caribbean pearl fisheries and other local suppliers when they refused to trade. The
Dutch West India Company (WIC), established in 1621, brought slaves from
Africa to work on profitable Dutch plantations in Suriname, the Guianas,
and Curaçao.[51]

But aggrandizers on the European continent the Dutch merchants were
not. They were often happy to sell to customers in any political realm, even
those who were considered enemies by their fellow countrymen.

Philip II of Spain—perhaps because of the soothing words he heard from the Dutch commercial class and the landed elite, many of whom were Catholics and willing to live with nominal subordination—gravely misjudged the depth of antipathy among the Dutch common people. In 1567 he appointed a new governor of the Spanish Netherlands, Duke of Alba, whose brutality in quelling unrest added fuel to the flames. A growing agglomeration of Calvinist rebels and the merchant marines, known as the "Beggars" because of a dismissive comment from a Spanish bureaucrat, launched guerrilla operations against the government from forests and the sea. "What, madam! Can it be possible that you are afraid of these beggars?" exclaimed an adviser to Duchess Margaret of Parma.[52] But the Beggars were a force to be reckoned with. In 1572 the rebel flag was spotted on five Dutch Sea Beggars ships near the Isthmus of Panama, near the "Spanish Indies."[53]

The Beggars attacked a succession of cities and towns in Holland and Zeeland, overpowering some of their defenses swiftly and forcing their city councils to join the revolt. Some towns, like Enkhuizen, invited the Sea Beggars in before the motley army even arrived; others, like Vlissingen, had Sea Beggar support in sufficient numbers to entreat their magistrates to take their side without a fight. Although only about 10 percent of Holland's population was Calvinist at that time, they were organized and motivated.[54] Moreover, their ranks were swollen by Huguenots fleeing the religious wars in France.[55] In 1572 the Beggars seized the ports of Brill, Bruges, Ypres, Oudenaarde, and other towns and replaced merchant-dominated municipal governments with radicals.[56] In 1574 the rebels used terrain to their advantage when they cut open a dike along the Maas River to block the advance of Spanish forces.[57]

Leadership of the revolt was not to remain in the hands of the Beggars, but the revolt made a populist of one of the richest and most powerful nobles in the Netherlands. William of Orange (sometimes known as William the Silent, 1533–84, and ancestor of the English king of the same name) was a magnate of enormous wealth and a duke in the Holy Roman Empire by virtue of his vast lands in the Low Countries and in the area of Orange, in southern France. The Duke of Orange himself was not a religious man, but his marriage in 1561 to the very rich and decidedly Lutheran Anna of Saxony (and niece of the prince elector and daughter of Maurice of Saxony, who had defeated Charles V in 1552) sidelined him from the Catholic Habsburg court in Brussels.[58] The military potency of religious zeal was not lost on this astute politician, and Philip Marnix of St. Aldegonde, William's leading pro-

Dutch Revolt

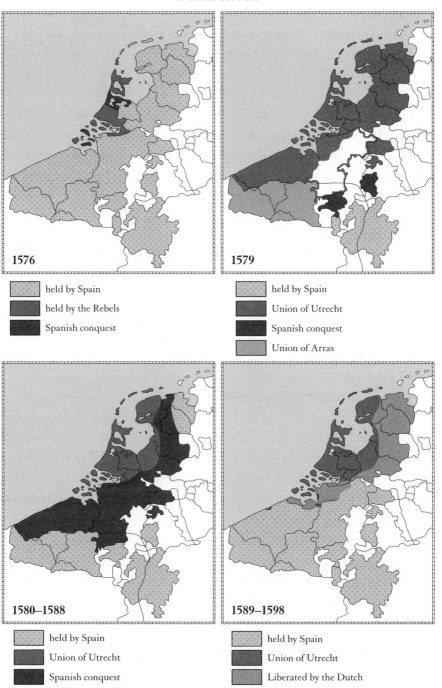

Changes in territorial control during the Dutch Revolt, 1576–98.

pagandist, helped turn Protestantism into the chief Dutch weapon against Catholic Spain.[59]

Orange was not the obvious leader for this movement, but the war against Habsburg Spain and the commoners manning the barricades, and not the intrinsic powers of the magnate class from whence he came, propelled the House of Orange into political leadership.

William of Orange united the northern and southern provinces in revolt in November 1576, when the gruesome carnage of a marauding horde of Spanish soldiers in Antwerp made temporary allies of the zealous and the reticent alike. When Orange failed to get the Protestant north and the Catholic south to agree to religious toleration, he moved the seat of his government from Brabant in the south to Holland in the north, where war zeal, Protestantism, and popular support for executive leadership were stronger.[60] In 1579 representatives of the seven provinces of Holland formed the Republic of the Seven United Provinces, marking the official beginning of the Dutch Republic.

After William of Orange died in 1584, his house remained the standard-bearer for the revolt and held the loyalty of many citizens for whom the ouster of Spain was paramount. Princes of the House of Orange were to become stadtholder, Dutch for "place holder," which in practice came to mean something closer to chief executive. Many merchants, however, remained cool to the war. The men of means who had come to control city governments resented the intrusion of town militias and their Sea Beggar allies during the height of the revolt and reclaimed their own authority on city councils as soon as a twelve-year truce was secured in 1609. Although the Spanish Habsburgs scored temporary victories from time to time, Spanish power to impose their rule died with the depletion of New World silver long before the Treaty of Münster in 1648 granted independence to the Netherlands at the end of the Thirty Years' War.[61]

This extinguished Spanish domination of the seven Dutch provinces, but the southern Catholic lands of present-day Belgium stayed with the Habsburgs. The peace also ended the claim of commoners on government. The size of city councils shrank, town militias were sidelined, and city governments once again became the preserve of prosperous merchants.[62] Once free of Spanish rule, the predominantly merchant leaders of Dutch municipal and provincial governments reasserted their privileges and imposed strict limits on the now-hereditary executive (stadtholder) House of Orange.

The Corpses of the Brothers de Witt, *attributed to Jan de Baen in 1672–75.*

The Dutch Republic that emerged from the revolt was a commercial aristocracy. The antiwar tendencies of the merchant class were sometimes spectacularly unpopular, as in 1672, when the de Witt brothers Cornelis and Johan, from a prominent Dutch trading family, were lynched and disemboweled by an angry Orangist mob. Their crime had been negotiating a peace settlement with England in 1654 behind the backs of the House of Orange, a settlement that contained a secret annex forbidding the Dutch ever to appoint William II's infant son as stadtholder.[63] It took eighteen years, but the House of Orange finally had its revenge.

More often, however, the merchant elite held the Orangists firmly in check. Without a need for the general public to defend the state militarily, only rich merchants retained the right to vote in elections. After the Netherlands ousted Spain, popular movements were replaced by aristocratic rule. The de Witt story is a reminder of populism's darker side, as well as its fragility.

✦ ✦ ✦

While the Dutch essentially rented commoners to fight off the Spanish Habsburgs, the Swedes did them one better in their fight against Danish rule in the fifteenth century. In 1434 the Swedish nobleman Engelbrekt Engelbrektsson led a predominantly peasant army against the Danes, who had continued to dominate Sweden off and on for a century. As part of an effort to gain support, the rebel leaders convened the first Swedish parliament (Riksdag) at Arboga (1435), which apparently contained a fourth estate composed of freeholding peasants along with the traditional three estates. Alone among European kingdoms, Sweden conceded formal representation to peasants, testimony to its desperate need for soldiers to fight the Danes.[64] Swedish military might was built on large conscription armies paid for in part by the villagers themselves, willing to send their sons and brothers, in exchange for a say in what wars were fought.

Like Henry VIII of England, King Gustavus Vasa of Sweden bought himself a measure of autonomy from the landed elite in 1545 when, declaring Sweden Protestant, he took the endowments of the parish churches.[65] The royal domain in Sweden went from 5.5 percent of all land in 1521 to 28.2 percent in 1560, but as in Tudor England, the crown had to give away lands to the nobility in exchange for their support. Thus spent, church lands in Sweden were not great enough to support royal absolutism, and the king remained hemmed in by all four estates: the nobility, the clergy (now Lutheran), burgers, and the peasant freeholders who formed the backbone of Sweden's military force.[66] Michael Roberts, a military historian of Sweden and father of the "military revolution" literature, has documented how the Swedish king Gustavus Adolphus imported the Dutch military model, based on well-drilled armies of commoners, to good effect.[67] All draft-eligible men, ages 15 to 40 (raised to 60 in 1617), were enrolled in lists at the village level, and depending on the need, those not drawn from the lists would provide monetary support for those who went to war.[68]

The military incorporation of the peasantry put the Swedish nobility in a relatively weak bargaining position. When he ran out of money in 1680, King Charles XI grabbed back the lands, formerly held by the crown, that his forebears had given the Swedish nobility, reducing the nobility's share of Swedish land from two-thirds to less than one-third of the total.[69] Thus did Sweden enter several decades of "populist royal absolutism" not unlike the coalition of commoner and stadtholder in the Dutch Republic under the

Dukes of Orange.[70] But when the Russians trounced the Swedish army in 1709, forcing Sweden into pacifist hibernation, the nobility seized the chance not only to clip the wings of the monarchy but to limit the role of commoners in the Riksdag as well. Sweden's so-called Age of Liberty that followed (1719–72) was an era of aristocratic constitutionalism that celebrated industry and property rights but not universal suffrage.[71]

Swedish politics in the eighteenth century centered on the rivalry between the Hats (industrial interests) and the Caps (various others, including the lower orders). For a brief period, beginning with the Caps' parliamentary majority won in 1764, the Swedish government reduced the power of the guilds, permitted coastal towns to engage in unregulated trade, and granted peasants the right to sell produce freely. In 1772 a swift coup d'état restored the nobility's supremacy under the guise of monarchical rule. Retreating from foreign military excursions, the aristocracy increased its domestic leverage by reducing both the king's need for troops and the people's ability to supply them.

✦ ✦ ✦

It is common to see the fifteenth and sixteenth centuries as the birth date of the modern territorial state, with monarchy its form and war its midwife. We have seen, instead, an array of vastly different possibilities of state organization beginning to emerge from the pressures of warfare.

Despite the efforts of the Stuarts, England never became a fully absolute monarchy. Lacking an independent source of funds or a shared sense of existential threat, English kings from the beginning had to get parliamentary consent for money with which to fight "unnecessary" offshore wars. In the Netherlands, the stadtholder, at first a noble like any other, began to look more like a monarch as he coordinated war efforts, but the merchants on whose money his efforts depended held him firmly in check. Wealthy citizens were able to secure property rights, institutionally safeguarded through parliamentary representation, and dismiss the commoners from government once the Habsburgs were ousted. Sweden's mass-conscription army allowed that small country to "punch above its weight," but once the Danish threat passed, the commoners were sidelined in Swedish politics as well. Not until a military conflict with Norway in the early twentieth century would Swedish commoners be invited back as full citizens. Without wars that required full manpower mobilization, the Netherlands became a merchant aristocracy with a weak "king," while Sweden reverted to an aristocratically dominated monarchy.

The island geography of England, and to some extent its equivalent in the Netherlands surrounded by moats and floodable plains and in Sweden surrounded by ice six months of the year, reduced the demand for protection and in equal measure weakened the monarch's hand. It also weakened the bargaining power of the general public, since its services were not needed for defending the homeland. The increasingly urban nobility in these trading countries grew rich from trade without having to defend the home turf.

Meanwhile in Italy, the birthplace not only of the Renaissance but also of new experiments in mixed government, an artistic explosion fueled by wealthy northern city-states also promoted political freedoms of certain kinds. Once home to the great landed empire of Rome, Italian cities, grown rich on silk production and trade, managed to push aside feudal lords in favor of communal or "home rule," at least for a time. But eventually, as we will see, oligarchs and foreign powers overwhelmed those cities that tried to retain their political independence.

Chapter Seven

_____

ITALIAN REPUBLICS

IN JUNE 1509, after a pitiless siege, Florence's new citizens' army brought Pisa to its knees.[1] Pisa's location at the mouth of the Arno River, Florence's artery to the sea, had given it strategic significance as the armies of France and Spain loomed ever larger on the horizon. The idea of creating a militia of citizen-soldiers in place of traditional mercenary forces was Niccolò Machiavelli's. Although Machiavelli is better known today as the author of *The Prince* (1513)—a treatise on how to rule with ruthless cunning—he was a proponent, based on his reading of the Roman Republic, of a more inclusive form of government that would support effective military mobilization.

Because Machiavellianism has become a byword for amoral opportunism, some readers are surprised to learn that Machiavelli advocated self-governance over autocracy. "A republic has a fuller life and enjoys good fortune for a longer time than a principality," he wrote, "since it is better able to adapt itself to diverse circumstances owing to the diversity found among its citizens than a prince can do."[2] After he was exiled to his family's farm outside Florence, he made several attempts to ingratiate himself with the family whose name is synonymous with power in Renaissance Italy, the Medici. He dedicated *The Prince* to the then-ruler of Florence, Lorenzo de' Medici, and wrote a play (*Mandragola*) to celebrate his wedding. In his *History of Florence* (1520–25), commissioned by the Medici pope Clement VII, Machiavelli described a city consumed by feuding clans, distracted by private and parochial interests, and rarely willing to fight to preserve its liberties.[3]

The *Discourses on Livy*, a book Machiavelli wrote while in exile, probably between 1513 and 1519, is a series of meditations on Livy's history of the early years of the Roman Republic, in which he reveals a longing that his native Florence remain free both of dictators and outside powers. The Roman Republic, suggested Machiavelli, offered a model to Florence and other Italian city-states for how to harness the people's passion for self-defense and military glory with which to fend off the unwanted encroachments of Spain, France, and the Holy Roman Empire. He believed that Florentine vitality could be recovered by adopting Rome's republican model—or his version of it—which featured a constitutional settlement that balanced aristocratic and popular forces, providing the basis for a strong citizens' militia.

The history of the Roman Republic was familiar to educated Italians during the Italian Renaissance. They knew that Rome in the late republic had been corrupted by vast inequalities of wealth and power, and that various factions had taken recourse to violent street fighting, often involving private armies of thugs. Machiavelli drew parallels between ancient Rome and the Italy of his day: the growing wealth of merchant families, the rising power of military captains, and the looming threat of foreign invasion. In Machiavelli's view, popular leaders in Rome including the Gracchus brothers, Marius, and Caesar had arisen in response to the growing oppression of the working and soldiering classes, which had upset the balance of popular and aristocratic elements in the Roman constitution. The purpose of these spokesmen for the people, as far as Machiavelli was concerned, was to restore the populace to its rightful place in the Roman constitution. Machiavelli's plan for constitutional restoration in Florence included the creation of a citizens' army that could defend against oppressive nobles; short terms and rotation in office for magistrates; and a central place for popular political institutions. Much more than the Romans had, Machiavelli seemed to favor an egalitarian franchise for a popular assembly, though not one including the poor and unskilled.

Machiavelli's take on Roman Republican history was not the dominant one at the time. Francesco Guicciardini and other aristocrats favored readings closer to Cicero's: popular leaders had undermined the Roman Republic by appealing to the mob and neglecting the natural and salubrious authority of the Senate and upper classes. Guicciardini's model for the republic was Venice, a system in which the lower classes were denied citizenship and the best men ruled peacefully.[4] The Medici no doubt preferred yet another interpretation of Roman history, one that saw Julius Caesar's assassination as the trigger for civil wars and that emphasized Emperor Augustus's role in the establishment of a peaceful and orderly government that left Rome's citizens free for private pursuits. They would have agreed with Dante who, in the *Inferno*, consigned Brutus and Cassius to the very lowest rings of Hell and granted Julius Caesar a more comfortable spot in Limbo, where he had hope of redemption.[5]

Machiavelli might have been fortunate to die in 1525, before the siege of Florence by the Medici and the final submission of the Florentine Republic to their autocratic rule in 1531. The aristocrats of his own class had by then appropriated the life and vocation of courtiers, and Guicciardini had gone so far as to assist the Medici and papal forces in the siege of Florence. Guicciardini had been no friend of the Medici in 1492, but by 1530 he had apparently reconciled himself to rule by that family. Like other aristocrats, he thought that masters ought to "accustom one's servants to a tight fist," and he bemoaned the unwillingness of ordinary Florentines to defer to the best men to rule the city.[6]

Machiavelli did not live long enough to see that the future of republican institutions lay either in the conservative republics such as Venice—which confined rule to a small group of families that were able to stave off dissolution for at least a couple of centuries more—or in the transplantation of republican ideas into postmedieval representative institutions based on elections rather than lottery. Like Montesquieu, who thought elections were conducive to elite control,[7] Machiavelli might have thought that such a transplanting could produce only an oligarchic state of the kind enjoyed by the Venetians, and such a future probably would not have appealed to him.[8]

Machiavelli's story, like Hegel's owl ("The owl of Minerva takes its flight only when the shades of night are gathering"), comes at the end of the story.[9] It is important to understand first how Italian republics emerged, and when they did, how they coped simultaneously with their external threats and with their fears of usurpation from within. They disappeared over the ensuing centuries, leaving Venice as the last remaining and very aristocratic republic.

✦ ✦ ✦

By the end of the twelfth century, northern Italy was dotted with towns and cities that had effectively become self-governing. The Holy Roman emperors who laid claim were far away (in Sicily, under Frederick II in the thirteenth century, but more typically in Germany) and were unable to sustain dominion despite repeated punitive expeditions and steady efforts at diplomacy. This posed a problem of legitimacy in every city: under the received medieval conceptions, no one had a clear right to rule.[10]

Moreover, by the thirteenth century, northern Italian cities had become among the most advanced economies in Europe. Trade and manufacturing grew rapidly, often based on the import of raw materials, which in turn drew migration into the cities and fueled the development of banks to finance these new ventures.[11] Unlike their continental counterparts, northern Italian cities enjoyed freedom from feudal restrictions on trade and factor mobility as well as from the taxes of centralizing states.[12] Free peasants were able to emigrate into cities or small towns to work or else to manufacture goods, especially textiles and dyes, in their own towns and farms. Landowners increasingly were rentiers rather than masters, many of whom also moved to

Renaissance Italy, 1494.

the cities, where they financed their peasants' new workshops or engaged in various other kinds of commerce.

Merchants and bankers came to control many of these cities and aimed to establish a peaceful environment in which to build wealth through trade and industry.[13] Alongside these leading families, guilds of craftsmen formed to organize production and recruitment, enforce professional norms, regulate product quality, and extend and protect markets. In Florence the early guilds included bankers, notaries and lawyers, physicians and chemists, merchants, wool manufacturers, and silk weavers. Guilds often fought with one another over economic, social, and political issues. New guilds sometimes formed and struggled for recognition within Florence's "guild republic."[14] While these tensions sometimes broke out into violent conflict, the urban guilds, their differences aside, had a collective interest in preventing competition from the countryside or from neighboring cities under Florentine control.[15] Florentine rule was famously oppressive toward the other Tuscan cities, as Venice was in the Veneto and Genoa in Liguria.[16]

Even after city-states came to dominate the countryside surrounding them, a remaining challenge was to manage the conflict among powerful and wealthy clans seeking advantage by catering to the middle class, principally members of the lesser guilds.[17] More inclusive governments, which alternated for a time with more oligarchic ones, were typically associated with certain policies: an armed urban militia to serve both in the city and in the army; the use of wealth taxes rather than reliance on excises; the use of lottery rather than election to select magistrates; large legislative councils; relatively open access to service as a magistrate; short terms of office; and antimagnate laws. As we know from John Najemy's magisterial history of Florence, each of these measures was usually reformed or eliminated as the governing class eventually shrank to a narrow oligarchy.[18]

For Florence as elsewhere, the thirteenth century was a period in which the middle class vied with the aristocracy for political control. In 1250, following a victorious battle against encroachments by Holy Roman emperor Frederick II, a committee of leading citizens reorganized the government around a system of twenty armed neighborhoods. Each neighborhood elected leaders and appointed a non-Florentine captain of the people who could summon the militia. The Florentine countryside was also organized in a way that made each district responsible for maintaining a militia. An executive body could propose legislation that would then have to be approved in legislative councils drawn from the neighborhoods, guilds, and districts.[19]

Guild leaders, who were elected to the legislative council, gave this government a representative quality. The landed elite, many of whom held titles from the pope or the Holy Roman emperor, were largely excluded from service on the legislative councils and completely absent from the executive body. Most members of the executive council came from families associated with the wealthiest rung of society, engaged in banking, trade, and law, but—unlike in later years, when the threats from the Holy Roman Empire waned—lesser guilds such as weavers, tailors, and shoemakers also had substantial representation. This constitutionally innovative government lasted until 1260, when Siena, aligned with the Holy Roman emperor, won a decisive battle at Montaperti and brought down the Florentine government. Although the forces were fairly evenly matched, the Florentine loyalist Dante Alighieri was convinced that a late defection to the imperial side by Bocca degli Abati and his followers tipped the balance, for which Dante gave him a place in the ninth circle of hell in his *Divine Comedy*.[20]

Thirty-three years later, in 1293, an extended set of twenty-one guilds formed the basis for a new guild federation, which then adopted a new written constitution, the Ordinances of Justice.[21] The twelve richer guilds nominated magistrates, but all twenty-one guilds had to approve them. Even more

Dante and His Poem, *by Domenico di Michelino, 1465.*

important, executive authority rested in the guilds. The new palace of the guild leaders, the Palazzo della Signoria (renamed the Palazzo Vecchio by the Medici when they moved to the Palazzo Pitti), dwarfed the towers of elite families sitting virtually in its shadow.

Guild government collapsed under the weight of uncontrollable rivalries. During the late 1290s warring factions produced so much violence that the pope was asked to intervene. The intervention failed, and a relatively inclusive government managed to struggle on for a few years in the interstices of civil war, before the richest families called a truce and prevailed over the rest once more.

It is no coincidence that during a period of elite government, in 1328, the Florentines devised an ingenious system of leadership selection to reduce factional rivalry among the powerful families. An elite council nominated a group of men, a somewhat larger body "scrutinized" them, and then the names of those surviving the scrutiny were placed in purses to be drawn by lottery each time a new magistrate was needed. The introduction of lottery allowed the narrow group of appointing officials to deny responsibility for choosing or not choosing a particular candidate for office—a useful device when disappointed office-seekers came from powerful and well-armed clans. One way or another, the elite ultimately controlled the nominating and scrutinizing committees.

Because the Florentine elite fiercely opposed wealth taxes, Florence financed its government, and especially its wars, predominantly with regressive excise taxes on certain commodities until 1300. But these taxes were ineffective because the public's demand for the taxed items was price elastic. Florence therefore turned increasingly to debt financing from local banking families, giving their banks substantial control over state policies by turning over to them taxes, state-granted monopolies, and other state resources as collateral. This meant that when Florence considered waging war, even a popular one, leaders were beholden to their bankers for the terms.[22]

Eventually Florence's debt-funded wars led to a disaster. Late in 1341 Florence suffered, in rapid succession, a major defeat to Pisa, the loss of papal accounts in Florentine banks, and a default on loans made to the English king Edward III to fund his invasion of France that started the Hundred Years' War. To resolve the ensuing crisis, the leaders turned over emergency powers, first to an ad hoc committee made up mostly of the leading banking families, then to a familiar and trusted foreigner, Walter of Brienne, who had been vicar under the Anjou duke Charles of Calabria a few years before.

Brienne turned out to govern differently from what his elite backers had expected. He did end the war with Pisa, but then he imposed a wealth tax, suspended interest payments on the public debt, and undertook various other reforms that were unpopular with the richest citizens and were correspondingly well received by the guilds. When he then demanded to be named magistrate for life, there was predictable support from the lower orders and opposition from the elite. Within a few months he was forced out of office in a bloody coup and replaced by a narrow government that abolished the guild-based constitution.[23] Matters did not end there. An outraged populace soon laid siege to the palace and forced government leaders to flee.

After brief military clashes among factions of the elite, a new guild-based government was established in 1342, and once again the twenty-one guilds played the leading role setting up a popular government.[24] As one rich citizen complained, the list of names in the lottery bags for executive roles now included "artisans, manual laborers and simpletons . . . to whom the republic mattered little and were even less capable of governing it."[25] In its five years in power, this so-called "popular" government managed to put the fiscal regime in order by consolidating the city's debts and partially defaulting on its loans to the big banks. These measures were disastrous for the bankers and existing bondholders, but they did create a substantial wealth transfer from the richest families and opportunities for "new men" to speculate in devalued paper.

The Florentine rich, resilient in the face of political encroachment, again narrowed the government with the help of an ad hoc committee with emergency powers. But the 1370s brought renewed labor unrest, partly on account of the Black Death in 1348 that wiped out a third of Florence's workforce. With labor shortages in key industries, the powerful wool guild, controlled by rich and powerful families, employed cartel practices to push down the wages of unskilled wool workers. With labor in short supply, however, wage suppression required more force and provoked popular reaction. The poorly paid wool workers, called the Ciompi, armed themselves and took over the government, forcing it to recognize three new guilds in 1378 that vastly outnumbered the membership in the existing guilds.

In response to the Ciompi Revolt, the government proposed to reorga-

Michele di Lando.

nize the now-twenty-four guilds into three sets of seven, fourteen, and three guilds, each with equal representation in the executive council. This constituted an immense redistribution of power away from the Florentine aristocracy. It was not to last. Following disputes among Ciompi leaders about the extent of constitutional reforms some months later, one of the Ciompi leaders, Michele di Lando, sided with the upper guilds to crush the radical wing of the Ciompi in a bloody battle in the Piazza della Signoria.[26] In 1382 the wealthy families in the wool business led an insurrection to install a new government that more thoroughly suppressed the Ciompi along with their elite supporters. Not only did the new order suppress obstreperous workers, it undermined the constitutional place of the guilds themselves.

Reflecting new political realities, republican theorizing in Florence took an elitist turn. Coluccio Salutati, the brilliant scholar of Roman legal rhetoric who served as Florence's chancellor from 1375 almost until his death in 1404, disavowed his earlier defense of the Ciompi Revolt. Ominously, in 1399 he published *De Tyranno*, an unvarnished defense of princely rule in times of civil unrest. In that book he described the Ciompi rebels as "sordid men whose quality of mind and amount of discretion is represented by their frightful rule of forty days in which this [human] plague reigned," implying that extreme measures were required to quell them.[27] Leonardo Bruni, another leading humanist of his day, described the post-1382 constitution of Florence as a pleasingly Aristotelian mix of democracy, aristocracy, and monarchy.[28] Florentine intellectuals were beginning to rediscover Cicero's conservative version of Roman republicanism, in which informal consultative gatherings, always dominated by elites and especially those skilled in Ciceronian rhetorical arts, could guide policies and generate social consensus along the way.

Given the shell-shocked conservatism of the post-Ciompi Florentine elite, it is no wonder that in 1401, when Florence was surrounded by hostile cities in the control of Milan's Visconti family, the Florentine government took out loans to pay for mercenaries instead of mustering local militias who might demand something in return. Military threat may motivate leaders to make domestic political concessions in exchange for bigger and more effective armies, but much depends on what the leaders fear they would lose from wider suffrage. That same year Giovanni di Bicci de' Medici founded the bank that would make that family's enormous fortune and permit it to dominate the financing of the republic.[29]

Florence made itself vulnerable to Medici control when aristocrats decided they had more to fear from the lower classes than from autocratic rule. From 1434, for the next sixty years, Cosimo de' Medici and then his son Piero and grandson Lorenzo ruled Florence, more through informal means than through actually holding office themselves. Cosimo forged extensive

Cosimo de' Medici, *by Agnolo Bronzino, before 1572.*

marriage alliances with the leading families and built a network of grateful clients throughout all the neighborhoods. He also cultivated close financial and political ties to the pope, to the Visconti, and especially to the mercenary leader and later usurper Duke of Milan Francesco Sforza, all of whom were always ready to provide military support to help suppress domestic dissent in Florence.

While their international alliances were vital, the Medici's principal means of maintaining power day to day was to control the council in charge of selecting members of councils and magistracies. They made frequent use of ad hoc committees and conventions to head off dangerous challenges from disgruntled elites in the traditional councils.

Outmaneuvered by the Medici, the Florentine elite became cut off from independent sources of power. The Medici, like many autocrats who skim from the rich to nourish their popular support, levied a wealth tax on mobile as well as landed property. With their coffers overflowing, they built churches and public buildings, established charities, commissioned work from nearly every artist in the city, and provided food subsidies and services to many ordinary people.

✦ ✦ ✦

The fractious Florentine elite fell under the sway of this very rich and well-organized family, but neither an aristocratic republic nor a local despotism was a match for the new continental powers that had emerged north of the Alps. Unlike the federated Holy Roman Empire, which had repeatedly failed to sustain military efforts in far-flung Italy, France and Spain had emerged as large and rich states with big armies. In 1494, on an expedition to make good on old dynastic claims in Naples, King Charles VIII brought the French army into Tuscany and billeted them in Florence for a month. Under threat of a sack, Piero de' Medici agreed to demands that Florence abandon its alliance with Naples and cede control of Pisa and several other towns as well. The wealthy families of Florence who had chafed under the Medici's wealth taxes then drove Piero "The Unfortunate" into exile, with the hope of replacing him with an aristocratic republic patterned after Venice.

The aristocracy was unable to sustain its advantage, however. The collapse of the Medici regime unleashed uncontrollable tumult, which produced a short-lived populist regime led by a Dominican priest named

Girolamo Savonarola, *by Alessandro Bonvicino.*

Savonarola. Physically unimposing but possessed of fiery zeal, Savonarola attracted enormous crowds to his impromptu sermons that, without naming names, seemed to accuse civic and church leaders of greed, hubris, sexual impropriety, and a host of other sins.

Savonarola took it as his mission to care not only about the hereafter but also about here-and-now improvements in the lot of society's downtrodden. He used his pulpit to urge that political nominations be opened to the populace, and he advocated a return to the lottery for the minor offices. Even more incendiary was his call for a popular convention in which neighborhoods and other bodies would be asked to submit proposals for a new constitution. While few of Savonarola's plans were adopted, his sermons and public appeals steered the process toward expanding the Great Council to over three thousand members to include at least the middle class. Significantly, the Great Council was the seat of legislative authority, including the power to approve taxes. The council's executive committee, which until 1499 had been an elected body, was chosen by lottery from among the council's members.

Savonarola's strength as a politician, his resolute commitment to principle, was also his weakness. He took on one too many enemies when he launched a moral crusade against the church and the corrupt papacy of

Alexander VI in particular. In 1495 Alexander ordered him to stop preaching and, after Savonarola's repeated defiance, excommunicated him in 1497.[30] The Florentine rich had their knives out for him because he had marginalized them politically; and the pope, who could not tolerate his criticisms of the church, had him arrested, tortured, declared a heretic, and executed.[31]

For ten years after Savonarola, Piero Soderini led a middle-class government under the auspices of which Niccolò Machiavelli took up the old republican cause of establishing a citizens' militia against the wishes of the old aristocratic families. Guicciardini complained that Soderini had pushed Machiavelli's proposal through the Signoria without consultation of the council.[32] Machiavelli's force of three thousand succeeded in taking Pisa in 1509, which mercenary armies had failed to do, but by 1510 the forces arrayed against Florence were gathering more strength than the city's militia alone could match. The papacy and the Medici conspired to attack Florence once again and found their chance in 1512, when a Spanish army forced the Soderini government to abandon the city. Medici partisans abolished the militia, dismantled the Great Council, and turned its meeting hall into a barracks fitted with a brothel and a tavern.[33]

Although the Medici were successfully reinstalled in Florence, they complicated matters for themselves when Giulio de' Medici, as Pope Clement VII, managed successively to alienate Francis I of France and Charles V of the Holy Roman Empire, leaving the path open for Spanish forces to sack Rome in 1527. In 1530 Clement forged a temporary alliance with Charles to besiege Florence, bringing the city to its knees after a year.

The Siege of Florence, *by Giorgio Vasari, c. 1560.*

The militia had fought well—although insufficiently against superior forces—while the mercenaries, as Machiavelli predicted, had betrayed the city. Many of the richest families had moved into the Medici camp, which, over-whelmed by continental powers, agreed to be absorbed in 1537 into a newly cre-ated Duchy of Tuscany, a vassal of the Holy Roman emperor. Not only was the age of merchant aristocracy over, Florentine autonomy had ended for all time.

The history of Florence illustrates a pattern of elite failure in Renaissance Italy: the richest families, who dominated trade and finance, recoiled at the prospect of making common cause with lower classes. The aristocrats chafed under rule by the Medici, but their refusal to ally with the middle class nar-rowed their base of political support at a time when Florence was constantly vulnerable to external threat. The prevailing theories of aristocratic repub-licanism were, instead, based on the hope that a narrow aristocracy could defend the republic without relying on a citizens' militia. While Florence was too small and too divided for Machiavelli's more expansive republican vision to work, his notion of a mobilized populace might have been success-ful in the context of peninsula-wide consolidated republic, strong enough to match the threats from large continental powers.

Florence is a constellation of mini-case-studies all by itself, showing that one territorial setting can give rise to an array of political configurations. Like the children's boxing toy with the weighted bottom, the merchant elite kept popping back up after being punched down by popular forces. The genius of the Medici was to capitalize on elite fatigue while at the same time insinuating themselves into the good graces of the bottom rungs of society. Their mistake, costly for Florence though less for themselves, was a failure to see that controlling the city did not give them sufficient powers to defend it from larger powers.

◆ ◆ ◆

If the Florentine merchant elite eventually collapsed from the effort of fend-ing off popular pressure, the Genoese rich never succeeded in stifling their internal rivalries long enough to rule supreme. Prominent noblemen and rich merchants such as the Spinolas and the Dorias dominated city councils, but almost incessant conflict among them created the conditions for competitive pandering to the populace, which they all loathed.[34] It was almost with relief that Genoa's messy oligarchy turned over the city's keys to the Spanish in

1528, under whose regime members of the Doria family continued to serve as fleet admirals—under the Spanish flag.

Still, the aristocratic elite's failure to end its civil strife was not for lack of trying and not entirely without success. They experimented with various methods of peaceful governance being tried elsewhere in northern Italy, including the delegation of the city's executive authority to an outside "manager" (*podest*à) with real but limited powers.[35] Rule by *podest*à imposed impartial justice, held powerful families back from the most egregious cases of self-aggrandizement, and set Genoa on a course of trade expansion. But as surely as walking on a tightrope is precarious, *podest*à were vulnerable to being toppled by one or another group of powerful families. By the fourteenth century, *podest*à were replaced by "captains of the people" who came from a succession of powerful families but often appealed to a fairly wide circle of the citizenry for support.[36]

That is not to say rich Genoese families did not prosper. Genoa had gained control of the surrounding territories, all the way up to the Ligurian Alps, that formed an almost half circle around it to the sea.[37] Ocean facing, Genoa became a great trading center until the sixteenth century, when the rise of Atlantic trade overshadowed the Mediterranean economies. Protected and prosperous, Genoa's armed fleet—which relied on a mixture of volunteers and drafted sailors—acquired Syracuse in Sicily as well as cities in North Africa and along the Black Sea, constantly in competition with Venice and Byzantium for control of markets.[38]

While a relatively small number of wealthy investors owned Genoa's bank, the House of Saint George (Casa San Giorgio), established in 1407, lays claim to being the world's first central bank because it acted as the lender of last resort and controlled the mint.[39] In a pointed demonstration that foreign takeover is not the worst fate that can befall rich citizens, Genoese bankers continued a flourishing business financing the Spanish crown after 1528. Genoese merchants and bankers rode the wave of Spanish prosperity from New World discoveries (Columbus, of course, was a Genoan) that lasted until New World gold and silver ran out at the end of the sixteenth century.[40]

✦ ✦ ✦

Milanese republicanism constitutes only one brief chapter in a long history of dictatorship. Milan sits in the large fertile plain of the Po River Valley, making it the first stop for any army that makes it over or around the Alps. From Roman times, the city lay near the crossroads of two trade routes: one from France and Genoa in the southwest to Friuli in the northeast, and the other across Alpine passes to Ravenna on the Adriatic coast. Milan did not become a major financial or commercial center in medieval times but profited from the demand for its local agricultural products and became known for textiles, arms, and metallurgy.[41] While merchant aristocracies of one kind or another governed Florence, Genoa, and Venice from the twelfth and thirteenth centuries, Milan came to be ruled in 1277 by the same Visconti family that had held the captaincy of the archbishop of Milan's guard. Milan's exposure on all four sides, not to mention the prosperity of the surrounding countryside eager for protection, were propitious for lordly rule.

The short-lived Milanese (Ambrosian) republic was born in 1447 after the unexpected death, without an heir, of Duke Filippo Maria Visconti. A group of aristocrats and intellectuals from the University of Pavia compacted with one another to form a free civic government, the Republic of St. Ambrose, named after the fourth-century bishop of Milan. This group of leaders, however, soon fell into feuding with one another, which played into the hands of Francesco Sforza, a mercenary warrior for the previous Visconti regime. Taking advantage of a Venetian attack on the city, Sforza betrayed the republic by besieging it himself. At the point of starvation, the city capitulated in March 1450 and made Sforza its duke. Not by coincidence both Visconti and Sforza, though hundreds of years apart, were militia captains who put Milan's military vulnerability in service of their personal ambitions.[42]

✦ ✦ ✦

Venice was as physically remote as Milan was exposed to invasion. What the world now experiences as a magical city of canals and palaces was once a small collection of swampy, malaria-infested offshore islands that served as the last refuge for coastal farmers and fisherfolk escaping slaughter from the Huns in the fifth century and the Lombards in the sixth.[43]

Poised to prance off the high balcony of St. Mark's Basilica in Venice today are four bronze horses of exquisite beauty and realism, sculpted by Greek artists in the fourth century BC. These horses, along with other priceless treasures from the ancient and early medieval worlds in the church's

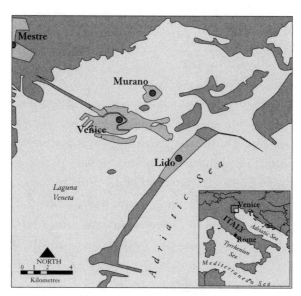

Venice and the Lagoon.

vault, are loot brought from Constantinople. There, in 1204, a fleet of two hundred Venetian ships transported knights from France and Flanders in the Fourth Crusade, a highly profitable detour on the way to the Holy Land.

As Venetian traders vied with the Genoese for domination of trade in the Mediterranean, North Africa, and the Black Sea, they were protected by their homegrown navy: the city government paid for the construction of ships, so important were they to the livelihood of Venice. On the eastern end of the largest island was the city's enormous arsenal and dockyard, where ships were built and outfitted as "public works": labor and materials were paid for by the city.[44]

As Venice grew rich, the city abandoned its conscription navy, drawn from neighborhood rolls or guild rosters, in favor of a mercenary navy. Unlike the Athenian citizens' navy that formed the core of the city's defense and therefore prosperity, Venice monetized its defense and disentangled it from citizenship, thereby undermining the common folk's claim to political participation. Thus began a gradual process of narrowing the political voice in Venice, culminating in what some historians term the *Serrata* of 1297, a rule that restricted the membership of the Great Council to "patrician" families.[45] The fifteen most prominent families accounted for 40 percent of the council's membership, chose relatively weak men to serve as their executive (the doge), and managed popular unrest with a combination of efficient suppression and financial generosity.[46]

The city subsidized charitable homes for widows and orphans, and the lavish ceremonies surrounding the doge and the cult of Saint Mark cultivated a proud Venetian identity that softened the hard edges of political exclusion. In the eighteenth century, Antonio Vivaldi composed much of his work for the all-female ensemble at the city-funded Ospedale della Pietà, a home for abandoned children where he was director of music. A visitor in 1739 wrote, "The most transcendent music here is that provided by the Ospedale. There are four of these, all of them for girls, illegitimate, orphans, or those whose relatives are not able to care for them. They are being brought up at the expense of the state and are being trained most especially to excel in music."[47]

The Venetian aristocracy chose its doge, who was to be executive for life, by way of a bewilderingly elaborate set of rules. These guidelines were designed to prevent family ambitions from degenerating into pandering to the masses of the same kind that undermined elite rule in Florence and especially Genoa. The doge selection took place in ten stages, the first nine of which produced electors for the next stage; no two members of the same family were allowed in the same stage. First, thirty names were selected by lot from the Great Council, a principally hereditary body of undefined size, usually between 500 and 1,000.[48] Next, these thirty elected nine people. These nine men chose forty by lot. The forty elected twelve. These twelve chose twenty-five by lot. The twenty-five elected nine. The nine chose forty-five by lot. These forty-five elected eleven. The eleven elected forty-one. The forty-one elected the doge, with a required supermajority of twenty-five.[49]

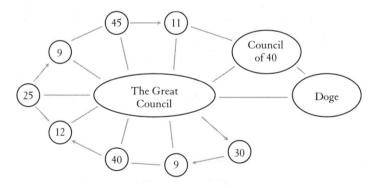

Procedure for electing the doge of Venice.

The interior of the Sala Maggior Consiglio. The Great
Council of Venice, *by Joseph Heintz der Jüngere, before 1678.*

Rig-proofing doge elections did not eliminate conspiracies, but power grabs were rare.[50] The rules were clever, but probably more important was Venetian geography. Because the lagoons' natural defense made the city nearly impossible to take in combat, disgruntled factions could not leverage support from the papacy, the Holy Roman Empire, Byzantium, or any other outside power to bankroll the coup attempts that were funded with regularity elsewhere. Even if, as Frederic Lane and William McNeill put it, the margin of Venice's "protection rent" declined as competitors developed large navies, Venice itself remained very hard to conquer. Venice also prospered by forming strategic alliances and playing the great powers against one another: first Byzantium, the Holy Roman Empire, and the papacy; later France and Spain.[51] The small scale of Venice's defensible territory underpinned a stable domestic majority in favor of the political status quo. *Il Serenissima* did not lack for men brimming with personal ambition, greed, and cunning, but it was a hard place in which to leverage them.

✦ ✦ ✦

Northern Italy, which had been the most productive area in Europe in the thirteenth century, lost its edge over the next three centuries, as the English and Dutch began producing woolen goods more cheaply.[52] Political impediments to trade and manufacture, impeding coordination over tolls, banking, and market regulation, might have undermined Italian competitiveness, but city-state identity blocked adaptation to the larger threats that would in time swallow them all.[53] Powerful cities disagreed about which of them should lead unification efforts because they were divided by institutional and ideological commitments that urban elites devised to defend their local rule.

The fate of the northern Italian city-states sheds light on the issue not only of territorial size but also of political bargains behind strategic choices. Republican self-rule was not a stop in the road toward democracy for self-protective reasons or for any others. As scholars have long pointed out, the commercial elite was in a better bargaining position than the landed elite to hold government accountable because merchants could withdraw their assets from domains that did not treat them well.[54] But nothing in the logic of "exit and voice" sets up a constitutional move from limited to mass franchise. Italy's short explosions of populist energy in medieval times spluttered and died in the cool political climate of merchant self-rule. Merchants preferred to govern themselves, and when they could not, they contracted with a prince or even capitulated to a foreign power rather than hand over the reins of government to their subject populations.

Military threats sometimes had discernible effects but rarely to the extent of convincing merchant elites of the benefit of democracy. Republican ideology, which enjoyed efflorescence in northern Italy and particularly in Florence around the time of the Renaissance, quite intentionally drew the lines of political participation around holders of wealth to exclude the working classes. Machiavelli's more radical republicanism, which advocated political broadening and the enlistment of citizens' militias, never gained widespread traction; merchants by and large opted instead to pay mercenaries to fight for them rather than to pay citizen-soldiers by granting them a political voice. In the short run, republican theorizing helped merchants coordinate local self-rule at the expense of peninsula-wide unity and to the exclusion of democracy.[55] In the longer run, however, city-republics were not viable.

Only Venice, barricaded within lagoons against the most formidable of foes, was untrammelled until Napoleon stormed through the gates in 1797.[56] Elaborate rules for selecting the Venetian doge confounded factional ambitions, affording the aristocracy a way to resist catering to broad groups of the populace (unlike in Cleisthenes' Athens) or conceding power to an autocrat able to maintain social control should they fail.

While history does not tell us plainly what would have happened in Venice if the lagoons had not spared the elite the choice between capitulation to a despot and wider enfranchisement, the other city-states provide clues. In Milan, where the landed and commercial families were unable to agree on how to share the spoils, local despotism came early. By contrast, Florentine merchants secured dominion over landed aristocrats by the thirteenth century, but when lower-middle-class guilds sought entry into the republic's hallowed halls in the Ciompi Revolt of 1378, the Florentine rich did not hesitate to bar their way. Machiavelli's call for wider enfranchisement in order to bolster Florence's military preparedness was a discordant voice in the chorus of republican theorizing of his day, and the ease with which the Medici took the reins of Florentine government is a measure of how much more the merchant elite feared popular rule than monarchy.

Genoa's periodic hiring of one-year dictators (*podestà*, who were city managers with extensive powers) tempered but did not eliminate feuding among tycoons who competitively rallied citizens to their side in exchange for political inclusion.[57] Genoa's accordion-like political opening and closing lasted until the Spanish conquest of 1528. The arc of history from the twelfth to the sixteenth centuries ran its course: merchant aristocracy gave way to authoritarian rule.

Chapter Eight

EASTERN LANDS IN
EARLY MODERN EUROPE

I N VOLTAIRE'S FAMOUS PHRASE, the Holy Roman Empire was "neither holy, nor Roman, nor an empire."[1] By the eighteenth century, in which Voltaire lived, it had become a fictional placeholder for Austrian geopolitical power. For smaller German realms and cities, it remained a hoped-for protection for local autonomy. But mostly it was scaffolding without a structure, left over from centuries of political redesign but not bothersome enough to anyone to be dismantled.

Eight centuries earlier, in 962 when the Saxon Otto the Great had himself crowned by the pope as "Emperor of the Romans," prospects looked excellent for the Holy Roman Empire. Combining his lands in the Harz Mountains of Saxony with the dwindling patrimony of Charlemagne, Otto had started out in 936 as king of Germany with only 375 square miles of farmlands, but he aimed for nothing short of the recreation of Charlemagne's empire. Using military means, marriages, and dynastic politics, he pushed his borders into eastern France and Burgundy and married his sister to the French king. After putting down Slavic and German uprisings, Otto turned to face the marauding Hungarian forces that were pounding western Europe. After defeating the Magyars at Lechfeld in 955, he arrived at Rome at the head of a conquering army, giving Pope John XII little choice but to name him Holy Roman emperor.[2]

Otto's friendship with the pope, such as it was, did not last long. A central

151

part of Otto's administrative strategy was to get control of the bureaucracy of the church, by appointing bishops and giving them the powers of counts throughout his realm. Soon Pope John XII began to conspire to depose him. Otto proved to be the more potent potentate. After forcing Pope John from office, he replaced him with a puppet and continued to expand his domains to the south and east, where he ultimately formed a marriage alliance with Byzantium. By 965 he was unquestionably the most powerful ruler in Europe.

There was, however, a catch to imperial power: Otto depended substantially on other landed lords for support. Like them, he lived off the revenues from land, principally in the form of labor and a proportion of produce, as well as tolls, fines, and a tax on immovable property. In this respect, he was no different from other feudal lords who collected the same kinds of revenues from their respective lands. The same remained true for the two dynasties that followed: the Salian (1024–1125) and the Hohenstaufen (1138–1254). Like Otto, Holy Roman emperors passed on to their sons a crown at the sufferance of "electors," the nobles of other great houses who were willing vassals but had no wish for an absolutist king.

The "perambulating kings" of the tenth and eleventh centuries traveled regularly to and from their lands, including Italy, where they claimed rights over Lombardy. On paper, they also laid claim to Charlemagne's lands in Burgundy; in reality, Burgundy could ignore pleas for money or help. Emperors provided strategically located monasteries and vassals with grants of properties and rights in exchange for political support and for provisions when their itinerary called for a stop.[3] They grabbed church lands when they could and appointed their protégés as clerics.

When Emperor Henry IV (1056–1106) refused to stop ordaining German priests and bishops on his own, the bloody Investiture Controversy between pope and emperor did not end until the Concordat of Worms, in 1122, provided a compromise that gave the emperor a veto over papal choices. The nobles, however, were the real winners. Emperors gave up nearly all the "colonial" lands east of the Elbe River to Knights of the Teutonic Order and to other vassals in exchange for support. In 1232 Frederick II agreed— though he had little effective choice in the matter—that the great nobles would become virtual princes in their own territories. Not only did the land concessions deplete the imperial coffers, it also consigned many German farmers who tilled those lands to effective serfdom.[4]

The Golden Bull of 1356 codified the selection rules for the Holy Roman emperor that had emerged from centuries of competition and alliance-building among noble houses: seven electors (the archbishops of the cities of Trier, Cologne, and Mainz, and the rulers of the Palatinate, Saxony, Brandenburg, and Bohemia) would choose the emperor. Although in theory the Holy Roman Empire remained an elective monarchy, from 1438 the Habsburg family maneuvered itself into effective dynastic control of the empire.[5]

The longevity of Habsburg hegemony over the empire (1438–1806) reflects not the power of the Habsburgs to enforce their will but rather the complacency (or corruptibility) of the largely autonomous nobility. The Habsburgs transformed the Archduchy of Austria into the empire's heartland, although it remained technically a fiefdom of the empire, as did the other German states.

In those imperial lands beyond Austria's grasp, power and wealth remained fluid until the Reformation. The Thirty Years' War, fueled by realigned and impassioned religious loyalties, created fertile ground for the emergence of centralized state authority in Brandenburg-Prussia as well as in Austria, but the war made it impossible for the German princes to find common ground. For another century and a half, the Habsburgs continued to preside over Austria and a rickety and divided German federation that included burgeoning nation-states within the fictional trappings of empire.[6] We already know the end of the story: Napoleon, after feigning retreat, crushed the combined Russian and Austrian armies at Austerlitz in 1805, then forced Holy Roman emperor Francis II to dissolve the empire.[7]

✦ ✦ ✦

Rather than assuming that absolutist monarchies were inevitable in eastern Europe, consider the years when alternatives to the nation-state, and particularly its monarchical form, remained possible. A betting person in the fourteenth century could reasonably have put money on German cities over kings and lords. Not until much later was it clear that large markets would have to be defended by large armies; in the meantime, weak governments were good for business because they did not tax effectively.

As in Italy, the Holy Roman Empire's loose lordship left ample opportunities for commercial interests to thrive. In the twelfth century the cities of Lübeck and Hamburg, on opposite sides of the Danish peninsula, built the sixty-one-mile-long Kiel Canal between them as an alternative to costly portage or dangerous sailing around the penninsula. Lübeck fishermen worked the herring spawning grounds off the coast of the lower tip of Sweden (at that time part of Denmark); Hamburg produced salt from mines at Kiel for brining and storing the herring. These cities, joined by others, formed what came to be known as the Hanseatic League (*Hanze* means "trade association" in German) in mutual defense against piracy and pillaging.

Besides herring and salt, the Hanseatic League came to specialize in low-profit, high-volume trade in other bulk commodities: grain, timber, honey, and amber. At its height, more than sixty cities were members,[8] and these cities controlled much of the countryside surrounding them. Lübeck remained the "Queen of the League" because of its strategic location connecting German towns to the Baltic by river, canal, and portage to the Atlantic.

Beginning in the fourteenth century the Hansa parliament, based in Lübeck, helped member cities coordinate contractual rules and enforce them. In 1356, for example, the league's cities collectively embargoed the city of Bruges for not agreeing to Hansa rules; Bruges capitulated a few years

HANSEATIC LEAGUE Land and Sea Trade Routes

The Hanseatic League in 1328.

later.[9] The Hansa's military consisted of voluntary contributions of ships, men, and funds from member towns, and the league expelled towns for refusing to submit levies agreed to by its diet. In practice, however, most campaigns were borne principally by the cities with the greatest stakes in the issue at hand. When Denmark grabbed Holstein (including the Kiel Canal) in 1367 and began charging for the use of the sound, the Hansa's war party was composed of the dozen or so towns most affected by the problem, along with Sweden, the Duke of Mecklenburg, and the Counts of Holstein, who opposed Denmark's ambitions.

The Hansa and its allies won the war against Denmark, but the Peace of Stralsund (1370) was no more than a brief pause in the changing geopolitical landscape that favored larger and more coordinated action than the Hansa could muster. Denmark absorbed Norway and Sweden in 1397 in the Union of Kalmar. Meanwhile English and Dutch traders, with their Atlantic-size ships, had no need of the Kiel Canal and could underprice and outperform Hanseatic merchants both on the carrying service and on the goods they carried. By the turn of the fifteenth century, most of the advantages the Hansa had won over Denmark in 1370, of promoting and protecting the trade of their member cities, had disappeared. Denmark's monarchy, thanks to lucrative tolls from the straits and to silver from Norway's Konigsberg mines, could buy military might without groveling to its estates.[10]

The Lübeck uprising of 1408 is a case study, to match that of the Dutch Republic, of fickle franchise extension. Saddled with an enormous debt from another (1404) war with Denmark, while simultaneously losing money against England and the Dutch, the Lübeck town council decided in 1406 to extend political representation to the lower orders who had been left out of city politics—craftsmen and artisans—in exchange for help in raising money to retire the debt. Two years later, when the plan had succeeded and city finances were back in balance, the council dismissed the newcomers. Furious, the craftsmen and artisans took to the streets and, with threats but no actual violence, sent fifteen of the twenty-three councilors into exile. In January 1408 an angry crowd threatened to attack the council's annual procession, and afraid for their lives, the council spokesman shouted from a window to the crowd, "You shall choose the council!" Similar uprisings took place soon thereafter in Rostock, Hamburg, and Wismar.[11]

The populist regime, which confiscated Lübeck exiles' property for public use, lasted until 1416, when the Holy Roman emperor declared all new Lübeck council members and supportive citizens to be imperial outlaws. The historian Rhiman Rotz reckons that the Holy Roman emperor Sigismund sold his decision on Lübeck to the highest bidder. Once implacably opposed to Denmark, the exiles persuaded Denmark to arrest Lübeck merchants in Danish waters.[12]

Happy for an opportunity to undermine the Holy Roman emperor, Pope John XXIII subsequently declared the imperial ban null and void.[13] A split Hanseatic League reached a skewed compromise: the status quo ante would be restored in Lübeck and in the copycat cities of Rostock, Hamburg, and Wismar, and the Lübeck council would pay restitution to the exiles for confiscated property. For punctuation, the Hansa declared that in the future rebels would meet with capital punishment.[14]

As in Sweden and the Dutch Republic before it, the narrowing of the franchise in Lübeck came with the loss of military capability and ambition. From this time, Lübeck neither acquired new territories nor led the Hansa to victories at sea. When Denmark claimed once again, in 1426, the right to toll shipping at the southern tip of Sweden and on the sound, the Hansa was incapable of responding, leaving the toll in place for four hundred more years.[15]

The Hanseatic League never recovered. In 1428 the nobility of Pomerania used an uprising in Stettin (a seaport in today's Poland) as an opportunity to subjugate that city. Complete control of the cities was elusive, but by the end of the fifteenth century the Pomeranian dukes succeeded. By 1498 all Pomeranian cities and towns had lost political and economic independence and were forced to pay higher tolls at Wolgast and Damgarten.[16]

Lacking coordination and the full participation of its members, Hanseatic cities were easy prey to the Dutch in 1441 as well as to the rural nobility in the surrounding countryside. The nobles of Brandenburg, Pomerania, and Poland waged a systematic campaign against cities along the Baltic coast and the rivers that connected to it. In 1442 the Brandenburg elector Frederick II took advantage of squabbling among the federated cities of Berlin and Cölln to seize those previously autonomous cities.

Emboldened by his success, Frederick II then forbade all cities in Brandenburg to participate in the Hanseatic League. Not only were cities then powerless to protect themselves, they were unable to call on the powers of the Holy Roman Empire to protect them. Even before the Thirty Years' War, the nominally imperial duchies along the Baltic were in fact landed aristocracies. When in 1488 nobles across the region gained for themselves a tax exemption for beer brewing, driving that and related industries out of cities into the countryside, the Hanseatic League and the Holy Roman Empire were both mere bystanders.[17]

Although a league of cities made good economic sense, the cities were often divided about particular military actions. The Holy Roman emperor, who had reasons to protect the cities from which he raised some revenues, was often powerless to provide them with protection. In 1469 England destroyed the Steelyard (a *stiliard* was a weighing beam), the Hanseatic trading post in London.[18] Cologne then swung opportunistically to the English side to protect its own trade.[19] In 1494 Ivan III of Russia closed the Hanseatic League's Novgorod office. Territorial princes were on the rise and hungry; cities were plums ripe for picking.[20]

Compared to the Hanseatic cities, the Free Imperial Cities farther to the south had the advantage of proximity to Habsburg Austria, which had an incentive to use the structures of the Holy Roman Empire to balance against the growing territorial states in the north. Augsburg, Nuremburg, Strasbourg, and literally hundreds of other urban centers in southern and southwestern Germany enjoyed extensive powers of self-government during the two or three centuries when imperial power was both sufficient to deter out-

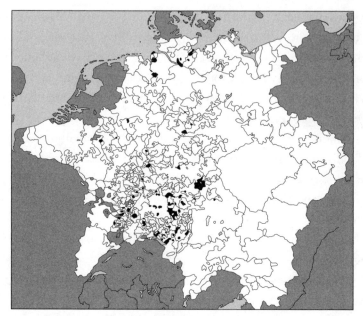

Free Imperial Cities enjoyed autonomy until, in the face of
peasant unrest, their nobility decided to join territorial
states in order to secure stability and property rights.

siders and insufficient to intervene.[21] But ultimately the Free Imperial Cities too were feeble contenders for territorial control. By the end of the Thirty Years' War, the burgeoning states of Brandenburg-Prussia and Saxony had enlarged themselves southward, and France seized the bishoprics of Metz, Verdun, Toul, and Strasbourg, as well as the cities of the Décapole: Colmar, Hagenau, Kaisersberg, Landau, Mülhausen, Münster, Oberehnheim, Rosheim, Schlettstadt, Selz, Türkheim, and Wessenburg.

Things might have turned out otherwise, but even without the threat of territorial absorption into Prussia or Saxony, the odds of maintaining urban power were low, as the German Peasants' War of 1525 would show.[22] Instead of fighting territorial princes, merchants and nobles joined forces to massacre nearly one hundred thousand farmers and miners who had taken up arms against centers of power and wealth.[23] Martin Luther and his followers, who judged the support of Protestant princes to be more crucial to the success of the Reformation than that of peasants, sided with the brutal repression.[24]

The rural and commercial elite decided they had more to lose at the hands of an energized peasantry than from one another, which played into the hands of territorial states that could offer stability and property rights. Allegiances thus clarified, German cities lost their independence, one by one.[25] One brief interlude was the Schmalkaldic War of 1546–47 in which several Lutheran imperial cities, including Bremen, Magdeburg, and Strasbourg, struggled in vain against the forces of Catholic Holy Roman emperor Charles. The Peace of Augsburg of 1555 gave religious control to territorial princes (*cuius regio, eius religio*: "whose realm, his religion"), ignoring the arguments of cities and towns for municipal sovereignty.[26]

The fatal flaw of the Augsburg "peace," which had sought to stanch the Reformation bloodbath, was that many territories remained religiously heterogeneous, setting the stage for another horrific war when groups of subjects would challenge the prince's "right" to choose a state church against historical practice. The Habsburg world, where many of the nobility were Protestant, even if opportunistically, was a powder keg awaiting a spark.[27]

The richest and largest Protestant domain was Bohemia, based in the great city of Prague. The Hradčany castle overlooked a distinguished university and magnificent aristocratic villas; across the Vltava River lay a vibrant commercial center. Prague had been, in fact, the capital of the Holy Roman Empire in 1355, when Charles IV was elected emperor. The city's prosperity was destroyed in the Hussite wars of 1419–37, during which the kingdom of Bohemia—in defense of the teachings of the proto-Protestant Jan Hus, whom the pope had burned at the stake for heresy in 1415—exhausted itself fighting five crusades launched against Bohemia by Pope Martin V for following this heresy.

The Holy Roman Empire's southeastern border crumpled in 1526, when the Ottoman Turks under Suleiman the Magnificent smashed through antiquated Hungarian cavalry lines at Mohács with artillery and muskets.[28] The Ottomans helped themselves to a large portion of Hungary, leaving the mountainous region of Transylvania to govern itself. A strip of land to the west and north was all that remained of the empire's Kingdom of Hungary.

As in Bohemia, the Reformation had taken root among the Hungarian and Transylvanian nobility, but the pragmatic archduke Matthias of Habsburg (later Holy Roman emperor, from 1612) forestalled secession with timely concessions.[29] In 1605 Stephen Bocskay (István Bocskai), a Calvinist nobleman who had led the Habsburg army in successive victories against the Ottoman Turks, switched sides in favor of the Turks to save his native Tran-

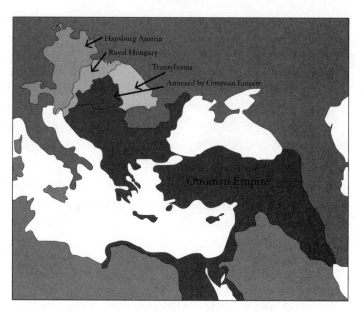

Partition of the Kingdom of Hungary in 1526.

sylvania from Habsburg domination. He also incited a peasant insurrection in Transylvania itself. To mobilize a large force, Bocskay promised tenant farmers (or outlaws and brigands, depending on your point of view) land rights with titles of nobility, creating a "warrior state." Recognizing the danger, Archduke Matthias guaranteed religious rights and acknowledged Bocskay as Prince of Transylvania in June 1606. Bocskay died in December later that year, possibly assassinated by his own chancellor Mihály Káthay, before the depth of this democratic commitment was tested.[30]

The zealously Catholic Ferdinand II who replaced Matthias as Holy Roman emperor in 1617 brought an end to an era of religious toleration throughout imperial lands. When Ferdinand began enforcing religious conformity at court, Protestant Bohemian nobles threw the new emperor's representatives out the window of Hradčany castle. This "defenestration," although landing the representatives more or less safely in a trash heap below the castle window, was a well-understood act of defiance.

The Bohemians miscalculated their chances of a quick military victory, not having factored in the strategic brilliance of the imperial commander Johann Tserclaes, Count of Tilly. In 1620 at White Mountain near Prague, imperial forces shredded both the defense and the morale of the Bohemians

The 1618 Defenestration of Prague, *by Václav Brožík, 1889.*

in a battle that lasted only about an hour. The Bohemian infantrymen had not even engaged when they saw their cavalry retreating and followed suit. Two years later, in 1622, Emperor Ferdinand III ordered all Calvinists and other non-Lutheran Protestants to leave the realm in three days or convert to Catholicism.[31] Most Bohemians converted; those who did not had their lands seized, and great numbers of them were killed.

The Thirty Years' War—a label that the seventeenth-century jurist and historian Samuel Pufendorf affixed to the ghastly succession of wars that ravaged Europe between 1618 and 1648—was fought, millions of lives later, more or less to a draw. Death toll estimates range from 3 million to 11.5 million, or 0.5 percent to 2 percent of total population. In some particularly hard-hit areas, two-thirds of the population died or fled.[32] The Holy Roman Empire was not up to the task of holding together a realm against powerful centrifugal forces of religion and economic disparity, and it ended the war as a shell, within which the Habsburg empire consolidated greater power over a smaller territory.[33]

One of the starring characters in the Thirty Years' War was also one of the greatest personal beneficiaries of the Bohemian defeat at White Mountain in 1620: Albrecht von Wallenstein, a Protestant Bohemian who had converted to Catholicism in 1606. Wallenstein, an orphan, nonetheless amassed a large fortune through his marriage to a Moravian widow with which he raised his own army regiments. Fighting on the side of the empire against the Bohemian rebels in 1620, he multiplied his wealth by confiscating the estates of the exiled Protestants. In 1624 he was rich enough to buy the Duchy of Friedland in Bohemia, whereby he became a prince of the empire with rights of a count palatine.[34]

The fact that Wallenstein had a leading role underscores that this war did not begin over interstate competition. Shifting coalitions of monarchs and military commanders used their own funds, or raised money on the same Dutch, English, and Italian financial markets, and raised armies from the same pools of mercenaries who were willing to fight for pay.[35]

Nor was it principally a war of religion. Various Protestant monarchs and princes such as Gustav Adolphus of Sweden and Christian of Denmark fought against the Catholic empire,[36] but so did Catholic France, when Austria seemed poised to seize European hegemony. The Protestant "Hague Coalition" of 1626 included Saxe-Weimar, England, Denmark, and the United Provinces of the Netherlands; the Protestant electors of Saxony and Brandenburg remained aloof. Sir James Turner related a maxim he learned in Germany: so long as "we serve our master honestly, it is no matter what master we serve."[37]

Wallenstein surveying a scene of devastation in the Thirty
Years' War, as depicted by John Ernest Crofts in 1884.

As terrible as the civilian toll was, the war lent momentum to political centralization rather than to franchise expansion because leaders were able to avoid large-scale mobilization by relying on mercenaries. There were some exceptions, as when the Swedish king Gustavus Adolphus widened the Swedish franchise to raise his own troops, or when the forces of Saxe-Weimar and Denmark appealed to the peasantry of Bohemia, Moravia, and Upper Austria in their war against Austria.[38] Millions of farmers and their families starved or were displaced when their fields were trampled in battle and when hungry soldiers ransacked their larders. In the village of Linden, northeast of Rothenburg in southwestern Franconia, the number of peasant households dropped 70 percent, from 1,503 in 1618 to 447 in 1641.[39] Habsburg armies took an estimated 30,000 horses, 100,000 cows, and 600,000 sheep from villagers following their victory at Nordlingen.[40]

Cities fared no better. In their occupation of the Archbisopric of Mainz, Swedish soldiers "self-provisioned" by helping themselves to food and shelter. The city lost a quarter of its dwellings, 40 percent of its population, and 60 percent of its wealth. Much of the fighting was carried out in intermittent skirmishes and strategic maneuvers designed to limit military casualties, but the civilian toll was catastrophic.[41]

By 1632, when the war ground to a stalemate, Swedish king Adolphus made overtures to Wallenstein for a truce, in exchange for which Wallenstein would receive the Duchy of Franconia. Wallenstein may have been tempted by the feelers. He had lost popularity among his men on account of exacting discipline. Moreover, in 1630 the Emperor Ferdinand III had removed him from command for fear of a coup; only Adolphus's success against Tilly at Breitenfeld (where Tilly was killed) forced the emperor to reinstate Wallenstein, at least temporarily. But before Wallenstein could accept Adolphus's proposition, Adolphus was killed while pursuing retreating Austrian forces at the Battle of Lützen.[42] Wallenstein nevertheless proposed peace talks to the emperor, who took the idea for treason. In January 1634 Habsburg loyalists assassinated Wallenstein along with his family and friends.[43]

❖ ❖ ❖

If most who died in the war were civilians who starved or perished of disease, a crushing financial burden also fell on states that had to maintain large, mostly mercenary armies. For a sense of scale, consider that 3,700 oxen and 753 vehicles were required for a train of ten siege guns and ten mortars. Twenty thousand horses consumed ninety tons of hay (400 acres of grazing) every day.[44] An army of 30,000 men required twenty tons of bread daily, and some combination of 1,500 sheep or 150 cows. Commanders struggled to keep armies big enough for the task but not so big that they could not be fed or controlled—an impossible balance to maintain. The historian Geoffrey Parker reckons that by 1648 there were about 200,000 men-at-arms out of a population of 12 to 15 million. This mobilization rate was not high by the standards of twentieth-century world wars, but it was unprecedented in its day.[45] In periods of truce, unemployed soldiers took what they wanted at gunpoint, a grave menace to civilian populations.[46]

The 1648 Treaty of Westphalia created the modern territorial state system as we know it today, mostly favoring monarchs over free cities.[47] Still, the delegations at the peace negotiations represented 194 European rulers, with entourages ranging from two hundred for the French to shared delegates for collections of cities.[48] Austria, Poland, and France dominated the new map of Europe, but Brandenburg-Prussia, Saxony, and Bavaria emerged as new powers.

The triumph of the territorial state was based on military advantage, not on superior economic efficiency. Brandenburg-Prussia inhibited the mechanization of linen manufacturing, as a way to protect the profits of feudal landlords from serf weaving.[49] In the 1500s Württemberg had been home to a thriving peasant business in weaving of light worsted cloths, but in subsequent decades state-sanctioned guilds blocked the introduction of new techniques or price flexibility, undermining their competitive edge.[50] The consolidated Duchy of Württemberg that emerged from the Thirty Years' War also enforced monopolies and corporate privileges. G.W.F. Hegel fumed about this earlier period from his nineteenth-century vantage point: "As long as Württemberg's peculiar burgher aristocracy existed . . . and this element of moral and intellectual degradation ensnaring the mass of the people [was] not destroyed, no true concept of law, freedom, and constitution could take root."[51] The economy was not more prosperous in the long run, but merchants and nobles temporarily raked in monopoly profits with which they paid taxes that funded state armies.

The most powerful state to emerge from the Holy Roman Empire, after Austria, was Prussia, which had, after Westphalia, the Great Elector Frederick William to lead it and the makings of an army strong enough to take on its Swedish and Polish neighbors.[52] At the start of the Thirty Years' War, the Electorate of Brandenburg had had only 10,000 square miles and a population of 350,000 (roughly the proportions of Vermont in 1917). East Prussia was a small duchy along the bleak shores of the Baltic, outside the perimeter of the Holy Roman Empire.[53] In the state's early years, the nobility generally refused to recognize officials from Brandenburg or Cleves, and vice versa, despite Prussia's legal unity. One result of effective decentralization was poorly coordinated military efforts and self-destructive abuse of local populations.

As the Great Elector Frederick William wrote in 1641, "We find that our military forces have cost the country a great deal and done much wanton damage. The enemy could not have done worse."[54] One of the Great Elector's first acts, when he took the throne of Prussia in 1640, was to dismiss the mercenaries in his army, who included Swedes, Scots, Irish, and Poles, in favor of a smaller infantry of his own subjects. He increased their pay to discourage pillaging. In the last years of the Thirty Years' War, he built an army of eight thousand men, with military heft that backed his claims to territories of East Pomerania, Magdeburg, Halberstadt, and Minden.[55]

Still, Prussia had no standing army. Following the Thirty Years' War, the noble estates refused to vote the Great Elector sufficient taxes to keep an army in times of peace. Junkers, as the Prussian landed elite were known, had grown rich from rising grain and livestock prices in the early seventeenth century and opposed market-disrupting wars. Although Swedish and Habsburg armies had swept through many of their villages in 1626, plundering and killing along their "self-provisioning" path of destruction, the Junkers themselves were largely unscathed and refused to pay taxes except for their own militia for local defense.[56]

The Great Northern War (1655–60) brought the elector another bargaining opportunity. When the nobility refused to pay new taxes (their preferred stance being to "trust in God and wait patiently upon events"), the elector collected taxes by military order without the explicit consent of the estates. In fact, he remained at the mercy of the nobility, for they controlled the vast proportion of taxable wealth, but he won them one by one by giving out new land titles tax free in exchange for new revenues.[57] His new army of nearly ten thousand won the Three Days' Battle for Warsaw in 1656; and although the nobility expected Frederick William's forces would be disbanded after the Northern War, the elector reduced them by half rather than disband them. "I have become convinced," he wrote, "that I owe the preservation of my position and my territory to God, and next to God, to my army."[58]

A problem for princes and nobles alike was the terrible labor shortage in the war's wake, but they favored opposite solutions. The grain-exporting nobility preferred to stay out of wars; its only use for a strong government was to help enforce peasant servitude under the unfavorable conditions (from their point of view) of land abundance and peasant scarcity. According to the famous hypothesis of the economic historian Evsey Domar, serfdom was harsh in Russia and eastern Europe generally precisely because labor scarcity required strict enforcement.[59]

The Great Elector, on the other hand, needed able-bodied men, this time for another war in 1674. He blamed the nobility for depopulation and rural poverty, and without consulting the estates, he decreed "by virtue of princely power and sovereign authority" that peasant farms must be granted six years of freedom from taxes, rents, and military quartering. But these were brave words from a mouth without a full set of teeth, so to speak. In practice, the outcome landed somewhere between the nobility's preference for forcing runaway peasants back onto their estates with harsh penalties, and the somewhat populist position of a monarch seeking military capacity on the international chessboard.[60]

Against the standard wisdom that the Prussian monarchy "confirmed and enlarged" the Junkers' privileges in the seventeenth century, the historian William Hagen provides considerable evidence that the stronger Prussian state in fact brought a measure of peasant relief.[61] The compromise seems to have involved the granting of monopoly rights over grain trade and beer production to the nobility at the expense of the towns, in exchange for taxes. As late as 1633, some towns, such as Königsberg, had declared peasant servitude to be a "hellish poison" and refused to hand runaway peasants back to their landlords. Even accounting for exaggerations about the harsh life of indentured servitude, we know that lords had an incentive to beat runaways within inches of their lives to make a point, if they ever caught them. The Holy Roman Empire, which had long established a claim on urban taxes, was incapable of protecting city or peasant against this combination of prince and lord.[62]

GROWTH OF BRANDENBURG–PRUSSIA 1600–1795

Ermeland

East Pomerania

West Pomerania

Duchy of PRUSSIA

West Prussia

New East Prussia

Osnabruck

BRANDENBURG

South Prussia

Minden

Magdeburg

Cleve

Mark

Silesia

New Silesia

Holy Roman Empire

Margravate of Brandenburg 1600

Duchy of Prussia 1600

Acquisitions 1600-1772

Territory acquired from Poland 1772-1795

Prussian military success and expansion coincided with the rise of monarchy and popular reforms.

The Great Elector's son, Frederick I, took over in 1688 and had himself crowned "King in Prussia" in 1701, in compensation for helping the empire fight Louis XIV of France. The Nine Years' War (1688–97) had pitted the Holy Roman Empire—in a "grand alliance" with William of Orange (now William III of England), Charles II of Spain, and an array of German princes—against the territorial ambitions of Louis XIV. The contested areas were ever growing, including borders between France and the Spanish Netherlands, the Rhineland, Savoy, and Catalonia, as well as the New World. The war succeeded in checking French ambitions: Louis XIV kept Alsace, including Strasbourg, but returned Lorraine to its duke, held on to the western half of the island of Hispaniola (Haiti), and relinquished territories east of the Rhine.

By appointing Frederick I "King in Prussia," the emperor all but gave up trying to treat Prussia—and the cities within its boundaries—as subordinate territories. It was only a matter of time before the Prussian royal family, the Hohenzollerns, appropriated the more meaningful title of "King *of* Prussia" by unopposed force.[63]

The Holy Roman Empire limped along until Napoleon's invasion in

1806, but by then Prussia and Habsburg Austria had been the real players for over a century. After Watereloo, the other German princes were free to negotiate their place between these two powers. While Austria remained the leading German power at the start of the eighteenth century, Frederick William I, the "Soldier King" (ruled 1713–40), embarked on a policy of army building that transformed Prussia into the most thoroughly militarized state in Europe. He established a system of primary schools, resettled devastated lands in East Prussia, and established the "canton" system for conscripting and training peasants (over the objections of the nobility), leaving to his son (the future Frederick the Great) a standing army of eighty thousand well-trained men and many more drilled reserves. Prussia soon announced itself as the Habsburgs' equal when Frederick, taking advantage of the powerful army his father left him, grabbed Silesia in the War of the Austrian Succession (1740–48).[64] He followed this by allying with the British against the French and Austrians in the Seven Years' War, in an unsuccessful attempt to acquire Saxony. But Frederick was not finished. In 1785 Prussia led a group of princes, including Hanover and Saxony, to shore up the old structures of the empire against the Habsburg emperor Joseph II's designs to exchange Habsburg possessions in the Spanish Netherlands (today's Belgium) for the Electorate of Bavaria.[65] By the end of the eighteenth century, Prussia was powerful enough to act without help from other German principalities. It agreed with Austria and Russia in 1792 to carve off large pieces of Poland among themselves.

The rise of powerful territorial states notwithstanding, the map of Germany continued to be dotted with smaller political entities long after the Thirty Years' War. In southern Germany, the Austrian fist in the imperial glove was still a potent counterweight to Prussia as well as to other princes with territorial ambitions.[66] At the same time, Bavaria's concern about Austrian ambitions prompted the Bavarian elector Maximilian to form an alliance with France at the end of the Thirty Years' War. At Westphalia, France's aim to cement German political fragmentation succeeded because it was consonant with the wishes of many middle-size German principalities for a counterweight to both Austrian and Prussian domination.

Napoleon's invasions of 1806 destroyed the Holy Roman Empire, but the devastation of Prussia was only temporary. It emerged after Waterloo in 1815 as a more homogeneously German state than it had ever been before and in a

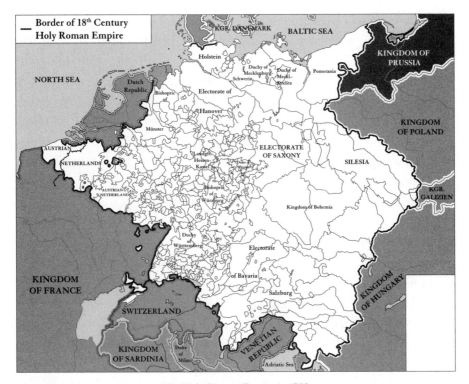

The Holy Roman Empire in 1789.

much more credible position to challenge Austrian leadership. Not until the 1860s—when Chancellor Otto von Bismarck united Prussian Junkers with southern and western industrialists in a protectionist logroll backed by an east-west railway system that could move troops to two fronts at once—did Prussia destroy Austrian and French resistance to German territorial consolidation under Prussian stewardship.

♦ ♦ ♦

Poland's republic of nobles enjoyed a remarkably democratic constitution, if only for the nobility. The Polish legislature (the Sejm) was governed by unanimity—the *liberum veto*—which gave every noble immense power to protect the status quo, although in 1764–66 the Sejm began using majority voting for some legislation. Nobles liked to say that their polity was an improvement on Heaven itself, since unanimity had been known on occasion to elude even God and his angels and Christ and his apostles. The Swiss political philosopher Jean-Jacques Rousseau admired the Polish constitution's protections of freedom but also saw the design flaw in the *liberum veto*: "It is hard to understand how a state so strangely constituted has been able to survive so long. . . . A body which exerts itself greatly to accomplish nothing; which is capable of offering no sort of resistance to anyone who tries to encroach upon it."[67] The extreme decentralization that protected the Polish Republic against internal tyranny exposed it to external defeat instead.[68] So strongly antipopulist and antimonarchical was the republic that it could not mobilize adequately for self-defense.[69]

Poland's military strategy, based on cavalry, had long avoided the need to arm the masses and instead reinforced the political power of the minor nobility. Even when cavalry fighting became obsolete against Russian and Prussian conscription armies in the eighteenth century, impoverished Polish minor nobility, faced with a loss in status and higher taxes, opposed arming an infantry that would put too many guns in the hands of too many peasants. The great magnates preferred instead to strike deals with their new Prussian and Russian overlords.

Poland had not always been a republic of nobles. Oral tradition has it that a warrior from the Polans tribe named Mieszko established the Piast dynasty in the tenth century, when he merged numerous western Slavic tribes to create a unified realm in today's Poland. Although historical accounts are sparse, it is easy to imagine that the broad plains of Poland, where settlers had the advantage of abundant lands but the disadvantage of few natural barriers, would have sought to protect their farmlands from invaders and would have been willing to throw their lot in with an energetic leader eager to organize mutual defense. Among the invaders was Holy Roman emperor Otto I "the Great" of Saxony seeking to expand eastward across the Elbe. Mieszko worked out an uneasy truce with the empire and even converted to Christianity to buy time.

From his base on the Warta and the middle and lower Vistula, Mieszko extended Polish boundaries to include the upper Vistula in the territory of Cracow, Silesia, and western Pomerania on the lower Oder.[70] But from its inception, the Polish monarchy struggled as much with its own warlords— who would become the nobility—as with the Holy Roman Empire and other external threats.[71] Poland's geographic vulnerability elevated the political importance of the citizens with enough land to commit horseback warriors to battle. Fending off three successive Mongolian invasions in the thirteenth century not only established the Polish cavalry (*husaria*) as a formidable military force but also entrenched the power of the landed elite in Polish politics.[72]

When the last Piast king, Casimir III, died in 1386 without a male heir, the Polish nobility blocked various claimants to the throne, agreeing finally to eleven-year-old Jadwiga and her fiancé, the Lithuanian grand duke Wladyslaw Jagiello. With larger combined forces, Poland and Lithuania defeated the highly trained and disciplined Teutonic Knights of Prussia in the 1410 Battle of Grunwald, ushering in Poland's Golden Age and creating an enormous empire between the two entities. Poland-Lithuania was known for its religious toleration, thriving cities, outstanding universities, and great art. In 1496, in exchange for money for wars, the king granted the nobility a law forbidding peasants to leave their villages without seigneurial permission.[73] But the workload was still manageable: in 1520 a peasant was required to perform one day's unpaid labor service each week on the lord's lands.

The personal union of the Kingdom of Poland and the Grand Duchy of Lithuania was replaced by an elective monarchy in the Union of Lublin of 1569, when the last Jagiello left no male heir. The Lithuanian magnates, who owned far larger tracts of land than the poor Polish nobility (*szlachta*), worried about a dilution of their influence in a formal entity but were appeased by the promise of a unit veto for every member of the legislature on any vote. The Lithuanian magnate Radziwill owned lands the size of present-day Belgium. By contrast, of the 120,000 or so Polish families in 1790, barely a quarter owned their land.[74]

The institutional hamstringing of the monarchy on the pretext of preserving "liberty, equality, and fraternity" (two centuries before the French but only for the nobility) governed Poland until 1791, when overwhelming external threats from Austria, Prussia, and Russia forced the nobility to concede more powers to the executive.[75] By then, however, the abandonment of the unit veto was too little too late.

The strengthening of the nobility at the expense of the monarchy was calamitous for Poland. As in Prussia and Pomerania, the nobility's monopoly in the production and sale of alcohol in Poland (*propinacja*) sapped the vitality of Polish towns and cities.[76] Alcohol sales as a proportion of estate income was insignificant in the sixteenth century but substantial by the eighteenth.

It also became a major source of employment for Jews. Landowners leased much of this business to Jewish merchants who had thrived under the Polish monarchy but now, under the republic of nobles, were squeezed into narrow lines of work. According to a census of Jews in 1764–65, about 80 percent of Jews living in villages and 14 percent of those in towns and cities were in the business of owning taverns selling landowners' alcohol.[77]

Peasants' labor obligations to manor lords doubled from one day a week to two or three days in the seventeenth century and to four days in seven by the eighteenth. The nobility's reluctance to pay for a standing army, perhaps from fear of arming peasants lest the guns be put to domestic use, kept the military too small for the job.[78] In 1717 Poland had only 24,000 men-at-arms, a fraction of the size of the armies being built by its neighbors. So dysfunctional was the Polish legislature that various of its members actually sold their votes to outside powers to block rearmament.

At the end of the eighteenth century, foreign powers were able to help themselves to large chunks of Poland in three successive assaults: 1772, 1792, and 1795. In the First Partition in 1772, Poland lost almost a third of its territory (81,500 square miles) and half of its population (four of its eight million) to a combined attack from Prussia, Russia, and Austria. Prussia took 14,000 square miles, including most of Poland's Baltic coastline on both sides of Gdansk. Russians seized 36,000 square miles, including Livonia and Belarus. The Habsburgs took 32,000 square miles north of the Carpathian Mountains, which they renamed the "Kingdom of Galicia and Ludomeria." (In the War of Spanish Succession, the Habsburgs had lost a province they had called Galicia in northern Spain, so the name was now available for this new acquisition. The former Galicia now lies divided between Poland and Ukraine.)[79]

Desperate for more latitude for military action, the Polish king Stanislaw August Poniatowski and his allies worked for years to eliminate the unit veto, the right of any single nobleman to block government initiatives. In his favor, the Russian protectorate established in Polish Ukraine was immensely unpopular in Poland. On the other hand, fighting against the reforms were the magnates who feared executive power and Polish populism more than foreign overlords.

For a time, the majority won. In May 1791 the legislature adopted a new constitution that eliminated the unit veto, expanded the franchise to include free men, and paved the way for a 10 percent tax on landed income. The 30

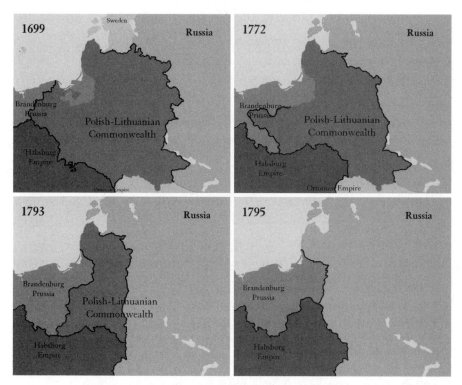

Poland's gridlocked republic of nobles allowed its neighbors to take its territory in the face of little military resistance. Its nobility even blocked populist reforms that would have allowed for more effective defense.

to 40 members of the legislature who opposed the new constitution were overwhelmed by the 140 to 150 who favored it, unit veto or not: "Only at six in the evening did the impatient assembly roar its approval at a gesture from the king, misunderstood as a sign that he was about to swear the oath to the new Constitution." The king was borne aloft to the church for the vow of obedience, while the rump remained behind, bewildered, in the empty debating chamber. The government was empowered to establish new executive organs, including a commission of police and an army commission in May 1792. In addition to the new land tax, the crown used its remaining lands as collateral for treasury bills to finance the army.[80] The plan was to build an army one hundred thousand strong by 1792.

Political reform in Poland struck fear into Prussian hearts. As one Prussian minister is reported to have written in alarm, "The Poles have dealt a fatal blow to the Prussian monarchy by bringing in a hereditary throne and a constitution better than England's. Sooner or later, Poland will take the west and perhaps even East Prussia from us."[81] Rather than wait for Poland to make its preparations, Prussia and Russia conspired once again to attack. In May 1792 Russia (invited by Polish magnates) invaded with 96,000 troops, quickly overwhelming the Polish-Lithuanian field army of still only 45,000 troops. Prussia and Russia again helped themselves to choice pieces of Polish territory, leaving Poland with less than one-third of the lands in its possession before the 1772 partition.

The Polish uprising that took place next is the stuff of romantic legend. Tadeusz Kościuszko, who had fought with the Americans in the Revolutionary War against Britain, led a group of military commanders in self-imposed exile in Leipzig to plan for an insurrection against Russian overlords. To build an army large and spirited enough for the task, he unilaterally issued a proclamation abolishing most forms of serfdom and granting peasants a wide array of civil liberties. Although the nobility blocked Kościuszko's measures from becoming law, by April 1794 he succeeded in rallying large numbers of peasants into his forces. The ragtag team was hopelessly outmanned and outgunned, and although they fought bravely with scythes and whatever else they could improvise from farm implements, their forces were

Kościuszko rallies his men, holding scythes, against the Russians at Raclawice on April 4, 1794.

vanquished within six months. In a last-ditch gamble, Kościuszko attacked the Russian army near Macieiowice on October 10, 1794, making a grand charge into their midst. Within minutes "he fell covered with wounds and all of his companions were killed or taken prisoner."

Kościuszko, seriously wounded, was taken to St. Petersburg, where Catherine the Great sentenced him to life in prison. He would outlive the empress and was released from prison in 1796 upon her death; he spent the rest of his days in exile, traveling to England, the United States, France, and finally Switzerland, where he died in 1817. In the meantime, however, without Kościuszko to lead them, the Polish army lost momentum. In a few days Warsaw capitulated, and at the nearby garrison of Praga "eight thousand Poles perished sword in hand, and the Russians having set fire to the bridge, cut off the retreat of the inhabitants. Above twelve thousand townspeople, old men, women, and children, were murdered in cold blood." His countrymen lamented Kościuszko's capture: "Kościuszko is no more; the country is lost!"[82]

Poland was once again partitioned, leaving behind a fraction of its former lands. But many of the magnates, who had opposed the Constitution of 1791, let alone the more radical changes proposed by Kościuszko, cut favorable deals with their new overlords. The new boundaries split the lands of one magnate family, the Zamoyskis, down the middle, but the Habsburgs excused the Zamoyskis from new Austrian customs duties. Judging from the income of Zamoyski lands, which peaked in 1778, they did well.[83] Russia, too, was generous to former Polish magnates, offering them the establishment of a Lithuanian Grand Duchy with its own constitution and government.[84]

✦ ✦ ✦

The history of modern central Europe to the nineteenth century is essentially a story of Germany's emergence as a militarized territorial state. Several other models of governance also ran but lost the race. Cities, the engines of commercial wealth in western Europe, died a slow death in the east, where they clashed with the interests of the more powerful landed aristocracy. Empires, of the Holy Roman and Habsburg variants, failed to elicit necessary levels of allegiance from far-flung constituents with conflicting interests. Poland, the republic of nobles, could not bring itself to arm the peasants to meet the perils of partition at the hands of more powerful neighbors.

Prussia alone—which adopted Sweden's model of village mobilization to build a standing army but without making Sweden's concession to peasant suffrage—outcompeted city, empire, and rural republic in the race for survival of the fittest. Unlike Austria and Poland, whose eastern borders required cavalry-centric modes of defense, Prussia was free to build a modern infantry around the newest technology and military organization.

Coaxing the nobility into largely symbolic and supportive roles, the Prussian monarchy became strong enough to roll back manorial control of the peasant population. This was the key to Prussia's military mobilization; and although it was not on Sweden's scale relative to population, it was enough for the wars of the day. Each new war pushed up the ratchet: the Thirty Years' War increased the price of labor, which weakened the nobility's ability to oppress peasants (without using a great deal of force); the Great Northern Wars gave the Prussian monarchy an opening to create a standing army, the advantages of which the War of Austrian Succession put on display; and Napoleon's invasion, by crippling Austria and Prussia, in fact gave the Prussians more latitude with which to weaken the rural aristocracy. The German constitutional monarchy that Bismarck forged out of the postrevolutionary turmoil would not survive the white-hot wars of the twentieth century, but it was a fit adaptation to its time.

The emergence of the Prussian territorial state, on par with France and Spain and England by the eighteenth century, demonstrates the importance of institutional responses to the changing requirements of survival. The Prussian monarchy was able to secure funding for its army from the grain-exporting nobility, while also protecting peasants from the worst abuses of agrarian oppression. The mobilizational demands on the peasantry were not so great as to raise the specter of universal male franchise, but the economic concessions were real. And the Prussian peasants formed the backbone of the Prussian army for two centuries.

These centuries of European warfare also highlighted both terrain and emerging technologies as co-shapers of political boundaries. Evolving instruments of war over this period, including guns for mass armies, bridge building, and railroad construction, reduced the height of mountains, narrowed the width of rivers, and shrank the size of continents. Napoleon's armies took Germany swiftly and even conquered Switzerland, at least on paper. But controlling the populations who were accustomed to living in rough terrain was another matter entirely.

Chapter Nine

————————

MOUNTAIN REPUBLICS

WHEN IT COMES TO MOUNTAINS, political maps can deceive. For centuries the Berbers of the Atlas Mountains, in today's Morocco and Tunisia, remained effectively independent of successive rulers who claimed sovereignty over them: Carthage, Rome, the Fatimid Dynasty of Egypt, and the Ottomans. Treacherous terrain provides protection by increasing the cost of conquest and by having less to grab. It is no wonder that nomads, mountain people, Laplanders, and swamp dwellers, not to mention renegades, pirates, and brigands, have taken shelter in inhospitable landscapes across the globe and throughout history to evade or at least soften external rule.

Where terrain is formidable enough to stop invaders in their tracks, geographically protected people have less need to give up taxes and freedom in exchange for protection from lords and kings. Economies of scale are small if armies and expensive equipment do little to enhance defense. To the extent that, with the help of terrain, each person in the community is an important and able defender as well as a voice that must be considered on questions of community protection, mountains and swamps should be propitious for democracy.

History has shown that people living in hard-to-reach places tend to govern themselves more or less democratically. For one thing, the population in an Alpine village or a swamp-dwelling community tends to be small enough to make do with informal rules and enforcement. For another, when it comes to defending themselves from the outside, the more everyone is needed to fight, the more these societies are likely to aim for near unanimity. Even majority rule is too thin a concept for group decision making when the alienation of a minority can be fatal. War, or the threat of war, can push in a democratizing direction when each person's contribution is vital, and defensible terrain can have that effect by leveraging each person's contribution to communal safety.

Mountains rarely stop invaders forever. New technologies and resources can degrade defensive advantages, exposing previously secure areas to attack. An Islamic state survived in Granada, at the base of the Sierra Nevadas, for 250 years after the Catholic kings of Castile began expanding southward, but even the Sierra Nevadas were not bulwark enough against the Spanish army in 1492.[1] Where defenders faced subjugation rather than expulsion or worse, heavy artillery deteriorated defenses even faster. The mountainous and swampy regions of Japan held out against the territorial unifiers in the sixteenth century, but only for a few decades. In other times and places, guerrillas have lasted for many decades, or governments have simply acknowledged the costs of conquest by leaving indigenous populations more or less alone.

Vulnerability to new military technologies is the least of it. The economic price of living in rugged terrain often outweighs the military benefits of conquest. Because cover-providing terrain also typically supports limited food production, daily life is generally more difficult. Indeed, the allure of markets, potential gains from trade, and even the prospect of moving to an easier life in richer lands make it tempting to leave. As the sturdy people of the French Pyrenees have long said, "He who works the mountain laughs for one year and cries for seven."[2] Linguistic anthropologists have identified the pattern that goes with this lament: people move to lower elevations while languages move up: successive generations of youth seek opportunities out in the world, and those left behind learn the lowland languages to access bigger markets.[3]

Recording his exploits in Gaul, Julius Caesar bragged about slaughtering thousands of migrating Helvetii, a Celtic tribe (living in today's Switzerland) who were looking for richer lands in Gaul.[4] Centuries later many Swiss whose mountain redoubts had protected them from the ravages of the Thirty Years' War migrated to the depopulated regions of Germany and eastern France in search of more fertile farmland.[5] By the nineteenth century a precipitously declining portion of the population in the Grisons, in the Eastern Alps, still spoke the local Romansch language, reflecting migration patterns and the voluntary adoption of German and Italian of those left behind.

Even today terrain's deep stamp on politics is visible. America's quagmire in Vietnam and the succession of Russian, British, and American failures to control Afghanistan are testimony to the enduring power of terrain. In the nineteenth century Afghanistan became a "tar baby" for Britain and Russia as they vied for influence in Central and South Asia—the harder they punched, the more they got stuck.[6] The various passes through the Sulimani Mountains were considered "gates" from Central Asia to India, ancient paths of conquest taken by the likes of Alexander the Great, Genghis Khan, Mahmud of Ghazni, Timur, and Babur, the founder of the Mughal Empire. In 1842 Afghans slaughtered better-equipped British forces who were poorly habituated to mountain navigation and warfare. Afghans on hillsides fired into British columns who made easy targets, marching through narrow valleys and ravines.[7] A larger British force returned to wreak vengeance but never managed to establish control.

In the nineteenth century the British failed to cultivate an Afghan national leadership with whom to negotiate because tribes and mullahs refused to get behind a single leader.[8] Afghanistan's rugged terrain is the geographical equivalent of a proportional representation electoral system: small groups resist joining a centralist majority party because they can survive in their own particular, in this case, geographical, niches. A degree of decentralization can be healthy for political and economic freedom,[9] but unlike many mountainous countries, Afghanistan lacks a large industrial or post-industrial economy that draws workers and professionals into cities from the countryside. The majority of the population remains illiterate, government infrastructure is minimal, and local authority structures rule, as they always have.

Most Afghans reacted to the military coup of 1973 with a collective yawn and to the subsequent foreign interventions, as to those of the past, with grim resignation.[10] More threatening to a peaceful and prosperous life than invasions and even smart bombs is Afghanistan's own failure to develop a public infrastructure and a national economy, both of which are hindered, though not to say ruled out, by the country's extreme geographic fragmentation.[11] Instead of havens of peace and prosperity, the high valleys have become safe areas for growing opium in the international narcotics market.[12]

Switzerland, on the other hand, is the world's best advertisement for rugged terrain. The Alps create a formidable natural barrier to would-be invaders, allowing inhabitants to govern themselves without trading taxes for defense. Mountain defense, courtesy of nature, made it possible for the Swiss to be both democratic and independent for millennia. Some decades later, in 1386, the Swiss attacked the Habsburgs at the Battle of Morgarten, winning their freedom and building a reputation as a nation of ferocious warriors. Fernand Braudel gave this a name—mountain freedom—and cites earlier sources for this idea: "Loys Le Roy, *De l'excellence du gouvernement royal*, Paris, 1575, writes, 'A country covered with mountains, rocks, and forests, fit only for pasture, where there are many poor men, as is most of Switzerland, is best suited for democracy.' "[13]

The potted history of Switzerland is partly romantic mythology, but there is more than a little truth in it. The run-up to Morgarten is two centuries long, beginning in the early twelfth century, when the three German-speaking "forest cantons" or self-defined districts of Schwyz, Uri, and Unterwalden banded together against territorially expansionist Habsburg dukes.[14] Their mountain valleys at the base of the high, central Alps were in the middle of nowhere and had been left largely alone by migrating tribes and land-hungry nobles. Nevertheless abbots and bishops of the church, often political appointees, established churches and monasteries throughout the region and converted the population to Catholicism.

The mountain cantons became earnestly Catholic but retained their long-standing tradition of choosing their own leaders and tribunals who made collective decisions about land use and dispute settlement. Living in the high Alps, however, was not for everyone, and the Habsburgs paid little attention until the twelfth and thirteenth centuries. Depending on the elevation and the position of the valley, weather can be extreme. Temperatures decrease by 10 degrees centigrade for every kilometer of increased altitude, so that 100 meters up a mountain is equivalent to 80 kilometers of latitude. Microclimates within the Alps also vary enormously by the depth of valleys and their orientation to the sun, to prevailing winds, and other factors.[15] Growing seasons are short, and the sparse vegetation means flocks and their herders have to cover considerable distances.[16]

Traveling with animals among pastures, through ravines, and over cliffs could be treacherous. The Alps glitter with glaciers hundreds of feet deep, and many are cracked and creviced. Avalanches in the winter and rockslides in the spring can be deadly. A rockslide at Bellinzona, near today's Ticino, Switzerland, blocked the Blegno River in 1512; two centuries later the dam burst open, flooding the valley below. In 1806 one of the summits of the Rossberg became sodden with heavy rains, causing a rockslide that killed five hundred people in the villages of Goldau, Boussingen, and Rothen near Lake Zug.[17] During World War I avalanches in the high Alps buried thousands of soldiers alive.[18]

Today at the watershed between Switzerland and Italy at the St. Gotthard Pass, the rushing torrent of the River Reuss creates a deep gorge. In the 1200s the first bridges were built there, creating the most direct route from Germany to Italy. The Habsburgs hungered for these newly strategic lands around St. Gotthard, and from their base just east of Lake Constance, they began purchasing or taking lands from monasteries and towns in the region.

Competing understandings of entitlement collided in a series of bloody encounters between the mountain dwellers and the Habsburg dukes. By oral tradition (and first published in written form in the 1470s), Wilhelm Tell incurred Habsburg rage when, in about 1307, he refused to bow before the ducal cap of Austria placed on a pole in the marketplace of Altorf. The bailiff sentenced him to shoot, from a considerable distance, an apple placed on the head of his son. After shooting the apple, Tell was being ferried off to prison for impudence (he had a second arrow, he had said, for the tyrant in case he had killed his son in error) when he killed his guards in an escape attempt.

A commemorative postcard depicting Swiss mountain
men defending against the Habsburgs at Morgarten.

A subsequent volley of violence between the Swiss and Habsburgs ended at the Battle of Morgarten in 1315 in Swiss favor.[19] Around fifteen hundred men of Schwyz, Uri, and Unterwalden, positioned on high ground at Morgarten, rained boulders and tree trunks onto an incoming force of some twenty thousand Austrian cavalry. Equipped with metal crampons on their shoes and wielding iron-studded clubs, the Swiss then clambered down the mountainside and set upon any of the cavalry who had not managed to escape, routing the entire force.[20]

Inspired by this victory of David and Goliath proportions, the three cantons solidified their bond, becoming known as the Swiss Confederation, to defend one another against all enemies and to eschew foreign assistance or arbitration.

By contrast, the lowland cities of Bern, Zurich, and Lucerne were conducive to agriculture but gave them no topographical advantage in warfare, and their interests with neighbors were principally to protect their commerce.

TERRITORIAL DEVELOPMENT OF THE OLD SWISS CONFEDERACY 1291–1797

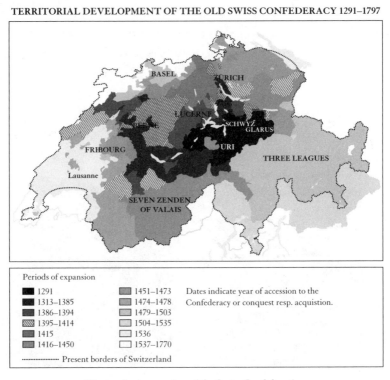

Periods of expansion

■ 1291	□ 1451–1473
■ 1313–1385	□ 1474–1478
■ 1386–1394	□ 1479–1503
▨ 1395–1414	□ 1504–1535
■ 1415	□ 1536
■ 1416–1450	□ 1537–1770

Dates indicate year of accession to the Confederacy or conquest resp. acquistion.

·········· Present borders of Switzerland

The gradual expansion of the Swiss Confederation,
beginning with the Alpine cantons in the center.

While the mountain cantons were at war with Habsburg dukes in the 1300s over grazing rights and tolls, the cities might well have worked out a relationship with the Holy Roman Empire that they could live with: imperial suzerainty and taxation in exchange for freedom to govern themselves as burgher aristocracies, Italian style. Some burghers favored just this kind of arrangement, and Basel, Soleure, and Schaffhausen in fact became Free Imperial Cities.[21]

As in Italy, Swiss cities had consolidated surrounding territories at the expense of feudal lords who were the titular owners. Aristocratic Swiss cities "rented" Swiss mountain boys rather than elevate their own underclass. The Swiss and the Habsburgs again clashed at Sempach in 1386, and though not on mountainous terrain, the Swiss prevailed again. The Austrians lost 2,000 men to 200 Swiss.[22]

In the rest of Europe, where new territorial states began testing their strength against the creaky-jointed Holy Roman Empire, geopolitics wobbled with the entrance of the "invincible" Swiss pikers and halberdiers. With eighteen-foot-long pikes, Swiss footmen could form an impregnable porcupine-like square that held cavalry at bay. The Swiss halberd was a weapon designed for attack: the hook on the end of the eight-foot shaft could pull a man from a horse; a spear could thrust between joints of armor; and an ax could hack through armor and bone.[23]

In a series of wars between 1474 and 1477, the Swiss Confederates helped the French to destroy Charles "The Bold" of Burgundy, a duke of the Holy Roman Empire with territorial ambitions.[24] When a French army with ten thousand Swiss mercenaries killed Charles at Nancy, the defeated Burgundians requested to join the Swiss Confederation, an offer the mountain cantons rejected for fear of diluting their weight in the union. Instead, the Swiss settled for peace and a small mountain of gold coins.[25]

Machiavelli, writing in the early sixteenth century, called attention to the military reassertion of infantry over cavalry. He knew firsthand about this renaissance of infantry-based warfare, a phenomenon in which he heard echoes of Republican Rome. He admired the valorous military democracy of the mountain cantons and saw glimmers of possibility for a militia-based defense of Italy. But instead of becoming an exportable model of self-defense that produced popular rule, the Swiss sold their military might to the highest bidder. Over the next few decades, with a large infantry army bolstered

Sixteenth-century engraving of Swiss pikemen by Hans Holbein the Younger.

by Swiss recruits, the French plowed through Italy and overran a succession of Italian principalities and city-states including Machiavelli's beloved Florence.[26] Ironically, by exporting their militia, the democratic Swiss propped up many a tyrant.

Men-in-arms became the Alpine cantons' most profitable export, twelve thousand of them signing up to fight for King Charles VIII of France in 1495. In vain did Swiss religious reformers such as Zwingli rail against the corrupting influences of mercenary traffic, along with prostitution and adultery. Money from military service was so substantial that it might have affected the way the cantons swung during the Reformation. The Catholic Alpine cantons had revenues enough from mercenary services without plundering church properties, whereas the lowland areas enriched themselves at the church's expense when they became Protestant.[27] According to the nineteenth-century historian of Switzerland Gaspard Vieusseux, "The number of adventurers in Switzerland had become so great that they could not all find employment in foreign service. [After Nancy] bands of idle and dissipated young men went about the country armed, living merrily as long as their share of the booty made in the war of Burgundy lasted."[28]

In 1506 Pope Julius II hired Swiss mercenaries to be his personal guards, a tradition honored to this day. The Holy Roman emperor Maximilian too coveted Swiss soldiers. Having granted the Swiss cantons independence from imperial taxes in 1499 (after failing to claim dominion over them even with the Swabian League's help), he further gave Switzerland official exemption from the jurisdiction of imperial courts in 1508 in exchange for Swiss troops.[29] Swiss military prowess, whether for homeland defense or for sale abroad, bought the Swiss political autonomy and neutrality in the centuries of European wars.[30]

Swiss mountain men were no doubt strong and brave, but their performance in fact was mixed.[31] The Swiss were on the losing side in the War of the League of Cambrai (1509–10), when they fought with the Papal States, Spain, and the Holy Roman Empire against Venice and France.[32] The spell of Swiss invincibility was broken at Marignano in 1515 when twelve thousand Swiss soldiers died on account of plunder-seeking disorganization and defeat.[33] To some extent, the benefits of geography in Swiss home territory had been mistaken for prowess. Probably not by coincidence, Scottish highlanders too were often found in foreign mercenary armies. They had a reputation for ferocity, and their upland villages tended to be poor.[34] Still, the Swiss had unmistakably proved that well-disciplined infantry could withstand and defeat heavy cavalry. What was not as clear was how infantry pikemen could compete with firearms, either as adversaries or replacements.

The invention of field artillery and firearms soon began to transform infantry-based warfare, putting a premium on training and organization that was developed not in Switzerland but in professional armies across Europe. The British statesman and historian Sir John William Fortescue tells of the blind Bohemian military genius John Zizka who in the fifteenth century successfully deployed artillery as a maneuverable arm in battle against Austrian and Hungarian knights, possible only because of discipline and organization.[35] The Dutch and Swedes perfected maneuver and discipline in the sixteenth century.[36]

During the same centuries that Switzerland was emerging as an independent and self-governing territorial state, dukes and lords of various kinds continued to hold Alpine Burgundy and Savoy in the western Alps, and Vorarlberg, Tyrol, and Liechtenstein in the east, where the mountains are more loosely knitted together and where river valleys provide passage. Mountains alone do not a mountain republic make. The rivalry among rul-

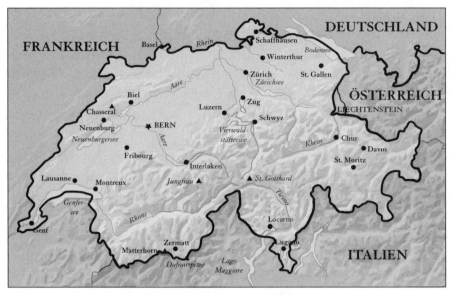

This topographical map of today's Switzerland shows
the ruggedness of the eastern canton of Graubünden.

ers for mountain passes and rivers with strategic value was intense, bringing larger armies than the pastoralists who lived there could withstand.

At the other end of Switzerland, the Eastern Alps, which straddle today's Swiss Canton of Graubünden (the Grisons) and Austrian Tyrol, are geographic neighbors with strikingly different political histories. On the modern map, Austria controls a narrow finger of territory along the Inn River Valley and beyond it through Vorarlberg to the Rhine, bordered by Germany to the north and Switzerland and Italy to the south—Austrian Tyrol. The Grisons of Switzerland push their own finger eastward just south of the Austrian finger at the headwaters of the Inn River. The labyrinthine valleys of the Grisons, like the Swiss cantons of the central Alps, nurtured strong traditions of self-government. But the city of Coire (Chur) at their base attracted conquerors from time immemorial because it stood at the crossroads of multiple paths between Germany and Italy. This combination, of an externally coveted city surrounded by self-governing mountain enclaves, created the conditions for centuries of attack, resistance, and civil war.

The valleys of the Eastern Alps had once been the thriving Roman province of Rhaetia, linking to Rome from about AD 50. Curia, now Coire (Chur), at the headwaters of the Rhine and one pass over from the Inn River, was its capital.[37] When Catholicism became the state religion of the Roman Empire in AD 380, Coire became the first Roman Catholic bishopric north of the Alps.[38] As Roman power waned, however, lowland valleys of Rhaetia became a vacuum for migrating Germanic tribes from the north, including the Alemanni. Like the Burgundians in western Switzerland, the Alemanni treated many of the preexisting inhabitants as subjects, allowing them to stay on their lands in exchange for labor and rent.[39]

The Franks conquered Coire in the sixth century, leaving surrounding lands to various vassals. The Magyars invaded in 925, and the Saracens in 940 and 954, who in turn were chased out by the Holy Roman Empire. Farmers in low, reachable valleys were forced to work for an overlord or placed themselves under the protection of bishoprics or monasteries on similar terms, a process by which the bishop of Coire gained jurisdiction over vast tracts of land. The Holy Roman emperor's claim to be the guardian and promoter of the true faith on behalf of the church did little to disguise the competition—for rents and taxes, for vassals, for men-at-arms—between the secular and spiritual authorities.

Coire's strategic location also enriched its commercial guilds, which sought to wrest control of the transit tolls from the Habsburgs in 1464. Lacking the necessary military heft, they failed. But in 1471 three groups of territories—the League of God's House, the League of Ten Jurisdictions, and the Gray League—formed the Alliance of the Three Leagues. It was tested a few decades later, in 1499, when it rallied to the cause of the Swiss Confederation against the Swabian League in today's southern Germany. The leagues formed a new federation that came to be known as the Grisons for the gray cloaks of the deputies who met alternately at Coire, Ilanz, and Davos.[40] Although the Grisons' strategic location on trade routes embroiled them in outsize conflicts over ensuing centuries, their rugged terrain enabled them to resist external domination, and they eventually joined the Swiss Federation in 1798 as the canton of Graubünden.

A curious fact about the Swiss Confederation is that it did not split apart at the sectarian seam in either the Reformation or the Thirty Years' War.[41] The confederation knew of this vulnerability and was saved by the extraordinary degree of cantonal autonomy.[42] The confederation survived because there was so little to it. The urban cantons of Bern, Geneva, and Zurich, controlled by aristocratic councils of burghers, embraced Protestantism early and, like Coire, gained fiscal autonomy by grabbing church assets.[43] City leaders granted commoners a modicum of political rights in times of military crisis, but conflicts between merchants on the one hand and the urban and rural poor on the other hardened the city burghers against the full male franchise of their Alpine brethren. Cities and their citizens wrangled constantly over taxes, wages, and currency values, not to mention representation.[44]

The Alpine cantons at the heart of the confederation retained their village-council democracy during centuries of engagement and economic integration with their urban allies, without either exporting their brand of politics to the cities or importing aristocratic republicanism.[45] In governments, as in firms or any other organization, democracy comes more naturally to groups whose members are relatively equally endowed, as in the rural cantons where lands remained principally in the hands of freeholding peasants.[46] The land was too poor to support a real nobility, so the social organization remained relatively flat.

The Alpine cantons also never considered abandoning Catholicism. Having established strong bargaining relationships with the church early on, they were not tempted to use Protestantism as an excuse to grab church lands. Although they were sparsely populated, their populist politics, about which they were almost as earnest as their religion, empowered them militarily and politically within the confederation since every man of fighting age participated in the cantonal militia.

It was not that the cantons got along harmoniously, once they settled on local religious autonomy. They cheered for opposite sides in the Thirty Years' War and fought as mercenaries against one another in foreign lands.[47] But locally they agreed on official neutrality and to leave each other alone.[48] The Swiss Confederation was rewarded at Westphalia with international recognition of independence and sovereignty.

The Swiss were asleep, a century and a half later, when Napoleon's post-revolutionary army showed up. This time Switzerland divided not along confessional or geographical lines but by wealth. Long-standing grievances by peasants and workers opened a chink in confederation armor through which French radical ideology found its mark.

Beginning in July 1794, a radical group of peasants and workers in Geneva, calling themselves the Revolutionists, seized the city's arsenal of heavy artillery, threw in prison the men of means, and grabbed their property.[49] Later on Napoleon's conquests against aristocracies in Austria and

Italy emboldened similar groups of rebels in Vaud, Zurich, Basel, and Aargau, while terrifying burghers about the prospects of social leveling.[50] The burghers were right to worry, for Napoleon moved with force and with the collaboration of many of the Swiss poor. In Basel the peasants went into open revolt, setting fire to the homes and castles of the rich. In Coire, when the wealthy citizens refused Napoleon's order to enfranchise their subject populations in Valtellina, Chiavenna, and Bormio bordering Italy, those districts were simply transferred, with the acquiescence of many who lived there, to Napoleon's new Cisalpine Republic in Lombardy.[51]

On the Austrian side of the Eastern Alps, across the border from the self-governing Grisons, the powerful estates—the nobility and the clergy—had always been the Habsburgs' partners in governance. Lords and abbots had substantial autonomy over their respective lands, including the right to defend themselves with their own militia. In some of the high mountain valleys of the Tyrol, this kind of federalism permitted village self-rule.[52] Tyroleans enjoyed more economic freedoms than those living in the lowlands of Austria.[53] But elsewhere, including in the lower valleys in the same mountains, bishoprics and noble houses had free rein.[54]

Some decades earlier, in the 1740s, the Empress Maria Theresa, anxious about growing Prussian military strength, instituted a series of state-building reforms including the creation of a centralized standing army. Other reforms pursued by her son, the Enlightenment emperor Joseph II, introduced mandatory elementary schooling and sought to weaken the ties of serfdom.[55] Those most threatened by Austrian centralizing initiatives were not the merchants in Bozen and Innsbruck, who happily operated monopolies in the transit business across the Alps, but the old Austrian nobility, for whom a stronger central state amounted to an erosion of ancient aristocratic freedoms and privileges.[56]

In 1798, with Napoleon eyeing the passes through the Eastern Alps to connect his theaters of war in the Rhineland and Italy, the nobles recognized the need for more preparedness than in the past, but still they resisted top-down state control. In a stroke of tactical brilliance, the Tyrolean estates forged a coalition with mountain peasants by resurrecting a religious movement called the Sacred Heart of Jesus. Dating back at least to the Counter-Reformation, the Sacred Heart movement was the Jesuits' answer to the Protestant promise of a close, personal relationship with God. The Tyrolean nobility conveniently disguised their fear of revolution behind the Sacred

A shrine of the Sacred Heart movement in Tyrol.

Heart movement, which portrayed the French as anti-Christian evildoers leading the world to perdition.[57]

Religious unity proved to be a more potent mobilizer against the French than did the Austrian "fatherland" or German nationhood because Austrian Tyrol encompassed Italian as well as German-speaking valleys.[58] In those areas, which he merely threatened and did not conquer, Napoleon inadvertently strengthened the old regime's cultural ballast.

In the west, Napoleon passed easily through French-speaking Vaud on his way to Bern, the economic if not political heart of Switzerland. Although the other cantons sent troops to stand with the Bernese, nearly all retreated at the first sign of French superiority.[59] Napoleon's propaganda was that of liberation, and for peasants, the new order sounded agreeable. For the Swiss rich, however, French conquest was an unmitigated disaster. France claimed for itself the Vaud and other territories contiguous to France, ravaged the countryside, carted off literally tons of accumulated gold and treasure from city vaults as war reparations, and levied new war taxes.[60]

Napoleon's offer of democracy fell on deaf ears in the mountain cantons, where internal democracy—including freedom from central taxes—was viewed as a birthright.[61] While Schwyz, Uri, and Unterwalden beat Napoleon's enormous, mobile, and well-equipped forces in three battles in 1798, they realized that their terrain-assisted manpower was no match for the

Napoleon at Great St Bernard Pass *by Edouard Castres.*

wealth of France, and they sued for peace before losing a war they could not possibly win.[62]

Every conquest results from a combination of factors, but in some instances military technology favors the offensive side to a degree that diminishes natural defenses. During the centuries leading up to the birth of the nation-state, the three game-changing technological advances were heavy artillery in the fourteenth and fifteenth century, the organized use of handheld guns in the sixteenth, and then in the eighteenth and nineteenth century the engineering know-how to convey large armies through previously insurmountable terrain. Each of these innovations diminished the value of remote and rugged terrain to some extent—although none really addressed the economic issue. Unless rugged areas offered some strategic advantage to an aggressor, it might not be worth the cost of conquering them. Napoleon accepted a deal with Schwyz rather than press his technological advantages and weaken his forces when there were larger and more dangerous enemies to subdue.

Advances in seafaring technology by the late fifteenth century quite suddenly put the whole world within range of European armies. The Europe-ans conquered South America by walking backward through a technological time warp. In 1536 Pizarro's band of some 250 Spanish sailor-soldiers brought the mighty Incan Empire to heel in a matter of months because their guns, to which Europe had already acclimated, inflicted unseen horrors on unsus-pecting South American victims. In addition, horses brought from Europe allowed the Spanish to chase down survivors, and Western diseases killed off many others. The Andes Mountains provided refuge for a few decades to a band of survivors, but their base of resistance was obliterated by 1572 with the help of subjugated Incans who knew the landscape as well as the rebels.[63]

In Japan, the holdouts against territorial unification—the monasteries and mountain communities that relied on terrain as their last defense—did not stand a chance against the large armies with heavy artillery and hand-held guns. Although they were among the last to capitulate, the renegades were eventually routed from their high mountain valleys and swamplands by the brute force of more men with more guns.[64]

◆ ◆ ◆

By 1798–1800, the war raged between Napoleon, who relied heavily on military engineering, and the Russians and Austrians. Napoleon's engi-neers created two military roads through Switzerland sturdy enough for artillery, in some cases cutting road out of sheer rock face: one through the Simplon Pass, for his movement from Geneva to Milan, and the other through Mont Cenis, for his attack on Turin from Lyons. One of the river gorges, sixty feet wide, required suspending a bridge over which the troops crossed.[65]

Nearly fifty years later, waves of revolution rippling across the continent once again divided the cantons along the ancient rural-urban lines. Austria and France, as temporarily resurrected forces of the ancien régime, encour-aged the confederation's original members to secede rather than to pay state-building taxes.[66] Forming a secessionist group called the Sonderbund, Uri and its allies managed to block the St. Gotthard Pass to Ticino, but the mountains had now come to play a far smaller part in Swiss warfare, given the economic integration between forest and urban cantons, and the techno-logical fixes for mountain navigation. The confederation, with an army of 94,000, took Fribourg with little popular resistance, then Lucerne with considerably more effort.[67] Both sides fought over Lucerne with heavy artillery, rifles, and howitzers from behind trenches and fortifications—a modern war on ancient ground. Schwyz, Uri, and Unterwalden capitulated as soon as the union forces took Lucerne.[68]

The Eastern Alps became a bloody battleground once again in World War I, as Austria and Italy fought over national boundaries that had been drawn in Austria's favor in 1815. At first, both sides were roughly matched in their use of terrain and technology, and the armies stalemated in Alpine trench warfare under brutal conditions that took many soldiers' lives from exposure. According to Otto Hahn, a German scientist, "The positions of the Italians were so strong that it would have been impossible to dislodge them with conventional weapons." The German answer was chlorine and phosphine gases. For the unsuspecting Italians dug into snowy trenches, the Germans' chemical attack in the early morning of October 24, 1917, was living hell. Five to six hundred men choked to death in the dense cloud of poison that settled into the trenches on that windless day, while others managed to flee for their lives. Having destroyed Italian resistance, the German and Austrian forces swept across the mountains to the Piave River, north of Venice.[69]

Other accounts corroborate Hahn's. Austria's German allies routed the Italians at Caporetto in November 1917, moving along the valley floor of the Isonzo River and trapping entire Italian battalions on the mountains. A twenty-five-year-old lieutenant of the Württemberg Mountain Battalion, Erwin Rommel (later one of Hitler's most valuable generals in World War II), played a key part in the mission's success by leading a flanking movement around and up a hill, to come down on the Italians from above and behind the front lines.[70] Austrian boundaries would have been redrawn deep into today's Italy if Allied forces had not pushed the Germans back with air strikes and ground attacks in 1918.[71] Technology more than terrain had driven the outcome of this war, and men were the fodder.

In World War II, Switzerland found itself surrounded by Axis powers: Mussolini allied Italy to Germany in 1938, and Austria was appended to Germany the same year; in 1940 Hitler's daring invasion of France through the Black Forest (against his officers' advice) succeeded.[72] Apparently, although little is known about these deliberations, Hitler considered invading Switzerland but decided it was not worth the trouble as long as Swiss banks accommodated the Nazis by storing their ill-gotten gold.[73] The Swiss had a backup

Young Rommel in Isonzo, 1917.

plan for Alpine guerrilla warfare had it come to that, but the long years of Alpine standoff during World War I must have given pause to both sides.[74] Terrain was made less formidable by technology, but it was still a nuisance.

Long before twentieth-century technology cut mountains down to size, the Alpine cantons knew, when they dissolved their civil war in 1848, that there was little point in holing up in the mountaintops without access to markets in the cities. The economic integration between the Alpine cantons and the cities had only deepened by the nineteenth century, improving the quality of life for both. The more general point is that the military advantages of forbidding terrain are inversely proportional to the gains from trade between the uplands and the lowlands.[75]

◆ ◆ ◆

Mountains and valleys form natural communities of complementary economic production across different elevations—for example, highlanders may sell milk to lowlanders in exchange for manufactured goods. But gains from trade require open borders, which political barriers often thwart. Cities in

Switzerland, Italy, and Germany tended to evolve into rival monopolists who compensated for the inefficiencies of protectionism by grabbing as much surrounding rural land as they could.[76] Nevertheless, peaceful relations among the Swiss cantons allowed villages in the high valleys to abandon rye and barley cultivation, on which they had relied for bread, in order to specialize in hay production for their dairy business. In less peaceful zones of the Alps, rural autarky remained the norm for considerably longer.[77] The upper Rhine, originating near Coire and flowing northward from the watershed into Germany, was an area of economic diversity crippled by tariffs and tolls of competing governments.[78]

Another example of mountain communities that became drawn into larger markets when political boundaries allowed is from the Pyrenees. In the fourteenth century, Sabartes was a virtually inaccessible 656-square-mile region in the French Pyrenees, surrounded on three sides by mountains.[79] It was home to some one thousand people scattered over 120 small villages in the high valleys along the Ariège River and its tributaries.[80] Some of the earliest mention of this region comes from the monks of St. Thibery, near Agde, who in 860 complained to the Count of Narbonne that the people of Sabartes were not paying their dues.[81] With the gradual disintegration of the Carolingian empire, local lords attempted to establish their territorial claims there, but with mixed success.[82] In the thirteenth century the Capetians vied with the church over Languedoc, including this area. Peasants regarded both with equal disdain: they were as likely to refuse to pay tithes to the church as they were to beat up the royal agents who came around to collect taxes.[83] These villagers lent support to the Albigensians, who were being hunted to extinction for heresy; when the Inquisition called on two hundred witnesses living in the Sabartes, they are reported to have resisted turning one another in. For supporting the heretics without remorse, Pope Clement V excommunicated the whole lot of them in 1312. Most of the Pyrenees remained steadfastly neutral during the Hundred Years' War and the War of Spanish Succession.[84]

Sabartes may represent an extreme case of inaccessibility. But even these remote valleys eventually wove themselves into the economic fabric of the larger region. The short growing season limited the possibility of agricultural self-sufficiency, and by the seventeenth century, logging pine along the Ariège for the royal navy was one of the region's principal sources of income.

The ruins of a fort at Lordat, once occupied by the
Albigensians, overlooking Sabartes and the Ariège valley.

There was little else, and the residents had become too poor, at least relative to the lowlanders, to cause much trouble. We know this because Louis
de Froidour spent three years in the French Pyrenees, from 1669 to 1671,
cataloguing forest lands and calculating fines for tree poachers and land
encroachers on behalf of Louis XIV and his revenue genius Jean-Baptiste
Colbert. Froidour found little evidence of the mountain people's legendary
ferocity: "[The village of Murat] is very depressed, and it gives a disadvan-
tageous view of a people who had once made a lot of noise."[85] The peasants
were if anything eager to help Froidour's team identify the secular and ecclesiastical lords who had been logging without permission. The crown and
the peasants shared an interest in stopping nobles from grabbing the forests
that belonged to the peasants, since the nobles were exempt from land tax
whereas the peasants were not.[86]

The crowns of Spain and France divided the Pyrenees between the two
of them in 1659 with the stroke of a pen—except for Andorra, a tiny autonomous realm of 191 square miles in the valleys of the Valira and its tributaries
that was not worth taking. The people of Andorra eked out a livelihood by
allowing access to their high pasturelands in the summer months in exchange
for wintering their own herds in lowland pastures. Andorra owed its inde-

pendence not to military might or to exceptional isolation—its valley was no better protected than any other—but to a bitter rivalry between the Count of Foix and the bishop of Urgell for passage through Andorra to the fertile lands of Roussillon, on the Mediterranean end of the Pyrenees; it ended in stalemate.[87] The competing lords agreed, through the Act of Paréage of 1278—an agreement subsequently adopted by the sovereigns of France and Spain—that each side should receive taxes in alternating years and that they should each get a share of military recruitment from the men of Andorra.[88]

Succumbing to taxation in exchange for participating in the market economy does not amount to wholesale political absorption or integration, but it deflates the image of supremely autonomous peoples thumbing their noses at territorial states. In one remote community after another, people gave up autonomy for wealth. If their resources were significant but they could not agree on how to use it, squabbling within their own ranks opened the door to external powers that could provide order at a price. A few nooks, like Andorra, were better at navigating the shoals of rivalrous predators to retain their autonomy. But most of the world, even its remote areas, came in time to look more like every place else.

◆ ◆ ◆

The medieval Swiss Alpine cantons are canonical examples of warlike democracies. History supplies others, only some of which we have reviewed here.[89] Places with terrain features that put them lower on the scale of defensibility than the Swiss Alps but above average, such as Classical Athens or the British Isles or Sweden or the Dutch Republic, also democratized in times of great threat but, when the danger passed, fell, at least for a time, under the sway of narrower political elites.

We can think of terrain as substituting for offensive technology: steep hills allowed Swiss mountain men to unhorse heavily armed Austrian cavalry with boulders and logs in 1315. But soon thereafter a series of technological revolutions substituted capital for labor. By increasing the demand for their labor, the infantry revolution of the thirteenth and fourteenth centuries may have improved the bargaining power of peasants for a short while, but the gunpowder and engineering revolution that followed fast on its heels increased the demand for money to pay for guns. Heavy artillery, handheld guns, roads, bridges, and tunnels all cost money, which in turn required new deals with those in society who have money to lend or with which to pay taxes. Not only did technology erode the protections afforded by terrain, it also elevated the owners of capital in constitutional bargains. Merchants cut better deals than peasants with the kings of the territorial states who used armies to supplant and money to buy off the nobility in the sixteenth and seventeenth centuries. The French Revolution was jet-propelled with vengeful, pent-up anger of peasants who paid taxes on almost everything while merchants were paying handsome sums—Versailles-worthy sums—to become tax-free nobles.

While technology made previously defensible mountain aeries vulnerable, the growing market economy in late medieval Europe and Japan increased the costs of isolation to their inhabitants. Peasants in remote villages felt poorer in relative terms because there was money to be made by specializing, trading, or emigrating. They were also poorer in absolute terms as population growth pushed communities up against one another, gave powerful people incentives to enclose traditionally communal lands needed for seasonal herding, and ramped up the demand for the enforcement of property rights on land and other assets. States offered protection services, and merchants invested in states that got progressively bigger until they hit up against a rival with equal expendable force per square mile. The winning Japanese warlord consolidated his rule, as did the monarchies of France, Spain, and Brandenburg-Prussia.

Many modern wars of insurgency still, as from time immemorial, seek to use the advantages of terrain for cover and maneuver; and they still, because they have to recruit and retain fighters, tend to have relatively horizontal decision-making structures.[90] Insurgency groups with money have access to new technologies of warfare and have adapted them to their use. But as with monarchies, independent sources of wealth such as natural resources or foreign support to bankroll guns and mercenaries can undermine the leadership's accountability to the rank and file. Externally funded guerrilla movements face less pressure to be democratic, but they are also fragile.[91] Centuries ago, a succession of French finance ministers working for a succession of French kings sought only to put the monarchy on firm financial footing, without realizing that the enormously lopsided burdens of taxation could prove to be more lethal than debt.

Napoleon's armies destroyed the tenuous balance among European territorial states with the sheer numbers of his men-at-arms, courtesy of the Revolution's legacy of the people's army. But neither Napoleon nor the Congress of Vienna, which tried to restore the ancien régime after his demise, grasped how feebly the states of Europe had knitted together the desire of merchants to secure their property and the interests of the burgeoning working class in a share of prosperity. It took the white-hot wars of the twentieth century, which required both money and manpower, to hinge them into a single coalition in favor of representative democracy.

Part III

WAR AND
DEMOCRACY

Chapter Ten

THE NINETEENTH-CENTURY PIVOT

A T TEN-THIRTY A.M. ON OCTOBER 7, 1870, Léon Gambetta soared over the tight Prussian siege of Paris in a yellow hot-air balloon to mobilize the French countryside for help.[1] Battered by heavy shelling, Parisian buildings were shattered, and its people were hungry. France's "L'Année Terrible" began on July 19, 1870, when Prussia declared war on France; in September the Prussians crushed the French army in a massive encirclement at Sedan and captured France's emperor, Louis Napoleon Bonaparte III. The city of Paris held out for some months more under the direction of the "Government of National Defense" that established itself in Napoleon's absence, waiting for Gambetta to return with fresh forces. Victor Hugo, one of Paris's most famous residents since publishing *Les Misérables* in 1862, captured the sense of defiance against Prussian bullying when he told a friend in November 1870, "I like Paris as it is today. I wouldn't have liked to see the Bois de Boulogne in the days when it was crowded with expensive carriages and fine horses, but now that it's a quagmire, a ruin, it appeals to me! It's grand."[2] Brave words when potatoes were scarce and Parisians were eating the elephants from the zoo.[3]

Although Gambetta's hot-air balloon landed safely in Tours, where he managed to raise an army of one hundred thousand, the effort was not enough to oust the Prussians. France's army in Lorraine surrendered at Metz on October 27. On January 28, 1871, France signed an armistice ending the war, ceding Alsace and Lorraine to Germany.[4] On February 8 national elections returned a divided parliament in which about two-thirds favored constitutional monarchy and one-third comprised radical republicans and socialists (with Léon Gambetta on that side).

The election results set the stage for more violence in Paris, this time a civil war. On March 18, 1871, the working class established its own government, called the Commune of Paris, under the socialist red flag in place of the tricolor. Two months later, on May 21, the troops that stormed Paris were French. Government soldiers spent the next week hunting down and slaughtering 25,000 Communards, giving no quarter.[5] Although the government took only a week to seize the city, it continued arrests and executions through early June.[6] Victor Hugo, sympathetic to the plight of the Communards but disapproving of the project, gave sanctuary and advocated amnesty.[7] The Impressionist painter Gustave Courbet got off lightly compared to many of his fellow Communards: he chose a life of exile in Switzerland over imprisonment for his alleged role in demolishing the Vendôme Column, which celebrated Napoleonic victories.[8]

The extreme gyrations in French politics in its "terrible year" illustrate how the nineteenth century shaped the subsequent history of democracy. In retrospect, it is possible to see two things that at the time were more or less enshrouded in smoke. The first was that industrialization had created a large pool of new workers dissatisfied with elite rule. The elite, however, liked the workers no better than the workers liked the elite. The institutions that we recognize today as central features of modern democracy—such as the electoral franchise and the legal protections of private property—did not come together easily. Much of the difficulty stemmed from investor and employer fears that a bigger franchise would empower workers while undercutting the elite's economic freedoms and property rights.

The second insight from the nineteenth century is that wars of national mobilization forced workers and employers to eventually reach a compromise for the sake of common defense. As states fought with one another, nationalism bubbled up, to some degree manipulated by governments but also with genuine, on-the-ground passion. Chest-thumping nationalist rhetoric was nearly loud enough to drown out the howls of leftist radicals and in fact won over many ordinary citizens. There is nothing inevitable about today's national boundaries or about representative democracy as their political form, but nineteenth-century military competition in Europe lies behind both.

From very different starting points, France and Germany converged on representative government by the end of the nineteenth century. France swung like a wild but slowing pendulum from a territorially large monarchy to a radical democracy, back to monarchy and then, by 1879, back to a moderate democratic republic. Germany, which began the period as a fragmented group of states teetering in precarious equipoise between Austria and the Holy Roman Empire, evolved more gradually and reluctantly under Prussian leadership into a constitutional monarchy with a legislature elected by universal male suffrage. Prussia's cabinet, unaccountable to the legislature, took fewer chances with representation, but even in Prussia the aristocracy took up new roles in national government or faced extinction.

One of the most memorable depictions of the extinction of traditional European aristocracy is Renoir's 1937 film *Le Grande Illusion,* in which the Prussian officer von Rauffenstein and French officer de Boeldieu struggle to balance their mutual affinity against their nationalist roles. Rauffenstein says wistfully in an unguarded moment, "Boeldieu, I don't know who will win this war, but whatever the outcome, it will mean the end of the Rauffensteins and the Boeldieus." Nineteenth-century wars replaced European aristocracy with mass politics and class compromise.

The French Revolution was the turning point, even though it collapsed after violence spiraled out of control. Still, the enormous armies created by the Revolution's mass mobilization gave Napoleon the force to threaten the world of the European monarchies. The First Coalition—of Austria and Prussia, soon joined by Spain, the Netherlands, Portugal, Tuscany, and Britain—resolved to restore order in Belgium and to launch a campaign to restore Louis XVI to his throne. While the coalition armies defeated the French in Belgium, the Prussian army's attempt under the Duke of Brunswick to reach Paris was thwarted at Valmy in 1792, where French artillery were able to force coalition armies to retreat behind the Rhine.[9]

Measured by casualties, Valmy was a minor engagement; measured by its psychological impact, it was a major French victory. Not only did the French army repel the Germans from France, but the very next day, as the news arrived in Paris, the newly elected National Convention abolished the monarchy, replacing it with a republic. In quick succession in 1793, the new government executed Louis XVI and formed the Committee of Public Safety as an executive body to protect France against external threats and internal

The Battle of Valmy, *by Horace Vernet, 1826. The blue-uniformed soldiers on the left were citizen volunteers, augmenting the professional soldiers in white on the right.*

rebellion. A few months later Robespierre joined the committee where, as a virtual dictator, he launched the Terror to eradicate promonarchical elements from French society.

Many French officers could see from Valmy that, although the volunteers fought well under fire, they were too few to secure their borders against so many hostile neighbors at once. When the National Convention declared war on numerous enemies, many officers abandoned their commissions and emigrated elsewhere in revulsion against the Revolution. Suddenly faced with a manpower shortage, the National Convention introduced conscription in 1793 over rural resistance. The number of conscripts proved insufficient even then, prompting the convention to take the radical step of mobilizing the entire French nation. Here is the key passage of the *levée en masse*:

> *From this moment until that in which the enemy shall have been driven from the soil of the Republic, all Frenchmen are in permanent requisition for the service of the armies. The young men shall go to battle; the married men shall forge arms and transport provisions; the women shall make tents and clothing and shall serve in hospitals; the children shall turn old linen into lint; the aged shall betake themselves to the public places in order to arouse*

the courage of the warriors and preach the hatred of kings and the unity of the Republic.

The *levée* enabled France to build an army on an unprecedented scale, reaching its peak of about 1.5 million in 1794, large enough to go on the offensive. The enormous force retook Belgium, where it reinforced the revolution there, and in quick succession invaded Spain, the Rhineland, Piedmont, and the Netherlands.[10] Every French person, young and old, male and female, was enlisted in the common cause of revolution, in the event that the homeland was invaded and the regular armies were insufficient. As the Revolution unfolded, guerrilla warfare did indeed break out in the Pyrenees and Cerdanya (encouraged but quite uncontrollable by the British), in Tyrol, in Russia, and even in Prussia under the French occupation after 1807.

Forced conscription met with resistance in the countryside, especially in the west, where Prussians were a distant threat. The newly established Committee of Public Safety turned its attention to suppressing counterrevolutionary forces, and perhaps ironically, the first example of a total war took place in the Vendée, which rejected the revolutionary ordinances against the church as well as against the *levée* itself. Over the next three years, successive French armies conducted brutal counterterrorist campaigns in the region, killing thousands of people.[11]

It was in this complicated political situation that the young Corsican artillery officer appeared onstage. Winning the admiration of Maximilien Robespierre's brother Augustin, Napoleon gained command of the artillery at the siege of Toulon and promotion to brigadier general at twenty-five years of age. Even after Robespierre fell from grace, Napoleon found ways to ride the swift currents of French politics.

The Constitution of 1795 charted a path between the Jacobins and conservatives by establishing a bicameral legislature elected on restricted suffrage, but it pleased no one. So unpopular was the new government that elections in 1797 returned royalist majorities in the chambers, even though the system of staggered terms meant the cabinet itself remained unchanged. Responding to the government's appeal for help, the army obligingly purged the royalists from the chambers. For two years the government worked in the lengthening shadows of the generals, until 1799, when Napoleon did away with formalities and put himself in charge. In the first of his plebiscites, voters accepted virtually unanimously the next constitution, which established Napoleon as first consul.

Napoleon was lucky that the wars of 1792–97 had left him a huge and experienced army and very good officers, with the dead wood largely cleared out. He was also a brilliant tactician who combined the use of mobile field artillery with audacious troop redeployments under shifting battlefield circumstances. This required that the soldiers be trained to maneuver in hostile environments, that they be willing to take initiatives, and that they have great confidence in their commander. Napoleon could see the battlefield and act quickly on that vision. His signature move during virtually all his battles, even at Waterloo, was to take advantage of his opponents' problems of communication and coordination and to quickly isolate and defeat one army before the others could assist. Speed was vital. The Austrian general Karl Mack von Leiberich, for example, thought it would take Napoleon more than a month to move 70,000 troops to Germany, but in fact it took him only thirteen days to arrive with 190,000 and surround the Austrians. Mack von Leiberich's entire army surrendered, leaving the French to face weakened Austrians at Austerlitz and late-arriving Russian allies.

Napoleon was a political genius as well, leveraging his popularity with his soldiers and in the general population. He knew that the French would be likely to support his armies as long as they paid for themselves, fighting their battles in Germany or Italy and extracting wealth from enemy or allied populations. Following the old model of Gustavus Adolphus, he had his armies live off the land rather than rely on supply trains. This required that his armies use different routes to battle so that they would not compete for resources. He also brought conquered peoples and allies into the French forces. By the time of the Russian campaign, half the army was not French, and the campaign's resources were drawn from former enemies or allies. He continued the revolutionary policies of "liberating" peasants from feudal restrictions while impressing defeated soldiers into his forces.

Napoleon, although a dictator, understood the military purposes to which he could put the egalitarian ideology of the French Revolution. Like U.S. president Abraham Lincoln's Emancipation Proclamation, the French promise of democracy was a secret weapon to undermine the solidarity of his enemies: it gave the underclass in every enemy state a stake in French victories. Once Napoleon's armies conquered a country, he imposed the so-called

Napoleonic legal code that gave people access to new legal rights and courts. He drastically rearranged the map of Germany and elsewhere, consolidating ecclesiastical states, small principalities, and free cities into larger confederations while weakening those powers still at war with him, including Austria. Behind these moves was always the threat of direct military occupation, but local leaders rarely took that course, preferring to adopt Napoleonic reforms and pay tribute when the collector showed up. In effect, he created a new kind of regime that combined the revolutionary idea of political equality with concentrated administrative authority. Would-be autocrats have been trying to copy Napoleon's playbook ever since.

◆ ◆ ◆

Eighteenth-century Prussia was such a country, as envious as it was fearful of Napoleon. Prussia was tiny, perhaps a third the size of France at the start of the century, but it had built and trained a large professional army for its size, mainly due to the Swedish threat in the seventeenth century. In the aftermath of the Thirty Years' War and in response to the aggression of King Charles of Sweden in the 1650s, the Prussian Great Elector Frederick William (1620–88) had created a permanent field army.[12] Adopting the Swedish "cantonal system" of mass conscription, the Great Elector's grandson, Frederick William I (1688–1740), transformed Prussia into a military state and doubled the size of the professional army. By Frederick William I's death, Prussia, the tenth-largest state by area in Europe, had the third-largest army.[13]

Frederick II ("The Great") who ruled Prussia from 1740 to 1786, combined diplomatic agility, the judicious use of military power, and firm authoritarianism at home. By the standards of the time, his policies were notoriously secular and liberal, attracting the likes of Voltaire to his court, even if his grab of Silesia from Poland in the Seven Years' War (1756–63) rubbed Voltaire's pacifism the wrong way.[14] Frederick the Great enjoyed music, literature, and philosophy, but he was at root a skilled opportunist when it came to politics. He was not interested in diluting his authority by conceding representational rights to Junkers or bureaucrats, let alone to the "people." Still, he protected peasant lands from aristocratic and commercial intrusion in order to ensure that the peasants were well fed and willing to serve in the military.[15] By the end of Frederick the Great's rule, Prussia had managed, more than most European powers, to create a bureaucratic and centralized "state" with an able and highly disciplined professional army.[16]

The French Revolution and the enormous army it created in France rocked a complacent Prussia to its foundations. Although France in 1801 was much larger, with a population of 29.4 million compared to Prussia's about 10 million, the Prussians had developed an exalted opinion of their own military excellence. Napoleon's destruction of Prussian armies at Jena in 1806 was a shocking humiliation, followed by the even more demoralizing French occupation of Prussia itself. Napoleon had already taken possession of the Rhineland several years earlier and had crushed Austria's army at Austerlitz in 1805. Napoleon set about rearranging the map of Germany by transferring territories away from Austria and then Prussia in favor of newly powerful middle-size German states, including Baden, Bavaria, and Saxony, and imposing administrative and legal reforms throughout Germany. He also extracted wealth and manpower from Germany, recruiting two hundred thousand German troops for his 1812 Russian invasion. While some of Napoleon's reforms were popular among progressives and citizens of the middle-size German states, they deeply distressed the Prussians.

The Prussians, who sat at the top table among Germans, felt the humiliation of French occupation most intensely. As the occupation became ever more onerous and humiliating, they were increasingly united in hatred of the French, a fact reflected in the formation of patriotic fraternities and gymnastic clubs, the purposes of which were to subvert the French occupiers while also reforming what they regarded as obsolete Prussian institutions. The Junker establishment, whose privileged position rested implicitly on its ability to deliver protection, came under new scrutiny.

In some desperation, Frederick William III (1770–1840) enacted a flurry of economic reforms. On August 23, 1807, he issued a cabinet order abolishing serfdom: "The abolition of serfdom has consistently been my goal since the beginning of my reign. I desired to attain it gradually; but the disasters that have befallen the country now justify, and indeed require, speedier action."[17] He gave Jews more citizenship rights and encouraged economic competition by restricting the monopolies of traditional guilds.

On the political front, Frederick William III turned to reformers such as Karl Freiherr vom Stein, who pushed for representative institutions. The king agreed to dissolve his circle of personal advisers in favor of a meritocratic board of ministers. He also agreed to the establishment of local elections, but Stein failed to persuade the king of the desirability of a national representative assembly to which the king and his cabinet would be accountable.[18] In 1808 Frederick William's chancellor, Karl August von Hardenberg, engineered the downfall of the reform-minded Stein, and with Stein went his plans for national representation. Wilhelm von Humboldt, an intellectual who had moved Prussian education in a more liberal direction, was shown the door a few years later.[19]

The last thing the Prussian military wanted was political reform that would make it accountable to a wider public, but it was more eager than anyone else to strengthen Prussia's military capacity. Two Prussian aristocrats, Gerhard von Scharnhorst and August Neidhardt von Gneisenau, pressed the army to reward ability and talent over lineage. From their base in the Military Reform Commission in 1807, they managed to purge the old officer corps of the recalcitrant, to create a corps of expert professionals.[20] They also installed the basis of what became the general staff system, instituting long-term military planning and consideration of evolving military doctrine.[21] The Junkers remained in control of the regular army, but some increasingly important parts, such as the artillery and engineering, were opened to educated bourgeois. The military reformers also dreamed up plans for a new militia, the *Landwehr*, to supplement the regular army.[22] This was too "French" for Frederick William III, who had little faith in the common people, the *Volk*. When he refused to institute a national conscription army to meet the French threat, a despairing Carl von Clausewitz and several other Prussian patriots resigned their commissions and went to St. Petersburg on their own to help the Russians fight Napoleon's advancing army.[23]

While Prussia dithered on the sidelines, Russia succeeded in driving back the French horde by 1813. Chagrined by Prussian passivity, the Prussian general Ludwig Yorck von Wartenburg acted without authorization to declare neutrality and refused to help the retreating French army hold off Russian pursuit. Frederick William III, while none too pleased at Yorck's insubordinate actions, reluctantly agreed to call up a general conscription army. But the new people's army was not to last. The king decommissioned the militia as soon as Waterloo dealt an end to the French threat.[24] He was simply not ready to accept the complicated politics of a mobilized public.

The coalition of assorted armies that defeated Napoleon in 1815 at

Waterloo forced France back to its borders of 1792 and placed Louis XVIII on the throne. Prince Klemens von Metternich, Austria's foreign minister who informally led the conservative coalition of European states, opposed a thorough dismantling of French military power. Metternich was worried that Russia had emerged as Europe's powerful savior, and he was equally wary of the rise of Prussia, which was Austria's majority competitor to lead the new Germany. He thought a strong France was vital to restoring the old order.[25] Louis XVIII, who must have felt some vertigo after France's tumultuous events, was eager to help build foundations for Europe's conservative restoration.

France's 1814 constitutional charter established a limited monarchy: the king would preside as head of state over a bicameral legislature, the upper house, which he would appoint, and the lower house, which would be elected by the richest one percent of the population. France's rich voters elected a preponderance of royalists (known as ultras) to the lower house. The elitist, somewhat more reform-minded "Doctrinaires," led by François Guizot, were flanked on their left by a smattering of liberal republicans and socialists.[26] The constitution granted the king the power to initiate legislation and to veto unwelcome parliamentary actions, but it required him to rule through the law. If he wanted to initiate a new policy, he would have to build majorities in the chamber, which meant he had to worry about elections and the opinions of at least some of the public.[27]

King Louis XVIII, though betrayed by the army during Napoleon's Hundred Days, seemed determined to put unpleasant events behind him and make the new constitutional arrangements work. He ended the violent antirevolutionary backlash in southern France, dissolved the right-wing chamber of deputies that had been elected after Waterloo, and generally sought a conservative course.[28] However, when his nephew Duc de Berri was assassinated in 1820—for which he blamed the liberals—Louis XVIII further narrowed the electorate.[29] He retained some of Napoleon's generals and high administrators as well as the Napoleonic legal code, but given his narrow political base, he preferred a small professional army drawn from volunteers.[30]

Louis XVIII's minister of war, Laurent de Gouvion-Saint-Cyr, who had been a marshal under Napoleon, drafted a limited recruitment law in 1818 to conscript by lottery only 40,000 of the 300,000 eligible pool of twenty-year-olds. Conscription was made politically palatable to the elite by permitting people to buy substitutes and by limiting the size of the army.[31] Saint-Cyr's provision for a trained reserve that could be called in for emergencies was scrapped, with the result that the standing army could not be reinforced in wartime unless the war was very long. What this implied for French military capacity was not to be fully revealed until 1870, when the French army, with no trained reserves to match the Prussian militia, was vastly outnumbered. France had ceded its mobilizational advantage for the sake of political elitism.

Charles X, who succeeded his older brother Louis in 1824, was even more reactionary. Charles refused to reconcile himself to the 1814 Charter and made every effort to slip the constitutional net. While Louis had positioned himself closer to the middle of the new political spectrum, Charles wanted nothing short of the ancien régime. Ignoring the wishes of François Guizot's Doctrinaires, who had gained seats in the ensuing elections, Charles appointed a royalist ministry. He responded to the legislature's refusal to enact repressive measures by closing liberal newspapers, dissolving the assembly, and demanding a further reduction in the size of the electorate. The aristocrat René de Chateaubriand defended the monarchy's reestablishment in words that echoed de Tocqueville's: "Absolute equality accommodates itself easily to despotism that levels everything, but is not compatible with a monarchy that establishes a distinction of powers."[32] The French aristocracy fancied itself the only legitimate check on royal power.

The result was a popular explosion in Paris in July 1830 that forced Charles to abdicate the throne. The legislature, narrowly based though it was, felt compelled to install a new monarch that would be more willing to work within constitutional confines. Symbolically this step was enormous: the crown had effectively become a creation of the elected assembly. The new monarch's title was not the traditional "King of France" but a new "King of the French" that rooted sovereignty in the nation rather than in his person.[33]

Still, the rejection of Charles X was not a move toward democracy. Rather, it marked the establishment of a new bourgeois oligarchy. France's richest men, who alone exercised the franchise, had elected the triumphant Doctrinaires and opposed a wider franchise. In their view, popular sovereignty could operate only through its institutional representative, parliament, which must be filled with men like themselves.[34] Their opposition to Charles

Fighting at the Hôtel de Ville, July 28, 1830, *by Jean-Victor Schnetz, 1833.*
"Les Trois Glorieuses" (the three glorious days, July 27–29) ended the brief
Bourbon Restoration and established King Louis-Philippe's "July-Monarchy."

X and his ministry was essentially a constitutional fight about parliamentary controls on the government that he had refused to accept.

The new king, Louis Philippe, doubled the franchise to 200,000 out of a population of 32 million, but politics in Paris and beyond continued to churn. The new government of "liberals" and republicans who argued endlessly over fine points of constitutional monarchy could not see that they were a mere bubble on a seething ocean of popular discontent over rising food prices and stagnating wages. On more than one occasion, the government wheeled out the newly reconstituted National Guard to maintain order.[35] The sitting members of parliament faced the grim prospect of elections on the expanded franchise in 1831, knowing that they would be held responsible for widespread economic hardship.

Compounding matters, capital cities across Europe were popping with insurrections, stimulated in part by the July 1830 tumult in France. Unlike the conservatives who held power in Paris, Euro-republicans thought the French should intervene on the side of liberty.[36] The Marquis de Lafayette,

Portrait of Gilbert Motier, the Marquis de Lafayette,
as a Lieutenant General, 1791, *by Joseph-Désiré Court, 1834.*

the French aristocrat who had been a general in the American Revolutionary War and a leader of the Revolutionary National Guard in France, advocated a French role in these struggles taking place in Belgium, Poland, and
Italy. "There exist certain natural rights inherent in every society," he argued
before the French Chamber of Deputies, "of which not only one nation but
not all of the nations together could not justly deprive an individual." These
rights were not "subject to the condition of nationality."[37]

Rather than stoke the flames of rebellion across Europe, however, the
French government sacked Lafayette, with predictable results. The Polish
army had led a popular revolt and formed a provisional republic for which
it sought French help, but when the help did not arrive, the Russians easily squashed the rebellion. Poland (again) ceased to exist as an independent
entity in 1832.[38] Back in France, the government replaced Lafayette with
Marshal Jean de Dieu Soult, who presided over a defensive military posture
more befitting the narrowly based regime it sought to preserve.

France's most striking effect on Germany in the nineteenth century was not the spread of revolutionary ideas there but the emergence of a German longing to unify as one great nation in the center of Europe capable of standing up to future threats of foreign interference, especially from France. The new German nationalism, which first took root among the educated middle classes and the young, ultimately drove Germany into the welcoming arms of Prussia, the only German state powerful enough to secure Germany against a looming Austrian empire.[39]

Germany had had its own groundswell of "liberalism" in the 1820s, springing from the cities and urban centers of the middle-size states (the *Mittelstaaten*), where the French had encouraged constitutions and elected legislatures.[40] But the liberals were not democrats. They sought freedom of activity including free trade, the antirevolutionary concerns of the well off.[41] Although liberals believed that financial independence and education could create citizens with the capacities for self-governance—an idealized German public, or *Volk*—they viewed wage laborers as an unenlightened and potentially dangerous mob. When, in July 1830, news of the fall of the Bourbon monarchy in France sparked popular revolts across Germany, the liberals took sides against the rising socialist parties. A partial exception was university students, some of whom kept revolutionary fires smoldering until the next flare-up in 1848.

The Sicilian revolt against the Bourbon regime in January 1848 might not have amounted to much there, had it not been for the smoldering discontent among industrial workers all over Europe. Unrest spread northward through Italy like brushfire, reaching France in February 1848 and Germany soon afterward. Louis Philippe, the French monarch since 1830, abdicated almost as soon as citizens swarmed the streets of Paris. The Second Republic was quickly declared, elections were held, and a new constitution was established that embodied universal male suffrage. The new government's radicals and conservatives, however, were unaccustomed to sharing government and battled for policy control in the National Constituent Assembly as citizens battled in the streets.[42] On June 23, 1848, when the legislature shut down government-funded "workshops" established around the country to boost employment, 170,000 citizens of Paris rushed to the barricades in protest. In response, the government dispatched over 100,000 soldiers to crush them. "June Days" bloodshed deepened the chasm between the liberals and the radicals, calling into question the compatibility of their economic aims and political visions.

Barricade on the Rue Soufflot, *by Horace Vernet, 1848.*

The next whiplashing event in French politics must have surprised the liberals, who thought they represented the voice of reason. On December 10–11, 1848, the voters gave a landslide victory to Louis Napoleon Bonaparte, nephew of Bonaparte himself. A hesitant speaker with ambiguous ideas, he nevertheless won support of the rich, eager for stability, and of the poor, hopeful that he would make good on promises to give work to the unemployed. Absent from Louis Napoleon's coalition were the liberals and republicans and the economic elite who above all else feared tyranny, of either the monarchical or the democratic variant. When Louis Napoleon doffed the democratic fig leaf in 1851 to establish his own dictatorship, Karl Marx wrote *The Eighteenth Brumaire of Louis Bonaparte,* referring to the date in the French Revolutionary calendar, November 9, 1799, when the first Bonaparte had seized power. Expressing the absurdity of a popularly elected dictator after so much blood had been shed for freedom, Marx wrote his famous addendum to Hegel's comment that history repeats itself: "[Hegel] forgot to add: the first time as tragedy, the second time as farce."[43]

To the east, conservatives responded to the political conflagrations of 1848 with the ferocious zeal of the desperate. In Vienna, university students led an uprising so formidable that the royal family fled and Metternich resigned in March 1848. Students kept order in the city with patrols and offered a variety of medical and legal services to workers who allied with them. The workers responded with generosity of their own, offering money from their wages to maintain the hodgepodge militia. Their combined forces were no match for the army, however, which crushed the Vienna uprising in October 1848.[44]

Domestic dissent was only a small part of Austria's problems. Austria fell into a civil war against its Hungarian partner, and its Italian subjects began to revolt. Metternich's Austrian-led international balance of power, established at the Congress of Vienna in 1815, unraveled into nationally colored skeins, beginning in Germany, where conservatives increasingly viewed Prussia and not Austria as capable of providing reliable protection from generalized disorder.

In Germany, liberals and radicals strived against each other as they sought to tame and master nationalism for their own purposes.[45] Workers and students took to the streets in the cities of Prussia, Baden, Bavaria, Saxony, and Württemberg, raising the specter of an uncontrollable beast. Students at the University of Berlin forced Rector Johannes Müller to resign when he circulated a petition pledging corporate loyalty to the king and opposition to an elected national assembly.[46] Some students in Berlin were

Troops firing into barricades at Alexanderplatz, Berlin, 1848.

even more radical than the workers. Gustav Adolf Schoffel, a student who had been expelled from Heidelberg in February 1848 for distributing Communist literature to Odenwald peasants, tried to organize a march on the palace in Berlin. He was imprisoned and died the following year in revolutionary battles in Baden.[47]

From May 18, 1848, to May 31, 1849, delegates of the German Confederation of states and principalities, an incipient pan-German body formed after 1815 that also included Austria, debated with one another at Paul's Church (Paulskirche) in Frankfurt until they sorted themselves into ideologically opposed camps. Their divisions arose even though they were mainly lawyers, judges, academics, and businessmen. Although there were no industrial workers, only one peasant, and just a few members of the lower middle class among them, some of the middle-class delegates worried that total exclusion of the lower orders would result in civil war.[48]

The fear of French-style chaos gave Prussia's William Frederick IV the strategic opening he was looking for: an opportunity to divide and conquer liberals and conservatives in his realm. He granted constitutional concessions to mollify the liberals, while squashing German radicals brutally and unequivocally. Once he put down the revolts, he rolled back even his modest

Frankfurt Assembly in Paulskirche, 1848, *by Leo von Elliott.*

constitutional promises—as his father had done in 1819—including the freedom of press he had granted only a few months earlier.[49]

With radicalism off the table, an emerging consensus among German liberals and conservatives prioritized the problem of how Germany would defend itself against France, a still powerful and apparently unstable state. Austria's polyglot empire had once seemed an asset on the world stage, but for leading Germany in an era of rising German nationalism, its multinational identity had become a liability. An unreconstructed Prussian monarchy, unencumbered by divided loyalties as Austria was, appeared to be the natural leader of German national unification.

Conservatives were back in the saddle across Europe in 1849. Louis Napoleon was secure, for the time being, in an antiradical moment. In Austria, archconservatives replaced the more moderate emperor Ferdinand and his adviser Prince Metternich. In Prussia, Frederick William IV granted a constitution in which wealth weighted the vote for the Prussian parliament and in which the military was accountable only to the monarchy. When the Frankfurt Parliament offered Frederick William IV the crown of a new imperial Germany in 1849, he dismissed it as a "dog collar" that he did not need to wear. He would lead Germany on his own terms.

✦ ✦ ✦

The revolutionary year of 1848 had sputtered inconclusively to a halt. After the fact, Marx's partner Frederick Engels saw the episode as premature, a failed prelude to "that great duel to the death between the bourgeoisie and the proletariat."[50] Instead, the "duel to the death" would be between Germany and France, elevating the political significance of nation over class.

First, however, Prussia and Austria came to blows over Prussia's rising command of German nationalism, a conflict that Prussia won handily in a seven weeks' war in 1866. There had been stops along the way of this winding path of national unification. With a very large army newly victorious in Hungary and Italy, Austria had forced Prussia to renounce its nationalizing ambitions in what German nationalists and liberals called the "humiliation at Olmütz" of 1850. But the wily Otto von Bismarck, whom King Wilhelm I had appointed minister-president of Prussia in 1862, understood that he must seize nationalism from German liberals if Germany were to have heft on the international stage. To win the support of the liberal-leaning southern states for his next move, to defeat France and retake the Rhineland, Bismarck offered a pan-German parliament.

With investments in railroads, fortifications, and recruitment, the German army was soon in a position to overwhelm the French in a swift war in 1870–71. The Prussian military commander Helmuth von Moltke "the Elder" used railroads to bring extensive artillery against French infantry, mostly negating the advantage of the French chassepot rifle. Moltke's forces managed to bottle up a French army at Metz and then completely devastate another one at Sedan, capturing more than one hundred thousand men and Napoleon himself. German armies then put Paris under siege.

In 1870, with Napoleon III in captivity, the humiliated and mortified French chose a republican Government of National Defense to defend Paris. Gambetta and his reenergized French forces battled German armies throughout France, requiring the Germans to divert siege forces to supply corridors elsewhere, but they failed to lift the siege of Paris.[51] German bombardments brought the city to its knees in early 1871, and to add to the insult, the Germans seized Gambetta's home province of Alsace. The Germans declared a new Reich, with King Frederick Wilhelm as Kaiser and Bismarck as chancellor.

The Germans required, as part of the armistice, that the French Republic hold elections immediately so that the Germans would have a legitimate negotiating partner. The result was an overwhelming conservative majority eager to make final terms with the Germans. They conceded Alsace-Lorraine and paid a large indemnity, and they agreed to a humiliating German victory march through Paris. The reaction in Paris was, in quick succession, the furious formation of the radical Paris Commune and its hasty repression.

Crucially, the Third Republic adopted universal male suffrage in 1875, along with other rules that lasted through the German invasion of 1940: a president, a chamber of deputies that selected a government, and a senate. Some important constitutional details were soon settled: Prime Minister Patrice de MacMahon insisted that the government was responsible to him rather than to the Chamber of Deputies and in 1877 forced the issue by dismissing the government and dissolving the chamber. The 1877 elections returned a republican majority to the chamber that forced MacMahon to resign.[52] Operationally the sovereign, with no other institution to veto its actions, the chamber enacted a series of statutes establishing rights of association and speech and separating church and state.[53] Nevertheless, governments tended to be unstable coalitions of liberals, conservatives, and radicals, somewhat reshuffled in each election.[54]

In Germany, Bismarck's wars against Austria and France had unified the nation as an empire under Prussian leadership. Like the French, Bismarck established universal male suffrage for elections to the Reichstag, rather than the wealth-weighted voting used in Prussia.[55] A German parliamentary majority could not vote a government out of power, but it could register discontent and hold up the passage of laws. Prussia remained the dominant state within Germany, its leading officials occupying the main cabinet and military posts. However, because Germany's constitution did not make the cabinet accountable to the Reichstag, Bismarck could pursue his foreign and military policies more or less with impunity. His wars with Denmark in 1864 and with Austria in 1866 had not been approved or funded by the Prussian Landtag, and it was clear that he could conduct future adventures in the same manner.

Liberal parties constituted the majority of the Reichstag as well as the parliaments of most of the German states (including Prussia), but liberals were deeply divided between the right, favoring a nationalist coalition with Bismarck, and the left, which opposed it. Liberals of all stripes were anti-Catholic and pushed a "cultural struggle" (*Kulturkampf*) to limit the political role of the church and religious orders. Bismarck, ever the pragmatist, went along with anti-Catholic policies as a price for support from the national liberals and pushed further, expelling the Jesuits from Germany and imposing new regulations on the church.

European countries were structured differently from one another at the end of the nineteenth century, in part because their vulnerability to external attack varied considerably.[56] Defensible terrain had everywhere and always put a thumb on the scale for political inclusion, while landlord-dominated agricultural lands lay at the other extreme.[57] War might have produced a robust nationalism capable of squeezing out the radicalism that emerged in France and Germany, but England demonstrated to the rest of Europe a less tumultuous path through the thicket of class politics.

◆ ◆ ◆

England was so sufficiently protected by water that the populace had never tolerated war mobilization without something in return, and parliamentary representation had developed early and steadily, particularly during periods of foreign war. The British Isles had the Channel to thank that the continent's nineteenth-century radicalism stopped at Calais. Although it is true that in 1817 the British government suspended habeas corpus and the right of public meeting to combat the "malignant spirit" that had allegedly wafted across the Channel following the revolution, English moderates as well as radicals objected to this kind of heavy-handedness, and Parliament restored habeas corpus within a year. Polite society was more disgusted than relieved by the "Peterloo Massacre" of 1819, in which a cavalry charge, intended to disperse crowds of 300,000 massed to protest bad economic conditions, killed 15 people and wounded 400 to 700.

England's Reform Act of 1832, which expanded the franchise from 500,000 to 813,000 (one in ten men), absorbed some of the demands for greater inclusion unleashed by wartime mobilization, but the wealthy and entitled were pleasantly surprised that the modestly expanded franchise did not create a redistributive state. Apparently it was possible to establish representative institutions that secured property rights even as the middle class joined the ranks of the represented. The perfect set of institutions that would give away as much as necessary (to be a great military power) but as little as

The Peterloo Massacre of 1819, *published by Richard Carlile in 1819.*

possible (to protect aristocratic privilege) was the holy grail for the nineteenth-century European elite.

The nineteenth-century British historian C. B. Roylance Kent blamed the English Radicals for delaying the reformist cause by undermining the Whigs' modest struggle against the landed aristocracy, who still dominated Parliament. Kent's criticism is only to notice that the Whigs did not wish to expand the franchise very far.[58] For employers who sat on the other side of distributional issues from workers, the Jacobin Terror was a bad advertisement of what universal suffrage might do. The Whigs in Parliament, identified with the urban middle and upper middle class, favored a modest franchise expansion to include all tax-paying households as a way to increase their numbers in the landowner-dominated Parliament. There were also not very many of them. It was joked that in the House of Commons the forty Whig members "might all have driven home together in a single hackney coach."[59]

The Radical organizer John Hunt dismissed the 1832 reform as a contemptible fraud upon the people—a middle-class enfranchisement: "A damnable delusion, giving us as many tyrants as there are shopkeepers."[60] Another Radical used even more colorful language to describe the new voters, slightly less wealthy but no less repugnant than the old elite: "The lion must give way to the rat, the tiger to the leech."[61] Radicals themselves, however, were so fraught through with racism and intolerance that they did not form a coalition with the Irish seeking full status. Some Radicals refused to participate in meetings between Whigs and Radicals when the Irish were invited.[62]

Meanwhile British mobilization against Napoleon had imposed large taxes on the people in blood and money. Britain's own "Levy en Masse" Act, passed in July 1803, promised "to drill every able-bodied man whether he liked it or not." The early Radical riots, including Peterloo, expressed economic despair and political disappointment in the wake of these sacrifices. But unlike on the continent, the government demobilized British troops after 1815, which the Radicals did not resist. The Manchester School of Radicalism was led by the so-called "little Englanders" John Bright and Richard Cobden who favored military neutrality and nonintervention.[63] Like the early Radicals, they feared that a standing army would be an instrument of domestic political coercion. Cobden noted that the army and navy were "the great preserve of the landlord class for their younger sons." If France took the whole of Africa, Cobden warned, it would only cause trouble for itself. Bright too believed that national defense was "a gigantic system of outdoor relief for the aristocracy." Nor were they were fans of the navy, believing that supremacy at sea was the source of British arrogance and dictatorial power at home and abroad.[64]

The Prussian elite, as we saw, had tried to resist parliamentary limits on monarchy. In Britain, where the elite already controlled Parliament, the struggle rather was to hold back the floods of popular demands for greater participation. In 1884 the Tory leader Benjamin Disraeli presided over one of Britain's largest franchise expansions, hoping for a happy marriage between British nationalism and Tory paternalism. The wife of the German socialist leader Wilhelm Liebknecht had translated Disraeli's *Sybil* into German as an honorable example of English Tory "socialism."[65] Without new wars to fight and new armies to muster, Britain had the luxury of trying out representation in small steps. A form of modern democracy gradually took shape, in which property holders tried out various ways to control democratic impulses through representation and lobbying behind closed doors. The final step of eliminating property and tax requirements to achieve universal male suffrage would not come until the new mobilizational pressures of World War I.

✦ ✦ ✦

In Russia, an almost entirely agrarian economy played into the hands of the great landholders who controlled most of the country's wealth. Like the Polish nobles of the late eighteenth century, they refused to accept the kind of reform that might have inoculated them against the revolution that swept Russia in 1917. Tsar Alexander II's emancipation of the serfs in 1861, after the Crimean War debacle, did not satisfy the vast number of peasants living on the poorest patches of land at the margin of subsistence. Instead Lenin, like Mao after him, improvised Marxism to incorporate peasant fury, at the bottom rungs of his vertical party structure. The Russian Revolution was bloody because the peasantry was divided, with richer farmers swinging right. Effective mobilization was surprisingly small for both the Reds and the Whites, but the Reds used support from the poorest farmers to their advantage. Lenin swept aside the prosperous farmers who opposed him with the armies he amassed from the discontented.[66]

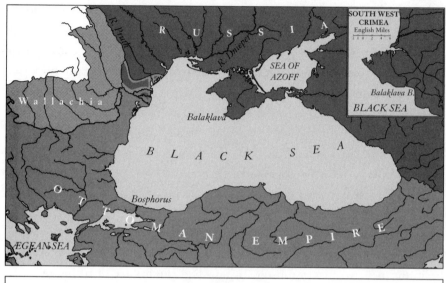

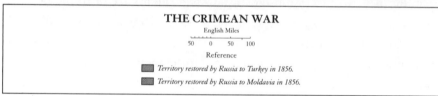

THE CRIMEAN WAR

English Miles

50   0   50   100

Reference

Territory restored by Russia to Turkey in 1856.

Territory restored by Russia to Moldavia in 1856.

Britain and France took the side of the Ottomans to stop
Russia's southward move to control of the Bosporus.

Understanding why so many Russian peasants remained at subsistence levels requires a deeper understanding of history. Russia had repelled Napoleon's invasion in 1812 with the help of its pitiless winter. The tables turned four decades later in the 1853–56 Crimean War, when the French and English easily thwarted Russia's territorial grab for warm-water ports in the Black Sea from the crumbling Ottoman Empire.[67] England's prime minister, Henry John Temple, Third Viscount Palmerston, did not wish Russia to get any closer to the prosperous British enterprise in India, although in Britain the war was so unpopular that the government recruited 10,000 Germans and other mercenaries to fight alongside 200,000 British soldiers.[68] France's Napoleon III joined with England in order to restore its place in Europe at the expense of two other former great enemies, Russia and Austria. French "radicals" saw an opportunity to weaken Russia while befriending England, whereas the "moderates" focused on the balance of power.[69]

Tsar Nicholas thought he could count on Austria, but it too was leery of

Russian expansion and refused to guarantee its neutrality. The tsar was instead forced to rely on peasant conscripts, including volunteers acting on well-timed rumors that fighting would free them from serfdom.[70] He raised an army of nearly 700,000 Russians to face nearly a million on the other side.[71] In addition to superior numbers of men-at-arms, the Allies benefited from more modern weapons, the telegraph, and Florence Nightingale, the nurse and social reformers who tended to the wounded on the Crimean battlefields. Better sanitation in English hospitals resulted in a smaller death toll: 22,181 Englishmen died out of an army of 97,864 men, relatively few of them in hospitals. By comparison, between Russia's destruction of the Turkish Black Sea squadron at Sinope in November 1853 and the Treaty of Paris that ended the war on March 30, 1856, an estimated 30,000 Russian soldiers were killed in battle, while hundreds of thousands died of disease and fatigue.[72] The British, too, were poorly officered (made legendary by Alfred Lord Tennyson's "Charge of the Light Brigade") and appallingly ill-equipped to deal with the Russian winter, but in addition to hospital sanitation, they had steam propulsion and iron armor for ships, and longer-range rifles.[73] Complicating matters for the Russians was the ambivalence of native Tatars about Russia's Christianizing mission.[74] The war was a complete mismatch. Although the allies did not demand a complete Russian withdrawal, they required Russia to demilitarize the Crimean Peninsula and points south, to restore the neutrality of the Bosporus.[75]

Startled by the undeniable evidence of Russia's economic and military backwardness, Alexander II insisted on making good on the rumors about abolishing serfdom to improve agricultural productivity and to release peasants for industrial work. The tsar said to the aristocrats in a speech of March 30, 1856, "All of you understand that the existing conditions of owning souls cannot remain unchanged. It is better to begin eliminating serfdom from above than to wait until it begins to eliminate itself from below."[76] At the same time minister of war Dmitry Milyutin reduced the years of compulsory service from twenty-five to six and introduced schooling for all conscripts.[77] Still, the officers and the rank and file lived in different social worlds. The command structure remained strictly hierarchical; although peasant soldiers fought bravely, they were not permitted to take any initiative, which accounts for the sudden deterioration of entire units upon the disappearance of their officers.[78]

In 1857, impatient with the landowners' foot-dragging, Alexander formed a secret committee of landlords to study the peasant question. Ultraconservatives on the committee included Prince Golitsyn, Prince Paskevih, Count Apraksin, and Count Shuvalov, as well as some representatives of the Polish magnates (from the Russian part of the partitions) in Lithuania and Belorussia. It was no good—the magnates refused to budge. Serfdom remained profitable for most Russian landlords up to the emancipation in 1861, refuting the thesis of Marxist Russian historians that Alexander II was merely rubberstamping a trend. Just before emancipation, 80 percent of serfs were in estates of 27,000 acres or more. Nearly half of all serfs belonged to nobles who "owned" more than five hundred male serfs each. Alexander gave up on the committee in August 1857.[79]

Alexander's next move, in 1858, was to commission his Ministry of Interior to take up the serfdom problem, involving 48 regional committees and 1,400 members. Weary of seeking aristocratic consensus, the tsar opened the session of the State Council in January 1861 with a peremptory announcement that "the matter of the liberation of the serfs I regard as . . . a question of life and death for Russia. . . . I am convinced of the necessity of a quick and sure conclusion of this matter. . . . Further delay can only arouse passions and lead to the most pernicious and disastrous consequences for the state as a whole and for the gentry in particular."[80] On February 19, 1861, Alexander II issued an edict giving personal freedom to twenty-three million serfs, just over one-third of the total population of Russia.

Tsar Alexander II's act of emancipation was marred by rearguard action of the landed elite who ensured that peasants got less than they had hoped. Peasants in villages all over Russia revolted in large numbers. In April 1861 a crowd of ten thousand former serfs in Voronezh province, for example, refused to pay their former masters anymore, in rent or labor. Government authorities arrested the ringleaders and flogged them publicly.[81] Official records show a decline in "disturbances" from 647 in April–June to 4 in October–November 1861, as peasants came to realize that there was nothing more the tsar was prepared to do for them—it had not been much, although it was more than freed American slaves got, it should be noted. According to the so-called "beggarly allotment," the landlord and peasant could voluntarily agree on an allotment of a smaller piece of land than decreed by law as long as the peasant did not have to pay for it. About half a million peasants opted for a tiny plot of debt-free land, but unable to sustain a livelihood on it, they gave it up for industrial jobs.[82]

By 1900, when revolutionary rumblings began, about one-quarter of all Russian agricultural income remained concentrated in the hands of the seven hundred largest landowners, and most peasants still worked the lands of others.[83] Russia's military defeat at the hands of the Japanese in 1905 sparked a new wave of peasant unrest, especially in the southwest. One contemporary reporter wrote that soldiers returning from Manchuria were dismayed by what they found: "There was nothing for them to eat, and no fuel for them to heat their huts." They were angry to learn that their families had not received allowances. "Why have we spilt our blood, if we do not have the land?" According to a report from one village, "The rich peasants and the poor peasants did not sympathize with the strikes, although they did not display energetic opposition either."[84] The poor peasants, in greatest need of earnings, reported to work as usual. The principal strikers were the middle peasants who could hold out for higher wages without suffering immediate losses.[85]

Thus was the stage set for the Russian Revolution. While the democratic compromise was emerging in the West, Russia succumbed to the authoritarian populism of Lenin's Bolsheviks. At least one enlightened tsar, Alexander II, had seen that serfdom was a ticking time bomb, but the landed aristocrats were intent on keeping as much of their land as possible, and they were politically strong enough to do so. Lenin overthrew them forcibly with the military arm of his highly organized revolutionary vanguard party. He knew better than to wait for the dictatorship of the proletariat to arise by public acclamation, for his vision of government "for the people" was incompatible with government "by the people" in more than a symbolic way.

✦ ✦ ✦

By century's end, both France and Germany had enormous standing armies with well-developed forms of recruitment, training, and promotion. Even more important, both had adopted representative government with universal suffrage—a first pass at stitching together the seemingly irreconcilable demands of the rich and the working class. The German kaiser remained freer of constitutional controls than the French leaders were. But as much as anything, it was nationalism, an outgrowth of the conflagration of war, that forged a cross-class alliance within countries in the place of the international class alliance that Marx so ardently championed.

Prussia's first response to the enormous new armies of Revolutionary France was to enlarge and professionalize its military. Like most states on the European continent at the beginning of the nineteenth century, Prussia maintained a standing army officered either by its own nobility or sometimes by nobility from other lands. However, its calamitous defeat at Jena in 1806 convinced Prussia's elitist military to conscript commoners and to open the officers' ranks to talent and skill. The public accepted the idea that the new militia, the *Landwehr*, fought for the nation and not merely for the dynastic interests of the prince.

Meanwhile the French onslaught took place during a time when the new technology of warfare, including faster-loading guns with accuracy at longer ranges, required longer and more intensive training. No longer fighting in lines in lockstep, armies broke into small mobile units that drew more deeply on soldiers' intellectual capacity and loyalty to respond flexibly to the shifting battlefield. In short, modern war by century's end required citizens. The Prussians, with their notion of the educated citizen (*Bildung*), took this idea as far as they could in an authoritarian state.

Ultimately, military responses alone were insufficient to meet the French challenge, and even the gleaming precision machine that was the Prussian military had to accept political changes that would motivate a whole German nation to fight. That is not to say that the new German constitution was designed for maximal battlefield effectiveness—far from it. The military insisted, all the way through World War I, that it should remain accountable only to the king. Rather, the checks on Prussia's constitutional monarchy, such as they were, emerged through the competitive jockeying of many players for advantage—the king, the nobles and military, the liberals, conservatives, and radicals—against the backdrop of threat-induced nationalism and romantic ideas about German culture and character.

To appreciate the momentous political transformations of the nineteenth century, consider that Europe in 1789 was still ruled by monarchs who claimed an absolute authority to rule that was given, somehow, by God. Not even Louis XIV would have thought that God picked him specifically to rule, but he might have thought that God sanctioned the Bourbons to rule in France by picking out a Protestant prince, Henry of Navarre, and accepting his confession and conversion as a sufficient submission for the crown. The Holy Roman emperor had a better story since he was, after all, elected as king of the Romans and then crowned emperor by the pope in God's name. God had guided the hands of the electors; but if not, there was a final check in the hands of His vicar on earth.

In the nineteenth century, popular sovereignty replaced supernatural legitimation. But the idea of a nation assenting to rule did not resolve fights over how to determine what the nation wanted or accepted. The venerable English formula "Grievances Before Supply" expressed the claimed position of the old estates. In 1789 France's Abbé Sièyes argued that the people were a body of indistinguishable citizens who collectively shared a common interest and had the right and authority to pursue it through their representatives. That this idea was mostly honored in the breach did not prevent elected parliaments, once they began appearing, from asserting it. It was in the nineteenth century that elections replaced dynastic succession, marriage, and war as the convention for leadership choice.

The old political elite had even more at stake in the question of who would vote and how much each vote would count. Giving the poor an equal political voice was terrifying not only to the very rich but also to the middle class. One way around it was to argue that legal equality did not imply equal *political* rights. Liberals and conservatives joined in imposing property qualifications on voting and even higher ones on officeholding. But in the end the real and deeply felt pride, humiliation, and determination to triumph helped to create a nation out of fractious people. It is hard to see how the squabbles over who got how much political say would have been resolved in a form of representative government without that incipient but powerful sense of national loyalty.

The fight over what elected officials would do, once in office, had been settled in England a century earlier, though there were still struggles for control over the cabinet. In France, parliament established its supremacy only in the 1870s, in response to the alarming ambitions and popularity of Boulanger, another would-be elective king. In Germany it was not until 1918, when the old Reich government was blamed for military adventurism, that the government became accountable to parliament. Unfortunately once again for Germany, the Weimar government was undone in the 1930s by a clause that gave the executive wide powers in emergencies. This proved a fatal flaw for German democracy, still fragile in the nineteenth century, when plunged into the whiter-hot wars of the twentieth.

Chapter Eleven

TWENTIETH-CENTURY WARS

OF FULL MOBILIZATION

B RITAIN, AN EARLY AND GRADUAL DEMOCRATIZER, withheld the vote from the poorest third of its male citizens until World War I. Then the Germans, in their rush to reach France, "raped Belgium" in August 1914, violating their neutrality and killing hundreds of suspected Belgian civilian guerrillas along the way. Horrified British citizens learned that German forces, encountering blown-up bridges and sniper fire at the River Meuse on August 4, killed dozens of townsfolk in riverside towns and destroyed hundreds of homes.[1] Between August 19 and 26, the rampage continued, with German soldiers taking the towns of Aarschot, Andenne, Tamines, Dinant, and Leuven with a ferocity intended to cow the Belgians into quick submission.[2] In Leuven they expelled the ten thousand residents after executing 248 of the most conspicuous and torched with gasoline the town's prized medieval library and collections.[3]

When news hit Britain, war was declared on Germany almost immediately.[4] Less than a month later, on September 2, 1914, Herbert Asquith's Liberal Party government created a War Propaganda Bureau under Liberal member of Parliament Charles Masterman from which to spread word of German viciousness. Some members of the private press such as Edward Tyas Cook of *The Times* of London refused to publish unverified reports from the front, about kittens nailed to church doors, schoolgirls stripped and raped en masse, and nurses having their breasts cut off; but other publishers

233

Britain's version of "Uncle Sam" was Herbert Kitchener, secretary of state for war.

boosted sales by representing the German invasion with pornographic imagery. The government's own inquiry into the truth of so-called eyewitness reports, chaired by former member of Parliament James Bryce, concluded in May 1915 that the Germans had indeed been guilty of countless atrocities.[5] The British War Office allowed a few journalists to serve as embedded war correspondents as long as their postings could be "guided" by army censors.[6]

Gory news from the front had, for the British government, two salutary effects. One was to impress the American government that the Germans were monsters. As Masterman wrote to Bryce about the Bryce Report on June 7, 1915, "Your report has *swept* America. As you probably know even the most skeptical declare themselves converted, just because it was signed by you."[7] The second was to electrify the British population in favor of fighting the Germans. The Liberal government had no plans to institute a draft, hoping instead on a steady stream of volunteers. They guessed correctly, and by November 1914 over a million men had responded to stomach-turning news, official recruitment posters, and women passing out white feathers to embarrass the hesitant.[8]

The pace of volunteering slowed, however, as reports of high casualties among British troops began to seep back home, despite the War Ministry's best efforts to control information from the front. By the end of November 1914, half the volunteers were wounded and 10 percent were dead.[9] As the prospect of a quick victory evaporated, so did the influx of English volunteers. On January 5, 1916, the cabinet introduced a conscription bill that would require military service of single males of ages eighteen to forty-one.[10] The imposition of conscription signaled British acceptance that this was a total war—a war between whole peoples—that would require everyone to do their part, especially the men who would be called up.

Once conscription was on the table, the public began to raise questions about the justice of unenfranchised British citizens spilling their blood. Britain's political parties fell over themselves to agree with this sentiment and on October 10, 1916, formed a thirty-six-person committee from both Houses to prepare a bill introducing universal male suffrage, as well as to extend the vote to women thirty and over (since the property requirement was the last fig leaf for excluding women). The first general election under universal male suffrage, held December 1918, is sometimes called the "atrocities election" because parties and candidates competed with one another to celebrate the costly contributions of British soldiers on the Western front.[11]

Britain, like other representative democracies that managed to mobilize both manpower and capital for a successful war effort, established an attractive model for the postwar world for decades to come. However, Nazi Germany, Japan, Soviet Russia, and Maoist China demonstrated that it was possible to raise vast armies in the modern world by instilling fear, promising economic benefits, and appealing to national pride, often all at the same time, meaning that there were other ways than franchise expansion to mobilize troops. Still, even countries that put large numbers of men-at-arms while repressing domestic dissent paid unintended tribute to the democratic model by publicly insisting that their governments embodied a more perfect blend of liberties. What else could Mao have meant by "democratic reforms" in 1959 when he crushed the Tibetan insurgency?

While twentieth-century wars proved to business interests and landholders that universal voting rights did not spell the end to secure property, this "democratic view" of the world did not come about overnight. Blood was spilled at the barricades of the nineteenth-century revolutions when the stakes of left-wing versus right-wing governments had seemed as high as life itself. The twentieth-century wars of full mobilization established instead that workers would be patriotic fighters and that businesses would pay taxes on income rather than to court inflation from runaway debt. The return on capital net of taxes and capital destruction actually fell below national growth rates during the twentieth-century wars and has only in recent years begun to exceed them.[12]

✦ ✦ ✦

World War I was a war in which Anglo-German animosity was not a foregone conclusion. Queen Victoria's ancestor George I, who ascended the throne as next of kin upon the death of Queen Anne in 1714, came from Hanover, Germany; Kaiser Wilhelm was Queen Victoria's nephew from Albert's side of the family. In addition, the economies of the two countries remained intertwined through extensive trade and finance. In fact, leading up to World War I, much of British trade was with France and Germany. British manufacturing and mining interests, geographically centered in northern England, was the Liberal Party's core constituency and favored peace with Germany on account of strong trade relations; the "gentlemanly investors" concentrated in London who constituted the base of the Tory Party were more belligerent toward Germany because a greater part of their business was with the empire than with Europe; and because they feared Germany's imperial ambitions.[13]

From 1905 to 1913 British trade with Russia was only half of what it was with Germany.[14] Large volumes of raw material imports from the British Empire, financed by the City of London, do not seem to have been a sore point for German industrialists.[15] German industry was booming, as were exports of manufactured goods. In 1905 Germany produced 24.3 percent of the world's iron ore that supplied a profitable steel milling industry. England had been the "motherland of technology" in the nineteenth century— Gottlieb Daimler studied engineering in England in 1861–63—but by 1914, for the first time, Germany accounted for a greater share of world manufacturing production than Britain.[16]

Had Germany been a pure parliamentary system, peace interests both there and in Britain might have prevailed. Germany under Kaiser Wilhelm was not, strictly speaking, an authoritarian regime. Bismarck had established universal male suffrage in 1871, confident that he could keep the socialist-

leaning workers and the antisocialist businesses in mutually debilitating competition. In 1912, long after Bismarck was gone, the Social Democratic Party
won over one-third of the votes, more than any two other parties combined.[17]
The parties' voices were muted but not silenced by the German constitution
that granted policy-making supremacy in military and foreign policy to the
emperor-appointed cabinet operating independently of the legislature.[18] Seeing how strenuously political parties attempted to influence policy through
debate and delaying tactics, many in Britain, not surprisingly, took heart in
Germany's international commercial engagement and diplomatic civility.[19]
As the British paper *Advocate of Peace* informed its readers in 1912, "The
German Reichstag has 397 members all told, of whom 110 members are
Social Democrats representing 4,250,000 electors. These would undoubtedly
put up a formidable fight against war on the floor of the Reichstag."[20]

Chancellor Theobald von Bethmann Hollweg said to a friend during
the war, "This war torments me. Again and again I ask if it could have been
avoided and what I should have done differently."[21] Confusing for Germany's
foreign partners was that, on military matters, the German high command
not only disregarded the legislature but also outweighed the cautious, if conservative, civilian wing of the German government—including Bethmann
Hollweg and the German ambassador to London Karl Max Lichnowsky.
The drift in German politics favored the impatience of General Helmuth
von Moltke "the Younger," who is reported as saying in a private meeting of
the German high command in December 1912 that he favored war and the
sooner it came the better.[22] He believed that all Europe was in an arms race
and that "war is possible now without defeat, but not in two years!"[23]

In the UK, Prime Minister H. H. Asquith's Liberal Party cabinet sought
to remain at peace with Germany, reflecting British manufacturing companies' interests in the prosperity of the European market as well as the
public's disinclination to concern itself with continental squabbles. British
public opinion had not pressed for war.[24] Instead, opposing sets of alliance
treaties—Britain with France and Russia arrayed against Germany with
Austria-Hungary and Italy—loaded the dice by increasing strategic complexity while narrowing avenues for diplomatic flexibility. As a result, it took
only a Serbian nationalist's assassination of the Austrian crown prince Franz
Ferdinand on June 28, 1914, in Sarajevo, to plunge the peoples of Europe
headlong into a bloodbath on a scale the world had never seen.[25]

The British foreign secretary Edward Grey struggled with German diplomats to find a way out: perhaps Germany might, after all, attack only Russia in response to Russian mobilization against Austria. As Grey was later to relay to the House of Commons, "It was reported to me one day that the German Ambassador [Lichnowsky] had suggested that Germany might remain neutral in a war between Russia and Austria, and also engage not to attack France, if we would remain neutral and secure the neutrality of France. I said at once that, if the German Government thought such an arrangement possible, I was sure we could secure it."[26] The rub was that Britain could not prevent France from making good on its own alliance with Russia.[27] With the alliances thus set in motion, Germany proceeded to launch a stunning two-front attack on France and Russia in August 1914 as soon as Russia invaded the Balkans.[28]

The French Revolution with its *levée en masse* had been a total war fought globally, but World War I stamped deeper on societies across Europe because of better military technology and logistics. Mobilizing at breakneck speed was politically disruptive for all combatant states, nowhere more so than in England, where avoiding continental entanglements had been common sense, broken only occasionally and for only the most serious of threats. England's balancing role on the continent was traditionally limited to the defensive goal of stopping others from infringing on English freedom and prosperity, now including British interests around the world. The English isles had become the seat of a great empire through its global exploits, colonizing lands too weak to fight back. Britain's conquests, centuries earlier than Germany's, made it a champion of the high moral principles of free trade and noninterference.

Britain declared war on Germany on August 4, 1914, as soon as Germany violated Belgian neutrality with a large-scale invasion heading for France.[29] Britain's wartime government mobilized manpower and money on an unprecedented scale, albeit in stages, as public support allowed. In the six weeks between the British declaration of war and the adjournment of the regular session of Commons on September 18, Parliament passed a series of bills strengthening the hand of the cabinet to prosecute the war. On August 6 Prime Minister Asquith received from Commons a vote of credit of one hundred million pounds for the war effort and a supplementary estimate for men in the army of half a million pounds.[30]

On August 7 Commons proposed, in the first of four Defence of the Realm Acts, that the government be given the power to turn people suspected of spying and sabotage over to the military, where they would be tried under court martial "in like manner as if such persons were subject to military law and had in active service committed an offense under section five of the Army Act." Reflecting the extreme reluctance with which the English were willing to give up individual rights and protections, Commons proposed immunity for the convicted from lifetime in prison or death on grounds that the punishments provided for in Section 5 of the Army Act were too dangerous a weapon to place in the hands of a court of summary jurisdiction.[31] The House of Lords went further, rejecting "this tremendous and unprecedented extension of military law" and managed to restore the right of trial to English-born British subjects; foreigners and foreign-born citizens they left under military jurisdiction.[32]

Reginald McKenna, whom Asquith appointed chancellor of the exchequer in May 1915, set about raising war revenue and apportioning it widely across society.[33] The "McKenna Rule," as old as the Glorious Revolution but given a new name, was the principle that the interest payments servicing government debt should not exceed tax revenues lest wars foster inflation and devalue private assets. For the English, wars required government debt, taxation, and the consent of those providing either. McKenna stated matter-of-factly to the Commons on June 21, 1915, "We shall have to find further money, and it is perfectly open to anybody to calculate what. They only have to reckon the time when . . . the mere interest on [government loans] will have exhausted all our surplus revenue, then . . . we must raise fresh taxes."[34]

Reflecting the cross-class composition of the government, revenues were raised both by increasing the number of citizens paying taxes and by raising marginal rates, especially at the upper end.[35] The wartime government more than doubled the tax base, raising the threshold for tax exemption to bring millions of "middle class" taxpayers onto the tax rolls.[36] The government also brokered a kind of labor-capital deal whereby unions agreed to refrain from strikes in exchange for which firms would be responsible for an extraordinary Excess Profit Duty (EPD) for extra returns attributable to the wartime economy.[37]

Although Parliament passed belt-tightening and rights-restricting wartime legislation of various kinds, Asquith's own Liberal Party began to break apart in opposition and disarray.[38] Even if Britain was able to adapt to the needs of war, the Liberal Party, long the champion of individual rights, was less supple. The "war party" among the Liberals and Unionists pushed Asquith aside; in December 1916 David Lloyd George formed a new cabinet without calling new elections, and Asquith took his seat in the opposition benches.[39]

While fighting a desperate war on the continent in 1917, the British government watched with concern the slow-motion collapse of the Russian tsarist government, from the February Revolution to the Bolshevik triumph on November 7.[40] The Russians dropped out of the war, and Germany's redirection of firepower westward would have been catastrophic for the Allied forces had the United States not entered the war in April 1917. Whitehall's sharper worry, however, was the spread of revolutionary agitation to the British labor movement at home. In the historian Eric Hobsbawm's view, although the Labour Party had initially supported the war, "the war had created a mood of revolt against capitalism among the rank and file of workers, such as the Labour moderates were for some years incapable of stemming. The November 1917 Bolshevik Revolution crystallized that mood round the symbol of Russia, and drove the British movement sharply leftward."[41] The Workers' Union, "the most hustling of the general labor unions," grew from a membership of 5,000 in 1910 to 350,000 in 1918.[42] Membership in the federation of unions was more than double that number.

The Harvest of Battle, *by Christopher Nevinson, 1919.*

It was against this background of labor agitation amid wholesale conscription, increased taxation, and rising prices that the coalition government introduced a suffrage expansion bill into the House of Commons in June 1917.[43] The bill, which Parliament passed on February 6, 1918, extended voting eligibility to all men over twenty-one by eliminating property requirements, and to all women over thirty.[44] This "Fourth Reform Bill" enlarged the British electorate by two million men and six million women—nearly a doubling of the voting public—with negligible opposition.

Without exception, the political parties espoused the high moral principle of fairness to the many fighting men who would otherwise return home from the grisly war without full rights of citizenship. Meanwhile universal male and almost-full female suffrage also softened labor radicalism. In the "atrocity election" of 1918 following the Armistice, the Labour Party won 21.5 percent of the vote (compared to about 13 percent for each of the two liberal factions) gaining 15 seats in Parliament over its previous 42. More to the point, the Labour Party became the second-largest party by moving in a centrist direction to widen its appeal.[45] Although the Liberals were nearly destroyed (those who refused to support the government dropping from 272 seats to 36) and Asquith himself lost his seat, the Unionist Conservatives gained even more than Labour, winning a third of the popular vote and increasing their seats from 271 to 379.[46]

In Moscow in March 1919, Lenin gave Labour a verbal thrashing at the first congress of the Communist International (Comintern) for accepting democracy: "The most democratic bourgeois republic is no more than a machine for the suppression of the working class by the bourgeoisie, for the suppression of the working people by a handful of capitalists."[47] Competing for votes, especially in a plurality system like Britain's, forced any party aspiring to rule to move to the political center. In continental countries with proportional representation systems, including Germany, Italy, and France, far left parties were able to survive, which breathed longer life into class divisions and produced bigger gyrations in politics until the postwar period.[48] Lenin did not see that from the point of view of the British working person, the right to the vote was a bird in the hand compared to the two in the bush promised by Communism.

Lenin became even more bilious at the second Comintern congress on August 6, 1920: "The Labour Party is a thoroughly bourgeois party, because,

Lenin speaks at the Second Congress of the Communist International, Petrograd, July 19, 1920.

although made up of workers, it is led by reactionaries, and the worst kind of reactionaries at that, who act quite in the spirit of the bourgeoisie. It is an organisation of the bourgeoisie, which exists to systematically dupe the workers with the aid of the British Noskes and Scheidemanns [the leaders of the German SPD whom he held responsible for the murders of Rosa Luxemburg and Karl Liebknecht and the destruction of their Communist "Spartacus Revolt"].[49]

The expanded British electorate did not expropriate owners of capital, as some might have wished and others had feared.[50] By war's end, the Labour Party sought to build a coalition of workers and middle class against the superrich through a levy on "dead" accumulations of wealth.[51] This produced from Conservatives a profusion of calculations, backed by Inland Revenue (tax officials), that taxing assets now would reduce income tax revenues and death taxes later.[52] The 1918 Conservative government rejected indirect taxes for fear of triggering social conflict and instead adopted a modest corporate income tax in 1920.[53] The tax (as in the United States) was not an instrument of income redistribution by a poorer electorate but a measure taken by a Conservative government to retire war debt, both to share widely the burdens of war and to prevent inflation that could undermine private assets in the future. Labour's first chance in government, from January to

October 1924, when it was heavily defeated, was likewise tentative in its search for fiscal solidity.[54]

+ + +

France, in World War I as so often throughout history, fought in self-defense against invaders. As with the British, the French required no hand wringing in the decision to fight; this was a war of survival, not of alliance politics or of forward defense. Rapid and full military mobilization was accepted with resignation, and a unity government was formed out of a fractious welter of political parties of left and right. A total of 8.7 million, or 75 percent of French men between twenty and fifty-five, would serve during the war; of them 1.3 million soldiers, or 3.4 percent of the French population, would die.[55]

All French men, irrespective of income and debt, already had the right to vote, having won it in the run-up to the previous war with Germany. The gravitational force of the Franco-German War pulled the French political pendulum—which after the 1789 Revolution had swung far to the left, then far to the right—back to the middle.[56] The elections after the adoption of universal suffrage resulted not in massive wealth redistribution but in a series of factory laws that improved working conditions.[57] In the early twentieth century Prime Minister Georges Clemenceau's Radical Party also tacked right to win business support and crushed a series of worker strikes. In reply to friends who had expected him to take the side of the striking workers, Clemenceau replied, "I am the same man I always was, but now I am on the other side of the barricade."[58] In 1905 two splinter groups formed the French Section of the Workers International (SFIO) in protest, but Germany's invasion of 1914 once again cemented a national unity government and undercut pacifist variants of socialism in France.[59]

Even as the war dragged on, France did not expand suffrage beyond its base of French-born fighting men, either to women, who were the mothers, sisters, and daughters of the dead, or to the North African and West African colonial subjects, who spilled their own blood for France. Sexism and racism ran deep, or at least many citizens worried about how the new voters would cast their ballots.[60]

As soon as early losses on the Western Front signaled that the war would be protracted and bloody, mass recruitment of soldiers in colonial French Africa began. The French military recruited 270,000 soldiers from Africa, including 85,000 from Algeria and 23,000 from Morocco.[61] Prime Minister Clemenceau undertook a second round of colonial conscription in November 1917. Anticolonialist though he was, Clemenceau had grown desperate while waiting for the Americans to arrive in force. All told, 450,000 Africans fought for France during the war, in addition to about 125,000 who were recruited to work in French factories. The French did not undertake African recruitment lightly, for local political activists in Algeria and Senegal in particular expected to win political concessions in exchange for supporting conscription. For the same reason, French colonists feared for their economic holdings in Africa.[62] They need not have worried. Although it is impossible to say what would have happened had the Americans not helped to bring the war to an end in 1918, only 256 Algerians gained French citizenship in connection with war-related reforms in the French colonies.[63]

Meanwhile Britain's adoption of nearly universal suffrage in 1918 on the heels of universal conscription is evidence that war strengthened the political hand of those supplying the resources with which to fight: the men supplying manpower in the trenches. The timing of Britain's final suffrage expansion is also consistent with a well-known argument that government widens the franchise to preempt revolution from below.[64] British labor was restive, and the Russian Revolution put the possible consequences of government unresponsiveness on full public display. But recall that the French elite revoked the franchise granted in the Revolution and viewed the 1830 and 1848 revolts with revulsion until war with Germany made common cause of manpower and money.

War and industrialization appear to be particularly potent in combination, as they were in France and Germany in the mid-nineteenth century. But sometimes governments manage to avoid both revolution and defeat with the use of coercion rather than making concessions.[65] Sometimes the fear of one's own population exceeds the fear of military defeat, as when the Polish aristocracy's reluctance to arm peasants hastened the demise of the Polish republic of nobles. Scandinavian countries adopted universal suffrage by the end of World War I, as did the United States and Britain, but the timing is deceptive: Denmark, Finland, Iceland, Norway, and Sweden sat out of the Great War. This would seem to impugn the idea that democratic consolidation in these countries came from war mobilization. Upon closer inspection, however, war played a role even there.

As we saw in the nineteenth century, military mobilization during the Napoleonic Wars had shaken European societies to their roots by unleashing energy for freedoms that in many industrializing countries put labor and capital on a collision course. Denmark, which remained substantially agrarian into the early twentieth century, was an exception. Indeed, Danes' "liberal" agitation for political freedoms and economic rights in 1848 carried them nearly to universal male suffrage in 1849, although the legislative power remained jointly vested in the king and parliament until a new constitution in 1901 established popular sovereignty.[66]

Danish suffrage expansion was helped, not hurt, by the common ground between the economic elite, who might worry about relinquishing privilege, and the commoners. Danish peasants were not in a revolutionary mood because from reforms beginning in the 1780s, many had become freeholders and now shared in the returns from grain and meat exports that found ready markets across Europe, especially Britain.[67] When war with Prussia broke out in 1848 over the Duchy of Schleswig, opposition in the Danish Rigsdag for full male suffrage gave way to enthusiasm for national mobilization.[68] Far from moderating the conflict, political liberals seeking greater domestic freedoms were also among the hawks on both sides of the border. The collapse of Danish military ambitions after defeat in the second Schleswig war undermined, for some decades, the smallholders and urban workers who held a majority in the Folketing, the legislature's lower house.[69] Then in 1901, in response to Norwegian and Swedish saber rattling, Denmark amended its constitution to vest legislative sovereignty formally in its more representative lower house.[70]

Norway too adopted full male enfranchisement decades before World War I. Regional conflicts had pushed universal male suffrage there along as well. Part of Denmark since the Union of Kalmar (1397), the victors in the Napoleonic Wars transferred Norway to Sweden in 1814, as Sweden's prize for joining forces against Napoleon. Norwegians, forced by rocky terrain to export fish and timber and carry goods on their merchant fleet for their livelihood, chafed at the union because Swedish trade policy hurt Norwegian exports.[71] As tensions rose between Norway and Sweden in the 1880s and 1890s, Norway's left party (Venstre) gained political ground on a combative platform of nationalism and separation from Sweden. In 1892 a coalition left-right government began a program of military readiness: it fortified the border and in 1898 bought four dreadnoughts from Great Britain. In 1898

Norwegian soldiers mobilized at the border with Sweden in 1905.

the Venstre government ordered universal military conscription and at the same time extended universal male suffrage. This got the attention of Sweden, which at four million citizens had twice Norway's population, but a war would have been costly.[72] After a Norwegian plebiscite on August 13, 1905, in which 99.5 percent of Norwegian male voters demanded dissolution of the union, Sweden conceded.[73]

Sweden, which had been the "hammer of Europe" during the Thirty Years' War, had meanwhile gone from being a full-franchise military-democracy—the only country of its day with a fourth estate for peasants in the national parliament—to a constitutional monarchy dominated by economic elites.[74] Sweden's abundant stores of iron ore powered its industrialization and created a class of industrialists, some of them of landed gentry origins, with a growing share of income and property.[75] Although Swedish peasants had retained control of the iron mines and small-scale smelting forges until the eighteenth century, international competition in iron production from Britain, Germany, and the United States pushed Swedish peasants out of the iron bar business and triggered a process of industrial consolidation in Sweden known as *bruksdoden,* "the death of the forges."[76] As peasants lost their supplemental income from mining, many emigrated;

between 1840 and 1915 over a million Swedes out of a total population of five million emigrated, many to the United States.[77]

Although Sweden remained the larger power, war against a newly militarized Norway would have been bruising at the very least. Weakened by the loss of manpower to emigration, the Swedish government overhauled its military recruitment system, instituting universal conscription in 1901. In 1906 a parliamentary commission recommended universal male suffrage, which the Swedish Riksdag adopted.[78] Women got the vote ten years later, in 1919.[79]

Finland became a duchy of Russia in 1809, during the Napoleonic Wars, after having been part of Sweden's "outback" for six centuries prior to that.[80] Nearly a century later, at the beginning of the twentieth century, Russia's attempt to absorb the Finnish militia into the Russian army's command structure ignited a Finnish separatist movement.[81] Without Russia's permission, the Finnish Diet in 1906 adopted universal suffrage for women and men over twenty-four who had no debt, but Finland's population of three million was no match for Russian overlords, even overlords in the throes of their own revolutionary chaos.[82] Finland might have continued on the peaceful path of Nordic democracy had it not been for its proximity to Russia, which precipitated a civil war in 1918, pitting Finnish "Reds" with Russian Bolshevik backing against "Whites" led by former officers of the Finnish Army.[83] The Whites won the war in three months with the support of German troops, who drove the Red Guard leadership into exile in Russia.[84] The White leader, General Carl Gustaf Mannerheim, suggested in his victory speech in Helsinki that the Finnish people consider anointing a strong leader who could remain above partisan strife, but general elections the following year in 1919 returned an array of political parties, among which the Social Democrats had the largest seat share.[85] The Scandinavian countries of Norway, Sweden, Denmark, and Finland all democratized in response to war.

✦ ✦ ✦

Twentieth-century Germany and Japan cut more directly against the proposition that mobilizing for modern war consolidated the democratic republican form of government by pulling capital and labor together into effective coalition. Both Germany and Japan moved in a democratic direction after World War I, but both succumbed to variants of authoritarian rule that presided over exceptionally successful war efforts. The experiences of these countries underscore the contingent nature of democratic politics and the possibility that, even in contemporary times, a population forfeits its bargaining leverage when it falls prey to fear, dread, anger, and even patriotism that strategic rulers employ to make virtue synonymous with support for the regime.

If Germany's military decisions in 1914 had been left to the civilians— Chancellor Bethmann Hollweg and Ambassador Lichnowsky, let alone the party leaders of the Reichstag—Germany probably would not have blundered into World War I. Even assuming that no one could have known in advance the blood price and material costs of the protracted war, or that the United States would come to the rescue of Britain and France, the enthusiasm for empire and ensuing competition with the British navy for control of the high seas was generated principally by the military itself.

Thucydides tried to make the case that democracies are especially prone to making catastrophic mistakes, as evidenced by Athens' rash decisions to slaughter the Mytileneans or to execute their best generals for letting Athenian sailors perish at sea. He might have been right that democratic publics are vulnerable to emotional arguments appealing to tribalist instincts, but democratic free speech has the countervailing possibility of bringing to light obvious logical flaws. The fantasy that Germany could stun the world to submission with lightning-fast grabs on two fronts bears the hallmarks of military men talking to one another in an echo chamber.

That, at least, was how things looked to many destitute, exhausted Germans at war's end. In July 1918 the Reichstag parties, spanning a wide political spectrum, had passed a Peace Resolution.[86] Knowing their impotence to act on it, they also called for the constitutional adoption of full parliamentary sovereignty in place of a monarchy with limited legislative accountability.[87] The question was how to bring the kaiser and his supporters to their knees. The parties were ready to take advantage of the political vacuum caused by General Erich Ludendorff's nervous breakdown at the end of September 1918. In October Kaiser Wilhelm fired Ludendorff, who alternated between tears and tirades against Jews and Social Democrats for embracing peace prematurely.[88] Changing military command was not enough to save Kaiser Wilhelm's militarist cabinet. The interim government, under the chancellorship of Prince Maximilian of Baden, which had already acceded to U.S. president Woodrow Wilson's Fourteen Points, collapsed when revolution broke out in Germany in November 1918.

1918 New York Times *front page reporting Germany's surrender and the end of the Great War.*

The New York Times's 42-point headlines on November 11, 1918, conveyed the chaos of the German vortex: ARMISTICE SIGNED, END OF THE WAR! BERLIN SEIZED BY REVOLUTIONISTS; NEW CHANCELLOR BEGS FOR ORDER; OUSTED KAISER FLEES TO HOLLAND. It began on November 4, when some eighty thousand sailors at Kiel mutinied rather than fight more pointless battles at sea; they were joined by workers in cities all over Germany, half a million in Berlin alone, striking for better conditions. Kaiser Wilhelm abdicated at the insistence of the Social Democrats and over the objections of the nonsocialist parties, but it was too little, too late to forestall months of bloodshed.[89] Apart from a small left-wing group that had been harassed and jailed during the war for its antimilitarist socialism, most of the Germans who took the revolutionary side in November 1918 wanted two objectives that were already in train but not yet fully visible: peace and democratization (or peace and bread, depending on whom you asked).[90] Friedrich Ebert, the leader of the Social Democratic Party who had formed a socialist-centrist legislative coalition, was in the unenviable position of suppressing the revolution violently with the help of the so-called Freikorps (paramilitary units) in return for the army's support of his government.[91]

The new democratic constitution that was promulgated on August 13, 1919 (named Weimar, after the city where the constitutional assembly met) had a short life.[92] With the wisdom of hindsight, it is easy to spot design flaws: a pure proportional representation system had the result of proliferating small parties that championed narrow interests, against which background the president's and the legislature's shared power to dismiss the cabinet set the stage for deadlock.[93] As the constitutional adviser Max Weber perhaps had intended, the game board tilted toward strong executives accountable directly to the people.[94] A humiliating defeat, the loss of territory, staggering war reparations owed to the French and the British, hyperinflation, and then a Great Depression that undercut prosperity with which to pay the reparations gave potential demagogues a steady stream of bad news with which to fuel public passions.[95]

Weimar successfully used the emergency powers in Article 48 of the new constitution to deal with the hyperinflation and from 1924 experienced a "golden" period even in the face of antisystem parties. It was not until the Depression hit in the early 1930s that the Nazis experienced large electoral gains and the senile president Hindenberg fatefully asked Hitler to organize a government. It did not help Weimar democracy that the constitution allowed the president to get things done with decrees over the heads of legislators tied up in knots.[96]

Hitler's intoxicating cocktails of intimidation and false hope won him 36.8 percent of the vote in the presidential election in March 1932 and 37.4 percent of the popular vote in the Reichstag elections of July 1932. Although President Paul von Hindenburg was elected to a second seven-year term in March 1932, Hitler's National Socialists gained a plurality of seats in the Reichstag in July.[97] From this political base, Hitler worked methodically to consolidate power. In January 1933 President Hindenburg appointed Hitler as chancellor, believing that only Hitler could control the four hundred thousand strong "brownshirts" or "storm troopers" (*Sturmabteilung*, SA).[98]

When the Reichstag building burned in February 27, 1933, the Nazis blamed Jews, Communists, and left-leaning politicians, whom they hounded and slaughtered. The public responded by giving Hitler an overwhelming Reichstag majority in the elections called on March 5, one week later. The

Hitler and Ernst Röhm reviewing the Nazi paramilitary storm troopers (also known as brownshirts) in Nuremberg in 1933.

following month Hitler ordered a nationwide boycott against all Jewish establishments in Germany. In October he withdrew from the Disarmament Conference and pulled Germany out of the League of Nations. At the end of June 1934, when Hitler killed more than eighty-five SA leaders including Ernst Röhm, whose street violence upset the German sense of order, Hindenburg thanked him.[99] Protected by Hindenburg's eagerness for domestic stability, Hitler also killed the conservative general and former chancellor Kurt von Schleicher and right-wing politician Gustav Ritter von Kahr.[100]

Upon Hindenburg's death a month later, on August 2, 1934, Hitler was unopposed in making himself Germany's sole executive; he combined the posts of president and chancellor.[101] Britain's prime minister Neville Chamberlain, in agreeing to German annexation of the Sudeten area of Czechoslovakia in September 1938, thought he was quenching a reasonable thirst, not fueling bottomless ambitions. Six months later, in March 1939, Hitler grabbed the rest of Czechoslovakia, in violation of the British-German understanding, and invaded Poland on September 1. Two days later, awakened to the danger of Hitler's territorial aggrandizement, Britain and France declared war on the Reich.[102]

By killing countless rivals and dissidents, Hitler had demonstrated his insistence on unswerving loyalty at the cost of death. When he reintroduced compulsory military service on March 16, 1935, he promised nothing in return but the opportunity to fight and die, if necessary, for the Fatherland.[103] In six years he expanded the army from the treaty-limited size of 100,000 men-at-arms to 3.6 million. Versailles had disallowed Germany to maintain an air force, but by 1938 the Reich had 385,000 airmen, more than 4,000 aircraft, and over 200,000 industrial workers in the production of airplanes and engines. The navy remained small compared to Great Britain's, although the number of sailors increased from 15,000 to 78,000 by 1939.[104]

With a combination of inducements and threats, Hitler corralled German heavy industry into his mad dash to war.[105] Some industrialists, particularly in Ruhr valley mining, supported the Nazis in hopes of quelling trade unionism; others hoped to benefit from getting rid of Jewish competition.[106] But some worried about the costs to business of Hitler's command-and-control populism. The German Federation of Chambers of Commerce warned in its monthly bulletin in October 1932 (before such public musings became a one-way ticket to the morgue), "The economy, employers and workers, may at best express their wishes; they have no means of seeing that these will be met even in their own organs. Their organizations will be turned into government departments, whose heads will be civil servants, and those they represent will have no legal right to choose or remove them. In the National Socialist programme the all-powerful 'total' state becomes a reality, economic self-government a mere form."[107]

In 1934 Horace Greeley Hjalmar Schacht, the Reichsbank president who had halted the explosive inflation in 1923 and Hitler's first minister of economics, introduced a "New Plan" giving the government control of foreign exchange and raw materials allocation, in order to reduce its external and internal deficits.[108] Schacht accommodated Hitler by creating a system of "mefo bills" (promissory notes) that artificially took some of the government deficit off the books.[109] Schacht also developed the autobahn system of highways crisscrossing Germany, but Hitler replaced him in 1936 with Hermann Göring, who expressed greater enthusiasm for centralized control of the economy in service of rapid rearmament than Schacht favored. Göring froze prices and set wages (the Nazis had already smashed trade unions in 1933), but rather than nationalize industry as the Soviets did, the Nazis controlled industrial production by rationing inputs, including raw materials and foreign exchange, and by quantitatively restricting the production of nonmilitary goods.[110]

The government's large military procurements, paid for by mefo bills, were at least partly responsible for a stunning bounce in corporate profitability: the rate of return on capital in Germany industry grew from the 1931 nadir of negative 7 percent to over 15 percent in 1935 and 17 percent in 1940.[111] For example, Interessensgemeinschaft (IG) Farben, a chemical company founded in 1926, grew to over two hundred thousand employees by the late 1930s producing explosives and synthetic fuel.[112] When the auto industry insisted that Hitler's wish for affordable family cars in wartime Germany was untenable, an enraged Hitler commissioned the willing engineer Ferdinand Porsche to build the Volkswagen Beetle with artificially cheap steel and aluminum; still the project failed, and not a single civilian was able to buy a Volkswagen during the war.[113]

Hitler's false sense of invincibility, exacerbated by successful gambles against Poland, France, and Russia, made him impervious to prudent advice on military strategy.[114] His decision in 1941 to exterminate all the Jews of Europe added a logistical nightmare to the war effort.[115] In October 1942 he insisted that Erwin Rommel's outgunned Panzer units defend the German position at El Alamein, Egypt, with the result that 59,000 of Rommel's 96,000 men were killed, wounded, or captured. Because Hitler refused to allow the Sixth Army to break out from Stalingrad when defeat was certain in early 1943, 194,000 of the 285,000 soldiers died.[116] Hitler's refrain was always the same: "It will not be the first time in history that the stronger will has triumphed over the enemy's stronger battalions. You can show your troops no other road than to victory or death."[117]

Many German military commanders could see that Hitler was pushing Germany off a cliff.[118] After several coup attempts failed, Hitler was left to insist, quite literally, on suicide.[119] By the time he took his own life on April 30, 1945, 4.5 million German soldiers had been killed or wounded, nearly 20 percent of the German male population of military age. Over five million Jews, along with Gypsies and other "undesirables," had perished in death camps. The Germans also killed millions of Ukrainians in their attempt to grab the Ukrainian "bread basket," millions of Poles, and millions of Soviet prisoners of war.[120] Retreating German armies from occupied lands left millions of German and local civilians to die at the hands of advancing Russian troops.[121] Obviously Hitler could not have accomplished so much violence without the complicity of a large number of people, including some of those who attempted, when the opportunity arose, to take him down. However history assigns responsibility, there is no gainsaying that Germany's mobilization of manpower and resources was a stupendous achievement, driven forward by the knowledge that the odds of victory grew steadily worse with time. Hitler did not need to restrict the franchise; he outlawed all political opposition.

Hitler was a madman, but Japan's role in World War II is a vivid demonstration of desperate gambles made by sane military leaders. In 1868 a group of rebels, mostly high-ranking bureaucrats from four western warlord domains, had overthrown the Tokugawa Shogunate in a virtually bloodless revolution. They restored Emperor Meiji as the titular head of the nation (hence "Meiji Restoration"), but they held tightly to the reins of power themselves as the emperor's privy councilors. Their short-term goal was to rid Japan of the unequal treaties that the Americans and British had foisted on them in the mid-1800s.[122] More ambitiously, they sought to forge a prosperous and powerful nation. Traveling the world for ideas on how to structure a government capable of carrying out these accomplishments, the Meiji oligarchs settled in 1891 on Bismarck's constitution, which subordinated parliamentary representation to the emperor, his cabinet, and his military.[123]

Sovereignty was vested in the emperor, who chose his prime minister and military chiefs from among the Meiji oligarchs and their protégés. As in Wilhelmine Germany, the military and civilian leaderships were formally accountable only to the emperor, who was more or less a figurehead, leaving the oligarchs in the driver's seat for all practical purposes. That, after all, had been their intention. As the oligarchs passed away, the military grew increasingly independent, given the constitutional provision that the military could use the previous year's budget in the event that parliament failed to pass a new one.

Still, parliament passed a bill of universal suffrage for men over twenty-five in 1925, enlarging the electorate from the small slice of propertied men that the Meiji constitution had enfranchised. The legislature could often hold up budget increases and repeatedly locked horns with the military over foreign policy and the budget needed to support it.[124] The final showdown took place in 1931 and 1932, when the military's Manchurian arm, the Kwantung Army, provoked Chinese forces to fight as a pretext for annexing Manchuria.[125] Rather than heed the parties' request for a diplomatic solution, the military launched a coup on May 15, 1932, killing Prime Minister Inukai Tsuyoshi. Admiral Saito Makoto became prime minister, ending Japan's prewar experiment with parliamentary democracy.[126]

Japan's massive business combines (*zaibatsu*) adapted, for the most part, to military rule by shifting production to armaments and war matériel. Like Germany, the military in 1937 created a Planning Agency (Kikakuin) through which to centralize control of raw materials, financing, production, and prices. Also like Germany, the government prohibited the payment of corporate dividends, to save more retained earnings for government-directed investment.[127] The South Manchurian Railway Company illustrates what

*A 1940 postcard showing the 10,000 kilometers of track
of Japan's South Manchuria Railway Company.*

could happen when the *zaibatsu* balked at the military's plans: the military found other willing partners. The South Manchurian Railway, which Japan had taken from Russian in the Russo-Japanese War of 1904–5, connected rich lodes of coal in western Manchuria to ports of Lushun, Andong, Yingkou, and Dalian for shipment to Japan.[128] In 1906 the Japanese government, with two of the largest Japanese *zaibatsu*, Mitsui and Mitsubishi, established a joint venture called the South Manchurian Railway Company to operate the mines, railway, hotels, schools, libraries, and hospitals for the Japanese colonists who would move from Japan and settle along the railway's "zone." Mitsui and Mitsubishi, for whom China proper was a large export market, pulled out of the venture when the Japanese military started a war with China in 1936. Nissan, an upstart company that took the place of Mitsui and Mitsubishi in Manchuria, became an industrial behemoth specializing in military production.[129]

The Japanese military government, lacking carrots, used "thought-guidance" and sticks to conscript an army of 5.5 million men out of a population of 73 million: it stoked patriotism through emperor-worship orthodoxy, fueled collective outrage at Japan's international pariah status with state-controlled propaganda, and spied on and bullied dissidents by military police with the help of a tight network of neighborhood associations.[130] Like Nazi Germany, Japan by war's end struggled to motivate soldiers to fight for a lost cause. Its military leaders were slow to recognize the hopelessness of the Pacific War against a richer and militarily superior United States, choosing instead to believe the timeworn falsehood of mind over matter.[131] Their only hope was that the Americans would become demoralized and overstretched as the Nazi regime pinned down Allied resources in Europe.

Down to the last few months of firepower and money by 1944, the military converged on the desperate thought that a massive attack of suicide bombers (*kamikaze*) on the U.S. fleets would dissuade an invasion of the Japanese islands. (The credit for the kamikaze idea goes to Onishi Takijiro, a navy vice-admiral who himself would commit suicide upon Japan's surrender ten months later, apologizing as he did so to the thousands of dead young pilots.)[132] Kamikaze pilots needed only minimal training: learning how to take off is far easier than mastering how to land. They would also need only half the fuel: the trip was one-way by design. On October 25, 1944, the American fleet off the coast of the Philippines was stunned by a succession

Japanese kamikaze pilots before leaving for combat.
1944. Kamikaze pilots, often university students drafted toward
the end of the war, were not given the choice to opt out.

of planes that began crash-diving, one after the other, into American ships. First an A6M Zero fighter struck the *St. Lo*, a U.S. escort carrier, killing 114 of its crew and sinking the ship in less than an hour. Scores of these human missiles kept coming, taking down 34 American ships in the Leyte Gulf. As demoralizing as this new weapon was to American seamen, it failed to halt the American advance. The United States lost 300 ships and 15,000 casualties to kamikaze attacks, a good ratio for the Japanese losses of 5,000 pilots. But the United States had enough reserve power to take the Philippines, Iwo Jima, and then Okinawa in the face of Japan's last-ditch, suicidal defenses.[133]

One unfortunate effect, for Japan, of the kamikaze attacks was to provoke American brutality in return, on the conviction that even Japanese soldiers waving white flags were tricksters prepared to defend their islands to the last man.[134] In the last months of the war, the U.S. Navy psychiatrist Alec Leighton struggled to convince the U.S. military that Japanese soldiers needed only assurances that they would not be harmed if they dropped their weapons.[135] Truman decided to drop the atomic bombs on Hiroshima and Nagasaki, one after the other on August 6 and 9, 1945, in part to spare American lives in the event of man-to-man combat with superhuman Japanese soldiers.

✦ ✦ ✦

It would be hard to make the case that Germany's and Japan's 1920s experiences with universal suffrage and parliamentary democracy influenced their strategies for military mobilization. The authoritarian regimes in those countries appealed directly to their publics over the heads of the party leaders of the previous democratic regimes, and they suppressed dissent ruthlessly, especially from the incipient trade union movements born of industrialization and nurtured by the popular vote. Even more strikingly, Russia and China managed to harness their publics to the yoke of heroic military efforts without experiencing a genuine democratic interlude other than fake elections.

These four cases suggest the limits of the logic that we lay out in this book, of military threat forcing leaders into a corner from which they can emerge only by granting broader political freedoms. Intimidation and brutality can substitute for political concessions, at least in the short run. The wartime leadership of Germany and Japan brooked no dissent to the bitter end. The revolutionary energy that pulsated through the Soviet Union and China in the 1940s and 1950s was more like a cattle prod to corral their own citizens than anything resembling accountability to mobilized masses.[136]

Lenin had expected that class warfare would destroy the White Army; he was irked that an urban-rural divide undermined his own efforts at Communist mobilization in the apolitical countryside.[137] Wealthier farmers declared themselves neutral and formed local militias to keep out the civil war.[138] In the end, although the Red Army recruited 5.5 million men, no more than half a million of those, it is estimated, were adequately trained and armed. According to historian Orlando Figes's calculations, no more men fought in the Russian civil war as a percentage of population than fought, for example, in the English civil war of the 1640s; and of those, many were fighting because of the free food.[139] Also like the civil war in Finland that was raging simultaneously, the Russian Revolution was fought between two groups of highly motivated partisans trying with limited success to mobilize the wider population.[140] The Soviets, viewed as urban snobs, got better at recruiting peasants against the White Army only by promising land redistribution.[141] Peasant support remained contingent on improved livelihood.

After the 1921 famine in Ukraine and southern Russia, Lenin backed off temporarily from forcing peasants to join collectives, but a decade later Stalin killed millions to collectivize agricultural production that would pay for Soviet industrialization.[142] His rationing system, designed to outsmart peasants' disinclination to supply all the grain they produced for central distribution, caused a famine in Ukraine and southern Russia, in which millions of peasants starved to death in 1932 and 1933. Some accounts say 7.5 million peasants starved, while other estimates go as high as 9 million.[143]

The Soviet Union under Stalin mobilized a larger percentage of its population during World War II than any other combatant state save Germany (16 percent of the Soviet population fought compared to 19 percent of Germany's). Soviet war deaths as a percentage of population were even greater than Germany's: 13 percent of Soviet citizens (25.6 million people, of whom 8.7 million were soldiers) compared to Germany's 9 percent (6.5 million, of whom 4.5 million were soldiers). Soviet production of munitions was also of heroic proportions, given its great cost to the civilian economy and consumption.[144] Between 1940 and 1942, as men, factories, and livestock were redirected to the war effort, supplies of food and basic goods fell by half or more; people grew weak and susceptible to disease. The situation in Leningrad, which was blockaded in 1942, was of course unspeakably worse.[145]

The Soviet Union's extraordinary war effort owes much to Germany's invasion, which terrified the people in its path. For them, this was a war of self-defense rather than an optional war of aggrandizement. If fear of invading armies was not enough, Stalin had demonstrated that, like Hitler, he would kill anyone he suspected of shirking or disloyalty. Millions of disobedient Soviet citizens were killed or subjected to soul-crushing deprivation in the gulag before, during, and after the war.[146]

For example, Alexander Solzhenitsyn, recruited into the Soviet army in 1941 at the age of twenty-three, was promoted to the rank of captain and fought, among other places, in the battles of Leningrad and Kursk. In January 1945, during the Battle of Königsberg, he was arrested and shipped to the Lubianka prison in Moscow, where he was interrogated and sentenced to eight years of imprisonment.[147] His crime: from the battlefield he had written letters to a friend, which were picked up by censors; in them he had criticized Stalin without mentioning his name. "I thought he had betrayed Leninism and was responsible for the defeats of the first phase of the war, that he was a weak theoretician and that his language was primitive. In my youthful recklessness I put all these thoughts down on paper."[148]

✦ ✦ ✦

Mao Zedong, like Lenin and Stalin, was a master manipulator of "revolution from above," in political scientist Theda Skocpol's phrase.[149] From the outset, Mao adapted Marxism-Leninism to China's rural demographics, against opposition from ideological purists. He clashed with leaders of the Chinese Communist Party in the 1920s, including founder Chen Duxiu and Zhang Guotao who, as literal followers of Marx and Lenin, nurtured the class struggle of urban workers. Mao remained undeterred after unsuccessful urban uprisings in Nanchang, Wuhan, and Guangzhou in 1925. In 1927 he wrote, "In a very short time, in China's central, southern and northern provinces, several hundred million peasants will rise like a mighty storm, like a hurricane, a force so swift and violent that no power, however great, will be able to hold it back."[150]

In 1934, pressed on all sides by Chiang Kai-shek's advancing Nationalist (Kuomintang or KMT) armies, Mao convinced his comrades to retreat on a "Long March" to the rugged mountains of Yunnan, with an army whose ranks swelled with peasant-soldiers willing to endure unimaginable hardships in the hopes of ousting China's landowning class.[151] On this trek to Yunnan, in southwestern China, and then to the caves of Yan'an in the northeast, where the Chinese Communist Party established its headquarters in 1935–38, Mao worked out his plan for guerrilla warfare: "The guerrilla campaigns being waged in China today are a page in history that has no precedent. Their influence will not be confined solely to China in her present anti-Japanese war but will be worldwide. . . . China is a country half colonial and half feudal. . . . These factors favor a protracted war; they favor the application of mobile warfare and guerrilla operations."[152]

Mao's genius was to abandon cities and railway zones that were Nationalist strongholds and the principal targets of Japanese occupation. At Stalin's urging, he held out an olive leaf to Chiang Kai-shek, and the two formed a short-lived United Front on December 25, 1937. All the while both sides competed for loyalty and troops for the inevitable showdown between them.[153] Once the Japanese left in 1945, China, like so many other postwar countries, became a scene of early Cold War shadowboxing: the United States funded Chiang's armies while the Soviet Union turned Manchuria's enormous stashes of Japanese armaments over to the Communists. In October 1949 the outmaneuvered Chiang Kai-shek fled to Taiwan with thousands of his men, leaving China to the Red Army.[154]

A population of disaffected peasants welcomed the Communist victory, but conspiracy theories and political struggles soon took millions of lives, as did famines exacerbated by collectivist experiments gone awry.[155] Mao, whose ascent to power had required dealing ruthlessly with rivals, seemed to thrive on continual uproar: mass meetings to expropriate the assets of the relatively well-off, public executions of dissidents, campaigns to promote one or another form of collective production or to root out one or another form of counterrevolutionary thought.[156]

The Korean War was China's first international challenge in the context of what Mao understood as American encirclement. According to a September 1950 pamphlet issued by the political department of the People's Liberation Army (PLA), "U.S. imperialists are trying to do the same as Japanese imperialists have done to China, namely, to seize Korea first and invade China second. . . . U.S. imperialists are the most dangerous enemy of the Chinese people."[157] The PLA's recruitment drive showcased KMT (Nationalist) defectors who described American involvement in the civil war against the Communists, recounted great atrocities committed by the Nationalists

Captured Chinese soldiers at the United Nations' prisoner-of-war camp at Pusan in Korea. Many of them were formerly KMT soldiers whom Mao sent to fight in Korea in exchange for promises of exoneration.

during the war, and then deflated the image of American military might by explaining that American troops were "spoiled playboys" who would wither in combat.[158] Nevertheless volunteers did not sign up as quickly as Mao wished; five successive mass campaigns not only raised the rhetorical decibel level to bullhorn proportions but also offered material incentives.[159] The Land Reform Law of June 1950 exempted the families of volunteers from the category of "landlord," who were designated political enemies for having leeched off of peasants. This favor, if delivered, would be worth real blood and money.[160]

Over a million soldiers in China's "volunteer army" helped Kim Il-sung fight UN troops to a standstill in Korea, but the price China paid was staggering. The Chinese used their superiority in numbers to compensate for inferior equipment—sometimes called "human wave" action by the U.S. troops. Caught up in ongoing ideological wars at home, Mao reneged on the promises made to the families of volunteers he deemed politically incorrect.[161] In 1958 he purged top army officers who were out of sync with his concept of perpetual revolution, undermining the PLA's attempts to develop a unified command structure capable of modern warfare.[162] As long as China faced no real external threat, Mao was free to use the PLA as a tool of his own domestic empire.[163]

✦ ✦ ✦

Unlike the revolutions of the nineteenth century, during the course of which antiauthoritarian liberals of the propertied classes became alarmed by the growing power of the working class, wars of the twentieth century pulled money and manpower together in collective self-defense. Britain's cross-class wartime government adopted full manhood suffrage and the corporate tax, one after the other, in recognition of national vulnerability in the face of the German threat. Setting aside class conflict to raise taxes helped the British government grapple with what could have been the serious inflation that was to plague postwar Germany. America instituted the corporate income tax during World War I in support of war matériel, but the physical distance across the Atlantic made it possible to undermobilize the American population and thereby to leave American blacks effectively outside the franchise in the southern states. Although France had already extended the right to vote to fighting men during the nineteenth-century struggle with Germany, there too the experience of the war nurtured a belief in cross-class coexistence and alternation in government.

Franchise extensions in Norway, Sweden, and Finland provide additional clues about the democratizing tug of war: workers' movements of the 1840s may have contributed to the demand for political voice, but the economic and landed elites were unmoved to make political concessions until national military exigencies increased the value of a patriotic and mobilized mass public. Norway gave its male citizens the right to vote in 1898 when it was gearing up for a war with Sweden; Finland adopted universal suffrage in 1906 during its fight with Russia; and Sweden adopted universal male suffrage in 1909 when fully enfranchised Norwegian citizens voted with near unanimity to secede from Sweden by force. Although the British enfranchisement of 1918 could be read as a prophylactic response of the elite to the frightening specter of possible contagion from the Russian Revolution, the Scandinavian countries—as a group, the most "social democratic" in the world today—expanded the franchise before that calculus was on the table.

Still, the collapse of democracy in Germany and Japan illustrates that, as in centuries past, coercion can substitute for democratic concession. Both countries also clearly ran into strategic and operational trouble by ignoring information that democratic structures would very likely have afforded their leaders. The problem was not only the delusions of a crazy man like Hitler; in Japan too, military planning was confounded by the refusal of low-ranked and vulnerable men at the bottom of a vertical ladder to provide, and then be blamed for, disagreeable information. With their security in office several steps removed from popular support, the military leadership was emboldened to take big and foolish gambles at enormous cost to Japanese citizens.

As in Germany and Japan, the Soviet and Chinese leaders mounted stupendous war efforts without giving away political control, but the differences between the Soviet and Chinese cases are telling. Germany's invasion of the Soviet Union in 1941 motivated Russian citizens to fight for their survival, greatly aiding Stalin's recruitment campaign. Mao had far more trouble raising the "People's Volunteer Army" to fight against "American aggression" on the Korean Peninsula, a situation to which he responded by threatening former Nationalist sympathizers with persecution unless they volunteered.

In both cases, the sheer size of their populations meant that enormous numbers of men were used as cannon fodder despite the regimes' tenuous basis of domestic support.

Barrington Moore, one of the most perceptive social historians of the twentieth century, blamed Russia's and China's agrarian economies for their failure to democratize: "no bourgeoisie, no democracy."[164] A commercial class might demand representation, but as we know from nineteenth-century history, economic elites could rarely overthrow monarchies on their own. Even so, they shunned the working class, whose interests partly collided with their own. More than fear of revolution from below, an external military threat was what shifted the calculus of the economic elite in favor of mass democracy. Experiments in wartime unity governments forged working relationships, trust, and institutions designed to protect each side from extreme versions of the other.[165] Moderation tends to replicate itself, but that is not the same thing as permanence. The expectations of shared interests and shared burdens that are the bedrock of modern politics are still shaped by military threats in discernible but sometimes surprising ways.

Chapter Twelve

_____

WAR, RACISM, AND CIVIL RIGHTS

IN THE UNITED STATES

I N DECEMBER 1944 HITLER WAS DESPERATE. He was emotionally shaken
not only by the Normandy landing in June and by an assassination attempt
in July but also by daily news of German setbacks on both the eastern and
western fronts. As his officers grew leery of his leadership, he became
ever more frantic. In making his second mad dash of the war through the

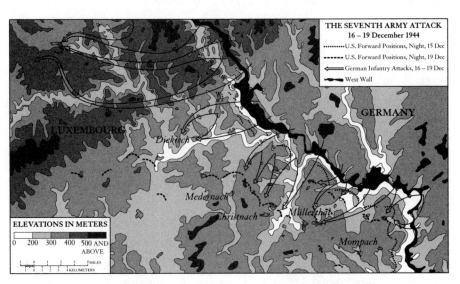

A topographical map of the Ardennes showing the hard terrain
through which the Germans attacked, against all odds.

265

Ardennes forest, he would pay for the prize of 75,000 American casualties with the lives and limbs of 80,000 to 100,000 German soldiers.

Ten days into the grisly Battle of the Bulge, heavy German fire pinned insufficiently supplied and frostbitten American soldiers to their locations in snowy fields and woods, General Dwight Eisenhower issued new orders: ask the African American soldiers in service roles in nearby units if they would be willing to fight at the front lines. More than 4,500 volunteered, many taking reductions in grade to join the war's first racially integrated combat units.[1] With their help and with further reinforcements from General George Patton's Third Army, the Americans turned the tide on January 7, 1945, when Hitler called for retreat.

From the outset, America's wartime mobilization was slow to include nonwhites: in every war until Vietnam, black soldiers were underrepresented in the military relative to their numbers in the population. Seen through the prism of race, the pattern suggests lack of imagination, stingy calculation, or both. Even at a cost to military mobilization, the United States was reluctant to arm the descendants of its former slaves if it meant offering them full suffrage and political rights. America could afford such discrimination because it enjoyed the luxury of "splendid isolation" from one or another ascendant neighbor. Moreover, because the United States is so large, the government need not extract much per capita to amass enormous military power. America was chary about extending rights because it could afford to be.

Periodically, looming threats have pushed the doors of American politics open. To overthrow the British, the American Revolution established the principle of universal white male suffrage in colonies that before the war, almost without exception, had property requirements on the British model.[2] Only Vermont, then a territory of New York hoping to attract to migrants, had granted the right to vote to every adult white man irrespective of financial means.[3] Putting aside the question of how "unfree" Americans really were under British rule, it was clear that throwing off the yoke of such a great power would require them to mobilize all their efforts.[4] Suffrage expansion in the colonies came almost at once, beginning with Pennsylvania's abolition of property requirements in 1776 in response to demands from the local militia.[5] About a third of the American states retained some property restrictions for years to come, but the politics of privilege became harder to defend.

The shortage of men-at-arms notwithstanding, the Americans did not emancipate—let alone enfranchise—their slaves. When in 1775 Britain's governor of Virginia, Lord Dunmore, seized the gunpowder magazine in Williamsburg and promised freedom to all slaves who joined "His Majesty's Troops," the colonists did not match the offer. Many slaves went over to the British, risking the brutality that faced them if they were caught. Thomas Jefferson reckoned that 30,000 Virginia slaves sought refuge behind British lines in 1778; South Carolina lost about 20,000 of its 80,000 slaves, between 1775 and 1783; Georgia lost 15,000, 75 percent of its total.[6] The southern colonies as well as most northerners were willing to pay the military cost of slavery; the plantation economy was a core southern value, and the Americans also banked on a British manpower shortage even more acute than their own. An estimated 5,000 blacks fought with the colonies against the British, but George Washington discouraged their recruitment when he became commander in 1775. Alexander Hamilton and Benjamin Franklin, among others, favored arming and enfranchising the slaves, but they were part of a small minority. Even antislavery John Adams yielded to southern opposition to a plan to free slaves who joined the Continental Army.[7] Thousands of miles from their own population base and dependent on Hessian mercenaries among others, the British tried, with little success, to recruit white tenant farmers with promises of a freeholder bounty in the event of British victory.[8]

States did not want to relinquish control of taxation any more than they wished to lose control of their local populations. The Continental Congress created the Continental Army in June 1775 without a source of funds other than the printing of money and the voluntary contributions of the states.[9] Without secure revenues with which to pay the interest on foreign loans, the congress found it hard to entice foreign lenders,[10] and the easily counterfeited printed money lost its value.[11] So poorly funded was the Continental Army that by 1783 some officers were owed six years of back pay. It took a soldiers' mutiny in Newburgh, New York, that year to frighten the states into granting temporary federal taxation authority.[12] With the war's end in sight, the states agreed to a federal tax for twenty-five years that would be restricted to paying war debts; for good measure, they insisted on appointing the collectors themselves.[13]

The excessive hopes generated by the American Revolution had produced a complicated mix of popular state governments in a loose confederation, scarcely capable of protecting their borders or their newly won freedom.

In the eighteenth century, educated Americans and Europeans alike thought "democracy" as a form of government was prone to degenerate into rule by mobs or demagogues. When Americans were haggling over a new constitution in 1787, the experiences of the Jacobin Terror in France were yet to come, but even as it was, the Founding Fathers were generally leery. One of the purposes of a strong federal government, in addition to promoting a more secure and prosperous country, was to check excessively democratic state governments. Key to the Constitution was the idea that the sovereign "people" played no direct role in governing. James Madison articulated this idea: "The true distinction between these [classical regimes] and the American governments, lies *in the total exclusion of the people, in their collective capacity*, from any share in the *latter*, and not in the *total exclusion of the representatives* of the people from the administration of the *former*." Madison was articulating ideas that had actually become quite common among liberal-minded eighteenth-century Europeans, such as Montesquieu and Kant, both of whom saw Athenian-style democracy—where the people retain the power to take any kind of action, judicial as well as legislative—as essentially despotic. Their institutional projects, like Madison's, required that the people's role in government be indirect and limited to selecting representatives. As Madison wrote in *Federalist* number 63, the Senate would be the body of "temperate and respectable citizens . . . to suspend the blow meditated by the people against themselves."

States, for their part, had been reluctant to share taxation authority with the federal government even during the darkest days of the Revolutionary War. The buzzsaw of public hostility toward their own state taxes in the 1780s changed their minds. The Constitution, passed in 1787 and ratified in 1789, enshrined permanent federal powers of taxation.

The owners of land and commercial wealth also came to see that the federal government needed good credit and strong taxing powers for national security reasons. Although Hamilton was unable to centralize government functions as much as he thought necessary, he was an architect of the "waterfront state," based on a strong navy and facing outward.[14] After much debate, compromise, and necessary obscuring of differences,[15] the state delegates to the Constitutional Convention drew fuzzy but discernible contours of a federal government that would take principal fiscal responsibility for national defense while remaining deferential to state powers and wishes.[16]

Local elites remained alert to possibilities of tyranny from above or below, and governments, federal and state, trod softly on their property. The franchise, widest during the revolutionary years, attenuated when the British threat passed and the well-to-do turned their attention to fending off mobocracy at home. The tumults of the 1780s, far from being the thin side of a populist wedge, motivated twelve state legislatures to pass laws to restrict the right of "paupers" to vote; many more retained literacy requirements.[17]

States' rightists accepted only so much federal authority and scuttled the Federalists' plans for a robust standing peacetime army. Congress also passed a law in 1792 barring African Americans from fighting in the U.S. Army.[18] Neither the nation-producing War of Independence nor the disquieting internal disorders of the 1780s changed many Americans' belief—like that of the "Country" opposition of late seventeenth- and eighteenth-century England—that standing armies were an "abomination."[19] The central government, they feared, might not share their views of what local expressions of freedom should and should not be tolerated. But providing some of what they wished for, such as lands belonging to Native Americans, required force.[20]

In 1791, when Native Americans thrashed separate expeditions by Generals Josiah Harmar and Arthur St. Clair in northern Ohio, Congress funded a force of three thousand men along a string of outposts where they posed little internal danger.[21] The American standing army thus had its roots, small at first, in the genocidal warfare on Native Americans. The British agreed to stop supporting Native Americans in the Jay Treaty, which was signed in 1794. The following year, in the San Lorenzo Treaty, Spain opened the Mississippi River to westward-bound settlers, trappers, and prospectors.[22]

The Napoleonic Wars' massive geopolitical earthquakes in Europe were felt as fairly big tremors in America. At the time, America's naval fleet of twenty-five ships engaged in an undeclared naval war with France to protect American trade with England, and the government took remarkable and unpopular steps to build a national army.[23] Still, the possibility of a French invasion of U.S. soil was not taken seriously, and even President John Adams, who as head of the Federalist Party was a hard-liner against France, wrote to former Massachusetts congressman (and soon to be his emissary to France) Elbridge Gerry on May 3, 1797, "Where is it possible for her to get ships to send thirty thousand men here? We are double the number we were in 1775. We have four times the military skill, and we have eight times the Munitions of War. What would 30,000 men do here?"[24] Some southern congressmen were terrified by the thought that a French force might invade from St. Domingue (now Haiti) in the Caribbean with an army of blacks to lead a slave insurrection in the American South, but that seemed far-fetched to the congressional majority.[25] Weighing the unlikely prospect of an external threat against unequivocal distrust of standing armies, Congress settled on a provisional army in May 1798 that could be commissioned in the event of imminent invasion.[26]

The following year, in March 1799, Congress authorized the president to conscript up to 30,000 more state militiamen in addition to the previous 10,000, as well as volunteer forces of up to 75,000 men.[27] President Adams had wished to build bipartisan support for the military by appointing both Federalists and Republicans to the military command, so he worried about the partisan backlash when George Washington accepted leadership of the army only on condition that arch-Federalist Alexander Hamilton be appointed to the number-two position.[28]

Republicans did indeed rear up against Hamilton's involvement, accusing the Federalists of building an army with which to establish a tyranny. In 1798 the Federalists, in a final but misguided attempt to stop a free fall in postwar support for their version of centralized national power and to undermine political opposition under the guise of national security, passed a set of bills known collectively as the Alien and Sedition Acts.[29]

The Federalists eventually lost far more support than they might have gained from silencing political competition.[30] Albert Gallatin, a Swiss American anti-Federalist congressman from Massachusetts who had won a Senate seat but was denied the right to take up office for not having met the residency requirement, was both a vocal opponent of the Alien and Sedition Acts and one of its key targets as an "alien." Gallatin drew attention to the similarity of the Federalists' tactics to Pitt's heavy-handedness in England at the beginning of the Napoleonic Wars: a "system of alarm . . . which, day after day, brings forth motions calculated to spread fears of imaginary dangers; which one day produces an alien bill; on the next . . . an unconstitutional sedition bill; and . . . grants military associations of one part of the people in order to suppress a supposed disaffection of the rest of the community."[31] In the elections of 1800, the voters repudiated the Federalists' opponent bashing by handing Thomas Jefferson's (and James Madison's)[32] Republican-Democrats a clean sweep of the presidency, the Senate, and the House.[33]

Contrary to the Federalists' propaganda about aliens and sedition, the French threat on American soil did not materialize. Instead, in 1803 the Louisiana Purchase, courtesy of France's financial desperation, doubled U.S. territory on the cheap. But Britain's rough-and-ready style of naval recruitment, which included grabbing American residents from ships on the high seas, and its interference with American trade with France, brought the United States and Britain once again to blows. President Jefferson, a dove toward France but anti-British, reorganized the small national army in 1802 (the Peace Establishment) and added to it in 1808 (the Additional Military Force), during the embargo crisis with Britain.[34]

Fighting Britain to protect U.S. trade was an odd thing to do, given that Britain was America's largest trading partner; French imports and exports were far down the list.[35] It was also odd for Britain to indulge in this distraction from opposing Napoleon on the continent. Had the pro-trade Whigs remained in power in Britain and the pro-trade Federalists in the United States, the two countries might have found a way to avert the war by honoring the neutrality of American shipping. The Jefferson and Madison administrations were eager to expel the British from Canada and to gain new territory, the Tories to check American expansion.[36] The agrarian pair, the British Tories and American Republicans, was a match made in hell. Both land-hungry and inclined to discount the costs to commerce, they went to war in June 1812. It is a testimony to the southern attachment to states' rights and to the dream of westward expansion that southern cotton exporters favored war against their biggest importer.[37] The South Carolinian freshman congressman John Calhoun urged pushing the British out of Canada, a view seconded by Thomas Jefferson from his exalted perch as president emeritus. The hope of quick victory and the westward expansion of slavery underpinned the coalition of planters and frontiersmen against the Federalists' "political economy of Anglophilia."[38]

In fact, the war became a quagmire, one so unpopular that Congress struggled to raise the necessary revenues. By 1814 the U.S. government was carrying a staggering national debt of $100 million, equal to a quarter of total gross domestic product. Before the war taxes had generally been raised through import duties, but even a doubling of the duties in 1812 brought in less tax revenue because trade had collapsed.[39] Madison's Republicans raised the rates on every excise tax imaginable: on goods, on houses, on slaves, and on land. Congress considered but dropped the idea of income and inheritance taxes when it became clear that that would be political suicide. Instead, they taxed trade even more.[40] Compared to Britain, which had adapted to Napoleon's threat by instituting a personal income tax in 1798, the American government was perennially broke and constantly behind on paying its soldiers.[41] Even so, Britain could not afford to fight the United States and Napoleon at the same time; the British public insisted on ending the war in a draw.[42]

Mustering men was almost as hard as raising money for this increasingly costly war.[43] The Madison administration nevertheless resisted the recruitment of blacks, who made up one in five of the U.S. population in 1810. Manpower shortages in the war against Britain eventually softened the opposition to putting black men in uniform, and the forces in Jackson's stand at New Orleans included two black regiments, one of mostly freemen and another of Haitian mercenaries. Each soldier who fought with Jackson was supposed to get 160 acres of land in addition to his pay, but forty years after the war black veterans still had not received their land, and slaves were returned to their masters, who were not bound by the military's promises.[44]

Meanwhile the British were more opportunistic in 1812 than they had been in 1776: they promised American slaves freedom in exchange for fighting under the Union Jack. Four thousand men escaped American slavery thanks to the British, and after the war they were resettled in the Caribbean or elsewhere over vociferous American objections. Some freemen resettled in Nova Scotia, and some in Trinidad, where their descendants are called "Merikans" to this day. Britain's three companies of black "Colonial Marines," speculated the British General Robert Ross, were "infinitely more dreaded by the Americans than the British troops," on account of the brutality they wished to avoid at the hands of former masters. Two hundred of the 4,300-man force that burned Washington were ex-slaves in British uniform.[45] From the Americans' point of view, enticing slaves from their masters was one of the chief British violations of the rules of war.[46]

For both the upstart nation and the distant behemoth, the War of 1812 dragged on too long. More eager to stop fighting than to score final points, the two sides signed a peace treaty at Ghent on December 14, 1814, bringing it to an end. But so slow was ship-borne communication that on January 8, 1815, several weeks after the truce, General Andrew Jackson fought and won a stunning victory in the Battle of New Orleans. Jackson's force of 4,000 men was small for Napoleonic battles on the continent but large for America at the end of Britain's attenuated supply chain, and British forces were running low on food and ammunition.[47] Although Jackson's victory owed much to heavy artillery and to the discipline of his army "regulars," he exaggerated the contributions of the militias for public consumption. Fortunately for both sides, the news of the peace treaty came before a spurt of patriotism could prolong the fighting. As Speaker of the House and peace emissary at Ghent, Henry Clay quipped, the Battle of New Orleans "wound up a disastrous and humiliating war in a blaze of glory."[48]

✦ ✦ ✦

In 1820 the U.S. military's general regulations once again excluded all blacks from enlistment, and men volunteered in such numbers to serve in the Mexican War that broke out in 1846 that further coaxing was not necessary.[49]

This, however, was to change in the Civil War, a conflict to which no other before or since has come close as measured by deaths as a proportion of the American population. Three-quarters of a million or more fighting-age men died in the Civil War out of a combined Union-CSA population of about 31 million.[50] By the end of the war, the stakes were so high for both sides that the Union and secessionist governments were eager to eke out more capacity from their respective populations. The asymmetry, of course, was that the South could not both give blacks the suffrage and maintain the system of slavery that was a principal war aim.

The CSA's vice president, Alexander Stephens, said on March 21, 1861, that the Confederacy was "founded . . . its foundations are laid, its cornerstone rests, upon the great truth that the negro is not equal to the white man; that slavery, subordination to the superior race, is his natural and normal condition. This, our new government, is the first, in the history of the world, based on this great physical, philosophical and moral truth."[51] The *Charleston Courier* scoffed at the talk, in the last desperate months of the war, of arming slaves as Confederate soldiers: "Slavery, God's institution of labor, and the primary political element of our Confederation of Government, state

sovereignty . . . must stand or fall together. To talk of maintaining independence while we abolish slavery is simply to talk folly."[52] Confederates refused
to exchange black Union soldiers in prisoner-of-war swaps. Instead the Confederates enslaved the captured black soldiers or, as at Fort Pillow in 1864,
killed them upon surrender.[53]

So deep was racism even in the North that President Lincoln almost
failed to get across how militarily valuable it might be to the Union cause if
southern black slaves were to flee the South en masse to fight for it.[54] To say
that many of Lincoln's Union officers were lukewarm about emancipation
would be an extreme understatement. General George Meade opposed it
on grounds that the rebels would fight with even greater rage and ferocity.[55]
General George McClellan of the Army of the Potomac harrumphed, in a
letter to Lincoln that was "moderate in tone, mutinous in substance," that
the Army of the Potomac would not fight for emancipation.[56] Once Lincoln
lined up the votes he needed in Congress, however, he ignored the reticence
of his officers and relieved some of them, including McClellan, of their commands.[57] He shared a secret draft of the Emancipation Proclamation with
his cabinet in July 1862 and tried to persuade them of the strategic value of
having both more men-at-arms and a virtuous cause for which to fight: he
had given emancipation "much thought and had about come to the conclusion that it was a military necessity absolutely essential for the salvation of
the Union."[58] Frederick Douglass made the link between fighting and citizenship in May 1863: "Once let the black man get upon his person the brass
letter, U.S., let him get an eagle on his button, and a musket on his shoulder
and bullets in his pocket, there is no power on earth that can deny that he has
earned the right to citizenship."

Lincoln knew that emancipation and black enlistment, let alone their
combination as a swap of one for the other, troubled southern Unionist
Democrats, whose help he sought to end the war and whose support, he
hoped, would help heal the Union postwar. At the request of Andrew Johnson, whom he appointed military governor of Union-controlled parts of
Tennessee in 1862, Lincoln exempted Tennessee from the emancipation of
slaves in Union territory. The Emancipation Proclamation, which Lincoln
announced in September 1862, to go into effect in January 1863, offered freedom for all blacks in southern states except for those states willing to join the

Union.[59] But Lincoln kept nudging. His letter to Johnson on March 26, 1863, is a lesson in the art of subtle persuasion:

> *I am told you have at least* thought *of raising a negro military force. In my opinion the country now needs no specific thing so much as some man of your ability, and position, to go to this work. When I speak of your position, I mean that of an eminent citizen of a slave-state, and himself a slave-holder. The colored population is the great* available *and yet* unavailed *of, force for restoring the Union. The bare sight of fifty thousand armed, and drilled black soldiers on the banks of the Mississippi, would end the rebellion at once. And who doubts that we can present that sight, if we but take hold in earnest? If you* have *been thinking of it please do not dismiss the thought.*[60]

Governor Johnson, soon to be Lincoln's vice-presidential running mate on the National Union ticket for the 1864 election, made no secret of his preference that blacks serve in menial and support roles so white men could fight. But Johnson relented and put 20,000 black men from Tennessee in blue, a significant percentage of the 179,000 black soldiers who fought in the Union Army. Strikingly but not surprisingly, in southern states, where African Americans accounted for nearly half of the population, the vast majority, nearly 4 million out of 4.4 million, were sidelined as slaves.[61]

Republicans won a landslide in the elections of 1866, in part because ten ex-Confederate states had not yet been readmitted into the Union. In February 1869 both houses of Congress passed a constitutional amendment forbidding the denial or abridgment of voting rights based on "race, color, or previous condition of slavery."[62] By February 1870 three-quarters of the states (28 of 37) had ratified it, making the Fifteenth Amendment the law of the land.

The Fifteenth Amendment added black men to the citizenry in 1870, but racist laws and practices tried to disenfranchise them in the South after a brief and incomplete "Reconstruction."[63] Congress's impeachment of Andrew Johnson for backing southern obstructionism was little more than a bump on the road to a century of second-class citizenship for black Americans. The Republican Party briefly used black enfranchisement as a political strategy for taking back the South, but public opinion in the North did not support

civil rights for blacks, causing the party to lose enthusiasm for the fight.[64]
White Democrats struggled to take back control of governorships and legislative majorities in the Deep South where, despite black majorities in some
districts, they campaigned to the theme song "The White Man's Banner." By
1877, southern whites had won back the Deep South states by, among other
things, violent thuggery. In the North racism extended to both Irish—one
million of whom had fled the Irish potato famine of 1847–48—and Italians,
who were derisively called "Guineas."[65]

    At the turn of the twentieth century, about 8.8 million of America's 76
million citizens were black; of them, 6.8 million lived in southern states.
Through a combination of intimidation, poll taxes, ballot stuffing, and literacy tests, white supremacists banned them from the polls wherever they
could, mostly in the South. One particularly brutal episode occurred on
Easter Sunday 1875, in Colfax, Louisiana, when an election dispute ended
with the murder of more than one hundred blacks. Armed with rifles and
a small cannon, the so-called White League, a self-appointed militia aim-
ing to reestablish white rule in Louisiana, attacked the Colfax courthouse,
where Republican freedmen sought to protect the ballots of the recent elec-

A bus station in Durham, North Carolina. Plessy v Ferguson *ushered
in the Jim Crow standard of "separate but equal" for black citizens.*

tion for governor and local offices.[66] The outnumbered blacks surrendered, after which the White League—which lost only three men—imprisoned and then murdered them.[67] Lynchings, on the order of one hundred a year in the 1890s, were designed to terrify blacks into quiet submission.[68] In case that was not enough, the Louisiana legislature passed a restrictive voter registration law that pushed black voter registration down from nearly 96 percent in 1896 to 1.1 percent by the following election. In *Plessy v. Ferguson* (1896) the Supreme Court ruled, meanwhile, that segregation did not violate the Constitution.[69]

Full military mobilization in the world wars would help reconfigure American society, but the 1898 Spanish-American War was not such a war. Triggered by an explosion on the USS *Maine* docked in Havana harbor that had been posted there to protect U.S. residents in Cuba, the war lasted only 114 days. The fight with Spain did not strain available stores of American money or manpower.[70]

In 1900 America's share of world GDP was still half of Great Britain's (America's 11 percent to Britain's 21 percent), but these great countries' vital statistics were moving in opposite directions.[71] Business leaders such as the steel magnate Andrew Carnegie and the banker W. W. Renwick welcomed additions to American military heft to secure bigger markets overseas.[72] Republican President William McKinley had won the 1896 election on promises to secure tariff protections for burgeoning American exporters and to protect vulnerable American import-competitors.[73]

It did not help the cause of black rights that the Spanish-American War's manpower requirements were light. When Congress declared war on Spain on April 20, 1898, it voted to augment the peacetime army of 65,000 with a volunteer army of 125,000 men based principally on quotas assigned to state militias.[74] A second round of recruitment in the summer of 1898 raised the army to 250,000, including ten additional volunteer regiments of blacks on account of their purported immunity to jungle diseases and summer heat.[75] That was before anyone suspected that the war would be over before most of these men ever set foot on a transport ship.[76]

Post-Reconstruction racism got in the way of recruitment. The first blacks mobilized for the war were the four black regiments of the regular U.S. Army, the so-called Buffalo Soldiers, formed just after the Civil War, who had been assigned to campaigns against the Indians in the West. The

U.S. military had kept these regiments out west to the extent possible, but racism followed them everywhere. According to a military surgeon's eyewitness account in 1897 at Fort Leavenworth, Kansas, several white soldiers preferred to be hung by their thumbs than to salute the black Buffalo Soldiers as required. The thumb-hangers finally relented when they were persuaded to salute the uniform, not the black man in the uniform.[77]

In the South, racism threw even bigger obstacles in the path of military recruitment.[78] Five southern states had dismantled the integrated state militias established during Reconstruction and created in their place separate all-white State Volunteer Troops and all-black National Guards. Jim Crow militia segregation allowed the states to use their all-white units to quell black labor unrest, as in the Thibodaux Massacre of November 1887, when ten all-white infantry companies and an artillery company of the Louisiana state militia broke the strike line at a sugarcane plantation, killing as many as fifty black workers.[79]

South Carolina failed to meet its quota for the Spanish-American War because it would not allow its all-black National Guard units to serve on behalf of the state. Georgia and Mississippi also refused to call up black units, disliking the idea of blacks in arms. The Alabama Third Regiment, a black battalion that had been expanded into a regiment under a white officer, never left the state.[80] One exception was North Carolina, where Republican Governor Daniel Russell created a black battalion with black officers.[81] Of the 250,000 soldiers recruited nationwide, southern resistance to putting black men in uniform resulted in the mustering of only 10,000 black soldiers.[82]

In the stateside military camps, where regiments assembled and prepared for deployment or were stationed on their way back home, black servicemen were often subjected to intolerable racial harassment, sometimes resulting in bloodshed. Black soldiers in transit to mustering camps were ordered out of "white only" restaurants, bars, parks, and public transportation.[83] At the embarkation camp in Tampa on June 6, 1898, twenty-seven black and three white soldiers were seriously injured in a fight.[84] At Camp Haskell near Macon, Georgia, later that year, four black soldiers from the Third North Carolina died under similar circumstances.[85] In December 1898 a black soldier from the Sixth Virginia wrote home from Camp Haskell describing his frustration at having to serve under white officers: "It is not so much a question of race or color for which [the members of the black regiment] now contend, but one of principle and they do not intend to have it violated so long as Negro men of capacity, integrity, and character can be found among the men of the regiment or in the state's broad domain. To be fair is all they ask."[86]

The black soldiers sent to Cuba, including the Tenth Cavalry who rode with Teddy Roosevelt's Rough Riders, impressed their officers in action. But they were expected, after combat duty, to undertake additional service work for the white troops. Edward Johnson relayed from eyewitness accounts in 1899 that

> *notwithstanding their heroic services, [the black Twenty-fifth Infantry] were still to be subjected, in many cases, to more hardships than their white brother in arms. When the flag of truce was, in the afternoon of July 3, seen, each man breathed a sigh of relief, for the strain had been very great upon us. During the next eleven days men worked like ants, digging trenches, for they had learned a lesson of fighting in the open field. The work went on night and day. The 25th Infantry worked harder than any other regiment, for as soon as they would finish a trench they were ordered to move; in this manner they were kept moving and digging new trenches for eleven days. The trenches left were each time occupied by a white regiment.*[87]

This small war against the decaying vestiges of Spain's empire in the western hemisphere—a "splendid little war," as Secretary of State John Hay called it—propelled the United States onto the world stage as an imperial power in possession of Cuba and Puerto Rico for minimal effort. In July 1898 the American navy destroyed the Spanish Atlantic fleet off Santiago, Cuba; a month later a U.S. force of 3,500 men landed in San Juan Hill, where they faced "only token resistance."[88]

It took the United States three more years to vanquish the Filipino independence fighters, under Emilio Aguinaldo, who resisted the American annexation of the Philippines. A thirty-year-old firebrand in 1898 who had helped to lead the Filipino revolt against Spanish rule, Aguinaldo played cat and mouse with American forces until he was captured on March 23, 1901, in his remote hideout on Luzon's rugged northwestern coast.[89]

Of the 120,000 American soldiers who fought in the Philippines, 4,000 were killed and 2,800 wounded. The black community, however, was first to call attention to the 200,000 Filipinos killed in the war, most of them civilians.[90] Henry Turner, senior bishop of the African Methodist Episco-pal Church, lambasted America's "unholy war of conquest" against "a feeble band of sable patriots."[91] While white soldiers commonly referred to Filipi-nos as "niggers," black soldiers, wrote General Robert Hughes from Manila, "mixed with the natives at once. Wherever they came together they became great friends. When I withdrew the darkey company [sic] from Santa Rita I was told that they shed tears over their going away."[92] Sergeant Patrick Mason, Company 1 of the Twenty-fourth Infantry, wrote to the *Cleveland Gazette* on September 29, 1900, "I feel sorry for these people and all that have come under the control of the United States. I don't believe they will be justly dealt with. . . . The poor whites don't believe that anyone has any right to live but the white American."[93] Infantry Sergeant James Loughry refers without self-consciousness in his diary entry to an attack on black troops who were felt not to be fighting aggressively enough against the Filipinos.[94]

The speed of Spanish capitulation was testimony to the decrepitude of the Spanish outpost more than to the magnificence of American military force, as yet "an imperial power with a provincial navy."[95] The manpower requirements of the war had been light, and the death of black soldiers did not soften their hostile treatment in the South. If anything, southern racists were more determined than ever to "put blacks back in their place."[96] The North Carolina Third Regiment, upon returning from Cuba, came in for harsh treatment in the southern media. The *Atlanta Journal* reported, in an article entitled "Happy Riddance,"

> *But for the promptness and pluck of several Atlanta policemen these Negro ex-soldiers would have done serious mischief at the depot. Those who under-took to make trouble were very promptly clubbed into submission, and one fellow more obstreperous than the rest, was lodged in the station house. With the exception of two or three regiments the Negro volunteers in the recent war were worse than useless. The Negro regulars, on the contrary, made a fine record, both for fighting and conduct in camp.*[97]

In November 1898 Democrats won the governorship and a legislative majority in North Carolina, the most Republican of the southern states. A week after the election, on November 10, two thousand racist thugs attacked the only black newspaper in North Carolina and violently ousted the biracial city council of Wilmington. The death toll of the attacks is unknown—estimates range from 6 to 100—but many black families fled Wilmington, never to return.[98]

James Vardaman was elected governor of Mississippi in 1903 on the campaign promise to lynch "every Negro in the state" if that was what it would take to maintain white supremacy.[99] By 1904 every former Confederate state had a poll tax to deter black voters from participating in elections.[100] Meanwhile Theodore Roosevelt, reelected president in 1904, blamed "black rapists" for lynchings and in 1906 gave dishonorable discharges to three companies of black soldiers who refused to rat on colleagues who had killed a white man.[101] In 1912 Vardaman won a landslide election for the U.S. Senate from Mississippi against sugar planter LeRoy Percy, who favored better treatment for blacks, perhaps on account of his need for labor, since black workers were leaving the state at a rapid clip in search of personal security.

But blacks found no escape; racial violence followed them on their northward trek. As over a million blacks moved north in the Great Migration between 1910 and 1930, they encountered anger and jealousy over scarce jobs.[102] William Howard Taft, formerly Roosevelt's war secretary, was the first Republican president (1909–13) to seek the southern racist vote on promises of federal noninterference in southern states.[103]

It was against this backdrop of continued racial violence that the United States entered World War I in April 1917. Three months later, in East St. Louis, a white mob, swollen by unemployed workers, rampaged through an African American neighborhood—unrestrained by the National Guard—leaving over forty people dead. Then in August the Third Battalion of the African American Twenty-fourth Infantry of the regular army was sent to guard a construction site for Camp Logan, a new National Guard facility near Houston. When they arrived, they soon clashed with Houston police. On one fateful day, August 23, 1917, the Houston police pistol-whipped a black soldier from the Twenty-fourth Infantry who tried to stop a police assault on a black woman. The same afternoon the police fired at Corporal Charles Baltimore, who had gone to the Houston police headquarters to seek release of another black soldier whom they had arrested and beaten.[104]

The infantrymen's response to Houston police brutality was swift: "Forget France, let's go clean up this goddamned city." That night about a hundred black soldiers set out in search of the offending police officers. In the ensuing fight with armed white civilians who rallied to the cause of the Houston police, seventeen whites and two black soldiers died.[105] The military's response was to hang twenty-one black soldiers who participated in the fight.[106]

Although many Americans were reluctant to participate in what they saw as a European war, few were as reluctant as black citizens. Black leaders wondered aloud why blacks should fight for a country that oppressed them. President of Tuskegee Institute Robert Russa Moton wrote to President Woodrow Wilson: "A number of people of prominence have approached me with reference to the attitude the Negroes would assume in case the country should go to war. I understand, also, that certain high officials of the Government have raised similar questions."[107]

Secretary of War Newton D. Baker was sandwiched between frustrated black citizens and influential racists such as (former governor) Senator James Vardaman of Mississippi, who opposed the recruitment of black troops. To placate obstructionists in Congress, the War Department created draft registration cards that indicated race so that African American conscripts could be segregated as soon as they were called up.[108]

The Wilson administration decided to form two African American combat units, the Ninety-second Division from new conscripts, and the Ninety-third from black National Guard units. For the first time, the War Department also established an officers' training camp for African Americans to lead African American troops. W.E.B. Du Bois, the Harvard-trained sociologist who had cofounded the National Association for the Advancement of Colored People (NAACP) in 1909, accepted a captaincy in the segregated American military. In the July 1918 issue of the NAACP journal *The Crisis*, Du Bois enjoined blacks to "forget our special grievances and close our ranks shoulder to shoulder with our own white fellow citizens and the allied nations that are fighting for democracy."[109] He also lamented that "we must choose then between the insult of a separate camp and the irreparable injury of strengthening the present custom of putting no black men in positions of authority."[110]

It is not that Du Bois was sanguine about American race relations. In a rebuke of President Wilson himself, he wrote in June 1918: "We raise our clenched hands against the hundreds of thousands of white murderers, rapists, and scoundrels who have oppressed, killed, ruined, robbed and debased their black fellow men and fellow women and yet today walk scot-free, unwhipped of justice, uncondemned by millions of their fellow citizens, and unrebuked by the president of the United States."[111] Still, Du Bois hoped that American citizens, seeing black soldiers fighting and dying for the country, would abhor the injustice of inequality.[112] Alice Dunbar Nelson, widow of the popular nineteenth-century black poet Paul Laurence Dunbar, also hoped that black sacrifice in the war could win respect and greater equality. She organized a Flag Day celebration on June 14, 1918, that attracted more than six thousand African Americans.[113]

On the other hand, the journalist and publisher of the *Boston Guardian* William Monroe Trotter spoke for many skeptics when he argued that "capitulation" had not worked against racism yet and that German atrocities posed no greater threat to blacks than southern lynch laws that continued to give whites virtual immunity from prosecution.[114] Hubert Harrison, president of the Liberty League and editor of the *New York Voice,* wrote that Du Bois's "Close Ranks" editorial sounded ominously like blacks should "consent to be lynched—'during the war'—and submit tamely and with commendable weakness to being Jim-crowed and disenfranchised."[115] Arthur Raper has estimated, in fact, that in the vast majority of lynchings, police officers at best stood by.[116]

On July 26, 1918, in response to relentless admonishing from the black community as well as some prodding from the U.S. military, President Wilson did publicly condemn lynching: "There have been many lynchings, and every one of them has been a blow at the heart of ordered law and humane justice. . . . I therefore very earnestly and solemnly beg that the governors of all the States, the law officers of every community, and, above all, the men and women of every community in the United States, all who revere America and wish to keep her name without stain or reproach, will cooperate—not passively merely, but actively and watchfully—to make an end of this disgraceful evil." Wilson's lofty words notwithstanding, however, Congress refused to pass an antilynching law.[117]

◆ ◆ ◆

The U.S. military may have been ahead of Congress on the lynching issue, but it had not moved beyond Jim Crow, which accompanied the military to Europe. Black soldiers were mustered principally to labor service rather than to combat roles. Those assigned to bear arms would be in "colored" units.[118] The military also attempted to place them under "racial quarantine" from white European women. The 904th Pioneers were ordered "not to talk to or be in company with any white woman, regardless of whether the women solicit their company or not."[119] In May 1919, angered to have supported a U.S. military effort that did not treat its black men with equality, Du Bois published a translation of the infamous memo written by French Colonel Jean L. A. Linard containing "secret information concerning the black American troops" conveyed to the French by the U.S. military authorities:

> *The increasing number of Negroes in the United States (about 15,000,000) would create for the white race in the Republic a menace of degeneracy were it not that an impassable gulf has been made between them.*
>
> *As this danger does not exist for the French race, the French public has become accustomed to treating the Negro with familiarity and indulgence.*
>
> *This indulgence and this familiarity are matters of grievous concern to the Americans. . . .*
>
> *We must prevent the rise of any pronounced degree of intimacy between French officers and black officers. . . . We must not eat with them, must not shake hands or seek to talk or meet with them outside of the requirements of military service.*[120]

In the eighteen months that the United States fought in World War I, about 4 million American troops were mustered, of whom 117,000 lost their lives; that figure includes an unbelievable 43,000 who died from the H1N1 flu pandemic that swept the camps in 1918. Although the war was a significant national effort, it remained remote for most Americans. Less than 4 percent of the American population of 110 million was in uniform, and the war deaths represented a loss of 0.13 percent of the population. By comparison, the British and Russians lost about 2 percent of their populations, and the French and Germans about 4 percent. Blacks made up 7.4 percent of the men conscripted into the U.S. military despite comprising about 9.9 percent of the U.S. population.[121]

World War I, if anything, worsened race relations back home. The combination of white hostility toward blacks in uniform and the refusal of black

French Military Mission   August 7, 1918
                        Confidential
            Concerning Black American Troops.

        1. It is well for French officers who are called upon to
command Negro American Troops, or to live near them, to understand
clearly the situation regarding the Negro in the United States.
They ought, therefore to learn of the things told in the following
note, and it is important that they be generally known and deseminated
It is the province of the French military authorities to inform
                                            civil
the French population, through the French military authorities,
at the cantonments of colored American troops upon this subject.

        2. The American point of view on the Negro question may seem
strange to the Frenchman, but the French have no right to discuss
what is known as prejudice. American opinion is unanimous upon
the Negro question and does not admit of discussion.

        The large number of Negroes in the United States , about
15,000,000, threatens the degeneration of the white race in the
Republic unless there is an inexorable separation between
blacks and whites.

        As this danger does not exist for the French people they
are accustomed to treat the Negro familarly and to accept attentions
from them.

        This indulgence on their part and this familarity profoundly
hurts the Americans. They consider it a blow to their national
doctrine. They fear that contact with the French will fill
American Negroes with ideas which the whites considers
intolerable. It is important that every effort be made to avoid profoundly estranging American opinion.

A memo from Jean L. A. Linard, written at the request of Americans,
warning French officers not to socialize with American blacks.

veterans to accept second-class citizenship exploded in the "red summer" of 1919.[122] Between April and September, twenty-six race riots in cities across the country left about one hundred blacks dead and thousands seriously wounded. In September in Omaha, a crowd of six thousand burned, beat, shot, and hanged Will Brown, an African American packinghouse worker. In the course of their rampage, they burned down the courthouse and attempted to lynch the city's mayor for defending him.[123]

Of the men lynched in that year, ten were in military uniform. Wilbur Little, an African American soldier, upon returning home to Blakely, Georgia, was met at the train station by a group of white men who stripped off his uniform. They killed him a few days later, when he defied their threats by again wearing his uniform in public.[124] In its 1919 annual report the NAACP urged "all Americans who love fair play" to recognize "that law-abiding colored people are denied the commonest citizenship rights."[125]

As the suffragist Alice Stone Blackwell had noted in 1897, many Americans shared the view that fighting for the country was a condition for full citizenship: "A favorite argument against equal suffrage is that women ought not to vote because they cannot fight."[126] The failure to address black disenfranchisement while accepting female suffrage in 1920 underscores the grotesque pull of American racism.[127]

Congress passed the Nineteenth Amendment on June 4, 1919. Just a year later, thirty-six state legislatures had ratified it, giving women the constitutional right to vote. To many blacks, it was deeply unjust that white women, who were not spilling their blood on the battlefields of Europe as black men had been doing, had leapfrogged them politically. Du Bois often found himself in the middle, arguing with blacks to support female suffrage, and with white women to resist the allure of racism.[128]

Women's suffrage coincided with an appreciation of women's wartime effort but did not, at least in the United States, reflect a sense of mobilizational urgency or a critical female role in the war effort. The suffragist movement straddled partisan politics in its efforts to gain a legislative majority.

The white women's procession in New York, 1917.

As *The New York Times* noted, leaders of the 1920 NAWSA convention in Chicago acknowledged both parties, thanking the Republican Party

> *"for having a Chairman [Will Hays] who is astute enough to recognize the certain trend of public affairs and to lead his party in step with the inevitable march of human progress." The resolution was adopted by a vote of 190 to 22, which was later made unanimous. Democratic women then introduced a resolution thanking Homer Cummings, Democratic National Chairman, for help he rendered their cause, and it, too, was adopted by unanimous vote.*[129]

Many southern supporters of female suffrage made no attempts to hide their hope and expectation that women voters would uphold white supremacy back home.[130] George Francis Train, the original financer of Susan B. Anthony's and Elizabeth Cady Stanton's publication *The Revolution,* for example, was both a racist Democrat and a female suffrage advocate. Henry Blackwell, in his 1867 pamphlet, argued for woman suffrage, showing there were more white women in the South than black men and women combined.[131]

Half a century earlier Anthony and Stanton, the women's movement founders, had been lukewarm about the Fifteenth Amendment, concerned that advocating for black men before women would set back the woman's cause. In 1895 Anthony personally asked Frederick Douglass not to attend the National American Woman Suffrage Association (NAWSA) convention in Atlanta for fear that his vocal commitment to black enfranchisement would be a distraction.[132] Meanwhile Frances Willard's temperance movement, though not antisuffragist, was off to the side and far more popular among women, mainly because it was seen as concerned with the "women's business" of protecting society from vice. The Women's Christian Temperance Union is estimated to have had 150,000 dues-paying members compared with NAWSA's 13,000 in 1890.[133]

To Du Bois's dismay, NAWSA tacked even more visibly in the direction of southern racism in the 1910s, when the Democrats controlled Congress and most southern state legislatures.[134] NAWSA's head in 1913, Alice Paul—a Quaker and an avowed racial egalitarian—planned a march on Washington in which black women would be relegated to a separate section, in deference to the southern suffragists and the southern legislatures whose support the organization sought for ratification. "We must have a white procession, or a negro procession, or no procession at all."[135]

The battle for ratification was fierce in the southern states. Senator Eward J. Gay of Louisiana proposed an amendment giving states, rather than the federal government, the power to enforce female suffrage. "Senator Gay said that from a survey of the States he could predict that thirteen States would not ratify the amendment, enough to block it. His amendment was defeated, 62 to 19." Gay was one of seventeen Democratic senators to vote against the amendment.[136] Antisuffrage organizations in the South made no secret of their concerns on behalf of white supremacy.[137] Southern Democrats openly worried that the South would "return to Reconstruction days" and that "Jim Crow legislation would be repealed."[138] Martin Calhoun, a descendant of John Calhoun, wrote, "Any southern state which ratifies this amendment will repudiate the principals [sic] for which the Confederate soldier struggled through four long years, and such a state should in all justice, dismantle every monument which has been erected to the heroic memory of 'the men who wore the grey.' "[139]

The Tennessee state legislature barely disagreed with Calhoun's sentiments, voting 51 to 49 in favor of the amendment on August 18, 1920, thereby becoming the thirty-sixth and last state needed for ratification. Although eight southern states (Alabama, Florida, Georgia, Louisiana, Mississippi, North Carolina, South Carolina, and Virginia) would not ratify the amendment until many decades later, they were forced to allow their female citizens to vote.

Some evidence suggests that the new female voters pushed governments toward more investment in education, health care, and various other public goods,[140] but civil rights for blacks, as the southern suffragists had promised, remained on the back burner. The historian Glenda Gilmore writes of white Democrats in North Carolina that "since their political religion was white supremacy, [they] began preaching it against woman suffrage even though the old sermon scarcely fit the sin." When the amendment was passed anyway, the women forgave them and voted Democratic along with the men who had tried blocking their right to vote.[141] Although the House of Representatives passed the Dyer Anti-Lynching Bill in 1922—which would have punished people convicted in federal courts of lynching and fined local governments that failed to protect its citizens—the Senate filibustered it to death. An anti-Klan plank was defeated at the Democratic Convention of 1924, reflecting the ideologically strange and sometimes chilly cohabitation of the northern and southern branches of the party for the sake of a legislative majority. William Joseph Simmons, an ex-garter salesman from Atlanta, breathed new life into a moribund Ku Klux Klan with aggressive propaganda and a membership drive in 1920 garnering one hundred thousand new members in six months. As the historian Richard Schaefer points out, the Klan's appeal was that it "offered a target for every frustration."[142]

Racism continued to limit American willingness to incorporate blacks into the U.S. military, placing a drag on manpower mobilization. Another resource needed for war was money from taxpayers. The substantial costs of World War I, though a lighter burden on the United States than on European economies, required heavy reliance on the income tax for the first time in U.S. history. During the War of 1812 Madison had proposed a national income tax to cope with the large war debt, but Congress rejected it. Lincoln's administration enacted the first federal income tax during the Civil War, again to deal with a crushing national war debt, though with large concessions to farmers. These taxes were repealed after the Civil War, and again the government resorted almost entirely to tariffs and excise taxes.[143]

American agricultural interests, accentuated by the Senate's built-in malapportionment in favor of agricultural states, had long preferred an income tax on the wealth of eastern industry and finance over the traditional American reliance on excise taxes and tariffs. Business temporarily lost its defender against income taxes when the Progressive movement splintered the Republican Party into agrarian and industrial wings at the turn of the century.[144] By way of the Sixteenth Amendment, Congress introduced a permanent income tax in 1909 (ratified in 1913) that, at the outset, accounted for a minuscule portion of government tax revenues but that during the war years swelled to over half of a much bigger government budget. Individual and corporate income taxes went from 16 percent of federal government revenues in 1916 to nearly 60 percent during 1917–20, taking the load off customs duties, although the Republicans cut taxes and decreased progressivity as soon as they returned to power in the 1920s.[145]

For many Americans, World War I was not worth the manpower and money required. Republican Warren Harding, campaigning on the proposition that Europe should deal with its own problems, won a stunning

62 percent of the popular vote in the 1920 election.[146] Although American banks had grown into a leadership position on world financial markets during and after World War I, most heavy industrial producers—of steel, railways, cars, and other machinery—were preoccupied with growing markets at home and had never warmed to Woodrow Wilson's heroic vision of American peacekeeping and leadership through the League of Nations.[147] As Connecticut senator Frank Brandegee, a Republican, told his colleagues, "Europe has been an armed camp and has been quarreling ever since the dawn of history."[148]

At an election rally in February 1920, Harding intoned that "many a European state is sorely menaced through distorted visions which come of warfare" and that therefore it would be better to "make Mexico safe and set it aglow with the light of new-world righteousness, than menace the health of the republic in old-world contagion."[149] Disappointment had also set in at the other end of the political spectrum. Walter Lippmann spoke for many disillusioned American liberals when he warned Europeans to rein in their postwar grudges: "If you make it a peace that can be maintained only by the bayonet, we shall leave you to the consequences and find our own security in this hemisphere."[150]

Once in office, Harding attempted to do just that: he notched back income tax progressivity and got busy raising tariffs to protect American businesses that cared more about blocking imports from foreign competitors than about promoting exports abroad.[151] Between 1921 and 1929 Harding and his successor Calvin Coolidge reduced defense spending from $2.6 billion to $0.7 billion.[152] The Teapot Dome scandal of 1921–24 was a metaphor for the times: Secretary of the Interior Albert Fall decided, with Harding's approval, to lease to private oil companies federal lands in Wyoming that had been set aside for the navy but for which there was no foreseeable military demand.[153]

Indeed, American isolationism did not protect the rest of the world from America. Mankind has yet to devise a better medium for economic contagion than the gold standard, to which fiscally anxious American administrations clung. When America's Roaring Twenties ended in a stock market meltdown in October 1929, depression spread through competitive tariff hikes,[154] "beggar thy neighbor" currency devaluations, and stringent monetary policy that dried up global liquidity.[155]

However much President Franklin Roosevelt may have understood that America was now embedded in the world and its economy, his sights were kept local by a strongly isolationist Congress centering on the western and midwestern Progressives whose votes he needed for his New Deal policies.[156] Roosevelt's inaugural address on March 1, 1933. put the accent on fixing what was broken at home: "Our international trade relations, though vastly important, are in point of time and necessity secondary to the establishment of a sound national economy. I favor as a practical policy the putting of first things first. . . . The emergency at home cannot wait."[157] In 1931 Herbert Hoover had wagged a finger at Japan for occupying Manchuria.[158] In late 1933 President Roosevelt purchased silver to boost western U.S. producers at cost to China's fragile economy, then on a silver standard.[159] When Hitler remilitarized the Rhineland in 1936, William Randolph Hearst defended American isolationism in the written version of shouting: "LET US CONTINUE TO KEEP OUT OF AFFAIRS THAT DO NOT CONCERN US. LET US PROVIDE ADEQUATELY FOR OUR NATIONAL DEFENSE. AND LET US STAY HOME AND MIND OUR OWN AMERICAN BUSINESS."[160] Helping European allies help themselves through "cash and carry" and "lend lease" loans was the best Roosevelt could do in the face of congressional opposition, based on hesitant public opinion, to entering the war outright.[161]

Roosevelt's priority to lift the economy out of the depths of depression

A Philip Randolph with Eleanor Roosevelt, 1946.

also came ahead of advancing civil rights at home.[162] He secured congressional support for the New Deal by letting southern Democrats ignore the Reconstruction amendments in their states; the courts, of course, had already pulled the amendments' teeth.[163] But mobilization for World War II put Roosevelt into a different frame of mind. First, A. Philip Randolph's March on Washington Movement was raising awareness of the hypocrisy of fighting for democracy abroad when millions of American blacks faced harsh job discrimination at home.[164] On June 18, 1941, Randolph, the charismatic leader of the Pullman porters union, told President Roosevelt (in a meeting brokered by Eleanor Roosevelt) that as many as a hundred thousand people were ready to gather in the capital to protest Jim Crow. The very next week President Roosevelt issued Executive Order 8802 stating, "There shall be no discrimination in the employment of workers in defense industries and in Government because of race, creed, color, or national origin."[165]

Political equality for blacks moved forward at least within the military. In 1944 the military proposed new legislation that would have given soldiers of every color the right to vote while deployed overseas. The rest of the country was not ready. Congress, led by Dixiecrats who feared what this would mean for Jim Crow, passed an emasculated version that preserved states' various voting restrictions.[166] In 1948 President Harry Truman endorsed military expediency when he abolished segregation in the military by executive order, but implementation was slow and uneven, as we shall see.

Americans watched Germany take Sudetenland, Austria, Poland, and France by 1940. But not until Japan attacked Pearl Harbor on December 7, 1941, did the American public get off the fence to intervene in "Europe's latest war."[167] In a broad cross-class compromise, Congress passed revenue legislation in 1942 that doubled the number of people paying taxes at the same time that it increased the tax rate for the rich.[168]

Eventually 16 million Americans, of a total population of 131 million, would serve in uniform during the war. Over 400,000 American soldiers would lose their lives, amounting to 0.32 percent of American population and three times the death rate of the First World War relative to population.[169] Still, this was a fraction compared to European countries, for which the war required mustering every able fighter and for whom their homelands were the theater of fighting. France lost 1.5 percent of its population; Germany, 3.5 percent (not including the millions of Jews they murdered from Germany and all over Europe), Italy and England each 1 percent, and Russia almost 15 percent. Tellingly, the American military never recruited blacks in numbers proportional to their place in the American population. Blacks registered for the draft in proportion to their numbers, but they never reached that proportion of American forces because of barriers to black enlistment.[170]

Before committing to war, Congress had created a peacetime conscription system in 1940, just in case.[171] The Selective Training and Service Act, which called for all men between the ages of 21 and 35 to register, from which pool the government would induct servicemen, explicitly proscribed racial discrimination.[172] Recruitment from the registration lists, however, was left to local offices of the Selective Service, which undermustered blacks relative to population, not only in the South. By 1948 three hundred thousand black enlistees had been denied admission on account of literacy tests and other hurdles.[173] The South and the border states disqualified over three-quarters of initial black inductees.

The problem, however, was not limited to the South. Secretary of War Henry Stimson acknowledged in his diary that the army had "adopted rigid requirements for literacy mainly to keep down the number of colored troops." Stimson's suggestion: find other ways to recruit illiterate but otherwise desirable whites from southern mountain states.[174] In 1940 the First Army Headquarters, responsible for New England, sent secret orders to its draft boards requesting that no blacks be inducted in the first draft, although Connecticut governor Raymond Baldwin had the order rescinded when he threatened to report it to President Roosevelt.[175]

Rather than nudge the services toward integration, Chief of Staff George C. Marshall told Roosevelt the problem was that there were not enough segregated training facilities for black draftees. In Puerto Rico, where the National Guard had previously been integrated, the War Department called for segregation.[176] Nor was the War Department's segregation policy far from mainstream American opinion. Roosevelt's Executive Order 9066 on February 19, 1942, to intern 120,000 Japanese civilians in desert camps was not widely recognized at the time as a grotesque civil rights violation of American citizens.[177] The Department of Agriculture had conducted public opinion surveys before the deportation in order to advise the president of the likely reactions.[178]

White supremacy in the U.S. military meant that black citizens were overlooked in the recruitment for soldiers. Frank Capra's forty-two-minute feature film commissioned by the War Department in 1944, *The Negro Soldier*, aimed to stir black patriotism and white admiration through the words of a black Protestant minister interspersed with scenes of black soldiers in combat, but black recruits who passed all the literacy and other tests, made it through training at segregated camps, and were deployed overseas typically found themselves in support roles rather than in combat duty.[179]

As in previous wars, black soldiers in training were harassed by camp guards as well as populations surrounding the camps. In 1941 army authorities found a black soldier lynched at Fort Benning, Georgia. Police brutality let to violence in Fayetteville, North Carolina. Forty-three black inductees fled harassment in Prescott, Arizona. Black soldiers at Fort Bragg, and at Camps Davis, Gibbon, and Jackson Barracks fought white soldiers and police.[180] In Muskogee, Oklahoma, four white military police barred John Hammond, a talent agent for the Columbia Broadcasting Company, from a dance hall near a black army training facility with the warning to stay away from "knife wielding N—s."[181] Joe Louis, who performed boxing exhibitions in military camps during the war, claims to have been appalled to see the poor conditions of the training facilities for black soldiers. As one black college student said in 1942, "The Army jim-crows us. The Navy lets us serve only as messmen. The Red Cross refuses our blood. Employers and labor unions shut us out. Lynchings continue. We are disfranchised, jim-crowed, spat upon. What more could Hitler do than that?"[182]

Charles Dryden, a Tuskegee airman, was incredulous that German POWs were treated better in some ways than he was: "From the day we arrived at this Godforsaken Walterboro Army Air Base in the piney woods of South Carolina, we had seen German prisoners of war, readily identifiable by the letters PW painted on the back of their fatigues in white paint, going into the 'White' side of the post exchange cafeteria and WE COULD NOT!" The Tuskegee officers were barred from the white officers' clubs and were often refused service in restaurants off base.[183]

When black soldiers were sent to fight, it was in segregated combat units. Army policy, stated in confidential 1937 War Department guidelines, was "not to intermingle colored and white enlisted personnel in the same regimental organization. This policy has proven satisfactory over a long period of years and to make changes would produce situations destructive to morale

and detrimental to the preparation for National defense."[184] The case of
Winfred Lynn, a black man who initially refused to serve in a segregated
unit, went all the way to the Supreme Court, which in 1945 dismissed it on
the technical grounds that Lynn was already serving in the army overseas.[185]
The southern press responded with outrage to blacks' demands for equality:
"There is no power in the world—not even all the mechanized armies of
the earth, Allied and Axis—which could now force the southern white people to the abandonment of the principle of social segregation."[186] Meanwhile,
to court black the vote, Roosevelt made Major Campbell Johnson executive
assistant to the office of the Selective Service, Colonel Benjamin Davis brigadier general, and Howard University Law School dean William Hastie civilian aide to the secretary of war.[187]

Not until 1943 did American military forces experience dire manpower
shortages; only then did the reluctance to enlist black soldiers give way to
active recruitment and deployment.[188] In the desperate, pitched Battle of the
Bulge, as we have seen, General Eisenhower sent in partially integrated units
to replace and augment fallen white ones.[189] In the ensuing all-out push to end
the war, all branches of the military partially integrated their combat units.[190]
Even in those darkest hours of 1944, however, southern states rejected stan-
dardized absentee ballots that would have made it easier for black soldiers
stationed overseas to vote in state and federal elections.[191]

Many southerners also did not want returning black soldiers to take the
"uppity" view that they should vote at home as well.[192] Just as the military
felt less pressure to integrate, returning soldiers and their families felt a new
sense of empowerment.[193] One white southerner observed, "It is as if some
universal message had reached the great mass of Negroes, urging them to
dream new dreams and to protest against the old order." A black veteran
agreed: "After having been overseas fighting for democracy, I thought that
when we got back here we should enjoy a little of it."[194] Thousands joined
the NAACP; hundreds of thousands tried to vote, many of whom were bru-
talized by locals trying to block them. Race riots in Columbia, Tennessee; a
quadruple lynching in Monroe, Georgia; and the blinding of black veteran
Isaac Woodard on his way home on a Greyhound bus by a sheriff in Bates-
burg, South Carolina, all occurred in 1946 as the soldiers came home.[195]

Opinion in the rest of the country, however, was turning. In April 1944
the U.S. Supreme Court overturned a Texas state law that authorized the

Democratic Party to choose its candidates with white-only primaries. As Arthur Krock wrote in *The New York Times*, "Neither [Justice Stanley Reed] nor [Justice Owen Roberts, the sole dissenter] mentioned the real reason for the overturn [of the all-white primary law]. It is that the common sacrifices of wartime have turned public opinion and the Court against previously sustained devices to exclude minorities."[196]

There was also electoral politics. Military victory relieved the military's immediate need for black manpower,[197] but Truman needed the black vote in the next election, especially after Dixiecrats from Mississippi and Alabama walked out of the Democratic National Convention in July 1948.[198] In his civil rights speech to Congress on February 2, 1948, Truman established a permanent Commission on Civil Rights, putting pressure on Congress to do its part:

> *The Federal Government has a clear duty to see that Constitutional guarantees of individual liberties and of equal protection under the laws are not denied or abridged anywhere in our Union. That duty is shared by all three branches of the Government, but it can be fulfilled only if the Congress enacts modern, comprehensive civil rights laws, adequate to the needs of the day, and demonstrating our continuing faith in the free way of life.*[199]

On the foreign policy front, Truman was vulnerable to foreign perceptions of racism that could undercut American effectiveness in the world. In a diary entry in 1945 he had written, "Propaganda seems to be our greatest foreign relations enemy. Russians distribute lies about us."[200] In fact, according to a State Department study, nearly half of Soviet propaganda against the United States put a spotlight on American racism, and Secretary of State Clark Clifford urged Truman to "stress the need for a federal Civil Rights program to cover every section of the United States, to prove to the world that the great benefits of American democracy are meant for all groups in the country." *Voice of America* gave Truman's 1948 civil rights address to Congress top billing.[201]

Truman's pace did not satisfy A. Philip Randolph, the elder statesman and known moderate in the black protest movement who, years earlier, had convinced Roosevelt to issue Executive Order 8802 to desegregate the defense industry. Randolph now threatened to lead a massive march on Washington

unless Truman took more concrete steps, beginning with official and immediate desegregation of the military. Worried about bad international public-
ity, Truman met with Randolph on March 22 to talk him out of it.[202] At that
meeting, Randolph warned that "the mood among Negroes of this country
is that they will never bear arms again until all forms of bias and discrimination are abolished." Truman stormed out of the meeting, responding hotly,
"I wish you hadn't made that statement. I don't like it at all."

They must have reached an understanding nevertheless, for Randolph
called off the march, and Truman, swallowing his pride, issued Executive
Order 9981 on July 26, 1948, mandating equal racial treatment in the military, effective immediately.[203] The key portion of the order reads: "1. It is
hereby declared to be the policy of the President that there shall be equality
of treatment and opportunity for all persons in the armed services without
regard to race, color, religion or national origin. This policy shall be put into
effect as rapidly as possible, having due regard to the time required to effec-
tuate any necessary changes without impairing efficiency or morale."[204]

The Korean War (1950–54), which cost about one-tenth of World War
II in number of American lives lost (36,000 compared to over 400,000), was
not an agent of radical change in the military, let alone in American society. In 1950 the UN commander in Korea, General Matthew B. Ridgway,
announced his intention to desegregate units in the combat zone; when the
war ended four years later, ten thousand black soldiers were still in segregated units.

A former Tuskegee airman, Charles Bussey, was a lieutenant in one of
those black units. When he and his vastly outnumbered battalion fended off
a North Korean attack at Yechon, he was awarded a silver medal for bravery
but not the highest the military could confer, the Medal of Honor. When he
asked a white officer why he received the lesser medal, he was told that "the
country does not need another Jackie Robinson."[205] Eisenhower, the general
who became president in 1952, helped things along by appointing Earl Warren and William Brennan to the Supreme Court, where they took aim at
Jim Crow in *Brown v. Board of Education* in 1954, but opinion is divided as
to whether Eisenhower knew what he was getting with those justices, and
progress was slow on other fronts.[206]

In May 1959 Dr. Martin Luther King Jr. challenged President Eisenhower to visit Tallahassee, Florida, to own up to the ongoing violence against

blacks, including the recent white gang rape of Betty Jean Owens, while black men were routinely lynched on trumped-up charges. "It is ironical that these un-American outrages occur as our representatives confer in Geneva to expand democratic principles. . . . It might well be necessary and expedient to appeal to the conscience of the world through the Commission on Human Rights of the United Nations."[207]

Vietnam was the first war with fully integrated combat units and black recruitment. It was also the first American war in which more black soldiers fought than was reflective of their proportion in the population. Blacks made up 11 percent of the American population and 12.6 percent of the soldiers serving in Vietnam. Black fatalities in Vietnam were 14.9 percent of the total, making them more likely to die than their white counterparts.[208]

Vietnam has the distinction of being the most unpopular war in American history. A 1969 Harris poll found that 80 percent of the respondents felt it had been a "mistake" for the United States to become involved. Annual Gallup polls showed steadily declining support until 1971, when they were discontinued.[209] Unable to sell the domino Communism theory to the baby boomer generation coming into draft-eligible age, politicians were in for a headache that turned into an incurable migraine.[210] As the military called for more troops in 1964, the Selective Service began to skimp on college and graduate school deferments, sparking middle-class outrage against the war in general and against the draft in particular.[211] Popular support declined with every new revelation of American casualties.[212]

Stateside, in what the legal historian Michael Klarman has called America's "unfinished business," the South continued to block legally enfranchised blacks from meaningful political participation. By the time President Lyndon B. Johnson nudged the House and Senate to pass the Civil Rights Act of 1964 and the Voting Rights Act of 1965, public opinion was ahead of Congress. Racism had by no means evaporated, but 80 percent of parents polled in 1964 did not object to sending their children to an integrated school—as long as the black children were below certain percentages of the class.[213]

Racism remained an obstacle to recruiting black soldiers in the South. Only 1.3 percent of members of draft boards were black, one-tenth of their proportion in the population. There were no black board members at all in Alabama, Arkansas, Georgia, Louisiana, Mississippi, and South Carolina until they responded to pressure from civil rights groups.[214] In 1966, partly to get around this problem, Defense Secretary Robert McNamara launched Project 100,000, purporting to provide upward mobility for inner city youth through military service. The plan was to relax mental and physical entry standards to active duty on grounds that underprivileged youth might have lacked educational opportunities needed to meet the regular standards.[215] About 40 percent of the some 350,000 men who enlisted through this project were African Americans.[216] To some black leaders, the program was a death sentence masquerading as social policy; to Congress, it was an unwelcome military foray into domestic politics. The program was put to rest after just a year in business.[217]

◆ ◆ ◆

The antiwar and civil rights movements partially overlapped, but they were not one and the same. For some years the NAACP, Martin Luther King Jr.'s Southern Christian Leadership Conference, and the National Urban League stood by President Johnson in gratitude for championing their cause in Congress, and they worried that antiwar rhetoric would undermine the mainstream coalition for civil rights they were trying to build. In 1965 Roy Wilkins of the NAACP hedged his bets: "Civil Rights groups do not have enough information on Vietnam or on foreign policy to make it their cause."[218] But in January 1966 the Student Nonviolent Coordinating Committee (SNCC) came out against the war. Many in the civil rights movement were increasingly frustrated by the "go along" strategy that had yet to produce a better livelihood for most blacks. Malcolm X, until his death in 1964, urged people to see that black nonviolence was not reciprocated.[219] Stokely Carmichael said of the distinguished but conciliatory Howard University professor Ralph Bunche, "You can't have Bunche for lunch!"[220]

On April 4, 1967, exactly a year before he was assassinated, Dr. King explained at Riverside Church in New York City why he too would now speak out against the war:

Over the past two years, as I have moved to break the betrayal of my own silences and to speak from the burnings of my own heart, as I have called for radical departures from the destruction of Vietnam, many persons have questioned me about the wisdom of my path. At the heart of their concerns this query has often loomed large and loud: "Why are you speaking about the

The Reverend Martin Luther King Jr. makes a speech
at a church in Selma, Alabama, March 27, 1965.

war, Dr. King?" "Why are you joining the voices of dissent?" "Peace and civil
rights don't mix," they say. "Aren't you hurting the cause of your people," they
ask? And when I hear them, though I often understand the source of their
concern, I am nevertheless greatly saddened, for such questions mean that the
inquirers have not really known me, my commitment or my calling. Indeed,
their questions suggest that they do not know the world in which they live.
. . . Somehow this madness must cease. We must stop now. I speak as a child
of God and brother to the suffering poor of Vietnam. I speak for those whose
land is being laid waste, whose homes are being destroyed, whose culture is
being subverted. I speak for the poor of America who are paying the double
price of smashed hopes at home, and death and corruption in Vietnam.[221]

Unlike veterans of past wars who returned home to gratitude and admiration, Vietnam veterans returned to a hostile public. Far from coming back
"all uppity," as southerners always feared, black soldiers often found themselves whiplashed by their patriotism and the derision they encountered.[222]

Nothing captures their impossible situation better than the grotesque celebrations of some white soldiers when Dr. King was assassinated on April 4, 1968, exactly one year after his "A Time to Break the Silence" speech. The situation of the black soldiers and veterans who were thus provoked to violent protest was tragic in a literal sense.[223]

Civil rights for blacks were hard fought, slow in coming, and somehow still fragile. The Civil Rights Act of 1964 and the Voting Rights Act of 1965 gave American blacks equality on paper that should have been secured by the Fifteenth Amendment but that southern states routinely ignored. Spelling out what equality means, and backing up a robust interpretation of those statutes in the courts and at the ballot box, remains a challenge of American politics.

Compared to advancing the cause of racial equality, lowering the voting age from twenty-one to eighteen was simple. In his 1954 State of the Union Address, President Eisenhower had publically urged Congress to amend the Constitution to grant voting rights to everyone eighteen and older. "For years our citizens between the ages of 18 and 21 have, in time of peril, been summoned to fight for America. They should participate in the political process

President Lyndon Johnson speaking to Senator Richard Russell,
who was leading a filibuster against the Civil Rights Bill in 1963.

that produces this fateful summons. I urge Congress to propose to the States a constitutional amendment permitting citizens to vote when they reach the age of 18." Republicans in Congress dragged their feet on lowering the voting age for fear they were on the wrong side of the "generation gap" that had opened up on questions of race, war, and Communism.[224]

By 1968 Congress could no longer ignore polls showing that two-thirds of Americans supported voting rights for eighteen-year-olds.[225] The backdrop was surging opposition to the Vietnam War, a war so reviled that the drafting of brothers and sons was increasingly intolerable. Congress, including its Republicans, had moved to the left as dovish senators replaced hawkish ones in a series of elections.[226] During the midterm election of 1970, John Gardner, Lyndon Johnson's secretary of health, education, and welfare, launched Common Cause to end the draft through electoral action.[227] In 1970 President Richard Nixon promised to end the draft to defuse the political fracas, and as he hoped, student antiwar protests stopped as soon as the draft ended.[228] The columnist Mike Royko noticed that "presto, the throbbing social conscience that had spread across America went limp."[229]

✦ ✦ ✦

For the majority of the population, North America has been a comfortable and safe place to live. Abundant resources and scant threat of invasion nurtured hair-trigger sensitivity about government in America's popular culture: stay out of our way unless requested. Sturdy self-reliance is of course largely a fantasy, judging from large, persistent agricultural subsidies and a ceaseless parade of political favoritism that comes in every flavor. Partisan competition is fierce in the balmy confines of centrism. Business has always been and continues to be treated well. With exceptions during the First and Second World Wars, when federal corporate income tax shot up to 4 percent and 8 percent of gross domestic product respectively, that percentage has hovered around 2 percent.[230]

America's geopolitical advantages have translated more easily into liberty than into "justice for all." To a degree seldom true elsewhere in the world, wars have been optional for the United States. When survival does not require the utmost from every man, woman, and child, the political and economic elites have the luxury of fighting limited wars that do not create obligations to political outsiders. Restricting wartime mobilization allows the dominant political coalition to withhold leverage from those who would trade the blood sacrifice of military service for political equality. The South dragged its feet on black conscription in every war to protect Jim Crow, and it succeeded for an extraordinarily long time because the costs to the republic were affordable. Still, the government increased taxes during the world wars and expanded the franchise to eighteen-to-twenty-one-year-olds during Vietnam, reshaping politics-as-usual for the sake of wider military mobilization.

Today America's twenty-first-century warfare on terror relies even less on native sons than ever before. Manned by enlisted men and mercenaries, powered by high-tech machinery, and financed by foreign-floated government debt, America's war machine is largely off the public's radar. In contrast to the rage young people expressed toward the Vietnam War in the 1960s, America's decades in Iraq and Afghanistan provoked more skepticism and dismay from old than from young citizens. The antiwar protester's scream has given way to a great, collective yawn.

CONCLUSIONS

ISTORY DOES NOT REPEAT ITSELF, but it rhymes, as Mark Twain is reputed to have said.[1] More precisely, history flows to recognizable rhymes and meters that can change over time and place for lots of reasons. This book has explored the conditions under which war has promoted one of the most cherished human values: democratic self-governance. Under some circumstances, when populations are sufficiently terrified of external enemies, rulers have been able to compel them to fight without sharing power, economic concessions, or anything else. This is the story of imperial China, of monarchical France, and of autocrats the world over. Autocrats appear to have found it relatively easy to force farmers who live in fertile and vulnerable plains to pay for the common defense through taxes, manpower, or both.

At the other topographical extreme, people who live in unapproachable terrain—places that are easy to defend such as mountains or islands or swamps—could refuse to be governed by an overlord at all. People in the Swiss Alps and in Southeast Asia's mountainous regions seem to have expected every man to help defend the community and to have been self-governing from ancient times. They had little use for "stationary bandits" (autocrats) offering protection either because they could handle the "roving bandits" (marauding armies) on their own, or because they were so poor no one bothered with them.[2]

Because most of the earth's topography falls somewhere between those two extremes, terrain alone only gets us so far in explaining the democratizing effects of war. Military technology, sometimes in combination with terrain, is a second factor that has influenced how much power a ruler must concede to his population to mobilize them. Democracy is more likely to emerge or survive when the prevailing military technology favors manpower, such as the extremely effective and rower-intensive Athenian trireme. The Roman iron panoply favored an infantry-based army, but the expense of the panoply gave effective political franchise only to the men who could afford to outfit themselves—essentially farmers who owned their land. Heavy cavalry warfare, which began to replace the Roman infantry (and light barbarian cavalry) from the 500s, favored the agrarian aristocracy with lands enough to breed and provision horses and to outfit the knights to ride them. Hand-held guns brought infantry back to center stage, but that military revolution launched the age of monarchies, not of democracies.

Monarchies took advantage of a third factor that could make the difference for a king between having to make democratic concessions or not: access to riches. For a couple of centuries, the Spanish monarchy lived in glory on New World precious metals and Dutch loans without catering to the masses. The French monarchy took a longer-term view, taxing commercial wealth in exchange for protecting merchant interests, which in turn gave the French king freedom from the landed aristocracy that had tethered him to mutual obligations with the men who were his heavy cavalry. Once freed from his vassals, at least relatively speaking, the French king could raise peasant armies, bought and paid for by taxes from his merchant class. He did not have to grant a wider franchise in exchange for this manpower because he could pay market wages.

Only the basic structure of our argument is timeless. In eighteenth-to-twentieth-century Europe a particular kind of war—wars of mass mobilization—gave rise to the particular kind of democracy that we now take for granted. We find war's deep stamp on modern democracy in the fusion of working-class demands for universal suffrage and elites' insistence on property protections sometimes known as "rule of law." Although pieces of the modern compromise are as ancient as Athens and Rome, the democracy favored by the masses and the aristocratic republicanism preferred by the rich have always had an uneasy, unsettled relationship, as we saw vividly from Rome to the Italian city-states. These tectonic plates still underlie democratic politics today, but the rift is cemented over with layers of democratic ideology, barely visible and infrequently interrogated.

TERRAIN/TECHNOLOGY

		Protected	Vulnerable
FINANCING	**Money**	**Property rights:** Dutch Republic England	**Absolutist Monarchy:** France Spain
	No Money	**Universal Suffrage:** Switzerland Sweden	

Terrain, technology, and resources have shaped the way communities felt and responded to military threats. The formidable natural defenses of the Swiss Alps enabled the inhabitants to self-govern for centuries. Most other places contracted with rulers for protection at one time or another, but autocracies are politically "wider" than aristocracies when manpower is needed to fight wars. During the more recent wars of total mobilization, many governments granted political concessions in exchange for even greater manpower mobilization.

Our story began in the fifth century BC in Athens, when Cleisthenes led a democratic coup against the Spartan-backed aristocracy. From the standpoint of military vulnerability, the peninsula of Attica, on which Athens stood, enjoyed some advantages of hilly terrain and ocean protection but not to the extent that farmers and fisherfolk could defend themselves with ease. Athenian aristocrats, who remained wealthier than the rest, continually lamented "mob rule" and repeatedly sought to restore elite-based government. Fortunately for Athenian democracy, the silver mines owned by the polity funded a navy of triremes that was foundational to Athens' trade-based economy and its military security.

As a city-state, Athens was physically small enough that its democracy was simply the gathering of five or six thousand male citizens (the entire population waxed and waned between 20,000 and 40,000) to make decisions in assembly, leaving out the women, slaves, and noncitizens who also lived in Athens. The difference between the Athenian model of direct democracy and our model of representative democracy today draws attention to democracy's multiple dimensions: depth, which captures how involved citizens are in self-government; and width, or what fraction of the population could be full citizens with the right to participate in those decisions. Athens was deep and fairly narrow on that scheme, while modern democracies are wide and shallow. Populist authoritarian governments today that hold elections of dubious integrity are shallower yet, not reaching the threshold necessary for real democratic accountability. Modern advanced democracies are deeper than electoral autocracies in several ways: leaders can be peacefully forced from office through elections and therefore need to present convincing justifications to citizens; a free press supplies relevant information for evaluating the incumbents and other candidates; and an opposition is free to present alternatives to reelecting incumbents. The figure below allows us to see regimes arrayed along two continua of depth and width.

Like Athens, the Roman Republic was a fierce warrior state that put political participation in service of military exploits. Compared to Athens, political participation was shallow because some functions of government were reserved for the unelected senatorial class, and it was narrow because voting was income-weighted, based originally on account of the cost of the iron panoply. The Republic's experiment with enfranchising conquered cities across the Italian Peninsula failed to protect the public from inordinate influence by the generals and their men who happened to be back in town from the latest campaign, or from the richest citizens who had time and money to travel to Rome. The Principate with which Augustus and his heirs

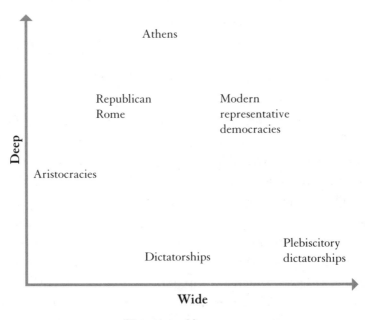

Dimensions of democracy.

replaced the Republic put a stop to genuine political assemblies, but like many dictatorships, it bought off the subject population with subsidies that the aristocracy would not have paid voluntarily.

Nevertheless, monarchies, aristocracies, and pure democracies are all prone to corruption and demise, suggesting an endlessly rolling wheel of constitutional forms (*anacyclosis*) as one type of government falls to another, in steady succession. As Polybius saw it, Rome's adaptation to military necessity, by combining democratic and aristocratic elements, was a possible fix. We think of Rome's experiment with "mixed government," in fact, as an earlier version of the constitutional bargain between manpower and money that lies at the heart of modern democracy.

The Roman Republic flourished for almost five centuries, but because we hope for durable arrangements, its demise gives us pause. The dictatorship that replaced the Republic took advantage of a vast reservoir of anger and alienation among Rome's poorest citizens. By some estimates, the income gap in Rome was no greater than it is in the United States today.[3]

Not for many centuries would the world's dominant powers incorporate elements of democracy. Monarchy and aristocracy took turns: the Roman Principate replaced the Republic for several centuries more, which in turn was replaced by feudal aristocracies that eventually fell to European monarchies in another six or seven centuries. Aristocracy, a system which by definition gives the vast majority of the population less of everything, was stable as long as aristocrats were able to fight their wars with only modest and coerced or bought contributions from peasants.

From about the fifteenth century, the effective use of gunpowder decisively tipped the balance away from the cavalry-dominated militaries of the previous five hundred years and in favor of mass armies. This had the effect of shifting political power upward to leaders who could finance and maintain such large armies. In principle, anyone could amass large gun-toting armies to destroy the castles and cavalry of the landed elite; in practice, those who solved the problem of raising money with which to buy big armies won this competition. Those were the men who could call themselves king.

Military competition would replace monarchy with representative democracy, but not before industrialization shifted power from landed elites (whom monarchs understood) to urban elites (whom monarchs managed less well). Monarchs, who were not particularly well equipped to bridge the widening gulf between industrialists and workers, dealt clumsily with the nineteenth-century explosions between them. Rare was the royalist like Bismarck who, by making war on neighbors, could pick his way through the thicket of domestic confrontation under an ideology of national unity. Even Bismarck was able to manage this only because he was willing to grant manhood suffrage in exchange for national loyalty.

In the few nooks and crannies where a direct voice in politics came by birthright, representative democracy had no immediate appeal either. Direct democracy, as the eighteenth-century Swiss philosopher Jean-Jacques Rousseau argued emphatically, is as close to an institutional embodiment of self-governance as man has yet devised.[4] Though Rousseau's concerns were elsewhere, the direct democracy of the Swiss alpine cantons, because it threatened industrialists who would never be a majority, was not a winner of the Polybian sweepstakes.

The constitutional mutation that allowed democracies to outperform monarchies was representation, a feature that the Greeks called "aristocratic." Political representation is not intended to favor aristocrats in any literal sense, but it is a vertical check on decision making that slows down the formation and implementation of majority views. In practice, it facilitated the transition to democracy for nineteenth-century aristocracies and autocracies by allowing leaders to try out democracy in gradations, by increasing the voter roster by increments of citizens' income and wealth, to test whether all hell would break loose. It did not produce deep democracy, partly because representation also tends to be aristocratic in another sense: rich citizens disproportionately show up to vote, to make their wishes known to their representatives,

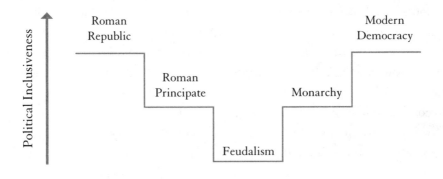

Historical junctures in state-types.

and to contribute money to political campaigns. The evolutionary metaphor captures the intuition that mutations—in this case, the institution of representation adopted to scale democracy up to large territorial size rather than to protect the property of the rich—can have surprising, unplanned effects.

The idea that an elected person could stand in for many voters, as a way to reconstruct democratic accountability in a large territory, was not designed with warfare in mind.[5] True, representation of the three estates—or in the rare instance of Sweden, the four "estates"—was a vestigial remnant of militarized feudalism that monarchies repurposed for national taxation and local administration. The constitutional historian Brian Downing's influential book stresses the medieval roots of democratic representation.[6] In fact, the struggles involved in reconstituting the medieval estates into modern representative government demonstrate that representation as a way to build cross-class coalitions was neither easy nor inevitable. The massive military threats of the nineteenth and twentieth centuries accomplished it.

Democratic representation's early theorists such as Sieyès and Kant advocated keeping monarchy but making monarchs politically accountable with the help of a legislature.[7] It took pragmatic state builders and military strategists such as Bismarck and Disraeli to see something else: a set of levers that could simultaneously motivate an entire population to support the nation, while retaining control of the actual decision-making power. In the 1867 British Reform Act, the Tory Prime Minister Benjamin Disraeli doubled the franchise from 14 to 28 percent of the adult male population by reducing the property qualification. Bismarck, with more pressing military aims, played an even bolder game when he introduced universal male suffrage in Germany to match the French. Still, he took the precaution of limiting parliament's role to an advisory one. Representation in the nineteenth century started small and, like a caged animal, was closely watched.

Representation paved the way for the national wars of the late nineteenth and twentieth centuries to fuse two constitutional pieces long in conflict: democratic suffrage and republican freedom. Early democratizers such as the United States and gradual franchise expanders such as Britain put on display for the rich strata in other countries the fact that the poor did not rush to expropriate the rich. In the hands of a savvy strategist like Bismarck, the institutions of representation, which could be modified and manipulated, were more of a tool than a constraint.

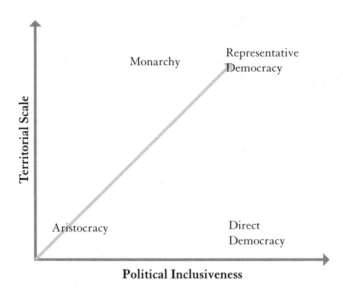

The military capacity of constitutional forms.

Nationalism was another crucial ingredient in the nineteenth-century evolution of modern democracy. It played the part of a bellows, both raising the forge's temperature and blowing smoke. Although the situation varied somewhat across countries, nineteenth-century nationalism not only intensified interstate competition but also created a romantic haze through which the wealthy saw, sometimes for the first time, the poorer classes as fellow citizens who would fight to achieve common goals rather than clamor for advantage at home.

Who was working the bellows to create national unity? Here the imagery of a purposeful actor loses traction, because the political nationalism that followed the French Revolution and the Napoleonic Wars was at least partly spontaneous combustion.[8] Intellectuals across the continent bundled national sentiment with calls for political freedom and civic engagement.[9] In Germany poets and philosophers produced misty-eyed paeans to the Fatherland, and in England a resurgence of interest in the legends of King Arthur and his court celebrated past glory.[10]

Still, some nineteenth-century politicians, chief among them Bismarck and Disraeli, were master manipulators of these national feelings. Bismarck exploited German sentiment that had been aroused at Jena in 1806 in opposition to Napoleon and stoked in 1848 by members of the Frankfurt Parliament who pressed for representative government.[11] As he intoned toward the end of the century, after Germany's victory against France,

> *The bond which holds us inseparably together was formed from a mixture of blood, wounds, and death on the battlefield of St. Privat, from deeds performed in common under the attack of the hereditary foe who threatened our nationality and had need to destroy our unity. . . . History reveals that unity is most firmly established by comradeship in war.*[12]

Bismarck's diplomatic sparring partner, British prime minister Disraeli, had similarly proud words for his countrymen:

> *Gentlemen, since the settlement of that Constitution [of 1688], now nearly two centuries ago, England has never experienced a revolution, though there is no country in which there has been so continuous and such considerable change. How is this? Because the wisdom of your forefathers placed the prize of supreme power without the sphere of human passions. Whatever the struggle of parties, whatever the strife of factions, whatever the excitement and exaltation of the public mind, there has always been something in this country round which all classes and parties could rally, representing the majesty of the law, the administration of justice, and involving, at the same time, the security for every man's rights and the fountain of honor.*"[13]

Viewing fellow citizens as compatriots through the prism of nationalism— with its focus on what the nation had in common rather than as class enemies—helped make democracy possible. It is important to see that nationalism is a military ideology: an ideology of mobilization against the enemy or outsider and that its rise in the nineteenth and twentieth centuries amounted to a kind of militarization of whole societies. In one country after another at the onset of World War I, the labor movement abandoned Lenin's plea for international worker solidarity and swung instead behind national cross-class compromise.

Electoral representation that replaced direct citizen democracy, against Jean-Jacques Rousseau's advice, made it possible for countries to call themselves democratic where citizens delegated the business of government to professional politicians. Although the accountability of politicians to their constituents depends in practice on a host of factors, both sociological and institutional, the core feature of representative democracy is the ability of voters, irrespective of income or any other attribute, to replace incumbents with challengers with relative ease.

Barrington Moore's study of the modern world has been captured in the aphorism, "No bourgeoisie, no democracy." Given that the middle classes generally opposed universal suffrage for fear of redistribution, however, it leaves us without an explanation for the jump from republican systems favored by the propertied classes to democracy in which poor voters have an equally weighted ballot. Competing arguments that stress the role of working classes, on the other hand, skip over the details of how the scattered and diffuse interests of the masses congealed, let alone how they could prevail over entrenched elite resistance.[14] Both kinds of arguments miss a crucial element: it was often the fear of outside enemies that pushed the sides together.

✦ ✦ ✦

If the modern democratic republic is a product of wars that required both manpower and money for success, it is time to take stock of what happens to democracy once the forces that brought it into being are no longer present. Understanding war's role in the creation of the modern democratic republic can help us recognize democracy's exposed flanks. If the role of the masses in protecting the nation-state diminishes, will the cross-class coalition between political inclusiveness and property hold?

Sentimentality about the past will not help. Protective terrain, which was once a boon to democracy in places like Switzerland and other mountainous communities, no longer plays a democratizing role. With some possible exceptions, new military and civil technologies have figuratively if not literally flattened terrain. Vulnerable locations like France that were prone to being governed as monarchies have nevertheless remained democratic since the full mobilizational wars of the nineteenth and twentieth centuries because of the protective shield of representative democracy. Today, no one would say that Paris is less democratic than the villages around the St. Gotthard Pass, or that the voters of Berlin have less clout than those in the Black Forest.

Healthy democracy in today's world requires an informed electorate and vigorous political competition. Educated citizens with the right to vote can hold their leaders accountable just as well as mountain men willing to charge with a bayonet-fitted gun. Although the accountability of politicians to their constituents depends in practice on a host of factors, both sociological and institutional, the core feature of representative democracy is the ability of voters, irrespective of income or any other attribute, to replace incumbents with challengers with relative ease. Universal access to good education is as important for citizens today as local militias were for citizens of yesteryear.

If concern about democracy's continued viability is one question, a second question is what is to become of the swaths of the world that were off the warpath in the fourteenth and fifteenth centuries when the European state was formed? Continued and intense warfare forged democracies with full enfranchisement and protected property rights in the Goldilocks zone: in countries that had already developed administrative capacity as monarchies, and where wars were horrendous but manageable with full mobilization. Perhaps for reasons Jared Diamond suggests—that migration follows agriculture because plants flourish in a narrow latitudinal band of growing conditions—vast portions of longitudinally arrayed Latin America and Africa had not organized themselves into strong nation-states by the time the western imperialists overran them in the fifteenth to nineteenth centuries with guns and new diseases.[15] With few exceptions, gun-equipped and monarchy-funded imperialist adventurers found people organized in constitutional forms that were small or poorly mobilized. By the nineteenth and twentieth centuries, Latin American and African aristocracies were able to negotiate independence with weary, half-hearted imperial overlords without having to raise the rabble and share political power with the general public. Colonial wars did not create strong states, let alone democratic ones.[16]

It would be grotesque to insist that states must undergo an authoritarian stage along the lines of European monarchical absolutism before becoming stable democracies, as Samuel Huntington has been understood to imply.[17] That policy advice, taken seriously by successive U.S. administrations, has produced Frankenstein monsters the world over: militarized aristocracies or dictatorships that have little reason to share power with their populations.[18]

The bad news is that in today's world, war has stopped functioning as a democratizing force. Among the great powers, expensive technology that substitutes for manpower has made the draft redundant or even trouble-some. Within insurgency groups that otherwise would have to be democratic to attract as many fighting men as possible, control of mineral wealth or religious orthodoxy allows them to run autocratically. Insurgencies that do not need to win the hearts and minds of the populations in which they operate bring all of the blights of bloodshed and destruction without the benefits of accountability. Democracy is not out of reach for these societies, but the path will be hard and war will not help them get there.

The good news is that we need not glorify wars. There is no point in mourning the unmooring of modern democracy from manpower wars if armed conflict today does not generally promote democracy and if democratic vigilance can secure freedom as reliably as threatening to spill blood.

There is, however, another source of optimism. Social science research shows an increase in the resilience of democracies (or of any regime type) as incomes rise above some threshold when citizens become satisfied with the status quo. If democracy is a luxury good that all humans seek upon securing physical safety and economic livelihood, perhaps prosperity alone can propel human societies toward self-governance without the blood costs of warfare to mend the divisions between them. That is the good scenario. There are bad scenarios too: societies that fail to address growing class divisions, like Republican Rome, can fall in on themselves; or societies rent asunder by conflicts over non-divisible goods such as religion or ethnicity will mire down in civil wars. Without a doubt, establishing state capacity and democracy at the same time is hard in practice because corruption that breeds in the crevices of weak institutions corrodes voter confidence. Thus is launched a vicious cycle that can undermine electoral accountability, when voters who believe that politicians are corrupt have no incentive to vote for the party touting the best policies.

Electoral democracies work best sitting atop fluid splits among the elite rather than in the presence of deep gulfs between classes, ethnicities, or religions on which politicians have an incentive to capitalize. One ancient theme that still rhymes today is that societies benefit the most from political competition, not from militarized authoritarianism. Democracy's best hope for emergence and survival in today's evolving world is for us to support prosperity, tolerance, and pluralism wherever we find it.

ACKNOWLEDGMENTS

W E OWE OUR FIRST DEBT OF GRATITUDE to a group of assiduous historians who talked with us over the ten-year period during which we researched and wrote this book. We do not hold them accountable for our interpretations and claims, but the book is far better than it would have been without the input of these wonderful scholars and friends. They include, among others, Virginia Aksan, Mary Beard, Eugenio Biagini, Rafe Blaufarb, Jeremy Black, William Cafferro, Henry Cohn, Sam Cohn, Thomas Conlan, Timothy Connell, Stephen Epstein, Ute Frevert, Karl Friday, Karin Friedrich, Robert Frost, Jan Glete, Mark Greengrass, William Harris, Marjolein 't Hart, Jonathan Haslam, Ann Hughes, Susumu Ike, Tsuguharu Inaba, Bela Karpossy, Andrew Lintott, Peter Lorge, Emily Mackill, Michael Metcalf, Ian Morris, John Najemy, Wilfred Nippel, Josiah Ober, David Parrott, Pasquale Pasquino, Maureen Perrie, Michael Rapport, Lucy Riall, Nathan Rosenstein, Walter Scheidel, Christine Shaw, Simonetta Soldani, Pierre Souyri, Jonathan Sperber, Kira Stevens, Barry Strauss, Kathleen Sullivan, Miles Taylor, Robert Toombs, Carol Richmond Tsang, Peter Wilson, David Wootton, and Dingxin Zhao.

For financial support, we extend our profound thanks to the Filomen D'Agostino and Max E. Greenberg Research Fund at NYU, Yale University's MacMillan Center for International and Area Studies, the Council on East Asian Studies, and the Leitner Program for Comparative and International Political Economy.

We also thank generous colleagues for advice at various stages: Robert Bates, Carles Boix, Gary Cox, Laura Engelstein, Glenda Gilmore, Paul

Kennedy, Andrew Lambert, David Mayhew, Kenneth Scheve, James Scott, Ian Shapiro, Rogers Smith, David Stasavage, Steven Wilkinson, and Daniel Ziblatt. For research support, we owe deep thanks to Luke Connell, Sajid Ghani, Yuchien Liu, Tess McCann, Megan Palmer, Radu Simion, and Lincoln Swaine-Moore. We are enormously grateful to Joshua Handelsman who improved the book's flow and readability, to Abraham Parrish and Stacey Maples at the Yale maps collection, Matthew Regan at Yale IT, and the Geography Department at Brigham Young University who provided us with invaluable materials and technical support. Enormous thanks to Pat Holl for humor, patience, and tenacity in supervising mapmaking and in tracking down picture and photo rights. Thanks also to Wendy Strothman of the Strothman Agency who persuaded us to write for a wider audience than our usual circle of academic colleagues, and Philip Marino, the supremely talented editor at Norton's Liveright, who tried to show us how.

NOTES

Introduction

1 The seventeenth-century alchemist Sir Kenelm Digby thought that he could heal wounds with "sympathy powder" made from iron sulphate. Miles, "Sir Kenelm Digby," 126.

2 Keyssar, *Right to Vote*.

3 Therborn, "Rule of Capital," 21–23.

4 Burnham, "Changing Shape."

5 Huntington, "How Countries Democratize," 589.

6 Peter Gourevitch pioneered the study of international effects on domestic policies ("The Second Image Reversed"). For domestic roots of foreign policy, see Reiter and Stam, *Democracies at War*; Russett and Oneal, *Triangulating Peace*; Ober, "Thucydides on Athens' Democratic Advantage"; Caverley, *Democratic Militarism*.

7 Mazower, *Hitler's Empire*.

8 Pericles, "Funeral Oration," as recounted by Thucydides in *Peloponnesian War*.

9 This is the very definition of demagoguery, which is Greek for "leading the people" or "leading the mob," depending on your political leanings: *demos* (people) and *agogos* (lead).

10 Aristotle, *Politics* IV through VI, especially 1292, 1305, 1318.

11 Literally "cycling upward," *anacyclosis*, ἀνακύκλωσις.

12 Polybius, "On the Forms of States," II.9.10–13, in *Histories,* Book VI.

13 Polybius, preface, *Histories,* Book VI.

14 Scott, *Art of Not Being Governed*.

15 Ibid.; Bates and Lien, "Note on Taxation"; Mancur Olson ("Democracy, Dictatorship, and Development") postulates a progression from "roving bandits" to "stationary bandits" as communities buy into the protection racket. Boix, *Democracy and Distribution*; Boix, *Political Order and Inequality*.

16 Braudel, *Mediterranean*; Scott, *Art of Not Being Governed*.

17 天高皇帝远 Tian gao huangdi yuan.

18 Tolstoy wrote in *Anna Karenina*, "All happy families are alike; each unhappy family is its own way."

CHAPTER I

The Twenty-First-Century Wars Without Citizen Armies

1 Gardner, "Lawyers Who Shaped America."
2 Caverley, *Democratic Militarism,* chap. 6; "A Decade Later, Iraq War Divides the Public," Pew Research Center for the People and the Press, March 18, 2013; Berinsky, *In Time of War*, 218; Berinsky, "Assuming Costs of War," 979; Ullman and Wade *Shock and Awe.*
3 Daggett, "Costs of U.S. Wars," 3.
4 Chan and Safran, "Public Opinion as a Constraint," 137–38.
5 These poll figures are the averages from Gallup, Zogby, Quinnipiac, ARG, Harris, Newsweek, CBS/NYT, CNN, AP/Ipsos, Fox, NBC/WSJ, ABC/WP, and Pew; Chiozza and Goemans, "Peace Through Insecurity," 443.
6 Caverley, *Democratic Militarism*, chap. 8.
7 Charles Rangel. "Bring Back the Draft," *New York Times,* December 31, 2002.
8 Reiter and Stam, *Democracies at War*, chap. 1.
9 Starr "War and Liberalism," 23.
10 Lyall and Wilson, "Rage Against Machines," 77, 99; Sechser and Saunders, "Army You Have," 506; Lyall, "Do Democracies Make Inferior Counterinsurgents?"
11 Baker and Stack, eds., *At War with Civil Rights and Civil Liberties,* 227.
12 Strong, "Fifty Years," 43; Lowe, "'Clear and Present Danger.'"
13 Strong, "Fifty Years," 42.
14 Baker and Stack, eds., *At War with Civil Rights and Civil Liberties*; Issacharoff and Pildes, "Between Civil Libertarianism," 23.
15 Reese and Lewis, "Framing War on Terror," 777; Gronke and Rejali, "U.S. Public Opinion on Torture," 441.
16 "Opinion Leaders Turn Cautious, Public Looks Homeward," Pew Research Center for the People and the Press, November 17, 2005.
17 Gronke and Rejali, "U.S. Public Opinion on Torture."
18 Hume, *Political Discourses*, I.V.7.
19 Viroli, *From Politics to Reason of State,* 196.
20 Ardito, *Machiavelli and the Modern State.*
21 Caverley, *Democratic Militarism*, chaps. 3–4.
22 Cline, review of Weight and Beach, 354.
23 Netto, "Malaysia's Three-Month National Service."
24 "Military Conscription Policy by Country," ChartsBin, http://bit.ly/1s721wr.
25 Jehn and Selden, "End of Conscription," 95.
26 Jorgensen and Breitenbauch, "Give Up Conscription?" 8.
27 Swiss Coalition Against Arms Trade, "Report on Exports of Arms," 3.
28 Efflandt, "Under Siege," 9.

29 Sechser and Saunders, "Army You Have," 506.

30 Nordhaus, Oneal, and Russett, "Effects of International Security Environment," 500.

31 Postwar U.S. defense spending as a percentage of GDP reached a low point in 2000 with the end of the Cold War, and it began rising after 9/11 in connection with the "War on Terror."

32 Bonvillian, "Connected Science Model," 207–10.

33 Chinn, "Preserving Combat Power."

34 Ibid.

35 Patman, "Globalisation," 970.

36 Schaub, Kristensen, and Pradham-Blach, "Long Time Coming," 12–13.

37 North Atlantic Treaty Organization, www.nato.int/cps/en/natohq/index.htm.

38 SAIC, "Typical Defense Contractor—Poor Pay, Poor Benefits, Horrible Hours, Antipathy Toward Home Life/Family," GlassDoor, n.d., http://bit.ly/1VVVfq5.

39 Commission on Wartime Contracting, *Transforming Wartime Contracting,* 22.

40 Ibid., 2.

41 "Protocol Additional to the Geneva Conventions of 12 August 1949, and the Protection of Victims of International Armed Conflicts (Protocol 1), 8 June 1977," Article 47, http://bit.ly/1skDhl2.

42 "Geneva Convention Relative to the Treatment of Prisoners of War, U.N.T.S. 135," University of Minnesota Human Rights Library, http://bit.ly/1NtkyNr; Hathaway et al., *Power to Detain*; Cohen, "Steelworkers Rethink," 155; Green, *Death in Haymarket*.

43 Commision on Wartime Contracting, *Transforming Wartime Contracting,* 25; Celik, Wolthuis, and Slagter, "War Profits"; Dzara, "Credibility Concerns"; Efflandt, "Under Siege," 12.

44 Efflandt, "Under Siege," 1.

45 Cameron, "Private Military Companies," 595; Pesce, "Private Contracting Gone Wrong?"; Bedard, Nelson, Saltzstein, and Spaziano, "US Supreme Court Bars."

46 Commission on Wartime Contracting, *Transforming Wartime Contracting*, 4–5.

47 Matt Apuzzo, "Trying to Salvage Remains of Blackwater Case," *New York Times*, May 12, 2014; House Committee on Oversight and Government Reform, Defense Contract Accountability, Institute for Domestic and International Affairs; Spencer Ackerman, "Blackwater Founder: My Company Could Have Prevented Benghazi Deaths," *Guardian*, November 22, 2013.]

48 Laub, "Taliban in Afghanistan."

49 Patman, "Globalisation," 974; Molly Crabapple, "Today Marks the 12th Anniversary of America's Guantánamo Prison Disgrace," *Guardian,* January 11, 2014; Lynch, "Truth and Lies"; Laub, "Taliban in Afghanistan."

50 Patman, "Globalisation," 974.

51 Kral, "Czech Republic and Iraq Crisis"; Hrobsky, "Public Opinion Divided."

52 Tago, "Democratic Friends Unreliable," 227.

53 McClure, "Coalition of Billing."

54 Matthew Day, "Poland Ends Army Conscription," *Telegraph*, August 5, 2008.

55 Tago, "Democratic Friends Unreliable," 228; Ormisson, "Public Opinion."

56 Simon Jeffery, "New Spanish Prime Minister Promises Iraq Withdrawal," *Guardian,* March 15, 2004.

57 Gvosdev, "Coalition of Billing"

58 David Stavrou, "The Debate over Swedish Troops in Afghanistan," Local.se, December 15, 2010, http://bit.ly/1s72D5j; "Iraq War Logs: The Response in Denmark, Sweden, and Norway," WikiLeaks Press, October 21, 2011, http://bit.ly/1UZdn1h.

59 Zakheim, *Vulcan's Tale,* 210; Jakobsen, *Nordic Approaches,* 180.

60 Iraq Coalition Casualty Count, iCasualties,org, 2009, http://bit.ly/1NtkGMZ.

61 "Casualties in Iraq: The Human Cost of Occupation," Antiwar.com, n.d., http://bit.ly/1qiB9IJ; Commission on Wartime Contracting, *Transforming Wartime Contracting,* 31.

62 Avant, "Mercenaries" 11.

63 Rebecca Traister, "Moore Interviewed Berg for 'Fahrenheit,'" *Salon*, May 27, 2004.

64 Catherine Lutz and Neta Crawford Lutz, "Bad Things Happened: The AfPak War at 12," *Huffington Post,* October 7, 2013; Chesser, "Afghanistan Casualties."

65 "Iraq War: 190,000 Lives, $2.2 Trillion," Costs of War Project, Brown University, March 14, 2013, http://bit.ly/1TbksqA; Commission on Wartime Contracting, *Transforming Wartime Contracting,* 56; "Evaluation of Development Support," Ministry of Foreign Affairs of Denmark, 96.

66 Hathaway et al., *Power to Detain,* 126.

67 Steyn, "Guantanamo Bay," 1.

68 Issacharoff and Pildes, "Between Civil Libertarianism"; Hathaway et al., *Power to Detain,* 176.

69 Marcel Berlins, "I Was Wrong about Steyn," *Guardian,* September 28, 2004.

70 Drew Desilver, "Most Young Americans Say Snowden Has Served the Public Interest," Pew Research Center, January 22, 2014; Jon Cohen, "Most Americans Back NSA Tracking Phone Records, Prioritize Safety Over Privacy," *Washington Post,* June 10, 2013; Susan Page, "Most Americans Now Oppose the NSA Program," *USA Today,* January 20, 2014.

71 Brennan Center for Justice, "The Voting Rights Act: A Resource Page," August 4, 2015, http://bit.ly/1FiMMoL.

72 Richard Wike, 2011; Springford, "Old and New Europeans United," 2003.

CHAPTER 2

War and Democracy in Classical Athens

1 That is the sanitized version of what he said, quoted in Proietti, *Xenophon's Sparta,* 10; Hale, *Lords of the Sea,* 222.

2 Semple, "Geographic Factors," 54; Bachteler, "Explaining Democratic Peace," 318.

3 Hale, *Lords of the Sea,* 222.

4 Hunt, *Slaves, Warfare, and Ideology in the Greek Historians,* 360.

5 Moles, "Xenophon and Callicratidas," 80.

6 Xenophon says shipwrecked; Diodorus Siculus, a Sicilian Greek writing three centuries later, says war dead.

7 Roberts, "Arginusae Once Again," 107.

8 McCoy, "Thrasyllus," 288; McCoy, "Thrasybulus and His Trierarchies," 319; Xenophon, *Hellenica*, 1.67.28; Roberts, "Arginusae Once Again," 107.

9 Strauss, "Democracy, Kimon"; Ober, *Democracy and Knowledge*; Pritchard, "Symbiosis Between Democracy and War."

10 Thucydides, *Peloponnesian War*, 7.73.

11 Morris, "Economic Growth"; Forrest, "Legislation in Sparta," 16; Evans, "Ancient Mesopotamian Assemblies," 115.

12 Rhodes, "Political Activity in Classical Athens."

13 Wallace, "Revolutions and New Order," 59; Old Oligarch, *Athenaion Politeia* (*AP*), 14.11, 16.2–3.

14 Herodotus, *Histories* (5.66, 69) suggests many of the Athenian aristocrats were executed. Ober, " 'I Besieged,' " 88.

15 Herodotus, *Histories* 5.

16 *Psephismata*; Raaflaub, "Introduction," in Raaflaub, Ober, and Wallace, *Origins of Democracy*, 4.

17 *Isegoria;* Nakategawa, "Isegoria in Herodotus."

18 Hansen, *Athenian Democracy.*

19 This suited Aristotle: "An agricultural population makes the best demos . . . for having no great abundance of wealth they are kept busy and rarely attend the Assembly." *Politics* 6.4.

20 Rhodes, "Political Activity," 143; Giffler, "Boule of 500," 224; Hansen, *Athenian Democracy*, 132.

21 The Greek word is *isonomia.* Aristotle, *Politics* 6.2.

22 Old Oligarch, *AP* 22.5; Develin and Kilmer, "What Kleisthenes Did"; Hansen, *Athenian Democracy*, 249; Raaflaub, "Introduction," in Raaflaub, Ober, and Wallace, *Origins of Democracy*, 5.

23 The Greek word is *dokimasia.*

24 The Greek word is *eisaggelia.*

25 Rhodes, "Eisaggelia in Athens," 105–8.

26 The Greek word is *euthana.*

27 See, for example, Hansen, *Athenian Democracy*, 220–24; Wallace, *Aeropagus Council*; Rhodes, "Eisaggelia in Athens"; Rhill, "Democracy Denied."

28 The Greek word is *dikasteria.*

29 Hansen, *Athenian Democracy*, 187.

30 Herodotus, *Histories* 3.82.

31 Herodotus, *Histories* 5.78–9.

32 Plutarch, *Life of Cimon,* 8.1.

33 Wallace, "Revolutions and New Order," 78.

34 Herodotus, *Histories* 6.132–36.

35 Old Oligarch, *AP*, 22.3.

36 Ibid., 22.7; Herodotus, *Histories* 6.87–93; 7.144.1–2; Thucydides, *Peloponnesian War* 1.14.1–2; Hale, *Lords of the Sea*; Frost, "Themistocles' Place," 117.

37 Plutarch, *Themistocles* 12; Herodotus, *Histories* 8.60; Hammond, "Battle of Salamis," 40; Robertson, "Decree of Themistocles," 44.

38 Peck, "Athenian Naval Finance."

39 Thucydides, *Peloponnesian War*, 2.85.2–3; Ober, "'I Besieged.'"

40 Raaflaub, "Breakthrough," 117; Aeschylus, *Persians*, 408–20; Thucydides, *Peloponnesian War*, 1.49.1–4; 7.62.3–4; Pritchard, "Symbiosis Between Democracy and War," 19.

41 Thucydides, *Peloponnesian War*, 1.143.5; Spence, "Pericles and Defense of Attika," 91.

42 Bonner, "Commercial Policy," 193.

43 Larsen, "Constitution of Peloponnesian," 267.

44 Morris, "Economic Growth in Ancient Greece."

45 Old Oligarch, *AP* 27.4.

46 Plutarch, *Aristeides*, 22, 27.

47 Thucydides, *Peloponnesian War*, 3.37.

48 Plato, *Laws*; Euben, "Battle of Salamis," 386; Plato, *Laws,* http://bit.ly/1TaTXqA.

49 Plato, *Laws*, 706c–707a.

50 In Greek, these were known as *liturgies*.

51 In Greek, *trierarchs*: Peck, "Athenian Naval Finance."

52 Giffler, "Boule of 500," 226.

53 Ober, "Defense of Athenian Land Frontier," 199–201.

54 Ibid., 221

55 Rhodes, "Political Activity," 139; O'Neill, "Exile of Themistocles," 335; Forrest, "Themistokles and Argos," 227.

56 Plutarch, *Cimon* 15.2

57 Old Oligarch, *AP* 26.2

58 Pericles was a descendent, on his mother's side, of Cleisthenes himself. Raaflaub, "Breakthrough," 113–14.

59 According to the Old Oligarch, Pericles introduced jury pay to clip the power of Cimon, who could buy a following with money. Raaflaub, "Breakthrough," 115; Plutarch, *Life of Pericles*; Hansen, *Athenian Democracy*, 7.

60 Wallace, "Revolutions and New Order," 80.

61 Hansen, *Athenian Democracy*, 90–94; Old Oligarch, *AP*, 1.2; Thucydides, *Peloponnesian War*, 1.142.6; 8.74–7; Pritchard, "Symbiosis Between Democracy and War," 27.

62 (*hetaireiai*) Rhodes, "Political Activity," 138; Mitchell and Rhodes, "Friends and Enemies," 22.

63 Finley, "Athenian Demagogues," 17.

64 Thucydides, *Peloponnesian War*, 8.68.

65 Caspari, "Revolution of Four Hundred," 5; Thucydides, *Peloponnesian War*, 8.67.

66 Thucydides, *Peloponnesian War*, 8.68.

67 Caspari argues, contrary to Thucydides' narrative, that the eviction of the old Boule preceded the convention at Colonus. "Revolution of Four Hundred," 10.

68 McCoy, "Thrasybulus and His Trierarchies," 314.

69 Finley, "Athenian Demagogues," 11; McCoy, "Thrasybulus and His Trierarchies."

70 McCoy, "Thrasyllus," 275.

71 Cloche, "L'affaire des Arginuses"; Roberts, "Arginusae Once Again."

72 Xenophon, *Hellenica* 2.2.24.

73 Rhodes, "Athenian Code of Laws," 93

74 Thucydides, *Peloponnesian War*, 8.67.3.

75 Hall, "Ephialtes, Areopagus," 323.

76 Raubitschek, "Heroes of Phyle," 284–85.

77 Hamilton, "Spartan Politics and Policy," 314.

78 Farrar, *Origins of Democratic*, 177; Ostwald, *From Popular Sovereignty*, 497 ff.

79 The *Graphe paranomon* was essentially a lawsuit that could be brought by any Athenian citizen against an Assembly decree (and/or its proposer) on grounds that it was inexpedient or illegal. When the Athenians made a distinction between laws and decrees upon restoring democracy after The Thirty, they called the procedure against laws (and/or its proposer) the *graphe nomon me epitedeion theinai*. We know more instances of *graphai paranomon* brought than *graphai nomon me epitedeion theinai*, reflecting the fact that the Athenians passed more decrees than laws. Rhodes, *Athenian Boule*; Rhodes, "Nomothesia"; and Hansen, *Sovereignty of the People's Court*.

80 Hansen notes that these codification and ratification procedures of the *nomothetai* bypassed the Assembly altogether. *Athenian Democracy*, 163.

81 *Graphe paranomon and graphe nomon,* respectively. Hansen *Athenian Democracy*, 168; Raaflaub, "Introduction," in Raaflaub, Ober, and Wallace, *Origins of Democracy,* 4; Farrar, "Power to People," 176.

82 Hansen, *Athenian Democracy*, 167.

83 *themosthetai.*

84 Rhodes, "Nomothesia," 56.

85 Potidaea in 432, Delium in 424, and Amphipolis in 423.

86 The steering committee of the *boule* was composed of randomly chosen *prytaneis*, with leadership of the steering committee rotating once a month among the tribes. Hale 2009: 230; Kagan, *Peloponnesian War*, 465.

87 Plato, *Apology* 25e–26a.

88 Ibid., 37a–b.

89 Plato, *Republic* VIII.562d.

90 Ibid., VIII.564d–11.565a, Alan Bloom's translation.

91 Plato, *Republic* IV 425, in Sihler, "Aristotle's Criticisms," 441.

92 Aristotle, *Politics*, IV.11.

93 Aristotle, *Politics* V.11.

94 Polybius, *Histories* 6.4.6–11.

95 See, for example, Pocock, *Machiavellian Moment*.

96 Kant, *Perpetual Peace,* sec. II.

97 Thucydides, *Peloponnesian War*, 1.70; Ober, *Democracy and Knowledge*.

98 The term "Corinthian assessment" is Ober's (*Democracy and Knowledge*, 17, 22). See also Strauss, "Thrasybulus and Conon"; Strauss, "Democracy, Kimon"; Strauss, "Memorandum for Workshop"; Pritchard, "Symbiosis Between Democracy and War," 31.

99 Knox, "Athenian 'Demos,' " 146.

100 Thucydides, *Peloponnesian War*, 4.27; Pritchard, "Symbiosis Between Democracy and War," 33.

101 Knox, "Athenian 'Demos,'" 146; Thucydides, *Peloponnesian War*, 5.26; Rhodes, "Political Activity," 137.

102 Ostwald, *From Popular Sovereignty.*

103 Thucydides, *Peloponnesian War*, 3.36–50

104 Finley, "Athenian Demagogues," 20; Strauss, "Thrasybulus and Conon"; Bruce, "Corcyraean Civil War," 115; Thucydides, *Peloponnesian War*, 3.91.

105 Quoted in Knox, "Athenian 'Demos.'"

106 Smith, *Athenian Political Art*, 9.

CHAPTER 3

The Glory That Was Rome

1 Lintott, *Constitution of Roman Republic*, 230–32.

2 Cicero, "Speech in Defense of Titus Annius Milo," translated by Charles Duke Yonge, 17, http://bit.ly/1Xpm5qb.

3 Drews, *End of Bronze Age,* stresses the discovery of iron in about 1200 BC in ushering in the age of infantry, since it was cheaper than bronze only affordable by the aristocracy.

4 Cincinnatus was one of eighty-five recorded dictators from 501 to 202 BC, after which the office of dictator was discontinued for 120 years. Only the Senate could invoke the dictatorship, and as the popular parts of the constitution gained strength in the overall institutional mix, the dictatorship fell into disuse for a time. Nippel, *Public Order.*

5 Never mind that Cincinnatus was staunchly conservative and always opposed to improving the situation of the plebeians.

6 Snodgrass, "Hoplite Reform and History," 119.

7 Drews, *End of Bronze Age*, 184–85.

8 Although the facts cannot be pinned down from available fragments of evidence, Livy credits King Servius Tullius with constructing an infantry built on military classes by property qualification. Livy 1.43, translation at http://go.mu.edu/2bPCsLL.

9 Seignobos, *History of Roman People*, 109; Polybius 10.17.11–13, referenced in Libourel, "Galley Slaves," 118; see also Livy 26.47.

10 Polybius 6.22, translated by http://penelope.uchicago.edu/Thayer/E/Roman/Texts/Polybius/home.html.

11 Ibid., 6.23.

12 Carey and Cairns, *Warfare in the Ancient World*; de Souza, "Parta Victoriis Tax," 141.

13 Zhmodikov, "Roman Republican Heavy Infantrymen," 74.

14 Nicolet, *World of the Citizen*, 89, 93.

15 Cornell, *Beginnings of Rome*, 256, sides with Momigliano, "Time in Ancient," against Raaflaub, "Politics and Society," in suggesting that the "sit-down strike" must have been instigated not by the hoplites but by the lowest classes of light-armed soldiers relegated to phalanx support. We do not take sides in this debate.

16 Polybius describes the workings of Rome's government during his day in Book V, at http://bit.ly/1TCgln7.

17 North, "Politics and Aristocracy," 285.

18 Mouritsen points out that the Roman Comitium was considerably smaller than the Athenian Pnyx and that most likely about 3,000 Roman voters could have cast their ballots in the pens in about 6.5 hours. *Plebs and Politics*, 23–35. Millar argues that the crowd was active and involved in deliberation that went beyond passive listening. *Crowd in Rome*. Morstein-Marx insists that these meetings do not merit the word *debate* even in a minimal sense of considering alternatives. *Mass Oratory*, 172–79.

19 As Polybius wrote, "Such is the cycle of political revolution, the course appointed by nature in which constitutions change, disappear, and finally return to the point from which they started. . . . And especially in the case of the Roman state will this method [of tracking mixed government systems through a cycle of competing pathologies] enable us to arrive at a knowledge of its formation, growth, and greatest perfection, and likewise of the change for the worse which is sure to follow some day. For, as I said, this state, more than any other, has been formed and has grown naturally, and will undergo a natural decline and change to its contrary." English translation available at Penelope. uchicago.edu. Scholars are divided on whether Polybius saw the Tiberius Gracchus tribunate, which came a decade after he wrote *The Histories,* as a harbinger of decline. Walbank, "Polybius on Constitution," 87.

20 Taylor, "Forerunners of Gracchi," 19; Boren, "Tiberius Gracchus," 362; Staveley, *Greek and Roman Voting*; Taylor, *Roman Voting Assemblies*.

21 Quoted in Taylor "Forerunners of Gracchi," 19; Boren, "Tiberius Gracchus," 362–64.

22 The Latin word for electoral bribery is *ambitus,* connected to the verb *ambitere* ("to go around canvassing") and the noun *ambition,* expressing the pursuit of fame to excess. Lintott, "Electoral Bribery," 1.

23 Scheidel calculates that Rome had a total citizen population of about a million in 234 BC, about a third of whom would have been adults. "Human Mobility I," 6–11. They would have been outnumbered three to one by the population on peninsular Italy including slaves. Peninsular Italy itself was a tiny fraction of the imperial population of 150 million.

24 Rosenstein, *Rome at War*, 137.

25 Scheidel, "Human Mobility I," 23.

26 Ibid.; Katz "Gracchi," 68; Plutarch's Tiberius 9, 4 ff; Rosenstein, *Rome at War.*

27 Livy, 22.57.12; 23.14.2 By the reign of Claudius, the free population of Italy was 7 million compared to 21 million slaves, up from (Brunt's guess) half a million slaves in 225 BC. Scheidel, "Human Mobility II," 64.

28 Katz, "Gracchi," 68.

29 A slave revolt in Sicily routed the Roman troops sent to crush them until additional troops were sent in 133–32 BC. Katz, "Gracchi," 70.

30 Boren, "Tiberius Gracchus," 359; Rosenstein, "Aristocrats and Agriculture."

31 Boren, "Tiberius Gracchus," 358.

32 Katz, "Gracchi," 68.

33 Lavery, "Cicero's 'Philarchia,'" 133.

34 On the dictatorship, see Broughton, *Magistrates of Roman Republic*, 141, and Nippel, *Public Order*.

35 Lushkov, "Narrative and Notice," 109; Silvalupus, "Politics and War."

36 Brunt, "Legal Issue in Cicero," 144.

37 Cicero's city of Arpinum, for example, was given citizenship without the vote in 188 BC.

38 Salmon, *Cause of Social War*, 120: "What the Sabellian gentry really wanted was, not to have their communities cut all ties with Rome, but to acquire Roman citizenship for themselves."

39 After the Gracchi, who were tribunes, there was a steady succession of consuls whom the Senate tried to chop down to size including Marius, Pompey, and Caesar. Also see Mary Beard, *The Roman Triumph*.

40 Ridley, "Dictator's Mistake," 211. Equites were taken back out of the Senate.

41 Batstone, "Cicero's Construction," 254.

42 Cicero, *De Re Publica* 1.67–68, quoted in Nelsestuen, "Overseeing," 168; George, "Lucan's Cato," 254.

43 Quoted in Mitchell, "Background of Roman Revolution," 316.

44 The tribunes' legislative powers were restored in 70 BC during Pompey's first consulship. Hardy, "Catilinarian Conspiracy in its Context," 155.

45 Smethurst, "Politics and Morality," 116; Murray, "Cicero and Gracchi," 297.

46 Lintott, "P. Clodius Pulcher," 159.

47 Quoted in Bennett, "Wit's Progress," 197.

48 Seager, "Clodius, Pompeius," 520–28; Robinson, "Cicero's References."

49 Quoted in Kelsey, "Cicero as a Wit," 9.

50 Smethurst, "Cicero and the Senate," 78.

51 Ayers, "Cato's Speech," 248.

52 Lavery, "Cicero's 'Philarchia,'" 142.

CHAPTER 4

A Millennium of Landed Aristocracy

1 MacDowall, *Adrianople*, 77.

2 Ibid., 80.

3 Burns, "Battle of Adrianople," 341; de Souza, "Parta Victoriis Tax," 206.

4 Rosenberger, "Gallic Disaster," 365.

5 Ibid., 366.

6 Deutsch, "Caesar and the Ambrones," 258; Polybius 1.20.1; Errington, *Dawn of Empire*, 102; Corbett, "Rome and the Gauls," 661; Polybius 2.23.9–10; Erdkamp, "Polybius, the Erbo Treaty," 510.

7 Carey and Cairns, *Warfare*, 89.

8 Hill, "Livy's Account," 245; Develin, "Voting Position," 160; Rowland, "C. Gracchus and Equites," 368.

9 Geary, *Before France*, 73. This arrangement broke down in the late empire as tribal leaders insisted on bringing whole units to serve under them.

10 Benedict surmises that the Senate sent Flaccus, a partisan of Gaius Gracchus, to get him out of Rome. "Romans in Southern Gaul," 40.

11 Ibid., 42; de Souza, "Parta Victoriis Tax," 154.

12 Caesar, *Gallic War* IV:33 and V:16; Moore, "A Vexed Passage in the Gallic War," 209; Darvill, *Prehistoric Britain,* 30; Black, "Sentius Saturninus," 7.

13 Tacitus, *Annals* 12.40.

14 Minor, "Bagaudae or Bacaudae?" 318–22.

15 Swain, "Caesar's Strategy," 72; MacDowall, *Adrianople,* 20; Brunt, "Princeps and Equites," 42.

16 Janz, "Chronology," finds evidence of wetlands in the Gobi into the early Bronze Age.

17 Heather, "Goths," 183.

18 MacDowall, *Adrianople,* 64.

19 Ibid.

20 Henri Pirenne argued that the Arabs drove the Roman Empire out of the Mediterranean, ending the trade with Gaul and consigning the Merovingians to poverty. But in fact the Arabs did not arrive until later, and there is plenty of evidence of continuing trade through Italian cities and Provence, as well as a new trade through the Russian river system. For a critique of Pirenne's thesis from the point of view of an Islamist scholar, see Dennett, "Pirenne and Muhammad," 165–90.

21 Bachrach, *Merovingian Military Organization.*

22 Fischer, *Laws of Salian Franks*; Geary, *Before France,* 92.

23 Collins, *Early Medieval Europe,* 63.

24 Geary, *Before France,* 115; Geary, *Myths of Nations,* 56.

25 Geary, *Before France,* 93–94, 152–54.

26 Umayyad expansion owed much to tolerance of cultural and religious differences in occupied lands. Collins, *Early Medieval Europe,* 298; Nicolle, *Poitiers AD 732,* 8, 30. By contrast, the Franks, though once proud of their "pagan" Nordic origins, prospered with the backing of the Church and coerced Catholic conversion (Moore, *A Sacred Kingdom,* 241; Einhard, and Notker the Stammerer. *The Life of Charlemagne,* 827.

27 Nicolle, *Poitiers AD 732,* 69.

28 Verbruggen, *Art of Warfare in Western Europe,* 277.

29 Bowlus, "Two Carolingian Campaigns," 121–25.

30 Bury, "Gambetta and Overseas Problems," 272; Fox, *Geographic Perspective,* 43; Andersen, Jensen, and Skovsgaard, "Heavy Plough."

31 Reynolds, *Fiefs and Vassals.*

32 Geary, *Before France,* 162.

33 Fox, *Geographic Perspective,* 43; Andersen, Jensen, and Skovsgaard, "Heavy Plough."

34 Hallam, *View of State,* 22.

35 Collins, *Early Medieval Europe,* 286; Pounds, *Historical Geography of Europe,* 173.

36 Pounds, *Historical Geography of Europe,* 225; Fox, *Geographic Perspective,* 44.

37 Some scholars call this the "feudal revolution." Reuter and Wickham, "'Feudal Revolution,'" 177.

38 Ohnacker, "What If," 184, 196. Louis's feuding sons broke apart the realm.

39 Bisson, "'Feudal Revolution,'" 6; Duby, *La Société aux XIe et XIIe siècles* (1971 ed.).

40 Bisson, "Medieval Lordship," 749; Bisson, "Feudal Revolution: A Reply," 208–25; White, "Feudal Revolution: Comment"; Barthelemy, "Debate: Feudal Revolution."

41 Goldberg, "Popular Revolt," 475.

42 Bowlus, *Battle of Lechfield*, 53.

43 For developments in Italy at roughly the same time, see Wickham, *Early Medieval Italy*.

44 North and Thomas credit the drop in the labor-land ratio and the rise of cities for the end of serfdom in the west. In our view, the rise of monarchy should share the spotlight. "Rise and Fall of Manorial System."

45 Froissart, *Chronicles* 1:138.

46 Tuchman, *Distant Mirror*, 182.

47 Historian Maurice Dommanget (*La Jacquerie*) believes the revolt covered a much wider area than has been generally believed, probably at least fourteen of France's present *Departements*; referenced in Braude, review of Dommanget, 189.

48 Green, "Last Century of Danegeld," 1.

49 The tax, known as the *Danegeld,* literally meant "Danish invasions."

50 Orderic Vitalis, *Ecclesiastical History* II 260, quoted in Green, *Aristocracy of Norman England*, 8.

51 Green, *Aristocracy of Norman England*, 8; Kapelle, "Domesday Book"; Green, review of Hingst, 1190.

52 Carpenter, "Second Century of English Feudalism."

53 Hatcher, "English Serfdom and Villeinage," 23.

54 Raimond, "Southey's Early Writings," 183; Ormrod, "Peasants' Revolt," 11, 22.

55 Campbell and Bartley, *England on the Eve*.

56 Hatcher, "English Serfdom and Villeinage," 38; see also Domar, "Causes of Slavery."

57 Hatcher, "English Serfdom and Villeinage," 38.

58 Thompson, *Economic and Social History of Europe*, 443–44.

59 Ibid., 446; Chodorow, "Ecclesiastical Politics," 614, 629.

60 Thompson, *Economic and Social History of Europe*, 452–53.

61 Ibid., 447.

62 Domar, "Causes of Slavery," 19.

63 Hagen, "Seventeenth Century Crisis"; Hagen, *Ordinary Prussians*; Foucault, *Discipline and Punish*.

64 Hunt, "Seventeenth Century Crisis," 49.

65 Ibid., 54.

66 Blum, "Rise of Serfdom," 835; Anderson, *Passages from Antiquity,* 253.

67 Lattimore, "Origins of Great Wall," 535.

68 Graff, *Medieval Chinese Warfare*; Li Feng, " 'Feudalism' and Western Zhou China," 144.

69 Dardess, "From Mongol Empire to Yuan Dynasty," 134; Williams, "Manchu Conquest," 153; Zhang, "Studies in Late Qing Dynasty."

70 Turnbull, *Mongolian Invasions*. Japan was barely touched by hostile forces before U.S. Commodore Perry steamed into Shimoda Bay in 1854 demanding refueling and trading rights.

71 Hall, *Government and Local Power in Japan*.

72 Batten, "Foreign Threat," 200; Asakawa, "Origin of the Feudal Land Tenure," 17.

73 Souyri, *World Turned Upside Down*.

74 Asakawa, "Some of the Contributions of Feudal Japan," 18.

75 Tsang, *War and Faith*; Souyri, *World Turned Upside Down*.

76 Conlan, *State of War*; and Conlan, "Instruments of Change."

CHAPTER 5

The Emergence of Monarchy in France and Spain

1 Hill, "Raymond of Saint Gilles," 265.

2 Strayer, *Medieval Statecraft*; Graham-Leigh, *Southern French Nobility*.

3 Aubrey, "Dialectic between Occitania," 1; Pegg, review of Graham-Leigh.

4 Strayer, *Medieval Statecraft*, 137; Bradbury, *Capetians*.

5 *La Chanson de la Croisade contre les Albigeois*, available online at http://bit.ly/1TL3IWE.

6 North and Thomas, "Rise and Fall of Manorial System"; Bean, "War and Birth"; Ames and Rapp, "Birth and Death of Taxes."

7 Pegg, review of Graham-Leigh.

8 Sherborne, "Hundred Years' War"; Postan, "Some Social Consequences," 2.

9 Firnhaber-Baker, "Seigneurial War," 37; Postan, "Some Social Consequences."

10 Henneman, *Royal Taxation*, 15.

11 Postan, "Some Social Consequences," 2; Henneman, *Royal Taxation*, 124, 283.

12 Henneman, "Financing," 276.

13 Ibid., 291; Villalon and Kagay, "Hundred Years War." In 1713 France ceded the area to Piedmont upon its defeat in the Spanish War of Succession. Pollard, *Marginal Europe*, 102.

14 Henneman, "Military Class," 951; Doyle, *Sale of Offices*.

15 Dewald, "Magistracy and Political Opposition," 69.

16 Benedict, "More than Market and Manufactory," 516.

17 Rothrock, "French Crown," 307; Hayden, "Deputies and Qualites," 514; Sturdy, "Tax Evasion," 550; Cohn, *Government in Reformation Europe*, 22; Henshall, *Myth of Absolutism*, 183; Major, "French Renaissance Monarchy," 44.

18 Cohn, *Government in Reformation Europe*, 17.

19 Benedict "Saint Batholomew's Massacres."

20 Harding, "Mobilization of Confraternities."

21 Wolfe, "Jean Bodin on Taxes." 269, 278; Dur, "Right of Taxation," 289; Meyer, "La Rochelle," 183; Jensen, "French Diplomacy," 46; Pegg, review of Graham-Leigh.

22 Hume, review of Willert, 578.

23 White, "From Privatized to Government-Administered," 636.

24 Montesquieu, *Spirit of the Laws*, 220.

25 Quoted in White, "From Privatized to Government-Administered," 647.

26 Hoffman, "Taxes and Agrarian Life," 55; Root, "Redistributive Role of Government," 351.

27 Bouton, review of Berce: 659; Salmon, "Peasant Revolt in Vivarais," 16.

28 Bonney, "Cardinal Mazarin," 832; Salmon, "Venality of Office," 22.

29 Brewer, *Sinews of Power*; North and Weingast, "Constitutions and Commitment"; Stasavage, *Public Debt*.

30 White, "From Privatized to Government-Administered," 652.

31 Ibid., 660.

32 Cohn, *Government in Reformation Europe*, 18.

33 Bisson, *Medieval Crown*, 9.

34 Ibid., 10.

35 Elliott, *Imperial Spain*, 34; Pierson, review of Klein, 257; Phillips and Phillips *Spain's Golden Fleece*.

36 Simpson, Griffiths, and Borah, "Representative Institutions," 230.

37 Bisson, *Medieval Crown*, 15.

38 Elliott, *Imperial Spain*, 40.

39 Freedman, "German and Catalan"; Elliott, *Imperial Spain*, 40.

40 Elliott, *Imperial Spain*, 84

41 Ames and Rapp, "Birth and Death of Taxes," 175.

42 Owens, "'By My Absolute Authority.'"

43 Rodriguez-Picavea, "Armies of Military Orders," 51.

44 Elliott, *Imperial Spain*, 119; Kamen, "Mediterranean and Expulsion," 45–46.

45 Asch, *Nobilities in Transition*, 128.

46 Espinosa, "Spanish Reformation," 4.

47 Nexon, *Struggle for Power*, 137.

48 Ibid.; Espinosa, "Spanish Reformation," 9.

49 Asch, *Nobilities in Transition*, 146.

CHAPTER 6

War and Representation in England, the Netherlands, and Sweden

1 Schultz, *Encyclopedia of American Law*, 439.

2 The quip has sometimes been attributed to parliamentary scholar A. F. Pollard, in describing Oliver Cromwell's Protectorate.

3 Turner, "William De Forz," 229.

4 Treharne and Sanders, *Documents of the Baronial Movement*, 72.

5 Madicott, *Origins of Parliament*, 233–76.

6 Harriss, "War and Emergence," 37.

7 Ormrod, "England in the Middle Ages," 20.

8 Henry V forced the French to recognize his son as the heir to the French Crown in the 1420 Treaty of Troyes but the French reneged when Henry died soon thereafter; see Parliament Rolls of Medieval England, http://bit.ly/27kiQEE.

9 Stow, review of Goodman and Gillespie, 476; Gillespie, review of Harriss, 139; Griffiths, review of Watts, 685.

10 Ormrod, "England in the Middle Ages," 38.

11 Menchi, "Rival Aversions," 14.

12 Alsop, "Innovation," 83; Cohn, *Government in Reformation Europe*, 17; Elton, "King or Minister?" 144; Brewer, review of Patterson; Henshall, *Myth of Absolutism,* 91; Koenigsberger, Mosse, and Bowler, *Europe in Sixteenth Century*, 292; Christianson, "Causes of English Revolution," 60; Gordon, "Collection of Ship-Money,"147; Ellis, *Ireland in Age of Tudors,* 343.

13 Beem, "Elizabeth's Wars," 568; Hinton, "Decline of Parliamentary Government."

14 Richards, " 'His Nowe Majestie,' " 73.

15 Harriss, *King, Parliament*; Brewer, review of Patterson; North and Weingast, "Constitutions and Commitment," and Stasavage, *Public Debt*, show how Parliament's victory in the 1688 Glorious Revolution further notched up England's ability to wage war.

16 Zaller, "Kingship," 122.

17 Cramsie, *Kingship and Crown Finance*, 80; Zaller, "Kingship," 122.

18 Clark, *Iron Kingdom*; Cramsie, *Kingship and Crown Finance*, 114.

19 Davis, "Religion and the Struggle for Freedom."

20 Lerner, "Impeachment, Attainder," 2070n45.

21 King, "Episcopate During Civil Wars," 523.

22 Parliament had their knives out for Wentworth for urging royal absolutism, calling him "libidinous as Tiberius, cruell as Nero, covetous as Cressus, as terrible as Phalaris, as mischievous as Sejanus." Quoted in Lerner, "Impeachment, Attainder, 2065.

23 Ibid., 2059.

24 Ibid., 2066.

25 Ibid., 2080.

26 Ibid., 2086. Ironically, monarchs had typically used bills of attainder against unfaithful nobles to seize lands and inheritance rights. Henry VIII got parliament to "attaint" nobles he distrusted.

27 Ibid., 2091.

28 Quoted in ibid., 2093.

29 Lambert "Opening of Long Parliament," 281.

30 Chayes, *Thieves of State*, 163.

31 Gentles, review of Dean and Jones, and Kishlansky, *Rise of New Model Army*.

32 Worden, "Bill for a New Representative."

33 Bushman, "English Franchise Reform," 40.

34 Hudon, "John Lilburne, Levellers," 687; Macpherson, *Possessive Individualism*.

35 Kishlansky, "Consensus Politics," 50.

36 Parkin-Spear, "John Lilburne," 288; Foxley, "John Lilburne," 850.

37 Full text available at http://bit.ly/2bPp7Vu. For debates about the role of the common law, see Dzelzainis, "History and Ideology," 270; Foxley, "John Lilburne," 850; Parkin-Speer, "John Lilburne," 287.

38 Worden, "Bill for a New Representative."

39 Woolrych, "Calling of Barebone's Parliament."

40 Donagan, "Web of Honour," 366; Clifton, "Popular Fear of Catholics," 23.

41 Brewer, review of Patterson; North and Weingast, "Constitutions and Commitment"; Stasavage, *Public Debt*; Pincus, *First Modern*; Cox, "Was the Glorious Revolution."

42 Cited in Cress, "Radical Whiggery," 46.

43 Schumpeter, "The March Into Socialism."

44 The full text of *Oceana* is available at http://bit.ly/1skEOra.

45 Cress, "Radical Whiggery," 46.

46 The full text of Sidney's 1698 "Discourses Concerning Government" is available at http://bit.ly/2bPoOtM.

47 Trenchard and Moyle, *Argument.*

48 Sluiter, "Dutch-Spanish Rivalry," 166.

49 Brandt, *History of Reformation.*

50 Pirenne, "Formation and Constitution," 484–85; Gould, "Crisis in Export Trade," 213.

51 Vink, "World's Oldest Trade," 132, 141, 145; Oostindie and Paasman, "Dutch Attitudes," 349, 353; Sluiter, "Dutch-Spanish Rivalry," 183; Renkema, review of Goslinga, 113.

52 Mets, *Naval Heroes*, 29.

53 Sluiter, "Dutch-Spanish Rivalry," 171.

54 Koenigsberger, "Organization of Revolutionary Parties."

55 Wilson, "Massacre of St. Bartholomew," 636; Sutherland, review of Christie.

56 Koenigsberger, "Organization of Revolutionary Parties," 345.

57 Israel, *Dutch Republic,* 181.

58 Dunthorne, "Resisting Monarchy," 125.

59 Asch, *Sacral Kingship*, 103.

60 Israel, *Dutch Republic*, 214; Wyntjes, "Family Allegiance," 51.

61 Israel, "Conflict of Empires," 71; Parker, *Thirty Years War.*

62 't Hart, "Cities and Statemaking," 666; Parker, "Attentive, Nonpartisan Reader," 58; Griffiths, "Revolutionary Character," 468.

63 See the painting by Jan de Baen, 1672–75, Rijksmuseum in Amsterdam.

64 Murray, "Peasant Revolt of Engelbrekt Engelbrektsson."

65 Cohn, *Government in Reformation Europe*, 12; Asch, *Sacral Kingship*, 104.

66 Maarbjerg, "Sweden, the First Modern State," 405.

67 Roberts, *Essays in Swedish History*; Riches, "Early Modern Military Reform," 355.

68 Riches, "Early Modern Military Reform," 356.

69 Maarbjerg, "Sweden, the First Modern State," 407.

70 Upton, "The Riksdag of 1680," 284.

71 Metcalf, "Challenges to Economic Orthodoxy," 254; Heckscher, "Place of Sweden," 13; Barton, "Gustav III of Sweden and the Enlightenment," 27; Sandelius, "Dictatorship and Irresponsible Parliamentarism," 365.

CHAPTER 7

Italian Republics

1 Najemy, *History of Florence*, 412.

2 Machiavelli, *Discourses* III.9.

3 Machiavelli, *History of Florence,* http://bit.ly/23NZ2EY.

4 Holmes, "Reading Order in Discord," 321–22, 327. The text of Francesco Guicciardini's

History of The Wars of Italy Book XIX is available at http://bit.ly/1skFbSI. His *History of Italy* is available as a free ebook at http://bit.ly/16XWTjo.

5 Baron, *Crisis of the Early Italian Renaissance*, chap. 3.

6 Holmes, "Reading Order in Discord," 317.

7 Montesquieu, *Spirit of the Laws*.

8 Ardito, *Machiavelli and the Modern State*.

9 Hegel, *Philosophy of Right*.

10 A ruler might appeal to the Emperor or pope, as in the case of the Visconti family who cozied up to the Holy Roman emperor to gain control of Milan, or the Medici of Florence, who generally relied on friendly popes. Alternatively, one could appeal to some underlying principle—such as the Justinian principle that "what touches all should be decided by all"—to justify local independent rule or even popular rule as long as they had the military might to back it up. Drew, "Immunity in Carolingian Italy," 183; Thompson, "German Feudalism," 462. Cassidy, "Simone Martini's," 156–57.

11 Lopez, "Hard Times"; Cipolla, "Economic Depression."

12 McNeill, *Venice*, 13; Jones, "Italian Estate," 18–32; Epstein, *Freedom and Growth*.

13 Goldthwaite, "Medici Bank," 6, 20.

14 Lane, *Venice*; Najemy, "Guild Republicanism," 55.

15 Epstein, *Freedom and Growth*; Shaw, "Memory and Tradition," 224.

16 Cohn, review of Bruni.

17 Bonadeo, "Role of the 'Grandi,'" 10.

18 Najemy, *History of Florence*.

19 Cohn, Review of *La città*.

20 Bowsky, "*Buon Governo* of Siena," 368.

21 Najemy, "Guild Republicanism," 58.

22 Najemy, review of Baron; Abularafia, "Southern Italy"; Goldthwaite, review of Brucker, Hale, Steinberg.

23 Becker, "Florentine Popular Government," 360.

24 Armstrong, *Usury and Public Debt*, ix–x.

25 Villani, quoted in Najemy, *History of Florence*, 139.

26 Winter "Plebeian Politics"; Cohn, Review of *La città*.

27 Translation by Jurdjevic, *Great and Wretched City*; Baron, *Crisis of the Early Italian Renaissance*; Bond, "Lucan Christian Monarchist," 485.

28 Najemy, "Civic Humanism."

29 Najemy, *History of Florence*, 191.

30 Shaw, "Memory and Tradition."

31 Najemy, *History of Florence*, 396.

32 "'The Gonfalonier began, with the authority of the signoria, but without consultation, to enroll soldiers in the contado' . . . In spite of the progress achieved in the contado and the positive reactions of the rural population, strong opposition continued in the city. During February influential citizens convened in several pratiche to discuss the arming of the countryside." Hörnqvist, "'Perché non si usa allegare,'" 154–57.

33 Najemy, *History of Florence*, 483.

34 Epstein, *Genoa and Genoese*, 257; Cole, "American Entry," 18.

35 Greif, "On Political Foundations"; Epstein, *Genoa and Genoese*, 88.

36 Epstein, *Genoa and Genoese*, 325–27.

37 Cole, "American Entry," 18.

38 Byrne, "Genoese Trade with Syria," 193; Greif, "On Political Foundations," 36; Epstein, *Genoa and Genoese*, 143.

39 Epstein, *Genoa and Genoese*, 279; Cole, "American Entry," 20.

40 Elliott, *Imperial Spain*, 192.

41 Sella, "Milan," 711–13.

42 Epstein, *Freedom and Growth*; Sella, "Milan," 714; Ianziti, *Humanistic Historiography*.

43 Ortalli and Scarabello, *Short History of Venice*, 8.

44 Davis, *Shipbuilders*, 179; Davis, "Slave Redemption," 460.

45 Rosch, "Serrata of the Great Council," 67–80.

46 Ibid., 68–69.

47 Lane, *Venice*, 271; Pincherele and Marblec, "Vivaldi and 'Ospitali,' " 300.

48 Rosch, "Serrata of the Great Council," 80.

49 Mowbray and Gollmann, "Electing Doge."

50 Ortalli and Scarabello, *Short History of Venice*, 52–53.

51 Lane, *Venice*, 124–35; McNeill, *Venice*, 19.

52 Rapp, "Unmaking of the Mediterranean Trade Hegemony."

53 Epstein, *Freedom and Growth*.

54 Hirschman, *Exit, Voice, and Loyalty*, Bates and Lien, "Note on Taxation"; Boix, *Democracy and Distribution*.

55 Ardito, *Machiavelli*.

56 McNeill, *Venice*, 229.

57 Epstein, *Genoa and Genoese*; Greif, "On Political Foundations."

CHAPTER 8

Eastern Lands in Early Modern Europe

1 "Ce corps qui s'appelait et qui s'appelle encore le saint empire romain n'etait en aucune maniere ni saint, ni romain, ni empire," in his 1756 *Essai sur l'histoire generale et sure le moeurs et 'esprit des nations,'* chap. 70.

2 Thompson, "Crown Lands," 361–62.

3 "Perambulating kings" is Brian Pavlac's rephrasing of John Bernhardt's book title, *Itinerant Kingship and Royal Monasteries in Early Medieval Germany, 936–1075* (review of Bernhardt, 882).

4 Thompson, *Crown Lands,* 366.

5 Whaley, *Germany and the Holy Roman Empire*, vol. 2, chap. 41.

6 Wines, "Imperial Circles," 2.

7 Whaley, *Germany and the Holy Roman Empire*, 2:213.

8 Walford, "Outline History of the Hanseatic League," 87.

9 Greif, Milgrom, and Weingast, "Coordination, Commitment," 760, 761; Dollinger, *German Hansa*, 63.

10 Knudsen and Rothstein "State Building in Scandinavia."

11 Rotz, "Lübeck Uprising," 12.

12 Ibid., 16.

13 This pope, a notorious scoundrel, was ordained for the ministry the day he took office and precipitated the Schism.

14 Rotz, "Lübeck Uprising," 16.

15 Ibid., 17.

16 Carsten, "Origins of the Junkers," 163.

17 Ibid., 38.

18 Walford, "Outline History of the Hanseatic League," 83.

19 Postel, "Hanseatic League."

20 Carsten *Essays in German History,* 37; Hagen, "Seventeenth Century Crisis," 315, 335.

21 Brady, *Turning Swiss,* 10, 17.

22 Machiavelli, *Discourses* 1:55; Brady, *Turning Swiss,* 21.

23 Brady, *Turning Swiss,* 40; Blickle, *Revolution of 1525*; Stalnaker and Ginsburg, "Auf Dem Weg Zu Einer Sozialgeschichtlichen"; Sreenivasan, "Social Origins," 38.

24 Freedman, "German and Catalan."

25 Brady, *Turning Swiss,* 16.

26 Schilling, "Reformation in Hanseatic Cities," 455.

27 Parker, *Thirty Years War,* 5.

28 Rudolf II, crowned Emperor and king of the Czechs, moved his imperial court back to Prague in 1583.

29 Seton-Watson's less charitable characterization of Matthias was that he was "a man of half measures . . . not sufficiently fanatical himself and . . . too hampered by the action of the Estates . . . to be capable of aggression against Transylvania." "Transylvania, II," 535.

30 Polisensky, *History*, 67.

31 Ibid., 62.

32 Parker, *Thirty Years War*, xii.

33 Evans *Making of Habsburg Monarchy*.

34 Valentin, "Wallenstein," 156.

35 Wallenstein himself lent over 6 million thalers to the emperor between 1621 and 1628.

36 Polisensky, *War and Society*, 170.

37 Parker, "Dynastic War," 175.

38 Polisensky, *War and Society*, 171.

39 Parker, "Dynastic War," 187.

40 Ibid., 147.

41 Deacon, review of Münkler and Camiller, 157.

42 Parker, "Dynastic War," 160.

43 Valentin, "Wallenstein," 159.

44 Parker, "Dynastic War," 161.

45 Ibid., 171.

46 Ibid., 160.

47 The Hansa and other Free Imperial Cities are a footnote in the Treaty of Westphalia, for most cities had been destroyed in the cross fire between territorial giants. The treaty

acknowledged the independence of free cities but such was the attenuation of Habsburg power that, in 1717, the imperial court refused to back this provision. Friedrich, *Other Prussia*, 63.

48 Parker, "Dynastic War," 159.
49 Ogilvie, *Institutions and European Trade*, 245.
50 Ibid., 243.
51 Quoted in McNeely, "Hegel's Württemberg Commentary," 348.
52 Prussia was technically Brandenburg-Prussia until 1701, for marriage brought the physically separated principalities of Cleves and Ravensberg in the Rhine Valley in 1614 and fused the electorate of Brandenburg with the heirless Duchy of Prussia in 1618.
53 Fay, "Beginnings of Standing Army," 765.
54 Ibid., 767.
55 Ibid., 768.
56 Hagen, "Seventeenth Century Crisis," 315.
57 Craig, *Politics*, 4.
58 Quoted in Fay, "Beginnings of Standing Army," 772; Mears, "Thirty Years' War," 123.
59 Domar, "Causes of Slavery."
60 Hagen, "Seventeenth Century Crisis," 325.
61 Hagen, "Seventeenth Century Crisis," revises the standard wisdom of aristocratic supremacy advanced by Blum, "Rise of Serfdom."
62 Schoffer, "Second Serfdom in Eastern Europe," 57.
63 Lynn, "States in Conflict," 179.
64 Manning, review of Satow, 458.
65 Blanning, "'That Horrid Electorate,'" 311.
66 Whaley, *Germany*, 202; Von Reden-Dohna, "Problems of Small Estates," S77.
67 Rousseau, *Government of Poland*.
68 McKenna, "Curious Evolution of the Liberum Veto"; Lukowski, "Recasting Utopia," 67.
69 Lukowski, "Recasting Utopia," 83.
70 Lang, "Fall of Monarchy," 627.
71 Ibid., 639.
72 Majewski, "Polish Art of War," 195.
73 Lukowski, *Liberty's Folly*, 48.
74 Quoted in ibid., 16.
75 Lukowski, "Recasting Utopia," 67.
76 Lukowski, *Liberty's Folly*, 29; Dynner, *Yankel's Tavern*.
77 Friedrich, *Other Prussia*, 52.
78 Lukowski, *Liberty's Folly*, 25.
79 Wolff, *Idea of Galicia*, 1.
80 Lukowski, *Liberty's Folly*.
81 Quoted in ibid., 253.
82 Williams, *Historians' History*, 99.
83 Lukowski, *Liberty's Folly*, 35.
84 Wandycz, *Lands of Partitioned Poland,* 55.

CHAPTER 9
Mountain Republics

1 Menocal, *Ornament of World*.
2 Blanks, "Regionalism," 222.
3 Nichols, *Linguistic Diversity*, 20.
4 Caesar, *Gallic Wars*.
5 Pounds, *Historical Geography*, 90.
6 The "tar baby" in Uncle Remus stories was a model Br'er Rabbit created out of tar to trick Br'er Fox.
7 Dupree, "Retreat of British Army," 54.
8 Nawid, "State, Clergy," 591.
9 Diamond, *Guns, Germs, and Steel*.
10 Dil, "Cabal in Kabul," 472.
11 John, "NGOs and Economic Recovery," 636.
12 Dil, "Cabal in Kabul," 469; Markham "Mountain Passes," 40–53.
13 Braudel, *Mediterranean*, 38.
14 Head, *Early Modern Democracy in the Grisons*, 27.
15 Hunt, *Alpine Archeology*, 8–9.
16 Ibid., 21.
17 "The Alps," 409; Walsh, Richer, and de Beaulieu, "Attitudes to Altitude," 447.
18 "Dec. 13, 1916: Soldiers Perish in Avalanche as World War I Rages," History.com, http://bit.ly/1WvCNoh.
19 Vieussieux, *History of Switzerland*, 38–51; Freedman, *Images of Medieval Peasant*, 192.
20 Vieussieux, *History of Switzerland*, 51.
21 Ibid., 63.
22 Ibid., 64–65.
23 Fortescue, *History of British Army,* 1:82.
24 Bradbury, *Capetians*, 61; Vieusseux, *History of Switzerland*, 99–100.
25 Borgeaud, "Switzerland and War," 873.
26 Zschokke and Zschokke, *History of Switzerland,* 129; Bonney, *European Dynastic States,* 84–87.
27 Kiernan, "Foreign Mercenaries," 76.
28 Vieusseux, *History of Switzerland*, 102.
29 Bonney, *European Dynastic States,* 95.
30 Korner, "Town and Country in Switzerland," 239.
31 Vieusseux, *History of Switzerland*, 85.
32 Zschokke and Zschokke, *History of Switzerland,* 129.
33 Fortescue, *History of British Army,* 1:83.
34 Worthington, *Scots in Habsburg Service,* 16.
35 Fortescue, *History of British Army,* 1:81; Mallett and Shaw, *Italian Wars, 1494–1559,* 103; Zschokke and Zschokke, *History of Switzerland,* 237.
36 Rogers, "Military Revolutions," 247.
37 Speidel, "Roman Army Pay Scales," 90.

38 Freund, "Ethnological Observations," 279; Kraas, "Decline of Ethno-Diversity," 46.

39 Vieusseux, *History of Switzerland*, 13.

40 Ibid., 18; Wilson, *Thirty Years War,* 160–61; Zschokke and Zschokke, *History of Switzerland,* 87, 105.

41 Zschokke and Zschokke, *History of Switzerland,* 141.

42 Ibid., 126; Vieusseux, *History of Switzerland,* 209.

43 Korner, "Town and Country in Switzerland," 239; Watt, "Reception of Reformation," 93, 97.

44 Zschokke and Zschokke, *History of Switzerland,* 226; Birnbaum, "Zwinglian Reformation," 28.

45 Wuarin, "Recent Political Experiments," 4; Vieusseux, *History of Switzerland,* 198.

46 Hansmann, *Ownership of Enterprise.*

47 Vieusseux, *History of Switzerland,* 210–11.

48 Zschokke and Zschokke, *History of Switzerland,* 177.

49 Ibid., 261; Sparrow, "Swiss and Swabian Agencies," 861–84.

50 Vieusseux, *History of Switzerland,* 229; Zschokke and Zschokke, *History of Switzerland,* 271.

51 Zschokke and Zschokke, *History of Switzerland,* 269.

52 Press, "Habsburg Court," S32.

53 Pollard, *Marginal Europe,* 103.

54 Cole, "Nation, Anti-Enlightenment," 479; Raybould, "Fascism in Tyrol," 408; Mac-Hardy, "Rise of Absolutism," 414.

55 Darden, *Resisting Occupation*; Kraas, "Decline of Ethno-Diversity," 43; Gordon, *Swiss Reformation,* 97; Evans, *Making of Habsburg Monarchy,* 447; Dickson, "Monarchy and Bureaucracy," 356.

56 Barber, "Maps and Monarchs in Europe," 97.

57 Cole, "Nation, Anti-Enlightenment," 489.

58 Ibid, 495; Ruehl, "'Time Without Emperors,'" 195.

59 Zschokke and Zschokke, *History of Switzerland,* 271.

60 Vieusseux, *History of Switzerland,* 239; Zschokke and Zschokke, *History of Switzerland,* 272.

61 Zschokke and Zschokke, *History of Switzerland,* 273.

62 Vieusseux, *History of Switzerland,* 242–45.

63 Orlove, "History of Andes," 50.

64 Souyri, *World Turned Upside Down*; Ferejohn and Rosenbluth, *War and State Building in Medieval Japan.*

65 "The Alps," 408–15.

66 Zschokke and Zschokke, *History of Switzerland,* 390; Altermatt, "Conservatism in Switzerland," 581; Duffield, "War of Sonderbund," 697.

67 Zschokke and Zschokke, *History of Switzerland,* 391.

68 Duffield, "War of Sonderbund," 692.

69 Hahn, *My Life,* 127.

70 Thompson, *White War,* 297–324.

71 Ibid., 362.

72 Tooze, *Wages of Destruction*.

73 Ganser, "British Secret Service," 558.

74 Ibid., 561.

75 Viazzo, *Upland Communities*, 185–91.

76 Ogilvie, *Institutions and European*; Epstein, *Freedom and Growth*.

77 Viazzo, *Upland Communities*, 184.

78 Scott, *Town, Country, and Regions*, 271.

79 Blanks, "Regionalism," 213; Mukerjee, "Great Forestry Survey," 240.

80 Blanks, ""Regionalism," 212.

81 Ibid., 216.

82 Wickham, *Mountains and City*, 135.

83 Blanks, "Regionalism," 219; Mukerjee, "Great Forestry Survey," 241.

84 Blanks, "Regionalism," 220; Peattie, "Study in Mountain Geography," 218.

85 Quoted in Mukerjee, "Great Forestry Survey," 240.

86 Ibid., 232; Whittlesey, "Andorra's Autonomy,"151.

87 Freedman, *Images of Medieval Peasant*, 185–90; Whittlesey, "Andorra's Autonomy," 147.

88 Whittlesey, "Andorra's Autonomy," 148; Peattie, "Study in Mountain Geography," 227.

89 Sutherland, "Guerrilla Warfare," 270.

90 Young, "Deciphering Disorder"; Weinstein and Humphreys, "Handling and Manhandling"; Staniland, "States, Insurgents, and Wartime Political Orders."

91 Mao, *Art of War,* 55.

CHAPTER 10

The Nineteenth-Century Pivot

1 Hugo, *Memoirs*, Sept. 20, 1849; Merriman, *Massacre*, 12; Foley and Sowerwine, *Political Romance,* 39; Lehning, "Gossiping about Gambetta," 240.

2 Quoted in Goncourt and Goncourt, *Journal*, Nov. 6, 1870; Rebecca L. Spang, "The Franco-Prussian War and the Commune" (lecture slides), http://bit.ly/1TL7NKz.

3 Hugo, *Memoirs*, January 12 1871.

4 Merriman, *Massacre*, 12.

5 Ibid., 155.

6 Ibid., 246.

7 Ibid., 188; Lodeman, "Victor Hugo," 98.

8 Merriman, *Massacre*, 249.

9 Blanning, *French Revolutionary Wars*.

10 Bell, *First Total War*.

11 Tilly, *Vendee*, 52.

12 Fay, *Rise of Brandenburg-Prussia to 1786*, 763; Eddie, *Freedom's Price,* 81; Frost, *Northern Wars*.

13 Clark, *Iron Kingdom*.

14 Ibid.; Voltaire's *Candide* (1759) takes square aim at Prussian militarism.

15 Wilson, "Origins of Prussian Militarism."

16 Clark, *Iron Kingdom*.

17 Quoted in Simon, *Failure of the Prussian Reform Movement*, 19.

18 Sheehan, *German History*, 289–99; Ford 1921: 512.

19 Simon, *Failure of the Prussian Reform Movement*, 221.

20 Sheehan, *German History*, 308–9.

21 Clark, *Iron Kingdom,* chap. 10.

22 Holborn, "Prusso-German School," 282–83.

23 Paret, *Clausewitz and State,* 225.

24 Sheehan, *German History*, 315; Holborn, "Prusso-German School," 282.

25 Kissinger, *World Restored*.

26 Allen, review of Craiutu, 647.

27 Artz, "Electoral System in France," 210.

28 Lewis, "White Terror," 109.

29 Artz, "Electoral System in France," 206.

30 Holroyd, "Bourbon Army," 529.

31 Porch, "French Army Law," 752.

32 Quoted in de Dijn, "Aristocratic Liberalism," 665.

33 Pilbeam, "Economic Crisis."

34 Pilbeam, "Emergence of Opposition," 12; Pilbeam, "Economic Crisis," 337.

35 Pilbeam, "Popular Violence."

36 van Duyse, cited in Tollebeek, "Historical Representation," 336; Vanhulle reports on the indigenous Belgian movement for prison reform. "Dreaming about Prison," 107.

37 Cited in Kramer, "Rights of Man," 523.

38 Ibid., 527; Scheifley, "Epic Genius," 84.

39 Davis, review of Flöter, 713.

40 Flockerzie, "State-Building and Nation-Building," 268.

41 Sheehan, *German History*, 198.

42 Higonnet and Higonnet, "Class, Politics, and Corruption," 207.

43 Marx, *Eighteenth Brumaire*.

44 Robertson, "Students on Barricades," 377.

45 Ludz, "Ideology, Intellectuals"; Hayes, "History of German Socialism," 63.

46 Hahn, "Junior Faculty," 882.

47 Robertson, "Students on Barricades," 375.

48 Meinecke, "Year 1848 in German History," 485–86.

49 Spalding, "Idiom of a Revolution," 60.

50 Paret, *Clausewitz and State,* 267.

51 Foley and Sowerwine, *Political Romance*; Lehning, "Gossiping about Gambetta," 248.

52 Winnacker, "Third French Republic," 396.

53 Rudelle, "Third French Republic."

54 Hovde, "French Socialism," 261.

55 Prussia retained its traditional three-class franchise for elections to the Prussian Landtag.

56 For an account of how domestic economic structure also constrained government action in this period, see Gourevitch, *Politics in Hard Times*.

57 Moore, *Social Origins*.

58 Kent, *English Radicals*, 129.

59 Ibid., 157.

60 Ibid., 279–80.

61 Holyoake in ibid., 333; ibid., 338.

62 Ibid., 157.

63 Kent, *English Radicals*, 384.

64 Ibid., 385.

65 Hayes, "History of German Socialism," 70.

66 Figes, "Red Army."

67 Clifton, "Crimean War," 166.

68 Ibid., 165.

69 Saab, Knapp, and Knapp, "Reassessment," 469, 477.

70 Moon, "Russian Peasant Volunteers," 696.

71 Dilke and Botassi, "Uprising of Greece."

72 The World Affairs Institute ("Crimean War") estimated that 75,000 of the 95,615 Frenchmen killed in the war (out of a French army of 436,144) in fact died from cholera, typhus, and infected wounds.

73 Chamberlain, "Florence Nightingale," 381; Clifton, "Crimean War," 166.

74 Kozelsky, "Casualties of Conflict," 882–90.

75 Ibid., 876; Harris, *British Military Intelligence*.

76 Pereira, "Alexander II," 104.

77 Bushnell, "Peasants in Uniform," 565.

78 Zenkovsky, "Emancipation of Serfs," 280; Bushnell, "Peasants in Uniform," 572.

79 Domar and Machina, "Profitability of Russian Serfdom"; Zenkovsky, "Emancipation of Serfs," 287; Pereira, "Alexander II," 106.

80 Pereira, "Alexander II," 111; Volin, "Russian Peasant," 47.

81 Pushkarev, "Russian Peasants' Reaction," 209.

82 Pereira, "Alexander II," 113.

83 Perrie, "Russian Peasant Movement," 139; Zenkovsky, "Emancipation of Serfs," 291; Volin, "Russian Peasant," 274.

84 Perrie, "Russian Peasant Movement," 137, 141.

85 Kingston-Mann, "Lenin and Challenge," 438.

CHAPTER 11

Twentieth-Century Wars of Full Mobilization

1 Zuckerman, *Rape of Belgium,* 23.

2 Lipkes, *Rehearsals*, 197; Horne and Kramer, *German Atrocities*, 136.

3 Wilson, "Lord Bryce's Investigation."

4 Adams, *Their Crimes*, 4.

5 Wilson, "Lord Bryce's Investigation," 370.

6 Gibbs, *Now It Can Be Told,* 8; Marquis, "Words as Weapons," 472–73.

7 Wilson, "Lord Bryce's Investigation," 370.

8 Flynn, *Conscription and Democracy*, 31.

9 Ibid.

10 Ibid., 33.

11 Farr, "Waging Democracy," 66.

12 Piketty, *Capital in the Twenty-First Century*, 355.

13 Narizny, "Political Economy of Alignment," 190, 205.

14 Papayoanou, "Interdependence, Institutions," 54–55.

15 Walker, "German Steel Syndicate," 393; "Diamond Cartel," 1407; Fremdling, "Anglo-German Rivalry."

16 Hewitson, "Germany and France," 572; McCreary, "Social Welfare and Business," 29; Usher, "Interpretations," 799; Walker, "German Steel Syndicate," 353; Streb, Baten, and Yin, "Technological and Geographical Knowledge," 347.

17 Sperber, *Kaiser's Voters*, 35, 209; Nettl, "German Social Democratic Party," 72; Marquis "Words as Weapons," 472; Nettl, "German Social Democratic Party," 85; Shand, "Doves Among the Eagles," 96.

18 Sperber, *Kaiser's Voters*, 190.

19 Nettl, "German Social Democratic Party," 65; Schonhardt-Bailey, "Parties and Interests," 303; Sherman, review of Tuchman, 463.

20 "Labor's International Action," 217.

21 Quoted in Jarausch, "Illusion of Limited War," 53; Lichnowsky, *My Mission*, 32.

22 Bucholz, review of *Helmuth von Moltke*, 469; Hewitson, "Germany and France," 573; Ferguson, *Pity of War,* 153.

23 Bethmann-Hollweg's paraphrase, quoted in Jarausch, "Illusion of Limited War," 54.

24 Marquis, "Words as Weapons," 470; Meyer, "Trade and Nationality," 247.

25 Clark, *Sleepwalkers*, 561; Levy, "Preferences, Constraints," 184.

26 *The Times Documentary History of the War: Diplomatic*, pt. 1–2, 438; Hewitson, "Germany and France," 578.

27 Clark, *Sleepwalkers*, 293.

28 *The Times Documentary History of the War: Diplomatic*, pt. 1–2.

29 Adams, *Their Crimes*, 4.

30 Fairlie, "British War Cabinets," 472.

31 Miller, "Foreign Government," 1073.

32 Quoted in ibid., 1074; "Defence of Realm," 197.

33 Nason and Vahey, "McKenna Rule," 290.

34 Nason and Vahey "McKenna Rule": 2.

35 Daunton "How to Pay for War," 889; Nason and Vahey, "McKenna Rule," 291.

36 Balderston, "War Finance," 233.

37 Maltby, "Showing a Strong Front," 148.

38 Flynn, *Conscription and Democracy*, 33; Keith Simpson, "First World War Commemoration," June 11, 2013, House of Commons, Hansard Parliamentary Archives, http://bit.ly/1qiGFuU.

39 Winter, "Arthur Henderson," 754; Fairlie, "British War Cabinets," 481.

40 Ferro, "Russian Soldier," 493; Von Laue 1971:117.

41 Hobsbawm, review of Graubard and Rogow, 168; Cole, "Recent Developments," 490–91; Maltby, "Showing a Strong Front," 151.

42 Cole, "Recent Developments," 488.

43 Maltby, "Showing a Strong Front," 149; Ogg, "British Representation of the People Act," 488.

44 "Representation of the People Bill," Feb. 6, 1918, http://bit.ly/29Jt8s2; Ogg, "British Representation of the People Act," 498–500.

45 Cole, "Recent Developments," 493.

46 "UK Election Statistics: 1918–2012," Research Paper 12/43, House of Commons Library, August 7, 2012, http://bit.ly/1TbpBPx.

47 Lenin, "Speech at Opening Session."

48 Ahmed, *Democracy and the Politics of Electoral System Choice*; France oscillated between proportional and majoritarian rules depending on who was in power and how urgently the right felt the need to fragment the left.

49 Hyde, " 'Please Sir, He Called Me Jimmy!' " 540; Elwood, "Lenin and Brussels Conference," 32; Schlesinger, *One Thousand Days*, 451–52; Lenin, "Opportunism and Collapse."

50 Roberts, "Popular Conservatism."

51 Daunton, "How to Pay for War," 904.

52 Ibid., 894–96.

53 Ibid., 917; Bank, *Anglo-American Corporate,* 11.

54 Thorpe, "Industrial Meaning," 92.

55 French, "Economic Conditions," 573; Schapiro, "How France Is Governed," 319.

56 Howorth, "Myth of Blanquism," 38.

57 Willoughby, "Labor Legislation in France," 392.

58 Quoted in Slosson, "Other Side of Barricade," 110.

59 Pinson, review of Weinstein, 544.

60 Teele, "Ordinary Democratization."

61 Forstner and Forstner, "France, Africa, and the First World War," 15.

62 Ibid., 15–16.

63 Ibid.

64 Acemoglu and Robinson, *Economic Origins.*

65 Przeworski, "Conquered or Granted?"

66 Svensson, "Parliament and Foreign Policy," 21; Henriksen, "Avoiding Lock-in," 59.

67 Henriksen, "An Economic History of Denmark"; Henriksen, "Avoiding Lock-in," 60–63.

68 "Peace Conference," 48.

69 Swensson, "Parliament and Foreign Policy," 23.

70 Ibid., 23–24; Pedersen, review of Dybdahl, 1339.

71 Heckscher, *Mercantilism*; Metcalf, "Challenges to Orthodoxy."

72 Thompson, "Norwegian Military Policy," 503.

73 Grytten, "Economic History."

74 Liedman and Persson, "Visible Hand," 260.

75 Gordon and Reynolds, "Medieval Iron," 112–13; Eriksson, "Advance and Retreat," 269; Agren, *Iron-Making Societies*, 77, 158.

76 Eriksson, "Decay of Blast Furnaces," 4; Eriksson, "Advance and Retreat," 281; Heckscher, *Mercantilism*; Gordon and Reynolds, "Medieval Iron," 116; Metcalf, "Chal-

lenges to Economic Orthodoxy," 259; Magnusson, "Economics and Public Interest," 251–52.

77 Akenson, *Ireland, Sweden,* 37–39, 70.

78 Harper, "Woman Suffrage," 67; Tilton, "Why Don't Swedish," 143, 156.

79 Harper, "Woman Suffrage," 67.

80 Stefansson, *Denmark and Sweden,* 323; Laitila, "Soldier, Structure," 54.

81 Hjerppe, "Economic History."

82 Waaranpera, "Finnish Civil War"; Stefansson, *Denmark and Sweden,* 411.

83 Casanova, "Civil Wars, Revolutions," 517; Smith, "Russia and Origins," 489, 497.

84 Casanova, "Civil Wars, Revolutions," 517.

85 Screen, "Marshal Mannerheim," 30.

86 Epstein, "Wrong Man in a Maelstrom," 225.

87 Ibid., 225.

88 Ibid., 218, 232. Ludendorff, as humiliated as he was furious, sneaked off to Scandinavia wearing a false beard and glasses, only to return as a Hitler supporter in the 1920s.

89 Epstein, "Wrong Man in a Maelstrom," 218.

90 Ibid., 240.

91 Lenin, "Murder of Liebnecht and Luxemburg."

92 Shepard, "New German Constitution," 35.

93 Shugart and Carey, *Presidents and Assemblies*; Myerson, "Political Economics."

94 Kennedy, Introduction to Schmitt, xviii.

95 Guinnane, "Financial," 5, 12; Gombrich, *Little History,* 275; Myerson, "Political Economics."

96 Kennedy, Introduction to Schmitt, xviii; Schmitt, "Dictatorship," 321n12; Myerson, "Political Economics"; Schmitt, "Dictatorship," 299.

97 Tooze, *Wages of Destruction,* xxiv; Thomsett, *German Opposition to Hitler,* 30.

98 Hinton, "'Triumph of Will,'" 49.

99 Ibid.; Thomsett, *German Opposition to Hitler,* 34.

100 Turner, "Myth of Chancellor," 678; Thomsett, *German Opposition to Hitler,* 39.

101 "Nazi Outlooks," 143.

102 Ibid., 144.

103 Ibid., 143.

104 Balsamo, "Germany's Armed Forces," 264.

105 Tooze, *Wages of Destruction,* 62–65.

106 Winkler, "German Society," 7–8.

107 *Deutsche Wirtschaftszeitung,* October 1932, quoted in Winkler, "German Society," 6.

108 Buchheim and Scherner, "Role of Private Property," 390; Thomsett, *German Opposition to Hitler,* 133–34.

109 Short for Metallurgische Forschungsgesellschaft, mefo bills were government promissory notes that amounted to forced loans. "Nuremburg Trial Defendants: Hjalmar Schacht," Jewish Virtual Library, http://bit.ly/1X7PNiN.

110 Buchheim and Scherner, "Role of Private Property," 399–402.

111 Tooze, *Wages of Destruction,* 109.

112 Ibid., 115–18.

113 Ibid., 155–56; Reich, "Ford Motor Company"; Silverstein, "Ford and the Führer."

114 Tooze, *Wages of Destruction*, 326.

115 Kershaw, " 'Improvised Genocide?' " 75; Gerlach, "Wannsee Conference," 760.

116 Thomsett, *German Opposition to Hitler*, 175.

117 Quoted in Balsamo, "Germany's Armed Forces," 272.

118 Mazower, *Hitler's Empire*, 527.

119 Thomsett, *German Opposition to Hitler*, chaps. 13–15.

120 Snyder, review of Holton.

121 Mazower, *Hitler's Empire*, 528.

122 Satow, *Diplomat in Japan*.

123 Malcolm, "Constitution of the Empire of Japan," 62–74.

124 Duus, *Modern Japan*.

125 Morck and Nakamura, "Frog in a Well," 414; Gordon, "China-Japan War," 140.

126 Large, "Nationalist Extremism," 533–56.

127 Morck and Nakamura, "Frog in a Well," 369, 422.

128 "Far Eastern Questions," 423.

129 Morck and Nakamura, "Frog in a Well," 421.

130 Garon, "State and Religion," 274; Gilmore, " 'We Have Been Reborn,' " 200.

131 Snyder, *Myths of Empire*.

132 Ohnuki-Tierney, *Kamikaze, Cherry Blossoms*, 15; Orbell and Morikawa, "Evolutionary Account of Suicide Attacks," 316.

133 Woodward, *Battle for Leyte Gulf*, 83.

134 Dower, *War Without Mercy*.

135 Barkow and Leighton, "Interview with Alec Leighton," 240; Gilmore, " 'We Have Been Reborn,' " 215.

136 Skocpol, "Social Revolutions," 152.

137 Figes, "Red Army," 172.

138 Ibid., 180.

139 Ibid., 184.

140 Ibid., 189.

141 Ibid., 208.

142 Lewin, "Immediate Background,"188; Livi-Bacci, "On Human Costs," 759.

143 Montefiore, *Young Stalin*; Matiash, "Archives in Russia," 36, 44.

144 Gatrell and Harrison, "Russian and Soviet Economies," 436–37.

145 Ibid., 440.

146 Ibid., 429.

147 Weerakoon, *Solzhenhitsyn*.

148 Ibid.

149 Skocpol, "Social Revolutions," 154.

150 Quoted in Womack, "Mao before Maoism," 104.

151 Womack, "Mao before Maoism," 105; Hu, "Mao, Lin Biao," 250; Lawrence, *China: The Long March,* 53–60.

152 Mao, *Art of War,* 65, 68; Hu, "Mao, Lin Biao," 266.

153 Salisbury, "Personnel and Far Eastern Policy," 362; Ah Xiang, "The Battle of Baizhang-guan Pass," http://bit.ly/1Xpq0Dg.

154 Kaufman, "Trouble in Golden Triangle," 446, 455.

155 Dikotter, *Mao's Great Famine*; Livi Bacci, "On Human Costs," 761.

156 Short, *Mao*, 437.

157 Quoted in Zhang, *Mao's Military Romanticism*, 190–91; He Di, "Most Respected Enemy," 150.

158 Zhang, *Mao's Military Romanticism*, 191.

159 Gittings, "Military Control," 92.

160 Ibid., 86.

161 Peisakhin and Pinto, "Army as the Forge"; Chang, *To Return Home.*

162 Ross, "Shaping the Chinese People's Liberation Army's Image," 26.

163 Forster, "Politics of Destabilization," 436; Hu, "Mao, Lin Biao," 253; Chen, "Tibetan Rebellion of 1959," 99.

164 Moore, *Social Origins of Dictatorship and Democracy.*

165 Stephens, "Class Formation."

CHAPTER 12

War, Racism, and Civil Rights in the United States

1 Johnson, "Black Soldiers of Ardennes."

2 Porritt, review of McKinley, 404; McKinley, *Suffrage Franchise*, 473.

3 Keyssar, *Right to Vote*, 15.

4 Anderson, *Crucible of War*; David Mayhew, personal communication 2014.

5 Keyssar, "Peculiar Institution," 13; Kozuskanich, "Pennsylvania, Militia," 119.

6 Franklin, "The North, the South," 20.

7 Chernow, *Alexander Hamilton*, 211–12; Elkins and McKitrick, *Age of Federalism,* 100.

8 Kim, "Impact of Chinese Relations," 341.

9 Baack, "Forging a Nation State," 640.

10 Ibid., 643–45.

11 Ibid., 643.

12 Chernow, *Alexander Hamilton*, 176–77; Kohn, "Inside History," 188.

13 Baack, "Forging a Nation State," 650; Kohn, "Inside History," 213; Maier, *Ratification*, 11.

14 Edling, *Revolution in Favor*, especially chap. 14; and Elkins and McKitrick *Age of Federalism,* 93.

15 Feer, "Shays's Rebellion," 405.

16 Vile, "Critical Role," 167.

17 Keyssar, *Right to Vote*, 49, 321–23; Engerman and Sokoloff, "Evolution of Suffrage Institutions," 898.

18 National Archives, www.archives.gov.

19 Elkins and McKitrick, *Age of Federalism,* 594.

20 Bickham, *Weight of Vengeance,* 42; Anderson, *Crucible of War,* 745–46.

21 Elkins and McKitrick, *Age of Federalism,* 438.

22 Ibid., 439–41.

23 Glover, "French Fleet," 235–36; Sharp, *American Politics in the Early Republic.*

24 Quoted in Elkins and McKitrick *Age of Federalism,* 597. Adams supported a strong navy but was unenthusiastic about a large army. Murphy, "John Adams," 234.

25 Elkins and McKitrick, *Age of Federalism,* 661.

26 Murphy, "John Adams," 236–37.

27 Ibid., 238.

28 Ibid., 242; Elkins and McKitrick, *Age of Federalism,* 599.

29 Dunn, *Jefferson's Second Revolution,* 107.

30 Mayhew, personal communication.

31 Quoted in Elkins and McKitrick, *Age of Federalism,* 598; Murphy "John Adams," 234; Wright, "Migration, Radicalism," 48.

32 Dunn, *Jefferson's Second Revolution,* 32; Elkins and McKitrick, *Age of Federalism,* 92.

33 Murphy, "John Adams," 234; Elkins and McKitrick, *Age of Federalism,* chap. 13.

34 Bickham, *Weight of Vengeance,* 27; Crackel, "Jefferson, Politics," 24.

35 Bickham, *Weight of Vengeance,* 25.

36 Ibid., 85.

37 Latimer, "South Carolina," 925.

38 Elkins and McKitrick, *Age of Federalism,* 123; Latimer, "South Carolina," 922.

39 Witte, *Politics and Development,* 67.

40 Ibid.; Lipsey 1994: 8.

41 Bickham, *Weight of Vengeance,* 85.

42 Ibid., 227.

43 Wingate, "Truth in Regard," 836.

44 Howe, *What God,* 14–15.

45 Stagg, "Soldiers in Peace," 84–92; Fabel, "Self-Help in Dartmoor," 169.

46 Fabel, "Laws of War," 204.

47 Howe, *What God,* 9.

48 Ibid., 9; Wingate, "Truth in Regard," 838.

49 May, "Invisible Men," 475.

50 Hacker, "Census-Based Count."

51 Quoted in Clark, "History Gives Lie."

52 *Charleston Courier,* January 24, 1865. In March 1865 the CSA did enlist several hundred black soldiers in a final act of desperation.

53 Pooley, "Shooing Geese," 88.

54 Full text available at TeachingAmericanHistory.org, http://bit.ly/1Ns5yPX; Gordon-Reed, *Andrew Johnson,* 76.

55 Clark, "History Gives Lie."

56 Pooley, "Shooing Geese," 91; Goldfield, *America Aflame,* 27.

57 Goldfield, *America Aflame,* 254.

58 From letter to Navy Secretary Gideon Welles, quoted in ibid., 261; Levine, *Fall of House of Dixie.*

59 "[A]ll persons held as slaves within any State or designated part of a State, the people whereof shall then be in rebellion against the United States, shall be then, thenceforward, and forever free."

60 Quoted in Pooley, "Shooing Geese," 96.

61 U.S. 1860 Census.

62 The March 13, 1869, issue of *Harper's Weekly* offers a timeline and assessment.

63 The Thirteenth Amendment abolished slavery in 1865; the Fourteenth Amendment (ratified in 1868) guaranteed equal protection under the law; the Fifteenth Amendment (ratified in 1870) prohibits discrimination in voting rights on the basis of "race, color, or previous condition of servitude."

64 Benedict, "New Look," 364; Vallely, *Two Reconstructions*.

65 Mayhew, personal communication; Vallely, *Two Reconstructions*; Goldfield, *America Aflame*.

66 Klarman, *From Jim Crow to Civil Rights*, 69; Kousser, *Colorblind Injustice*; Kousser, *Shaping of Southern*; Vallely, *Two Reconstructions*.

67 Foner, *Reconstruction*, 437.

68 Klarman, *Unfinished Business*, 77–79.

69 Ibid., 17.

70 Saldin, "Strange Bedfellows," 37.

71 Kennedy, *Rise and Fall of the Great Powers*.

72 Halpern, "Solving 'Labour Problem,'" 39.

73 Schott, "Louisiana Sugar," 266; Granitz and Klein, "Monopolization," 1; Kuznets, "Proportion of Capital Formation," 523.

74 Bailey, "Splendid Little Forgotten War," 194; Rayburn, "Rough Riders," 114.

75 Gatewood, *Smoked Yankees*, 11.

76 Fischer, "American War."

77 Parker, "Evolution," 224.

78 Gatewood, *Smoked Yankees*, 6.

79 Halpern, "Solving 'Labour Problem,'" 23; Bailey, "Splendid Little Forgotten War," 196.

80 Gilmore, "Black Militias," 53; Bailey, "Splendid Little Forgotten War," 207.

81 Johnson, *History of Negro Soldiers*; Williams, "War in Black and White," 7; Maybry, "Negro Suffrage," 96; Kousser, *Shaping of Southern Politics*, 224.

82 Parker, "Evolution," 224.

83 Gatewood, *Smoked Yankees*, 11.

84 Murray, "Black Regular Troops," 56.

85 Gilmore, "Black Militias," 54.

86 Gatewood, *Smoked Yankees*, 143–44; Gilmore, "Black Militias," 52.

87 Johnson, *History of Negro Soldiers*.

88 Mortimer and Loughrey, "James J. Loughrey's Diary," 79.

89 Totanes, review of Bain, 112.

90 Saldin, "Strange Bedfellows," 46.

91 Gatewood, *Smoked Yankees*, 13.

92 Ibid., 14.

93 Ibid., 257.

94 Mortimer and Loughry, "James J. Loughrey's Diary,"; Gatewood, *Smoked Yankees.*

95 Skowronek, *Building a New American State*, 85; Dodge, review of Wheeler, Lodge, Bigelow, and Roosevelt, 382.

96 Gilmore, "Black Militias," 54.

97 Johnson, *History of Negro Soldiers.*

98 Williams, "War in Black and White," 7; Maybry, "Negro Suffrage," 96; Kousser, *Shaping of Southern Politics*, 224; Cecelski and Tyson, *Democracy Betrayed.*

99 Klarman, *From Jim Crow to Civil Rights*, 66.

100 Kousser, *Shaping of Southern Politics*, 63.

101 Klarman, *From Jim Crow to Civil Rights*, 79.

102 Abernethy, "Race Riot," 431.

103 Klarman, *From Jim Crow to Civil Rights*, 67.

104 Reich, "Soldiers of Democracy,"1485.

105 Steptoe, *Dixie West,* 20; Reich, "Soldiers of Democracy," 1485.

106 Christian, "Houston Mutiny," 112.

107 Mennell, "African-Americans," 277.

108 Ibid., 276.

109 Du Bois, "Close Ranks," 111.

110 Du Bois, "Perpetual Dilemma," 270.

111 Du Bois, "Thirteen," 114.

112 Ellis, " 'Closing Ranks,' " 113.

113 Davis, "Not Only War," 478; Jordan, " 'Damnable Dilemma,' " 1572; Hart, "Cry in Wilderness," 74.

114 Ellis, " 'Closing Ranks,' " 113.

115 Quoted in ibid., 115.

116 Jordan, " 'Damnable Dilemma,' " 1574; Klarman, *From Jim Crow to Civil Rights*, 122.

117 King and Smith, *Still a House Divided,* 64.

118 Lewis, *W.E.B. Du Bois*, 355.

119 Quoted in Lentz-Smith, *Freedom Struggles,* 100.

120 Du Bois, "Documents of the War," 16–17; see also Lentz-Smith, *Freedom Struggles*, 103.

121 Murray, "Blacks and Draft," 1971: 59; Nalty, *Strength for Fight*, 112.

122 Davis, "Not Only War," 478; Nalty, *Strength for Fight*, 125.

123 Menard, "Lest We Forget," 154.

124 Capozzola, "Only Badge Needed," 1375; Davis, "Not Only War," 477.

125 The Tenth Annual Report of the NAACP for the year 1919, full text available at the Gilder Lehrman Center for the Study of Slavery, Resistance, and Abolition, http://bit .ly/1skL6XV.

126 Blackwell, "Military Argument," 54.

127 Smith, "Beyond Tocqueville," 559.

128 Pauley, "Du Bois on Woman Suffrage," 395.

129 "Suffrage Wins in Senate; Now Goes to States," *New York Times,* June 5, 1919.

130 Pauley, "Du Bois on Woman Suffrage," 391.

131 McDaneld, "White Suffragist Dis/Entitlement," 251.

132 Butler, "Frederick Douglass," 832; Pauley, "Du Bois on Woman Suffrage," 391.

133 Marilley, "Frances Willard," 123.

134 Pauley, "Du Bois on Woman Suffrage," 398; Kraditor, *Ideas of the Woman Suffrage Movement*.

135 Bland, "New Life in an Old Movement," 666.

136 "Suffrage Wins in Senate; Now Goes to States," *New York Times*, June 5, 1919.

137 Reid, "Racism, Manhood," 9.

138 Ibid., 24.

139 Quoted in ibid., 25.

140 Miller, "Women's Suffrage, Political Responsiveness"; Mehotra, "Lawyers, Guns," 179; Lott and Kenny, "Did Women's Suffrage"; Iversen and Rosenbluth, *Women, Work, and Politics*.

141 Gilmore, *Gender and Jim Crow*, 216.

142 Schaefer, "Ku Klux Klan," 147.

143 Witte, *Politics and Development of the Federal Income Tax*, 67–74.

144 Burnham, "Changing Shape," 25; Morgan and Prasad, "Origins of Tax Systems," 1354–60; Witte, *Politics and Development of the Federal Income Tax*, 74.

145 Witte, *Politics and Development of the Federal Income Tax*, 79; Brownlee, "Wilson and Financing," 204.

146 Adler and Encyclopaedia Britannica, *Syntopicon*, 335.

147 Frieden, "Sectoral Conflict," 70-71; Abramson, *Spanning the Century*, 236.

148 Quoted in Adler and Encyclopaedia Britannica, *Syntopicon*; Janick, "Senator Frank B. Brandegee," 434.

149 Reprinted in Schortemeier, *Rededicating America,* 188, from an address at a Republican rally in Columbus Ohio on February 23, 1920.

150 Lippman, *Political Scene*, 81.

151 Brownlee, "Wilson and Financing," 204; Goodykoontz, "Edward P. Costigan," 413–17.

152 Keller, "Supply-Side Economic Policies," 782.

153 Waller, "Business and Initiation," 349–52; Bates, "Teapot Dome Scandal," 308.

154 Callahan, McDonald, and O'Brien, "Who Voted for Smoot-Hawley?" 683; Frieden, "Sectoral Conflict," 63; Tooze, *Wages of Destruction*, 27.

155 Kindleberger, *World in Depression*; Eichengreen, "International Policy Coordination"; Temin, *Lessons from Great Depression*; Simmons, *Who Adjusts?*; Parker, *Economics of Great Depression*; Smith, "Isolationism, Devil," 61.

156 Beard and Beard, *America in Midpassage*, 452–53.

157 Rosenman, *Public Papers of Franklin D. Roosevelt,* 2:11–16.

158 Current, "Stimson Doctrine," 515–20.

159 Friedman, "Roosevelt, Silver, and China," 100.

160 Hearst in *Examiner*, March 11, 1936, quoted in Carlisle, "Foreign Policy Views," 221.

161 Donovan, "Congressional Isolationists," 306–7; Tooze, *Wages of Destruction*, 306.

162 Katznelson, *Fear Itself*; Mayhew, personal communication.

163 Klarman, *Unfinished Business*; Klarman, *From Jim Crow to Civil Rights*.

164 Gilmore, *Defying Dixie*, 356; Knauer, *Let Us Fight*, 14.

165 Executive Order 8802: Prohibition of Discrimination in the Defense Industry, Ourdoc-
     uments, gov, http://1.usa.gov/1Tb8Qr5; Knauer, *Let Us Fight.*
166 Katznelson, *Fear Itself*, 222.
167 Ibid., 285; Grill and Jenkins, "Nazis and American South," 669.
168 Witte, *Politics and Development of the Federal Income Tax*, 117–35.
169 Leland and Oboroceanu, "American War," 2.
170 Murray, "Blacks and Draft," 64.
171 Harrison, "Resource Mobilization," 184; O'Neill, *Interwar U.S. and Japanese.*
172 Section 4 (a): In the selection and training of men under this act, there shall be no dis-
     crimination against any person on account of race or color.
173 Murray, "Blacks and Draft," 62; Saldin, "Strange Bedfellows," 109.
174 McGuire, "Desegregation of Armed Forces," 149.
175 Ibid.; Flynn, "Selective Service," 18.
176 Flynn, *Conscription and Democracy*, 103; Flynn, "Selective Service," 21.
177 Togami and Hansen, review of Shepherd and Adams, 115; Dudziak, "Desegregation as
     Cold War Imperative," 66.
178 Sides "Public Opinion Polling."
179 Sitkoff, "Racial Militancy," 668; the entire film is available on YouTube.
180 Sklaroff, "G.I. Joe Louis," 975.
181 Quoted in ibid., 964.
182 Quoted in Sitkoff, "Racial Militancy," 665.
183 Quoted in Dryden, *A-Train,* 176, 228.
184 Quoted in McGuire, "Desegregation of Armed Forces," 149.
185 Murray, "Blacks and Draft," 64–65.
186 Mark Ethridge, publisher of the *Louisville Courier-Journal*, quoted in Klarman, *From
     Jim Crow to Civil Rights*, 180.
187 McGuire, "Desegregation of Armed Forces," 150.
188 Lawrence, "Thirty Years," 1; for stories of the Buffalo Soldiers of the 92nd Division sent
     to Italy, see "Experiencing War: Stories from the Veterans History Project," Library of
     Congress, http://bit.ly/26OTXJz.
189 Kersten, "African Americans," 15.
190 Ibid., 17.
191 Katznelson, *Fear Itself*, 219; Knauer, *Let Us Fight*, chap. 4.
192 Klinkner and Smith, *Unsteady March*, 193.
193 Nalty, *Strength for Fight*, 217.
194 Quoted in Klarman, *From Jim Crow to Civil Rights*, 181.
195 Myers, *Black, White and Olive Drab*; Riehm, "Forging the Civil Rights Frontier," 55.
196 Quoted in Klinkner and Smith, *Unsteady March*, 193.
197 Klarman, *From Jim Crow to Civil Rights*, 185.
198 Lawrence, "Thirty Years," 4.
199 Harry S. Truman, "Special Message to the Congress on Civil Rights," Feb. 2, 1948,
     American Presidency Project, http://bit.ly/29C2pd4.
200 Quoted in Skrentny, "Effect of Cold War," 245.

201 Ibid., citing Nichols, *Bleeding Kansas*, 9; Clifford Memo 1947, http://www.hks.harvard .edu/case/3pt/rowe.html. Truman carried seven of the eleven Dixie states.

202 Fairclough, "King and War in Vietnam," 23; Kornweibel, review of Anderson, 471.

203 "Transformation of Racial Views," 30.

204 Segal, "Diversity in Military," 532.

205 "After 4 Decades, a Battle."

206 Kahn, "Shattering Myth," 47; Klarman, *From Jim Crow to Civil Rights*, 232.

207 Quoted in McGuire, " 'It Was like All of Us,' " 921.

208 Butler, *Oxford Companion*; Gartner and Segura, "Race, Casualties," 116.

209 Lunch and Sperlich, "American Public Opinion," 25–26, 33.

210 Westheider, *Vietnam War*, 33; McGarrah, review of Topmiller, 767.

211 Flynn, *Conscription and Democracy*, 77; Saldin, "Strange Bedfellows," 193; Foley, *Confronting the War Machine*, 129.

212 Mueller, *War, Presidents*, 70; Hammond, "Press in Vietnam," 312.

213 Burstein, "Public Opinion, Demonstrations," 162.

214 Westheider, *Vietnam War*, 33.

215 Franck and Weisband, *Foreign Policy by Congress*, 92.

216 Greenhill, "Don't Dumb Down."

217 Flynn, *Conscription and Democracy*, 154; Hersh, "Lieutenant Accused."

218 Quoted in Fairclough, "King and War in Vietnam," 25; Hall, "Response of the Moderate Wing," 669.

219 Cone, "Martin and Malcolm," 177.

220 Quoted in Holloway, "Ralph Bunche," 125.

221 Quoted in Bromwich, "King's Anti-War Speech"; Klarman, *Unfinished Business*, 189; Westheider, *Vietnam War*, 33; Berinsky, *Silent Voices*, 123.

222 Laufer, Gallops, and Frey-Wouters, "War Stress and Trauma," 79.

223 Westheider, *Vietnam War*, 33.

224 Page and Brody, "Policy Voting," 995; Cultice, *Youth's Battle*; Franck and Weisband, *Foreign Policy by Congress*.

225 Beck and Jennings, "Lowering Voting Age," 379; Jehn and Selden 2002: 95.

226 Burstein and Freudenburg, "Ending the Vietnam War," 991; Page and Brody, "Policy Voting," 985.

227 Lazarus, *Genteel Populists*, 191.

228 The draft did not officially end until June 1973.

229 Quoted in Bacevich, "Absent History," 80.

230 Witte, *Politics and Development of the Federal Income Tax*, 124; "T11-0105—Baseline Tables: Effective Tax Rates by Cash Income Percentile; Baseline: Current Policy, 2013," Tax Policy Center, 2011, http://tpc.io/1UZkO8t.

Conclusions

1 There is no evidence that Twain actually said these words although he was fascinated by historical recurrences.

2 Olson, "Democracy, Dictatorship, and Development."

3 Scheidel and Friesen, "Size of the Economy," 70.

4 Rousseau, *Social Contract* I.IV; Rousseau, *Discourse on Inequality* SD 25–26; Rousseau, *Government of Poland*; Douglass, "Rousseau's Critique," 742–43.

5 Pitkin, *Concept of Representation.*

6 Downing, "Constitutionalism"; Downing, *Military Revolution.*

7 Sieyès, *Third Estate*; Kant, *Perpetual Peace.*

8 Anderson, *Imagined Communities*, 30; Colley, "Whose Nation?" 100.

9 Colley, "Whose Nation?" 106; Palmer, *Age of Democratic Revolution.*

10 Kohn, "Arndt and the Character."

11 Pflanze, "Bismarck and German Nationalism," 550–51.

12 Quoted in ibid., 559, from Bismarck's speech to the Dresden Choral Society in 1890.

13 Benjamin Disraeli, speech in Manchester, April 3, 1872.

14 Rueschemeyer, Huber, and Stephens, *Capitalist Development.*

15 Diamond, *Guns, Germs, and Steel.*

16 Herbst, "War and State in Africa," 117; Centeno, "Blood and Debt"; Posado-Carbo, "Limits of Power."

17 Huntington, *Political Order.*

18 Luckham, "Democracy and Military."

BIBLIOGRAPHY

Abadie, Alberto, and Javier Gardeazabal. "The Economic Costs of Conflict: A Case Study of the Basque Country." *American Economic Review* 93, no. 1 (2003): 113–32.

Abernethy, Lloyd. "Race Riot at East St. Louis." *Journal of the Illinois State Historical Society* 57, no. 4 (1964): 431–33.

Abramson, Rudy. *Spanning the Century: The Life of W. Averell Harriman, 1891–1986.* New York: Morrow, 1992.

Abularafia, David. "Southern Italy and the Florentine Economy, 1265–1370." *Economic History Review* 34, no. 3 (1981): 377–88.

Acemoglu, Daron, and James Robinson. *Economic Origins of Dictatorship and Democracy.* New York: Cambridge University Press, 2009.

Adair, Douglass. "'That Politics May Be Reduced to a Science': David Hume, James Madison, and the Tenth Federalist." *Huntington Library Quarterly* 20, no. 4 (1957): 343–60.

Adams, J. E., ed. *Their Crimes.* London: Cassell, 1917.

Adams, Julia. "Trading States, Trading Places: The Role of Patrimonialism in Early Modern Dutch Development." *Comparative Studies in Society and History* 36, no. 2 (1994): 319–55.

Adler, Selig. "Isolationism Since 1914." *American Scholar* 21, no. 3 (1957): 335–44.

Adler, M. K., and Encyclopaedia Britannica, Inc. *A Syntopicon of Great Books of the Western World.* Chicago: Encyclopaedia Britannica, 1952.

Africa, Thomas W. "Phylarchus, Toynbee, and the Spartan Myth." *Journal of the History of Ideas* 21, no. 2 (1960): 266–72.

"After 4 Decades, a Battle for Recognition of a Soldier Still Goes On." *New York Times,* April 25, 1994.

Agren, Maria, ed. *Iron-Making Societies: Early Industrial Development in Sweden and Russia, 1600–1900.* Providence, RI: Berghahn Books, 1998.

Ahmed, Amel. *Democracy and the Politics of Electoral System Choice: Engineering Electoral Dominance.* New York: Cambridge University Press, 2013.

Akenson, Donald. *Ireland, Sweden, and the Great European Migration, 1815–1914.* McGill–Queen's University Press, 2011.

Allen, Barbara. "Review of Liberalism under Siege: The Political Thought of the French Doctrinaires by Aurelian Craiutu." *Publius* 35, no. 4 (2005): 646–48.

Allen, Robertson. "Games Without Tears, Wars Without Frontiers." In Koen Stroeken, ed., *Wars, Technology, Anthropology.* New York: Berghahn, 2012.

"The Alps," *North American Review* 38, no. 83 (1834): 405–25. Cornell University Library, http://bit.ly/1TT1xTS.

Alsop, J. D. "Innovation in Tudor Taxation." *English Historical Review* 99, no. 390 (1984): 83–93.

Altermatt, Urs. "Conservatism in Switzerland: A Study in Antimodernism." *Journal of Contemporary History* 14, no. 4 (1979): 581–610.

Ames, Edward, and Richard T. Rapp. "The Birth and Death of Taxes: A Hypothesis." *Journal of Economic History* 37, no. 1 (1977): 161–78.

Andersen, Thomas B., Peter S. Jensen, and Christian V. Skovsgaard. "The Heavy Plough and the Agricultural Revolution in Medieval Europe." *Journal of Development Economics* 118 (2016): 133–49.

Anderson, Greg. *The Athenian Experiment: Building an Imagined Political Community in Ancient Attica, 508–490 B.C.* Ann Arbor: University of Michigan Press, 2003.

Anderson, Myrdene. "Transformations of Centre and Periphery for the Saami in Norway." *Anthropoligica* 29, no. 2 (1987): 109–30.

Anderson, Perry. *Lineages of the Absolutist State.* London: New Left Books, 1974.

———. *Passages from Antiquity to Feudalism.* London: New Left Books, 1975.

Anderson, Benedict. *Imagined Communities: Reflections on the Origin and Spread of Nationalism.* London: Verso, 1983.

Anderson, Fred. *Crucible of War: The Seven Years' War and the Fate of Empire in British North America, 1754–1766.* New York: Knopf, 2000.

Andrew, C. M. and A. S. Kanya-Forstner. "France, Africa, and the First World War." *Journal of African History* 19, no. 1 (1978): 11–23.

Ardito, Alissa M. *Machiavelli and the Modern State:* The Prince, The Discourses on Livy, *and the Extended Territorial Republic.* New York: Cambridge University Press, 2015.

Aristotle. *The Politics.* Translated with an introduction by T. A. Sinclair. London, Penguin Classics, 1962.

Armstrong, E. "Review of *Die Anfänge der Fugger (Bis 1494)* by Max Jansen." *English Historical Review* 23, 92 (1908): 778–79.

———. "Review of *Jakob Fugger der Reiche: Studien und Quellen, I* by Max Jansen." *English Historical Review* 27, no. 107 (1912): 564–66.

Armstrong, Hamilton Fish. "Where India Faces China." *Foreign Affairs* 37, no. 4 (1959): 617–25.

Armstrong, Lawrin. "The Politics of Usury in Trecento Florence: The Questio de Monte of Francesco da Empoli." *Mediaeval Studies* 61, no. 1 (1999): 1–44.

———. *Usury and Public Debt in Early Renaissance Florence: Lorenzo Ridolfi on the Monte Comune.* Toronto: Pontifical Institute of Mediaeval Studies, 2003.

Artz, Frederick. "The Electoral System in France during the Bourbon Restoration, 1815–30." *Journal of Modern History* 1, no. 2 (1929): 205–18.

Asakawa, K. "Some of the Contributions of Feudal Japan to the New Japan." *Journal of Race Development* 3, no. 1 (1912): 1–32.

Asakawa, K. "The Origin of the Feudal Land Tenure in Japan." *American Historical Review* 20, no. 1 (1914): 1–23.

Asch, Ronald G. *The Thirty Years War: The Holy Roman Empire and Europe, 1618–48.* London: Palgrave, 1997.

———. *Nobilities in Transition: 1550–1700.* New York: Oxford University Press, 2003.

———. *Sacral Kingship Between Disenchantment and Re-enchantment: The French and English Monarchies, 1587–1699.* New York: Berghahn Books, 2014.

Ashworth, A. E. "The Sociology of Trench Warfare 1914–18." *British Journal of Sociology* 19, no. 4 (1968): 407–23.

Aubrey, Elizabeth. "The Dialectic between Occitania and France in the Thirteenth Century." *Early Music History* 16 (1997): 1–53.

Aulitsky, Herbert, Helmut Heuberger, and Gernot Patzelt. "Mountain Hazard Geomorphology of Tyrol and Vorarlberg, Austria." *Mountain Research and Development* 14, no. 4 (1994): 273–305.

Austin, M. M. "Greek Tyrants and the Persians, 546–479 B.C." *Classical Quarterly* 40, no. 2 (1990): 289–306.

Auxier, George W. Middle Western Newspapers and the Spanish American War, 1895–1898." *Mississippi Valley Historical Review,* 26, no. 4 (1940): 523–34.

Avant, Deborah. "Mercenaries." *Foreign Policy* 143 (2004): 20–28.

Ayers, Donald. "Cato's Speech against Murena." *Classical Journal* 49, no. 6 (1954): 245–53.

Baack, Ben. "Forging a Nation State: The Continental Congress and the Financing of the War of American Independence." *Economic History Review* 54, no. 4 (2001): 639–56.

Bacevich, Andrew J. "Absent History: A Comment on Dauber, Desch, and Feaver." *Armed Forces & Society* 24, no. 3 (1998): 447–54.

Bachrach, Bernard. *Early Carolingian Warfare: A Prelude to Empire.* Philadelphia: University of Pennsylvania Press, 2001.

———. "The Idea of the Angevin Empire." *Albion: A Quarterly Journal Concerned with British Studies* 10, no. 4 (1978): 293–99.

———. *Merovingian Military Organization.* Minneapolis: University of Minnesota Press, 1972.

Bachteler, Tobias. "Explaining the Democratic Peace: The Evidence from Ancient Greece Reviewed." *Journal of Peace Research* 34, no. 3 (1997): 315–23.

Bailey, Harris Moore. "The Splendid Little Forgotten War: The Mobilization of South Carolina for the War with Spain." *South Carolina Historical Magazine* 92, no. 3 (1991): 189–214.

Bailyn, Bernard. "Political Experience and Enlightenment Ideas in Eighteenth-Century America." *American Historical Review* 67, no. 2 (1962): 339–51.

Baker, Thomas E., and John F. Stack, Jr., eds. *At War with Civil Rights and Civil Liberties.* Lanham: Rowman & Littlefield, 2006.

Balderston, T. "War Finance and Inflation in Britain and Germany, 1914–1918." *Economic History Review* 42, no. 2 (1989): 222–44.

Balfour, Major-General. "On the Military Conscription of France." *Journal of the Statistical Society of London* 30, no. 2 (1867): 216–92.

Balot, Ryan. "Democratizing Courage in Classical Athens." In David Pritchard, ed., *War, Democracy and Culture in Classical Athens*. New York: Cambridge University Press, 2010.

Balsamo, Larry. "Germany's Armed Forces in the Second World War: Manpower, Armaments, and Supply." *History Teacher* 24, no. 3 (1991): 263–77.

Balslev, Uffe. "The Danish Case: International Involvement as the Small State's Remedy for Great Power Dominance." In Laurent Goetschel ed., *Small States Inside and Outside the European Union,* 107–24. Boston: Kluwer, 1998.

Bank, Steven. *Anglo-American Corporate Taxation: Tracing the Common Roots of Divergent Approaches*. New York: Cambridge University Press, 2011.

Barber, Benjamin. "How Swiss Is Rousseau?" *Political Theory* 13, no. 4 (1985): 475–95.

Barber, Peter. "Maps and Monarchs in Europe, 1500–1800." In Oresko, Gibbs, and Scott, eds., *Royal and Republican Sovereignty in Early Modern Europe*. New York: Cambridge University Press, 1997.

Barkow, Jerome, and Alec Leighton. "Interview with Alec Leighton." *Anthropologica* 31, no. 2 (1989): 237–61.

Baron, Hans. "Imperial Reform and the Habsburgs, 1486–1504." *American Historical Review* 44, no. 2 (1939): 293–303.

Baron, Hans. *The Crisis of the Early Italian Renaissance*. Princeton: Princeton University Press, 1966.

Bartels, Larry M. "The American Public's Defense Spending Preferences in the Post-Cold War Era." *Public Opinion Quarterly* 58, no. 4 (1989): 479–508.

Barthelemy, Dominique. "Debate: The Feudal Revolution." *Past & Present* 152 (1996): 196–205.

Barton, H. A. "Gustav III of Sweden and the Enlightenment." *Eighteenth-Century Studies* 6, no. 1 (1972): 1–34.

Bates, David. "Normandy and England after 1066." *English Historical Review*. 104, 413 (1989): 851–80.

Bates, Leonard. "The Teapot Dome Scandal and the Election of 1924." *American Historical Review* 60, no. 2 (1955): 303–22.

Bates, Robert. *Prosperity and Violence: The Political Economy of Development*. New York: W. W. Norton, 2001.

Bates, Robert, Avner Greif, and Smita Singh. "Organizing Violence." *Journal of Conflict Resolution* 46, no. 5 (2002): 599–628.

Bates, Robert, and Da-Hsiang Donald Lien. "A Note on Taxation, Development, and Representative Government" *Politics & Society* 14 (1985): 53–70.

Batstone, William. "Cicero's Construction of Consular Ethos in the First Catilinarian." *Transactions of the American Philological Association* 124 (1994): 211–66.

Batten, Bruce. "Foreign Threat and Domestic Reform: The Emergence of the Ritsuryō State." *Monumenta Nipponica* 41, no. 2 (1986): 199–219.

Baxter, Stephen B. "Recent Writings on William III." *Journal of Modern History* 38, no. 3 (1966): 256–66.

Bean, Richard. "War and the Birth of the Nation State." *Journal of Economic History* 33, no. 1 (1973): 203–21.

Beard, Charles, and Mary Beard. *America in Midpassage*. New York: Macmillan, 1939.

Beard, Mary. "Lucky City." *London Review of Books* 23, no. 16 (2001): 3–6.

———. *The Roman Triumph*. Cambridge; Harvard University Press, 2009.

Beck, Paul Allen, and M. Kent Jennings. "Lowering the Voting Age: The Case of the Reluctant Electorate." *Public Opinion Quarterly* 33, no. 3 (1969): 370–79.

Becker, Marvin B. "Economic Change and the Emerging Florentine Territorial State." *Studies in the Renaissance* 13 (1966): 7–39.

———. "Florentine Popular Government (1343–1348)." *Proceedings of the American Philosophical Society* 106, no. 4 (1962): 360–-82.

———. "Some Aspects of Oligarchical, Dictatorial, and Popular Signorie in Florence, 1282–1382." *Comparative Studies in Society and History* 2, no. 4 (1960): 421–39.

Bedard, Julie, Timothy Nelson, Susan Saltzstein, and Jennifer Spaziano. "US Supreme Court Bars Extraterritorial Application of Alien Tort Statute." 2013, http://bit.ly/1V4bUa8.

Beede, Benjamin, ed. *The War of 1898 and U.S. Interventions, 1898–1934: An Encyclopedia*. London: Routledge, 1994.

Beem, Charles. "Elizabeth's Wars." *Sixteenth Century Journal* 37, no. 2 (2006): 568–70.

Behrens, Betty. "A Revision Defended: Nobles, Prsivileges, and Taxes in France." *French Historical Studies* 9, no. 3 (1976): 521–27.

Beik, William. *Absolutism and Society in Seventeenth Century France: State Power and Provincial Aristocracy in Languedoc,* Cambridge: Cambridge University Press, 1985.

Bell, David A. *The First Total War: Napoleon's Europe and the Birth of Modern Warfare*. London: Bloomsbury, 2007.

Benedict, Coleman H. "The Romans in Southern Gaul." *American Journal of Philology* 63, no. 1 (1942): 38–50.

Benedict, Michael. "A New Look at the Impeachment of Andrew Johnson." *Political Science Quarterly* 88, no. 3 (1973): 349–67.

Benedict, Philip. "More than Market and Manufactory: The Cities of Early Modern France." *French Historical Studies* 20, no. 3 (1997): 511–38.

Benedict, Philip. "The Saint Batholomew's Massacres in the Provinces." *Historical Journal* 21, no. 2 (1978): 205–25.

Bennett, H. "The Wit's Progress: A Study in the Life of Cicero." *Classical Journal* 30, no. 4 (1935): 193–202.

Benton, John. "The Revenue of Louis VII." *Speculum* 42, no. 1 (1967): 84–91.

Berinsky, Adam. "Assuming the Costs of War: Events, Elites, and American Public Support for Military Conflict." *Journal of Politics* 69, no. 4 (2007): 975–97.

———. *In Time of War: Understanding American Public Opinion from World War II to Iraq*. Chicago: University of Chicago Press, 2009.

———. *Silent Voices: Public Opinion and Political Participation in America*. Princeton: Princeton University Press, 2004.

Bickham, Troy. *The Weight of Vengeance: The United States, the British Empire, and the War of 1812*. New York: Oxford University Press, 2012.

Birnbaum, Norman. "The Zwinglian Reformation in Zurich." *Past & Present* 15 (1959): 27–47.

Bisson, Thomas. "The 'Feudal Revolution.'" *Past & Present* 142 (1994): 6–42.

———. "The Feudal Revolution: A Reply." *Past & Present* 155 (1997): 208–25.

———. *The Medieval Crown of Aragon*. London: Oxford Clarendon, 1986.

————. "Medieval Lordship." *Speculum* 70, no. 4 (1995): 743–59.

Black, E. W. "Sentius Saturninus and the Roman Invasion of Britain." *Britannia* 31 (2000): 1–10.

Black, J. B. "Queen Elizabeth, the Sea Beggars, and the Capture of Brille, 1572." *English Historical Review* 46, no. 181 (1931): 30–47.

Black, Samuel, ed. Soul Soldiers: *African Americans and the Vietnam Era*. Pittsburgh, PA: Pittsburgh Regional History Center and the Smithsonian Institution, 2007.

Blackshire-Belay, Carol. "German Imperialism in Africa: The Distorted Images of Cameroon, Namibia, Tanzania, and Togo." *Journal of Black Studies* 23, no. 2 (1992): 235–46.

Blackwell, Alice Stone. "The Military Argument." In Carrie Chapman Catt, ed., *The Ballot and the Bullet*. Philadelphia: National American Woman Suffrage Association, 1897.

Bland, Sidney. "New Life in an Old Movement: Alice Paul and the Great Suffrage Parade of 1913 in Washington, D.C." *Records of the Columbia Historical Society* 71/72 (1971–72): 657–78.

Blanks, David. "Regionalism in Medieval Languedoc: The Pays de Sabartès." *Historical Reflections / Réflexions Historiques* 19, no. 1 (1993): 209–28.

Blanning, T. C. W. *The French Revolutionary Wars, 1787–1802*. London: Arnold, 1996.

————. " 'That Horrid Electorate' or 'Ma Patrie Germanique'? George III, Hanover, and the Fürstenbund of 1785." *Historical Journal* 20, no. 2 (1977): 311–44.

Blickle, Peter. *The Revolution of 1525: The German Peasants' War from a New Perspective.* Translated by Thomas A. Brady, Jr., and H. C. Erik Midelfort. Baltimore: Johns Hopkins University Press, 1981.

Blind, Karl. *Germany and the Schleswig-Holstein Question*. London: Trubner, 1862.

Bloch, Marc. *Feudal Society,* vol. 2, *Social Classes and Political Organization*. Translated by L. A. Manyon. Chicago: University of Chicago Press, 1971.

Blough, Roy. "Problems of Corporate Taxation in Time of War." *Law and Contemporary Problems* 10, no. 1 (1943): 108–20.

Blum, Jerome. "The Rise of Serfdom in Eastern Europe." *American Historical Review* 62, no. 4 (1957): 807–36.

Boehm, Laetitia. "Burgundy and the Empire in the Reign of Charles the Bold." *International History Review* 1, no. 2 (1979): 153–62.

Bogacz, Ted. "War Neurosis and Cultural Change in England, 1914–22: The Work of the War Office Committee of Enquiry into 'Shell-Shock.' " *Journal of Contemporary History* 24, no. 2 (1989): 227–56.

Bohdanowicz, L. "The Muslims in Poland: Their Origin, History, and Cultural Life." *Journal of the Royal Asiatic Society of Great Britain and Ireland* 3 (1942): 163–80.

Boix, Carles. *Democracy and Distribution*. New York: Cambridge University Press, 2003.

————. *Political Order and Inequality*. New York: Cambridge University Press, 2015.

Boix, Carles, and Susan Stokes. "Endogenous Democratization." *World Politics* 55, no. 4 (2003): 517–49.

Bonadeo, Alfredo. "The Role of the 'Grandi' in the Political World of Machiavelli." *Studies in the Renaissance* 16 (1969): 9–30.

Bond, Christopher. "Lucan the Christian Monarchist: The Anti-Republicanism of the *De Tyranno* and the *De bello civili*." *Renaissance Studies* 20, no. 4 (2006): 478–93.

Bonhomme, Jacques. "The Franchise in Germany." *Social Democrat* 10, no. 5 (1906): 284–90.

Bonner, Robert. "The Commercial Policy of Imperial Athens." *Classical Philology* 18, no. 3 (1923): 193–201.

———. "Xenophon's Comrades in Arms." *Classical Journal* 10, no. 5 (1915): 195–205.

Bonney, Richard. "Cardinal Mazarin and the Great Nobility during the Fronde." *English Historical Review* 96, no. 381 (1981): 818–33.

———. *The European Dynastic States, 1494–1660.* New York: Oxford University Press, 1991.

———. *The Rise of the Fiscal State in Europe, 1200–1815.* New York: Oxford University Press, 1999.

Bonvillian, William. "The Connected Science Model for Innovation: The DARPA Role." In Sadao Nagaoka, Masayuki Kondo, Kenneth Flamm, and Charles Wessner, eds., *21st Century Innovation Systems in Japan and the U.S.: A Decade of Change.* Washington, D.C.: National Academies Press, 2009.

Boren, Henry. "Tiberius Gracchus: The Opposition View." *American Journal of Philology* 82, no. 4 (1961): 358–69.

Borgeaud, Charles. "Switzerland and the War." *North American Review* 200, no. 709 (1914): 870–78.

Born, Lester K. "What is the Podestà?" *American Political Science Review* 21, no. 4 (1927): 863–71.

Bosworth, Brian. "Athens' First Intervention in Sicily: Thucydides and the Sicilian Tradition." *Classical Quarterly* 42, no. 1 (1992): 46–55.

Bouton, Cynthia A. Review of *History of Peasant Revolts: The Social Origins of Rebellion in Early Modern France* by Yves-Marie Berce. *Journal of Social History* 26, no. 3 (1993): 658–60.

Bowlus, Charles. *The Battle of Lechfield and its Aftermath.* Burlington, VT: Ashgate, 2006.

———. "Two Carolingian Campaigns Reconsidered." *Military Affairs* 48, no. 3 (1984): 121–25.

Bowman, Timothy. "The Ulster Volunteer Force and the Formation of the 36th (Ulster) Division." *Irish Historical Studies* 32, no. 128 (2001): 498–518.

Bowsky, William. "Florence and Henry of Luxemburg, King of the Romans: The Rebirth of Guelfism." *Speculum* 33, no. 2 (1958): 177–203.

Bowsky, William. "The *Buon Governo* of Siena, 1287–1355: A Medieval Italian Oligarchy." *Speculum* 37 (1962): 368–81.

Bradbury, Jim. *The Capetians: Kings of France, 987–1328.* London: Hambledon Continuum, 2007.

Brady, Thomas. *Turning Swiss: Cities and Empire, 1450–1550.* Cambridge, UK: Cambridge University Press, 1985.

Brandt, G. *The History of the Reformation and other Ecclesiastical Transactions in and about the Low Countries,* London, 1720; reproduced in University of Leiden, 2010, "The Revolt of the Netherlands, 12: The Image-breaking in Antwerp, Flanders, Tournai, Holland, Utrecht, and Friesland," http://bit.ly/1RUa1Jy.

Braude, Beatrice. "Review of *La Jacquerie* by Maurice Dommanget." *French Review* 46, no. 1 (1972): 188–89.

Braudel, Fernand. *The Mediterranean and The Mediterranean World in the Age of Philip II.* 2 vols. Translated by Siân Reynolds. London: Collins, 1972–73.

Brewer, Derek. Review of *Negotiating the Past: The Historical Understanding of Medieval Literature* by Lee Patterson. *Speculum* 64, no. 3 (1989): 751–53.

Brewer, John. *The Sinews of Power: War, Money and the English State, 1688–1783,* Cambridge: Harvard University Press, 1988.

Bromley, J. S. "The Rise and Fall of the Dutch Republic." *Historical Journal* 22, no. 4 (1979): 985–95.

Bromwich, David. "Dr. King's Anti-War Speech," 2008, http://bit.ly/242UGNg.

Brooks, Sydney. The Real Problem of Alsace-Lorraine." *North American Review* 206, no. 744 (1917): 695–704.

Broughton, T. R. S. *Magistrates of the Roman Republic.* New York: American Philological Association, 1951.

Brown, Elizabeth A. R. "Taxation and Morality in the Thirteenth and Fourteenth Centuries: Conscience and Political Power and the Kings of France." *French Historical Studies* 3, no. 1 (1973): 1–28.

———. "The Tyranny of a Construct: Feudalism and Historians of Medieval Europe." *American Historical Review* 79, no. 4 (1974): 1063–88.

Brown, J. E. T. "Hannibal's Route across the Alps." *Greece and Rome* 10, no. 1 (1963): 38–46.

Brownlee, Elliot. "Wilson and Financing the Modern State: The Revenue Act of 1916." *Proceedings of the American Philosophical Society* 129, no. 2 (1985): 173–210.

Bruce, I. A. F. "The Corcyraean Civil War of 427 B.C." *Phoenix* 25, no. 2 (1971): 108–17.

Brucker, Gene. "Bureaucracy and Social Welfare in the Renaissance: A Florentine Case Study." *Journal of Modern History* 55, no. 1 (1983): 1–21.

Brunt, P. A. "The Legal Issue in Cicero, *Pro Balbo*." *Classical Quarterly* 31, no. 1 (1982): 136–47.

———. "Nobilitas and Novitas." *Journal of Roman Studies* 72 (1982b): 1–17.

———. "Princeps and Equites." *Journal of Roman Studies* 73 (1983): 42–75.

Brustein, William, and Margaret Levi. "The Geography of Rebellion: Rulers, Rebels, and Regions 1500–1700." *Theory and Society* 16, no. 4 (1987): 467–95.

Buchheim, Christoph, and Jonas Scherner. "The Role of Private Property in the Nazi Economy: The Case of Industry." *Journal of Economic History* 66, no. 2 (2006): 390–416.

Bucholz, Arden. *Moltke and the German Wars, 1864–1871.* New York: Palgrave Macmillan, 2001.

———. Review of *Helmuth von Moltke and the Origins of the First World War* by Annika Mombauer. *Central European History* 37, no. 3 (2004): 468–72.

Burhop, Carsten, and Guntram Wolff. "A Compromise Estimate of German Net National Product, 1851–1913, and Its Implications for Growth and Business Cycles." *Journal of Economic History* 65, no. 3 (2005): 613–57.

Burnham, Walter D. "The Changing Shape of the American Political Universe." *American Political Science Review* 59, no. 1 (1965): 7–28.

Burns, T. S. "The Battle of Adrianople: A Reconsideration." *Historia* 22 (1973): 336–45.

Burrell, Robert. "Breaking the Cycle of Iwo Jima Mythology: A Strategic Study of Operation Detachment." *Journal of Military History* 68, no. 4 (2004): 1143–86.

Burstein, Paul. "Public Opinion, Demonstrations, and the Passage of Antidiscrimination Legislation." *Public Opinion Quarterly* 43, no. 2 (1979): 157–72.

Burstein, Paul, and William Freudenburg. "Ending the Vietnam War: Components of

Change in Senate Voting on Vietnam War Bills." *American Journal of Sociology* 82, no. 5 (1977): 991–1006.

Bury, J. P. T. "Gambetta and Overseas Problems." *English Historical Review* 82, no. 323 (1967): 277–95.

Bushman, Richard. "English Franchise Reform in the Seventeenth Century." *Journal of British Studies* 3 (1963): 351–56.

Bushnell, John. "Peasants in Uniform: The Tsarist Army as a Peasant Society." *Journal of Social History* 13, no. 4 (1980): 565–76.

Butler, Broadus. "Frederick Douglass by William McFeely." *Presidential Studies Quarterly* 22, no. 4 (1991): 830–35.

Butler, John Sibley. *An Oxford Companion to Military History*. New York: Oxford University Press, 1999.

Byrne, Eugene H. "Genoese Trade with Syria in the Twelfth Century." *American Historical Review* 25, no. 2 (1920): 191–219.

Caesar, Julius. *The Gallic War*. Trans. Carolyn Hammond. Oxford: Oxford University Press, 2008.

Caferro, William. *John Hawkwood: An English Mercenary in Fourteenth Century Italy*. Baltimore: Johns Hopkins Press, 2006.

———. "War and Economy in Renaissance Italy." *Journal of Interdisciplinary History* 39, no. 2 (2008): 167–209.

Cain, P. J. and A. G. Hopkins. "Gentlemanly Capitalism and British Expansion Overseas: New Imperialism, 1850–1945." *Economic History Review* 41, no. 1 (1987): 1–26.

Cairns, Huntington. "Plato's Theory of Law." *Harvard Law Review* 56, no. 3 (1942): 359–87.

Callahan, Colleen M., Judith A. McDonald, and Anthony Patrick O'Brien. "Who Voted for Smoot-Hawley?" *Journal of Economic History* 54, no. 3 (1994): 683–90.

Campbell, Bruce. "Benchmarking medieval economic development: England, Wales, Scotland, and Ireland, circa 1290." *Economic History Review* 61, no. 4 (2008): 896–948.

Campbell, Bruce M. S., and Ken Bartley. *England on the Eve of the Black Death: An Atlas of Lay Lordship, Land and Wealth, 1300–49*. Manchester: Manchester University Press, 2006.

Cameron, Lindsey. "Private Military Companies: Their Status under International Humanitarian Law and Its Impact on Their Regulation." *International Review of the Red Cross* 88, no. 863 (2006): 573–98.

Capozzola, Christopher. "The Only Badge Needed Is Your Patriotic Fervor: Vigilance, Coercion, and the Law in World War I America." *Journal of American History* 88, no. 4 (2002): 1354–82.

Carey, Brian, and John Cairns. *Warfare in the Ancient World*. Barnsley: Pen & Sword, 2005.

Carlisle, Rodney. "The Foreign Policy Views of an Isolationist Press Lord: W. R. Hearst and the International Crisis, 1936–41." *Journal of Contemporary History* 9, no. 3 (1974): 217–27.

Carpenter, David A. "The Second Century of English Feudalism." *Past & Present*, no. 168 (2000): 30–71.

Carrithers, David. "Not so Virtuous Republics: Montesquieu, Venice, and the Theory of Aristocratic Republicanism." *Journal of the History of Ideas* 52, no. 2 (1991): 245–68.

Carsten, F. L. *Essays in German History*. London: Hambledon Press, 1985.

———. "The Origins of the Junkers." *English Historical Review* 62, no. 243 (1947): 145–78.

————. *War Against War: British and German Radical Movements in the First World War.* Berkeley: University of California Press, 1982.

Casanova, Julian. "Civil Wars, Revolutions, and Counterrevolutions in Finland, Spain, and Greece (1918–1949): A Comparative Analysis." *International Journal of Politics*, Culture, and Society 13, no. 3 (2000): 515–37.

Caspari, M. O. B. "On the Revolution of the Four Hundred at Athens." *Journal of Hellenic Studies* 33 (1913): 1–18.

Cassidy, Brendan. "Simone Martini's 'St. Martin and the Emperor' and Contemporary Italian Politics." *Zeitschrift für Kunstgeschichte* 70, no. 2 (2007): 145–58.

Castelot, E. Review of *Das Zeitalter der Fugger; Geldkapital und Creditverkehr im 16 Jahrhundert* by Richard Ehrenberg. *Economic Journal* 8, no. 29 (1898): 100–2.

Caverley, Jonathan. *Democratic Militarism: Voting, Wealth, and War.* New York: Cambridge University Press, 2014.

Cawkwell, G. L. "Athenian Naval Power in the Fourth Century." *Classical Quarterly* 34, no. 2 (1984): 340.

————. "The Crowning of Demosthenes." *Classical Quarterly* 19, no. 1 (1969): 163–80.

————. "The Decline of Sparta." *Classical Quarterly* 33, no. 2 (1983): 385–400.

————. "Notes on the Failure of the Second Athenian Confederacy." *Journal of Hellenic Studies* 101 (1981): 40–55.

Cecelski, David, and Timothy Tyson, eds. *Democracy Betrayed: The Wilmington Race Riot of 1898 and Its Legacy.* Chapel Hill: University of North Carolina Press, 1998.

Celik, Ali, Loess Wolthuis, and Marieke Slagter. "War Profits from the Iraq War: The Dirty Games of Contractors." Working Paper, Erasmus University, 2008.

Centeno, Miguel Angel. "Blood and Debt: War and Taxation in Nineteenth-Century Latin America." *American Journal of Sociology* 102, no. 6 (1997): 1565–605.

Chamberlain, Muriel. "Florence Nightingale: Letters from the Crimea, 1854–1856." *Victorian Studies* 42, no. 2 (2000): 379–81.

Chan, Steve, and William Safran. "Public Opinion as a Constraint against War: Democracies' Responses to Operation Iraqi Freedom." *Foreign Policy Analysis* 2 (2006): 137–56.

Chang, David. *To Return Home or Return to Taiwan: Conflicts and Survival in the Voluntary Repatriation of Chinese POWs in the Korea War,* Dissertation in the Department of History, University of California San Diego, 2011, http://bit.ly/1RUlCs5.

Chayes, Sarah. *Thieves of State: Why Corruption Threatens Global Security.* New York: W. W. Norton, 2015.

Chen, Jian. "The Tibetan Rebellion of 1959 and China's Changing Relations with India and the Soviet Union," *Journal of Cold War Studies* 8, no. 3 (2006): 54–101.

Chernow, Ron. *Alexander Hamilton.* New York: Penguin Press, 2004.

Chesser, Susan. "Afghanistan Casualties: Military Forces and Civilians." Washington, DC: Congressional Research Service, 2012.

Chinn, David. "Preserving Combat Power when Defense Budgets Are Falling." McKinsey & Co. Insights and Publications, 2013, http://bit.ly/1MNKRNS.

Chiozza, Giacomo, and H. E. Goemans. "Peace Through Insecurity: Tenure and International Conflict." *Journal of Conflict Resolution* 47, no. 4 (2003): 443–67.

Chodorow, Stanley. "Ecclesiastical Politics and the Ending of the Investiture Contest: The

Papal Election of 1119 and the Negotiations of Mouzon." *Speculum* 46, no. 4 (1971): 613–40.

Christian, Garna L. "The Houston Mutiny of 1917." *Trotter Review* 18, no. 1 (2009): 112–14.

Christiansen, Niels Finn. "Denmark: The End of the Idyll." *New Left Review* 1, no. 144 (1984): 1–33.

Christianson, Paul. "The Causes of the English Revolution: A Reappraisal." *Journal of British Studies* 15, no. 2 (1976): 40–75.

Christopherson, A. J. "The Provincial Assembly of the Three Gauls in the Julio-Claudian Period." *Historia* 17, no. 3 (1968): 351–66.

Cipolla, Carlo. "Economic Depression of the Renaissance?" *Economic History Review* 16 (1964): 519–24.

Clark, Christopher. *Iron Kingdom: The Rise and Fall of Prussia, 1600–1947*. Cambridge, MA: Harvard University Press, 2006.

———. *The Sleepwalkers: How Europe Went to War in 1914*. London: Allen Lane, 2012.

Clark, Truman. "History Gives Lie to the Myth of Black Confederate Soldiers." *Houston Chronicle,* August 29, 1999.

Clifford, Clark. *Counsel to the President: A Memoir.* New York: Random House, 1991.

Clifton, Robin. "The Crimean War, 1853–1856." *Victorian Studies* 44, no. 1 (2001): 165–67.

———. "The Popular Fear of Catholics during the English Revolution." *Past & Present*, no. 52 (1971): 23–55.

Cline, Peter. Review of *The Right to Belong: Citizenship and National Identity in Britain, 1930–1960* by Richard Weight and Abigail Beach. *Albion* 31, no. 2 (1999): 353–55.

Cloche, P. "L'affaire des Arginuses." *Review Histoire* 130 (1919): 5–68.

Coffey, David. In Spencer C. Tucker, ed., *Encyclopedia of the Vietnam War: A Political, Social, and Military History*. Oxford, UK: ABC-CLIO, 1998.

Cogan, Marc. "Mytilene, Plataea, and Corcyra Ideology and Policy in Thucydides, Book Three." *Phoenix* 35, no. 1 (1981): 1–21.

Cohen, Steven. "Steelworkers Rethink the Homestead Strike of 1892." *Pennsylvania History* 48 (1981): 155–77.

Cohn, Henry, ed. *Government in Reformation Europe, 1520–1560*. New York: Harper and Row, 1971.

Cohn, Samuel. *Creating the Florentine State: Peasants and Rebellion, 1348–1434*. Cambridge, UK: Cambridge University Press, 1999.

———. Review of *La città divisa: Le Parti e il bene commune da Dante a Guicciardini* by Francesco Bruni. *Speculum* 80, no. 3 (2005): 848–50.

Cole, G. D. H. "Recent Developments in the British Labor Movement." *American Economic Review* 8, no. 3 (1918): 485–504.

Cole, Laurence. "Nation, Anti-Enlightenment, and Religious Revival in Austria: Tyrol in the 1790s." *Historical Journal* 43, no. 2 (2000): 475–97.

Cole, Wayne. "American Entry into World War II: A Historiographical Appraisal." *Mississippi Valley Historical Review* 43, no. 4 (1957): 595–617.

Colley, Linda. "Whose Nation? Class and National Consciousness in Britain, 1750–1830." *Past & Present* 113, no 1 (1986): 97–117.

Collins, Roger. *Early Medieval Europe, 300–1000*. New York: St. Martin's, 1991.

Commission on Wartime Contracting in Iraq and Afghanistan. *Transforming Wartime Contracting: Controlling Costs, Reducing Risks. Final Report to Congress*. Washington, DC, 2011.

Comstock, Alzada. "British Income Tax Reform." *American Economic Review* 10, no. 3 (1920): 488–506.

———. "Excess Profits and Corporation Taxes in Great Britain." *Bulletin of the National Tax Association* 6, no. 1 (1920): 7–9.

Cone, James. "Martin and Malcolm on Nonviolence and Violence." *Phylon* 49, nos. 3 /4 (2001): 173–83.

Conlan, Thomas C. "Instruments of Change: Organizational Technology and the Consolidation of Regional Power in Japan, 1333–1600." In John A. Ferejohn and Frances McCall Rosenbluth, eds., *War and State Building in Medieval Japan*, 124–58. Stanford: Stanford University Press, 2010.

———. *State of War: The Violent Order of Fourteenth-Century Japan*. Ann Arbor: Center for Japanese Studies, University of Michigan, 2003.

"Conscription in England During the Napoleonic War." *Minnesota History Bulletin* 1, no. 2 (1915): 55–57.

Coolidge, W. A. B. "The Republic of Gersau." *English Historical Review* 4, no. 15 (1889): 481–515.

Cooper, J. P. "A Revolution in Tudor History?" *Past & Present* 26, no. 1 (1963): 110–12.

Corbett, J. H. "Rome and the Gauls, 285–280 B.C." *Historia* 20 (1971): 656–64.

Cornell, Timothy. *The Beginnings of Rome*. London: Routledge, 1995.

"Count Munster, the German Ambassador in Paris." *Spectator,* July 4, 1891, p. 9.

Cox, Gary. "Was the Glorious Revolution a Constitutional Watershed?" *Journal of Economic History* 72, no. 3 (2012): 567–600.

Crackel, Theodore. "Jefferson, Politics, and the Army: An Examination of the Military Peace Establishment Act of 1802." *Journal of the Early Republic* 2, no. 1 (1982): 21–38.

Craig, Gordon A. *The Politics of the Prussian Army, 1640–1945*. Oxford: Oxford University Press, 1955.

Cramsie, John. *Kingship and Crown Finance Under King James VI and I, 1603–1625*. Rochester: Boydell Press for the Royal Historical Society, 2002.

Cress, Lawrence D. "Radical Whiggery on the Role of the Military: Ideological Roots of the American Revolutionary Militia." *Journal of the History of Ideas* 40, no.1 (1979): 43–60.

Cultice, Wendell. *Youth's Battle for the Ballot: A History of Voting Age in America*. Westport, CT: Greenwood, 1992.

Current, Richard. "The Stimson Doctrine and the Hoover Doctrine." *American Historical Review* 59, no. 3 (1954): 513–42.

Daggett, Stephen. "The Costs of U.S. Wars." Congressional Research Service, 7-5700, RS22926, 2010.

Dahl, Robert. *Polyarchy*. New Haven, CT: Yale University Press, 1971.

Darden, Keith. *Resisting Occupation: Mass Schooling and the Creation of Durable National Loyalties*. New York: Cambridge University Press, 2015.

Dardess, John. "From Mongol Empire to Yuan Dynasty: Changing Forms of Imperial Rule in Mongolia and Central Asia." *Monumenta Serica* 30 (1972–73): 117–65.

———. Review of *The Military Establishment of the Yuan Dynasty* by Ch'i-Ch'ing Hsiao. *International History Review* 1, no. 3 (1979): 439–41.

Darvill, Timothy. *Prehistoric Britain*. London: Routledge, 1987.

Daunton, Martin. "How to Pay for the War: State, Society and Taxation in Britain, 1917–24." *English Historical Review* 111, no. 443 (1996): 882–919.

———. *Trusting Leviathan: The Politics of Taxation in Britain, 1799–1914*. Cambridge, UK: Cambridge University Press, 2001.

David, E. "The Oligarchic Revolution at Rhodes, 391–89 B.C." *Classical Philology* 79, no. 4 (1984): 271–84.

Davies, J. K. *Athenian Propertied Families, 600–300 B.C.* Oxford, UK: Oxford University Press, 1971.

———. *Wealth and the Power of Wealth in Classical Athens*. New York: Arno Press, 1981.

Davis, David. "Not Only War Is Hell: World War I and African American Lynching Narratives." *African American Review* 42, nos. 3/4 (2008): 477–91.

Davis, John. "Review of Jonas Flöter, *Beust und die Reform des Deutschen Bundes, 1850–1866: Sächsischmittelstaatliche Koalitionspolitik im Kontext der deutschen Frage. Journal of Modern History* 76, no. 3 (2004): 713–14.

Davis, J. C. "Religion and the Struggle for Freedom in the English Revolution." *Historical Journal* 35, no. 3 (1992): 507–30.

Davis, Robert C. *Shipbuilders of the Venetian Arsenal: Workers and Workplace in the Preindustrial City*. Baltimore: Johns Hopkins University Press, 1991.

———. "Slave Redemption in Venice, 1585–1797." In John Martin and Dennis Romano, eds., *Venice Reconsidered: The History and Civilization of an Italian City State, 1297–1797*. Baltimore: Johns Hopkins University Press, 2000.

Deacon, Roger. Review of *The New Wars* by Herfried Münkler and Patrick Camiller. *Theoria: A Journal of Social and Political Theory* 111, Democracy and Power (2006): 156–60.

de Dijn, Annelien. "Aristocratic Liberalism in Post-Revolutionary France." *Historical Journal* 48, no. 3 (2005): 661–81.

"Defence of the Realm: Habeas Corpus." *Michigan Law Review* 16, no. 3 (1918): 196–97.

Delbruck, Hans. *History of the Art of War* (1920), 4 vols. Translated by Walter J. Renfroe. Lincoln: University of Nebraska Press, 1990.

Dennett, Daniel. "Pirenne and Muhammad." *Speculum* 23, no. 2 (1948): 165–90.

de Parieu, M. Espuirou and Frederick Hendriks. "John De Witt; or Twenty Years' Interregnum in Stadtholdership of the Seventeenth Century." *Assurance Magazine, and Journal of the Institute of Actuaries* 8, no. 4 (1859): 205–31.

Desch, Michael. "War and Strong States, Peace and Weak States?" *International Organization* 50, no. 2 (1996): 237–68.

de Souza, Philip. "Parta Victoriis Tax: Roman Emperors as Peacemakers." In Philip de Souza and John France, eds., *War and Peace in Ancient and Medieval History*. Cambridge: Cambridge University Press, 2008.

Deutsch, Monroe E. "Caesar and the Ambrones: (Suetonius Iulius ix.3)." *Classical Philology* 16, no. 3 (1921): 256–59.

Develin, Robert. "The Voting Position of the Equites after the Centuriate Reform." *Rheinisches Museum für Philologie* 122, no. 2 (1979): 155–61.

Develin, Robert, and Martin Kilmer. "What Kleisthenes Did." *Historia* 46, no. 1 (1997): 3–18.

deVries, Kelly. *Guns and Men in Medieval Europe.* Burlington, VT: Ashgate, 2002.

———. "The Lack of a Western European Military Response to the Ottoman Invasions of Eastern Europe from Nicopolis (1396) to Mohacs (1526)." *Journal of Military History* 63, no. 3 (1999): 539–59.

———. *Medieval Military Technology.* New York: Broadview Press, 1992.

———. "On the Modernity of the Dutch Republic." *Journal of Economic History* 33, no. 1 (1973): 191–202.

Dewald, Jonathan. "Magistracy and Political Opposition at Rouen: A Social Context." *Sixteenth Century Journal* 5, no. 2 (1974): 66–78.

Dewey, P. E. "Military Recruiting and the British Labour Force During the First World War." *Historical Journal* 27, no. 1 (1984): 199–223.

Diamond, Jared. *Guns, Germs, and Steel: The Fates of Human Societies.* New York: W. W. Norton, 1997.

"The Diamond Cartel." *Yale Law Journal* 56, no. 8 (1947): 1404–19.

Dicey, Edward. *The Schleswig-Holstein War.* London: Tinsley Brothers, 1864.

Dickins, G. "The True Cause of the Peloponnesian War." *Classical Quarterly* 5, no. 4 (1911): 238–48.

Dickson, P. G. M. "Monarchy and Bureaucracy in Late Eighteenth Century Austria." *English Historical Review* 110, no. 436 (1995): 323–67.

Dikotter, Frank. *Mao's Great Famine: The History of China's Most Devastating Catastrophe, 1958–1962.* New York: Walker, 2010.

Dil, Shaheen F. "The Cabal in Kabul: Great-Power Interaction in Afghanistan." *American Political Science Review* 71, no. 2 (1977): 468–76.

Dilke, Charles and Demetrius Botassi. "The Uprising of Greece." *North American Review* 164, 485 (1897): 453–61.

Diller, Aubrey. "Scrutiny and Appeal in Athenian Citizenship." *Classical Philology* 30, no. 4 (1935): 302–11.

Dobb, Maurice. *Studies in the Development of Capitalism.* London: Routledge, 1946.

Dodge, Theodore Ayrault. Review of *The Santiago Campaign, 1898* by Joseph Wheeler; *The War with Spain* by Henry Cabot Lodge; *Reminiscences of the Santiago Campaign* by John Bigelow; *The Rough Riders* by Theodore Roosevelt. *American Historical Review* 5, no. 2 (1899): 376–82.

Dollinger, Philippe. *The German Hansa.* Stanford: Stanford University Press, 1970.

Domar, Evsey. "The Causes of Slavery or Serfdom: A Hypothesis." *Journal of Economic History* 30, no. 1 (1970): 18–32.

Domar, Evsey, and Mark Machina. "On the Profitability of Russian Serfdom." *Journal of Economic History* 44, no. 4 (1984): 919–55.

———. "The Profitability of Serfdom: A Reply." *Journal of Economic History* 45, no. 4 (1985): 960–62.

Dommanget, Mauric. *La Jacquerie.* Paris: Maspero, 1971.

Donagan, Barbara. "The Web of Honour: Soldiers, Christians, and Gentlemen in the English Civil War." *Historical Journal* 44, no. 2 (2001): 365–89.

Donovan, John. "Congressional Isolationists and the Roosevelt Foreign Policy." *World Politics* 3, no. 3 (1951): 299–316.

Douglass, Robin. "Rousseau's Critique of Representative Sovereignty: Principled or Pragmatic?" *American Journal of Political Science* 57, no. 3 (2013): 735–74.

Dower, John W. *War Without Mercy: Race and Power in the Pacific War.* New York: Random House, 1986.

Downing, Brian M. "Constitutionalism, Warfare, and Political Change in Early Modern Europe." *Theory and Society* 17, no. 1 (1988): 7–56.

———. *The Military Revolution and Political Change: Origins of Democracy and Autocracy in Early Modern Europe.* Princeton: Princeton University Press, 1992.

Doyle, William. *Venality: The Sale of Offices in Eighteenth-Century France.* New York: Oxford University Press, 1996.

Drew, Katherine Fischer. "The Immunity in Carolingian Italy." *Speculum* 37, no. 2 (1962): 182–97.

Drews, Robert. *The End of the Bronze Age: Changes in Warfare and the Catastrophe ca. 1200 B.C.* Princeton: Princeton University Press, 1993.

Dryden, Charles. *A-Train: Memoirs of a Tuskegee Airman.* Tuscaloosa: University of Alabama Press, 1997.

Du Bois, W. E. B. "The Perpetual Dilemma." *Crisis* 13, no. 6 (1917): 270–71.

———. "Close Ranks." *Crisis* 16, no. 3 (1918): 111.

———. "Documents of the War." *Crisis* 18, no. 5 (1919): 16–21.

———. "Thirteen." *Crisis* 15, no. 3 (1918): 114.

Duby, Georges. *La Société aux XIe et XIIe siècles dans la Region Maconnaise.* Paris: A. Colin, 1955. Reproduced with changed pagination in 1971.

Dudziak, Mary. "Desegregation as a Cold War Imperative." *Stanford Law Review* 41, no. 1 (1988): 61–120.

Duffield, W. B. "The War of the Sonderbund." *English Historical Review* 10, no. 40 (1895): 675–98.

Duncan, Lauren. "The Psychology of Collective Action." In Kay Deaux and Mark Snyder, eds., *The Oxford Handbook of Personality and Social Psychology.* New York: Oxford University Press, 2012.

Dunn, Susan. *Jefferson's Second Revolution: The Election Crisis of 1800 and the Triumph of Republicanism.* Boston: Houghton Mifflin, 2004.

Dunthorne, Hugh. "Resisting Monarchy: The Netherlands as Britain's School of Revolution in the Late Sixteenth and Seventeenth Centuries." In Robert Oresko, G. C. Gibbs, and H. M. Scott, eds., *Royal and Republican Sovereignty in Early Modern Europe.* New York: Cambridge University Press, 1997.

Dupree, Louis. "The Retreat of the British Army from Kabul to Jalalabad in 1842: History and Folklore." *Journal of the Folklore Institute* 4, no. 1 (1967): 50–74.

Dur, Philip. "The Right of Taxation in the Political Theory of the French Religious Wars." *Journal of Modern History* 17, no. 4 (1945): 289–303.

Durr, David. "The Cadre Division Concept: The 106th Infantry Division Revisited." A Study Project for the U.S. Army War College, 1992.

Duus, Peter. *Modern Japan.* 2nd ed. Boston: Houghton Mifflin, 1997.

Dynner, Glenn. *Yankel's Tavern: Jews, Liquor, and Life in the Kingdom of Poland.* Oxford University Press, 2014.

Dzara, Daniel. "Credibility Concerns Mar Iraq Reconstruction." *Public Contract Law Journal* 34, no. 2 (2005): 435–41.

Dzelzainis, Martin. "History and Ideology: Milton, the Levellers, and the Council of State in 1649." *Huntington Library Quarterly* 63, no. 1–2 (2005): 269–87.

Eddie, S. A. *Freedom's Price: Serfdom, Subjection, and Reform in Prussia, 1648–1848.* New York: Oxford University Press, 2013.

Eddy, Samuel K. "The Cold War Between Athens and Persia, ca. 448–412 B.C." *Classical Philology* 68, no. 4 (1973): 241–58.

———. "Four Hundred Sixty Talents Once More." *Classical Philology* 63, no. 3 (1968): 184–95.

Edling, Max. *A Revolution in Favor of Government: Origins of the U.S. Constitution and the Making of the American State.* New York: Oxford University Press, 2003

Efflandt, Scott. "Under Siege: How Private Military Companies Threaten the Military Profession." Research project, U.S. Army War College, 2013, http://bit.ly/1RzQsaP.

Eichengreen, Barry. "International Policy Coordination in Historical Perspective: A View from the Interwar Years." In Willem Buiter and Richard Marston, eds., *International Economic Policy Coordination.* New York: Cambridge University Press, 1985.

———. "The Political Economy of the Smoot-Hawley Tariff." In R. L. Ransom, P. H. Lindert, and R. Sutch, eds., *Research in Economic History.* Greenwich, CT: Westwood, 1989.

Einhard, and Notker the Stammerer. *The Life of Charlemagne.* Ed. and trans. David Ganz. New York: Penguin Classics, 2008.

Elkins, Stanley, and Eric McKitrick. *The Age of Federalism: The Early American Republic, 1788-1800.* New York: Oxford University Press, 1993.

Elliott, J. H. "A Europe of Composite Monarchies." *Past & Present* 137, no. 1 (1970): 48–71.

———. *Imperial Spain 1469–1716.* London: Penguin Books, 1963.

Ellis, Steven. *Ireland in the Age of the Tudors, 1447–1603.* London: Longman, 1998.

Ellis, Mark. "'Closing Ranks' and 'Seeking Honors': W. E. B. Du Bois in World War I." *Journal of American History* 79, no. 1 (1992): 96–124.

Elton, G. R. "King or Minister? The Man Behind the Henrician Reformation." In Henry J. Cohn, ed., *Government in Reformation Europe, 1520–1560.* New York: Harper and Row, 1971.

Elwood, R. C. "Lenin and the Brussels 'Unity' Conference of July 1914." *Russian Review* 39, no. 1 (1980): 32–49.

Engerman, Stanley. "Slavery and Emancipation in Comparative Perspective: A Look at Some Recent Debates." *Journal of Economic History* 46, no. 2 (1986): 317–39.

Engerman, Stanley L., and Kenneth L. Sokoloff. "The Evolution of Suffrage Institutions in the New World." *Journal of Economic History* 65, no. 4 (2005): 891–921.

English, Richard. "Himalayan State Formation and the Impact of British Rule in the Nineteenth Century." *Mountain Research and Development* 5, no. 1 (1985): 61–78.

Epstein, Klaus. "Wrong Man in a Maelstrom: The Government of Max of Baden." *Review of Politics* 26, no. 2 (1964): 215–43.

Epstein, Steven A. *Genoa and the Genoese, 958–1528.* Durham: University of North Carolina Press, 1996.

Epstein, Stephan R. *Freedom and Growth: The Rise of States and Markets in Europe, 1300–1750.* London: Routledge, 2000.

———. *The Rise and Decline of Italian City States.* Department of Economic History, London School of Economics, Working Paper no. 51/99, 1999, http://bit.ly/29zgxEO.

Erdkamp, Paul. "Polybius, the Erbo Treaty, and the Gallic Invasion of 225 B.C.E." *Classical Philology* 104, no. 4 (2009): 495–510.

Eriksson, Gosta. "Advance and Retreat of Charcoal Iron Industry and Rural Settlement in Bergslagen." *Geografiska Annaler* 42, no. 4 (1960): 267–84.

———. "The Decay of Blast Furnaces and Iron Works in Vaster Bergslagen in Central Sweden 1860–1940." *Geografiska Annaler* 35, no. 1 (1953): 1–10.

Errington, R. M. *The Dawn of Empire: Rome's Rise to World Power.* London: Hamilton, 1972.

Espinosa, Aurelio. "The Spanish Reformation: Institutional Reform, Taxation, and the Secularization of Ecclesiastical Properties Under Charles V." *Sixteenth Century Journal* 37, no. 1 (2006): 3–24.

Euben, J. Peter. "The Battle of Salamis and the Origins of Political Theory." *Political Theory* 14, no. 3 (1986): 359–90.

"Evaluation of Development Support to Afghanistan." Ministry of Foreign Affairs, Denmark, 2012.

Evans, Geoffrey. "Ancient Mesopotamian Assemblies: An Addendum." *Journal of the American Oriental Society* 78, no. 2 (1958): 114–15.

Evans, R. J. W. *The Making of the Habsburg Monarchy 1550–1700. An Interpretation.* London: Oxford University Press, 1979.

Everitt, Anthony. *Cicero: The Life and Times of Rome's Greatest Politician.* New York: Random House, 2003.

Fabel, Robin. "The Laws of War in the 1812 Conflict." *Journal of American Studies* 14, no. 2 (1980): 199–218.

———. "Self-Help in Dartmoor: Black and White Prisoners in the War of 1812." *Journal of the Early Republic* 9, no. 2 (1989): 165–90.

Fairclough, Adam. "Martin Luther King, Jr., and the War in Vietnam." *Phylon* 45, no. 1 (1984): 19–39.

Fairlie, John. "British War Cabinets." *Michigan Law Review* 16, no. 7 (1918): 471–95.

"Far Eastern Questions." *Advocate of Peace Through Justice* 83, no. 12 (1921): 418–24.

Farr, Martin. "Waging Democracy: The British General Election of 1918 Reconsidered." *Cerecles* 21 (2011): 65–94.

Farrar, Cynthia. *The Origins of Democratic Thinking: The Invention of Politics in Classical Athens.* Cambridge, UK: Cambridge University Press, 1988.

———. "Power to the People." In Kurt A. Raaflaub, Josiah Ober, and Robert Wallace, eds., *Origins of Democracy in Ancient Greece.* Berkeley: University of California Press, 2007.

Farris, Wayne. *Heavenly Warriors: The Evolution of Japan's Military, 500–1300.* Cambridge: Harvard University Press, 1992.

Fay, Sidney. "The Beginnings of the Standing Army in Prussia." *American Historical Review* 22, no. 4 (1917): 763–77.

———. *The Rise of Brandenburg-Prussia to 1786.* Malabar, FL: Kriegr Publishing, 1937.

Fearon, James, and David Laitin. "Ethnicity, Insurgency, and Civil War." *American Political Science Review* 97, no. 1 (2004): 75–90.

Feer, Robert. "Shays's Rebellion and the Constitution: A Study in Causation." *New England Quarterly* 42, no. 3 (1969): 388–410.

Fenoaltea, Stefano. "The Rise and Fall of a Theoretical Model: The Manorial System." *Journal of Economic History* 35, no. 2 (1975): 386–409.

Ferejohn, John, and Frances Rosenbluth. *War and State Building in Medieval Japan.* Stanford: Stanford University Press, 2010.

Ferguson, Niall. "Germany and the Origins of the First World War: New Perspectives." *Historical Journal* 35, no. 3 (1992): 725–52.

———. *The Pity of War: Explaining World War I.* London: Allen Lane, 1998.

Ferro, Marc. "The Russian Soldier in 1917: Undisciplined, Patriotic, and Revolutionary." *Slavic Review* 30, no. 3 (1971): 483–512.

Figes, Orlando. "The Red Army and Mass Mobilization during the Russian Civil War, 1918–1920." *Past & Present,* no. 129 (1990): 168–211.

Figueira, T. "Sitopolai and Sitophylakes in Lysias' 'Against the Graindealers': Governmental Intervention in the Athenian Economy." *Phoenix* 40, no. 2 (1986): 149–71.

Finlay, Robert. "Fabius Maximus in Venice: Doge Andrea Gritti, the War of Cambrai, and the Rise of Habsburg Hegemony, 1509–1530." *Renaissance Quarterly* 53, no. 4 (2000): 988–1031.

Finley, Moses. "Athenian Demagogues." *Past & Present* 21, no. 1 (1962): 3–24.

Firnhaber-Baker, Justine. "Seigneurial War and Royal Power in Later Medieval Southern France." *Past & Present* 208 (2010): 37–76.

Fischer, Hannah. "American War and Military Operations Casualties: Lists and Statistics." Congressional Research Service Report for Congress, Department of the Navy Library, Knowledge Services Group, 2005.

Fischer, Kathryn. *The Laws of the Salian Franks.* Philadelphia: University of Pennsylvania Press, 1991.

Fitzpatrick, Matthew. *Liberal Imperialism in Germany: Expansionism and Nationalism, 1848–1884.* New York: Bergahn Books, 2008.

Flockerzie, Lawrence. "State-Building and Nation-Building in the 'Third Germany': Saxony after the Congress of Vienna." *Central European History* 24, no. 3 (1991): 268–92.

Flynn, George. "Selective Service and American Blacks During World War II." *Journal of Negro History* 69, no. 1 (1984): 14–25.

———. *Conscription and Democracy: The Draft in France, Great Britain, and the United States.* Westport: Praeger, 2002.

Foley, Michael S. *Confronting the War Machine: Draft Resistance during the Vietnam War.* Chapel Hill: University of North Carolina Press, 2003.

Foley, Susan, and Charles Sowerwine. *A Political Romance: Léon Gambetta, Léonie Léon, and the Making of the French Republic, 1872–1882.* Basingstoke, UK: Palgrave Macmillan, 2012.

Foner, Eric. *Reconstruction: America's Unfinished Revolution, 1863–1877.* New York: Harper Perennial Modern Classics, 1988.

Ford, G. S. Review of *Der Preussische Verfassungskampf vor Hundert Jahren* by Paul Haake. *American Historical Review* 26, no. 3 (1921): 512–13.

Forrest, W. G. "Legislation in Sparta." *Phoenix* 21, no. 1 (1967): 11–19.

———. "Themistokles and Argos." *Classical Quarterly* 10, no. 2 (1960): 221–41.

Forsdyke, Sara."Revelry and Riot in Archaic Megara: Democratic Disorder or Ritual Reversal." *Journal of Hellenic Studies* 125 (2005): 73–92.

Forster, Keith. "The Politics of Destabilization and Confrontation: The Campaign against Lin Biao and Confucius in Zhejiang Province." *China Quarterly*, no. 107 (1986): 433–62.

Forstner, Andrew, and A. S. Kanye-Forstner. "France, Africa, and the First World War," *Journal of African History* 19, no. 1 (1978): 11–23.

Fortescue, John W. *A History of the British Army*. London: Macmillan, 1899–1930.

Foucault, Michel. *Discipline and Punish: The Birth of the Prison*. New York: Random House, 1979.

Fox, Edward Whiting. *History in Geographic Perspective: The Other France*. New York: W. W. Norton, 1971.

Foxley, Rachel. "John Lilburne and the Citizenship of 'Free-Born Englishmen.'" *Historical Journal* 47, no. 4 (2004): 849–74.

Franck, Thomas M., and Edward Weisband. *Foreign Policy by Congress*. Oxford: Oxford University Press, 1979.

Franklin, John H. "The North, the South, and the American Revolution." *Journal of American History* 62, no. 1 (1975): 5–23.

Fraser, Peter. "British War Policy and the Crisis of Liberalism in May 1915." *Journal of Modern History* 54, no. 1 (1982): 1–26.

Freedman, Paul. "The German and Catalan Peasant Revolts." *American Historical Review* 98, no. 1 (1993): 39–54.

———. *Images of the Medieval Peasant*. Stanford: Stanford University Press, 1999.

Fremdling, Ranier. "Anglo-German Rivalry on Coal Markets, 1850–1913." Research Memorandum, Groningen Growth and Development Center, 1995.

French, A. "Economic Conditions in Fourth-Century Athens." *Greece and Rome* 38, no. 1 (1991): 24–40.

French, David. "Watching the Allies: British Intelligence and the French Mutinies of 1917." *Intelligence and National Security* 6, no. 3 (1991): 573–92.

Freund, William. "Ethnological Observations Made on a Journey Through the Rhaetian Alps." *Journal of the Ethnological Society of London* 4 (1854): 268–84.

Friday, Karl. *Hired Swords: The Rise of Private Warrior Power in Early Japan*. Stanford: Stanford University Press, 1992.

———. "They Were Soldiers Once: The Early Samurai and the Imperial Court." In John Ferejohn and Frances Rosenbluth, eds., *War and State Building in Medieval Japan*. Stanford: Stanford University Press, 2010.

Frieden, Jeffrey. "Sectoral Conflict and Foreign Economic Policy, 1914–1940." *International Organization* 42, no. 1 (1988): 59–90.

Friedman, Milton. "Franklin D. Roosevelt, Silver, and China." *Journal of Political Economy* 100, no. 1 (1992): 62–83.

Friedrich, Karin. *The Other Prussia: Prussia, Poland, and Liberty, 1569-1772.* Cambridge University Press, 2000.

Fritschy, W. "A 'Financial Revolution' Reconsidered: Public Finance in Holland During the Dutch Revolt, 1568–1648." *Economic History Review* 56, no. 1 (2003): 57–89.

Fritzsche, Peter. "Did Weimar Fail?" *Journal of Modern History* 68, no. 3 (1996): 629–56.

Froissart, Jean. *Chronicles* (1322–77). Translated by John Bourchier. Edited by G.C. Macaulay. London: Macmillan, 1904.

Frost, Frank J. "Themistocles' Place in Athenian Politics." *California Studies in Classical Antiquity* 1 (1968): 105–24.

Frost, Robert. *The Northern Wars: War, State, and Society in Northeastern Europe, 1558–1721.* New York: Longmans, 2000.

———. "Ordering the Kaleidoscope: The Construction of Identities in the Lands of the Polish-Lithuanian Commonwealth Since 1569." In Len Scales and Oliver Zimmer, eds., *Power and the Nation in European History.* New York: Cambridge University Press, 2005.

Galbraith, V. H. "Penrose Memorial Lecture. Runnymede Revisited." *Proceedings of the American Philosophical Society* 110, no. 5 (1966): 307–17.

Ganser, Daniele. "The British Secret Service in Neutral Switzerland: An Unfinished Debate on NATO's Cold War Stay-Behind Armies." *Intelligence and National Security* 20, no. 4 (2005): 553–80.

Ganshoff, F. L. *Feudalism*, 3rd ed. New York: Harper, 1964.

Gardner, Kathryn. "Lawyers Who Shaped America: Sandra Day O'Connor." *America Inns of Court,* January–February 2012.

Garner, J. W. "A Record of Political Events." *Political Science Quarterly* 19, no. 4 (1904): 717–48.

Garon, Sheldon M. "State and Religion in Imperial Japan, 1912–1945." *Journal of Japanese Studies* 12, no. 2 (1986): 273–302.

Gartner, Scott Sigmund, and Gary M. Segura. "Race, Casualties, and Opinion in the Vietnam War." *Journal of Politics* 62, no. 1 (2000): 115–46.

Gatewood, Willard. *Smoked Yankees and the Struggle for Empire.* Fayetteville: University of Arkansas Press, 1987.

Gatrell, Peter, and Mark Harrison. "The Russian and Soviet Economies in Two World Wars: A Comparative View." *Economic History Review* 46, no. 3 (1993): 425–52.

Gaustad, Edwin. "Restitution, Revolution, and the American Dream." *Journal of the American Academy of Religion* 44, no. 1 (1976): 77–86.

Gauvain, Auguste. "Five Years of French Policy in the Near East." *Foreign Affairs* 3, no. 2 (1924): 277–92.

Geary, Patrick. *Before France and Germany.* New York: Oxford University Press, 1988.

———. *The Myths of Nations: The Medieval Origins of Europe.* Princeton: Princeton University Press, 2002.

Gelderblom, Oscar, and Joost Jonker. "Completing a Financial Revolution: The Finance of the Dutch East India Trade and the Rise of the Amsterdam Capital Market, 1595–1612." *Journal of Economic History* 64, no. 3 (2004): 641–72.

Gentles, Ian. Review of *The Parliaments of Elizabethan England* by D. M. Dean and N. L. Jones. *Albion* 23, no. 4 (1991): 730–32.

————. "The Struggle for London in the Second Civil War." *Historical Journal* 26, no. 2 (1983): 277–305.

George, David B. "Lucan's Cato and Stoic Attitudes to the Republic." *Classical Antiquity* 10, no. 2 (1991): 237–58.

Gerlach, Christian. "The Wannsee Conference, the Fate of German Jews, and Hitler's Decision in Principle to Exterminate All European Jews." *Journal of Modern History* 70, no. 4 (1998): 759–812.

Gibbs, Philip. *Now It Can Be Told.* New York: Harper & Brothers, 1920.

Gibson, Craig. "Sex and Soldiering in France and Flanders: The British Expeditionary Force along the Western Front, 1914–1919." *International History Review* 23, no. 3 (2001): 535–79.

Gibson, Hugh. "Switzerland's Position in Europe." *Foreign Affairs* 4, no. 1 (1925): 72–84.

Giffler, Martin. "The Boule of 500 from Salamis to Ephialtes." *American Journal of Philology* 62, no. 2 (1941): 224–26.

Gillespie, James L. Review of *Henry V: The Practice of Kingship* by G. L. Harriss. *Speculum* 62, no. 1 (1987): 137–39.

Gilmore, Allison B. " 'We Have Been Reborn': Japanese Prisoners and the Allied Propaganda War in the Southwest Pacific." *Pacific Historical Review* 64, no. 2 (1995): 195–215.

Gilmore, Glenda. "Black Militias in the Spanish-Cuban/American War." In Benjamin R. Beede, ed., *The War of 1898 and U.S. Interventions in 1898–1934: An Encyclopedia.* London: Routledge, 1994.

————. *Defying Dixie: The Radical Roots of Civil Rights, 1919–1950.* New York: W. W. Norton, 2008.

————. *Gender and Jim Crow: Women and the Politics of White Supremacy in North Carolina, 1896–1920.* Chapel Hill: University of North Carolina Press, 1996.

Gittings, John. "Military Control and Leadership, 1949–1964." *China Quarterly*, no. 26 (1966): 82–101.

Given-Wilson, Chris, et al., eds. *The Parliamentary Rolls of Medieval England, 1275–1504.* http://bit.ly/1XbQhmi.

Glover, Richard. "The French Fleet, 1807–1814: Britain's Problem and Madison's Opportunity." *Journal of Modern History* 39, no. 3 (1967): 233–52.

Goldberg, Eric. "Popular Revolt, Dynastic Politics, and Aristocratic Factionalism in the Early Middle Ages: Saxon Stellinga Reconsidered." *Speculum* 70, no. 3 (1995): 467–501.

Goldfield, David. *America Aflame: How the Civil War Created a Nation.* New York: Bloomsbury, 2011.

Goldsworthy, Adrian. *How Rome Fell.* New Haven, CT: Yale University Press, 2009.

Goldthwaite, Richard. "The Medici Bank and the World of Florentine Capitalism." *Past & Present* 114, no. 1 (1987): 3–31.

————. Review of *The Civic World of Early Renaissance Florence* by Gene Brucker; *Florence and the Medici: The Pattern of Control* by J. R. Hale; *Fra Girolamo Savonarola, Florentine Art, and Renaissance Historiography* by Ronald M. Steinberg. *Journal of the Society of Architectural Historians* 38, no. 4 (1979): 386–87.

Gombrich, E. H. *A Little History of the World.* New Haven, CT: Yale University Press, 2005.

Goncourt, Edmond de, and Jules de Goncourt. *The Journal of the de Goncourts.* Ed. Julius West. London: Thomas Nelson and Sons, ca. 1915.

Goodykoontz, Colin. "Edward P. Costigan and the Tariff Commission, 1917–1928." *Pacific Historical Review* 16, no. 4 (1947): 410–19.

Gordon, Bruce. *The Swiss Reformation*. New York: Manchester University Press, 2002.

Gordon, David M. "The China-Japan War, 1931–1945." *Journal of Military History* 70, no. 1 (2006): 137–82.

Gordon, M. D. "The Collection of Ship-Money in the Reign of Charles I." *Transactions of the Royal Historical Society* 4 (1910): 141–62.

Gordon, Robert, and Terry Reynolds. "Medieval Iron in Society-Norberg, Sweden." *Technology and Culture* 27, no. 1 (1986): 110–17.

Gordon-Reed, Annette. *Andrew Johnson: The American Presidents: The 17th President, 1865–1869.* New York: Times Books, 2011.

Gosse, Edmund. "Norway Revisited." *North American Review* 167, no. 504 (1898): 534–42.

Gould, J. D. "The Crisis in the Export Trade, 1586–1587." *English Historical Review* 71, no. 279 (1956): 212–22.

Gourevitch, Peter. *Politics in Hard Times: Comparative Responses to International Economic Crises.* Ithaca, NY: Cornell University Press, 1986.

———. "The Second Image Reversed: The International Sources of Domestic Politics." *International Organization* 32, no. 4 (1978): 881–912.

Graff, David. *Medieval Chinese Warfare, 300–900.* London: Routledge, 2002.

Graham, A. J. "Thucydides 7.13.2 and the Crews of Athenian Triremes." *Transactions of the American Philological Association* 122 (1992): 257–70.

———. "Thucydides 7.13.2 and the Crews of Athenian Triremes: An Addendum." *Transactions of the American Philological Association* 128 (1998): 89–114.

Graham, Dominick. "The British Expeditionary Force in 1914 and the Machine Gun."

Graham-Leigh, Elaine. *The Southern French Nobility and the Albigensian Crusade.* Woodbridge, UK, and Rochester, NY: Boydell and Brewer, 2005.

Granitz, Elizabeth, and Benjamin Klein. "Monopolization by 'Raising Rivals' Costs': The Standard Oil Case." *Journal of Law and Economics* 39, no. 1 (1996): 1–47.

Gras, N. S. B. "War and Business: Four Century-Long Struggles." *Bulletin of the Business Historical Society* 20, no. 6 (1946): 165–89.

Graubard, Stephen. "Military Demobilization in Great Britain Following the First World War." *Journal of Modern History* 19, no. 4 (1947): 297–311.

Green, James. *Death in the Haymarket: A Story of Chicago, the First Labor Movement, and the Bombing that Divided Gilded Age America.* New York: Pantheon Books, 2006.

Green, Judith. *The Aristocracy of Norman England.* Cambridge, UK: Cambridge University Press, 1997.

———. "The Last Century of Danegeld." *English Historical Review* 96, no. 379 (1981): 241–58.

———. Review of *The Written World: Past and Place in the Work of Orderic Vitalis* by Amanda Hingst. *English Historical Review* 127, no. 528 (2012): 1190–91.

Green, Louis. "Changes in the Nature of War in Early Fourteenth Century Tuscany." *War and Society* 1, no. 1 (1983): 1–24.

Greenhalgh, P. A. L. "Aristocracy and Its Advocates in Archaic Greece." *Greece and Rome* 19, no. 1 (1972): 190–207.

Greenhill, Kelly. "Don't Dumb Down the Army." *New York Times.* February 17, 2006.

Greif, Avner. "On the Political Foundations of the Late Medieval Commercial Revolution:

Genoa During the Twelfth and Thirteenth Centuries." *Journal of Economic History* 54, no. 2 (1994): 271–87.

Greif, Avner, Paul Milgrom, and Barry Weingast. "Coordination, Commitment, and Enforcement: The Case of the Merchant Guild." *Journal of Political Economy* 104, no. 4 (1994): 745–76.

Griffiths, Gordon. "The Revolutionary Character of the Revolt of the Netherlands." *Comparative Studies in Society and History* 2, no. 4 (1960): 452–72.

Griffiths, Ralph A. Review of *Henry VI and the Politics of Kingship* by John Watts. *English Historical Review* 113, no. 452 (1998): 685–87.

Grill, Johnpeter Horst, and Robert Jenkins. "The Nazis and the American South in the 1930s: A Mirror Image?" *Journal of Southern History* 58, no. 4 (1992): 667–94.

Gronke, Paul, and Darius Rejali. "U.S. Public Opinion on Torture, 2001–2009." *PS*, July 2010, 437–45.

Grubb, James S. "When Myths Lose Power: Four Decades of Venetian Historiography." *Journal of Modern History* 58, no. 1 (1986): 43–94.

Grytten, Ola H. "The Economic History of Norway." EH.Net Encyclopedia, edited by Robert Whaples, March 16, 2008.

Guicciardini, Francesco. *The History of Italy* (1537).Translated and edited by Sidney Alexander. New York: Macmillan, 1969.

Guinnane, Timothy. "Financial Vergangenheitsbewaltigung: The 1953 London Debt Agreement." Yale University Working Paper, 2004.

Gvosdev, Nikolas. "Coalition of the Billing—First Past Due Notice." *National Interest*, April 14, 2004.

Habicht, Christian. "Athens, Samos, and Alexander the Great." *Proceedings of the American Philosophical Society* 140, no. 3 (1996): 397–405.

Hack, Harold M. "Thebes and the Spartan Hegemony, 386–382 B.C." *American Journal of Philology* 99, no. 2 (1978): 210–27.

Hacker, David. "A Census-Based Count of the Civil War Dead." *Civil War History* 57, no. 4 (2011): 307–48.

Hagen, William. *Ordinary Prussians: Brandenburg Junkers and Villagers, 1500–1840*. New York: Cambridge University Press, 2002.

———. "Seventeenth Century Crisis in Brandenburg: The Thirty Years' War, the Destabilization of Serfdom, and the Rise of Absolutism." *American Historical Review* 94, no. 2 (1989): 302–35.

Hagglof, Gunnar. "A Test of Neutrality: Sweden in the Second World War." *International Affairs* 36, no. 2 (1960): 153–67.

Hahn, Erich. "The Junior Faculty in 'Revolt': Reform Plans for Berlin University in 1848." *American Historical Review* 82, no. 4 (1977): 875–95.

Hahn, Otto. *My Life: The Autobiography of a Scientist*. Translated by Ernst Kaiser and Eithne Wilkins. New York: Herder and Herder, 1970.

Hale, John R. *Lords of the Sea: The Epic Story of the Athenian Navy and the Birth of Democracy*. New York: Penguin, 2009.

Haliczer, Stephen. "The Castilian Aristocracy and the Mercedes Reform of 1478–1482." *Hispanic American Historical Review* 55, no. 3 (1975): 449–67.

Hall, John W. *Government and Local Power in Japan: A Study on Bizen Provice, 500–1700*. Princeton: Princeton University Press, 1966.

Hall, Lindsay G. H. "Ephialtes, the Areopagus and the Thirty." *Classical Quarterly* 40, no. 2 (1990): 319–28.

Hall, Simon. "The Response of the Moderate Wing of the Civil Rights Movement to the War in Vietnam." *The Historical Journal* 46 (September 2003): 669–701.

Hallam, Henry. *View of the State of Europe During the Middle Ages.* London: John Murray, 1853.

Halpern, Rick. "Solving the 'Labour Problem': Race, Work and the State in the Sugar Industries of Louisiana and Natal, 1870–1910." *Journal of Southern African Studies* 30, no. 1 (2004): 19–40.

Hamilton, Charles D. "Spartan Politics and Policy, 405–401 B.C." *American Journal of Philology* 91, no. 3 (1970): 294–314.

Hammond, N. G. L. "The Battle of Salamis." *Journal of Hellenic Studies* 76 (1956): 32–54.

———. "Diodorus' Narrative of the Sacred War and the Chronological Problems of 357–352 B.C." *Journal of Hellenic Studies* 57, no. 1 (1937): 44–78.

Hammond, William. "The Press in Vietnam as Agent of Defeat: A Critical Examination." *Reviews in American History* 17, no. 2 (1989): 312–23.

Hansard Parliamentary Archives. http://www.hansard-archive.parliament.uk/

Hansen, Mogens Herman. *The Athenian Democracy in the Age of Demosthenes: Structure, Principles, and Ideology.* Translated by J. A. Crook. Norman: University of Oklahoma Press, 1991.

———. *The Sovereignty of the People's Court in Athens in the Fourth Century B.C. and the Public Action against Unconstitutional Proposals.* Odense: University of Odense Press, 1974.

Hansmann, H. *The Ownership of Enterprise.* Cambridge: Belknap Press, 1996.

Harding, Robert R. "The Mobilization of Confraternities against the Reformation in France." *Sixteenth Century Journal* 11, no. 2 Catholic Reformation (1980): 85–107.

Hardy, E. G. "The Catilinarian Conspiracy in its Context: A Re-Study of the Evidence," *Journal of Roman Studies* 7 (1918): 153–228.

Harper, Ida Husted. "Woman Suffrage throughout the World." *North American Review* 186, no. 622 (1907): 55–71.

Harris, Stephen. *British Military Intelligence in the Crimean War, 1854–1856.* London: Frank Cass, 1999.

Harrison, Mark. "Resource Mobilization for World War II: The U.S.A., U.K., U.S.S.R., and Germany, 1938–1945." *Economic History Review* 41, no. 2 (1988): 171–92.

Harriss, Gerald L. *Henry V: The Practice of Kingship.* New York: Oxford University Press, 1985.

———. *King, Parliament and Public Finance in Medieval England to 1369.* Oxford: Clarendon Press, 1975.

———. "War and the Emergence of the English Parliament, 1297–1360." *Journal of Medieval History* 2, no. 1 (1976): 35–56.

Harriss, Gerald L., and Penry Williams. "A Revolution in Tudor History?" *Past & Present* 31, no. 1 (1965): 87–96.

Hart, Betty. "A Cry in the Wilderness: The Diary of Alice Dunbar-Nelson." *Women's Studies Quarterly* 17, nos. 3/4 (1989): 74–78.

Hartmann, Susan. "Transforming Women, Transforming Politics: The U.S. Woman Suffrage Movement." *Reviews in American History* 26, no. 2 (1998): 390–94.

Hatcher, J. "English Serfdom and Villeinage: Toward a Reassessment." *Past & Present* 90 (1981).

Hathaway, Oona, et al., *The Power to Detain: Detention of Terrorism Suspects After 9/11,* Yale Law School Legal Scholarship Repository, 2013. http://bit.ly/1SMd8ng.

Haupt, George. *Socialism and the Great War: The Collapse of the Second International.* Oxford: Clarendon Press, 1972.

Hayden, Michael J. "Deputies and Qualites: The Estates General of 1614." *French Historical Studies* 3, no. 4 (1964): 507–24.

Hayes, Carlton. "The History of German Socialism Reconsidered." *American Historical Review* 23, no. 1 (1917): 62–101.

Haynes, Robert. "The Houston Mutiny and Riot of 1917." *Southwestern Historical Quarterly* 76, no. 4 (1973): 418–39.

Head, Randolph. *Early Modern Democracy in the Grisons.* Oxford: Oxford University Press, 1995.

Heather, Peter. "The Goths." *Speculum* 74, no. 1 (1999): 182–84.

———. "The Huns and the End of the Roman Empire in Western Europe." *English Historical Review* 110, no. 435 (1995): 4–41.

Heckscher, Eli. *Mercantilism.* London: George Allen & Unwin, 1935.

———. "Multilateralism, Baltic Trade, and the Mercantilists." *Economic History Review* 3, no. 2 (1950): 219–28.

———. "The Place of Sweden in Modern Economic History." *Economic History Review* 4, no.1 (1932): 1–22.

He Di. "The Most Respected Enemy: Mao Zedong's Perception of the United States." *China Quarterly,* no. 137 (1994): 144–58.

Hedin, Robert, ed. *The Zeppelin Reader: Stories, Poems, and Songs from the Age of Airships.* Iowa City: University of Iowa Press, 1998.

Hegel, Georg Wilhelm Friedrich. *Elements of the Philosophy of Right.* Translated and edited by Allen W. Wood. Cambridge: Cambridge University Press, 1991.

Hencken, Hugh. "Syracus, Etruria and the North: Some Comparisons." *American Journal of Archaeology* 62, no. 3 (1958): 259–72.

Henneman, John Bell. "The Black Death and Royal Taxation in France, 1347–1351." *Speculum* 43, no. 3 (1968): 405–28.

———. "Financing the Hundred Years War." *Speculum* 42 (1967): 275–98.

———. "The Military Class and the French Monarchy in the Late Middle Ages." *American Historical Review* 83, no. 4 (1978): 946–65.

———. "Nobility, Privilege and Fiscal Politics in Late Medieval France." *French Historical Studies* 13, no. 1 (1983): 1–17.

———. *Royal Taxation in Fourteenth-Century France: The Captivity and Ransom of John II, 1356–1370.* Philadelphia: American Philosophical Society, 1976.

Henriksen, Ingrid. "Avoiding Lock-in: Cooperative Creameries in Denmark, 1882–1903." *European Review of Economic History* 3, no. 1 (1999): 57–78.

———. "An Economic History of Denmark." EH.Net Encyclopedia, edited by Robert Whaples. October 6, 2006, http://bit.ly/24QxGkd.

Henshall, Nicholas. *The Myth of Absolutism: Change and Continuity in Early Modern European Monarchy.* London: Longman, 1992.

Herbst, Jeffrey. "War and the State in Africa." *International Security* 14, no. 4 (1990): 117–39.

Hersch, Seymour. "Lieutenant Accused of Murdering 109 Civilians." *St. Louis Post-Dispatch*, November 13, 1969.

Heurlin, Bertel. "Danish Security Policy." *Cooperation and Conflict* 17 (1982): 237–55.

Hewitson, Mark. "Germany and France before the First World War: A Reassessment of Wilhelmine Foreign Policy." *English Historical Review* 115, no. 462 (2000): 570–606.

Higonnet, Patrick, and Trevor Higonnet. "Class, Politics, and Corruption in the French Chamber of Deputies, 1846–1848." *French Historical Studies* 5, no. 2 (1967): 204–24.

Hill, H. "Livy's Account of the Equites." *Classical Philology* 25, no. 3 (1930): 244–49.

Hill, John H. "Raymond of Saint Gilles in Urban's Plan of Greek and Latin Friendship." *Speculum* 26, no. 2 (1951): 265–76.

Hill, Joseph A. "The Prussian Income Tax." *Quarterly Journal of Economics* 6, no. 2 (1892): 207–26.

Hillerbrand, Hans. "The Reformation in the Cities." *Journal of Modern History* 50, no. 1 (1978): 162–67.

Hinton, David. "'Triumph of the Will': Document or Artifice?" *Cinema Journal* 15, no. 1 (1975): 48–57.

Hinton, R. W. K. "The Decline of Parliamentary Government under Elizabeth I and the Early Stuarts." *Cambridge Historical Journal* 13, no. 2 (1957): 116–32.

Hirschman, Albert O. *Exit, Voice, and Loyalty: Responses to Decline in Firms, Organizations, and States.* Cambridge: Harvard University Press, 1970.

Hirst, Derek. "The Failure of Godly Rule in the English Republic." *Past & Present* 132, no. 1 (1991): 33–66.

Hjerppe, Riitta. "An Economic History of Finland." EH.Net Encyclopedia, edited by Robert Whaples, February 10, 2008.

Hobsbawn, E. J. Review of *British Labour and the Russian Revolution, 1917–1924* by Stephen Richards Graubard and *The Labour Government and British Industry, 1945–1951* by A. A. Rogow. *Science and Society* 23, no. 2 (1959): 168–71.

Hoffman, Philip. "Taxes and Agrarian Life in Early Modern France: Land Sales, 1550–1730." *Journal of Economic History* 46, no. 1 (1986): 37–55.

Hoffman, Richard C. *Land, Liberties, and Lordship in a Late Medieval Countryside: Agrarian Structures and Change in the Duchy of Wroclaw.* Philadelphia: University of Pennsylvania Press, 1999.

———. "The Rise of the Polish Monarchy: Piast Poland in East Central Europe." *Speculum* 49, no. 3 (1974): 573–75.

Holborn, Hajo. "The Prusso-German School: Moltke and the Rise of the General Staff." In Peter Paret, ed., *Makers of Modern Strategy.* Princeton: Princeton University Press, 1986.

Holladay, James. "Hoplites and Heresies." *Journal of Hellenic Studies* 102 (1982): 94–103.

———. "Medism in Athens 508–480 B.C." *Greece and Rome* 25, no. 2 (1978): 174–91.

Holloway, Jonathan Scott. "Ralph Bunche and the Responsibilities of the Public Intellectual." *Journal of Negro Education* 73, no. 2 (2004): 125–36.

Holmes, Olivia. "Reading Order in Discord: Guicciardini's Ricordi." *Italica* 76, no. 3 (1999): 314–34.

Holmes, Stephen. "Aristippus In and Out of Athens." *American Political Science Review* 73, no. 1 (1979): 113–28.

Holroyd, Richard. "The Bourbon Army, 1815–1830." *Historical Journal* 14, no. 3 (1971): 529.

Horne, John, and Alan Kramer. *German Atrocities 1914: A History of Denials*. New Haven, CT: Yale University Press, 2001.

Hörnqvist, Mikael. "'Perché non si usa allegare i Romani': Machiavelli and the Florentine Militia of 1506." *Renaissance Quarterly* 55, no.1 (2002): 148–91.

Hovde, Brynjolf. "French Socialism and Franco-German Relations, 1893–1914." *Journal of Political Economy* 35, no. 2 (1927): 261–77.

Howe, Daniel Walker. *What God Hath Wrought: The Transformation of America, 1815–1848*. New York: Oxford University Press, 1994.

Howorth, Jolyon. "The Myth of Blanquism under the Third Republic (1871–1900)." *Journal of Modern History* 48, no. 3 (1976): 37–68.

Hrobsky, Martin. "Public Opinion Divided as the Czech Parliament Approves a Bill Which Could see Troops Involved in a Possible War with Iraq," Radio Praha, January 7, 2003.

Hu, Chi-hsi. "Mao, Lin Biao and the Fifth Encirclement Campaign." *China Quarterly*, no. 82 (1980): 250–80.

Hubatsch, Walther. "Albert of Brandenburg-Ansbach, Grand Master of the Order of Teutonic Knights and Duke of Prussia, 1490–1568." In Henry J. Cohn, ed., *Government in Reformation Europe, 1520–1560*. New York: Harper and Row, 1971.

Hudon, Edward G. "John Lilburne, the Levellers, and Mr. Justice Black." *American Bar Association Journal* 63, no. 6 (1974): 686–88.

Hughes, Ann. "The King, the Parliament, and the Localities During the English Civil War." *Journal of British Studies* 24, no. 2 (1985): 236–63.

Hughes, Christopher. *Switzerland*. New York: Praeger, 1975.

Hugo, Victor. *Memoirs of Victor Hugo*. Project Gutenberg, http://bit.ly/29HNRgF.

Hume, David. *Political Discourses*. Edinburgh: Fleming, Kincaid, and Donaldson, 1752.

Hume, Martin. Review of *Henry of Navarre and the Huguenots in France* by P. F. Willert. *English Historical Review* 9, no. 35 (1894): 578–80.

Hunt, Patrick. *Alpine Archeology*. New York: Ariel Books, 2007.

Hunt, Peter. "The Slaves and the Generals of Arginusae." *American Journal of Philology* 122, no. 3 (2001): 359–80.

———. *Slaves, Warfare, and Ideology in the Greek Historians*. New York: Cambridge University Press, 1998.

Hunt, Verl. "The Rise of Feudalism in Eastern Europe." *Science and Society* 42, no. 1 (1978): 43–61.

Huntington, Samuel. "How Countries Democratize." *Political Science Quarterly* 106, no. 4 (1991): 579–616.

———. *Political Order in Changing Societies*. New Haven, CT: Yale University Press, 1968.

Hurst, Michael. Review of *The Liberal Imperialists: The Ideas and Politics of a Post-Gladstonian Elite* by H. C. G. Matthew. *Historical Journal* 17, no. 3 (1974): 665–68.

Hyde, Samuel. "'Please Sir, He Called Me Jimmy!': Political Cartooning Before the Law: 'Black Friday,' J. H. Thomas, and the Communist Libel Trial of 1921 Communist Libel Suit." *Contemporary British History* 25, no. 4 (2011): 521–50.

Hyde, Walter Woodburn. "The Ancient Appreciation of Mountain Scenery." *Classical Journal* 11, no. 2 (1915): 70–84.

Hyndman, H. M. "Clemenceau, the Man and His Time." *North American Review* 209, no. 763 (1919): 852–54.

Ianziti, Gary. *Humanistic Historiography Under the Sforzas: Politics and Propaganda in Fifteenth-Century Milan.* New York: Oxford University Press, 1988.

Israel, Jonathan. "A Conflict of Empires: Spain and the Netherlands 1618–1648." *Past & Present* 76, no. 1 (1977): 34–74.

———. *The Dutch Republic: Its Rise, Greatness, and Fall: 1477–1806.* New York: Oxford University Press, 1998.

Issacharoff, Samuel, and Richard Pildes. "Between Civil Libertarianism and Executive Unilateralism: An Institutional Process Approach to Rights During Wartime." *Theoretical Inquiries into Law* 5, no. 1 (2004): 1–45.

Iversen, Torben, and Frances Rosenbluth. *Women, Work, and Politics: The Political Economy of Gender Inequality.* New Haven: Yale University Press, 2010.

Jakobsen, Peter. *Nordic Approaches to Peace Operations.* New York: Routledge, 2006.

Jakobsson, Sverrir. Review of *Taxes, Tributes and Tributary Lands in the Making of the Scandinavian Kingdoms in the Middle Ages* by Steinar Imsen. *Journal of English and Germanic Philology* 112, no. 4 (2013): 550–52.

James, Alan. *The Origins of French Absolutism, 1598–1661.* London: Pearson, 2006.

James, Robert Rhodes, ed. *Winston S. Churchill: His Complete Speeches, 1897–1963,* vol. 3, *1948–1949.* New York: Chelsea House, 1974.

Janick, Herbert. "Senator Frank B. Brandegee and the Election of 1920." *Historian* 35, no. 3 (1973): 434–51.

Janz, Lisa. "Chronology of Post-Glacial Settlement and Subsistence Among Gobi Desert Hunter-Gathers and Their Role in the Neolithization of Mongolia and China." PhD dissertation, University of Arizona, 2011.

Jarausch, Konrad H. "The Illusion of Limited War: Chancellor Bethmann Hollweg's Calculated Risk, July 1914." *Central European History* 2, no. 1 (1969): 48–76.

Jeffery, L. H., and Paul Cartledge. "Sparta and Samos: A Special Relationship?" *Classical Quarterly* 32, no. 2 (1982): 243–65.

Jehn, Christopher, and Zachary Selden. "The End of Conscription in Europe?" *Contemporary Economic Policy* 20, no. 2 (2002): 93–100.

Jensen, De Lamar. "French Diplomacy and the Wars of Religion." *Sixteenth Century Journal* 5, no. 2 (1974): 23–46.

Joesten, Joachim. "The Scramble for Swedish Iron Ore." *Foreign Affairs* 16, no. 2 (1938): 347–50.

John, Elijah. "NGOs and the Economic Recovery of Afghanistan." *Development in Practice* 11, no. 5 (2001): 633–36.

Johnson, Edward. *History of Negro Soldiers in the Spanish-American War, and Other Items of Interest.* Raleigh, NC, 1899.

Johnson, Gerald K. "Black Soldiers of the Ardennes." *Soldiers: The Official U.S. Army Magazine,* February 1981.

Jones, Edgar. "The Psychology of Killing: The Combat Experience of British Soldiers During the First World War." *Journal of Contemporary History* 41, no. 2 (2006): 229–46.

Jones, Peter J. "An Italian Estate, 900–1200." *Economic History Review*, new ser., vol. 7 (1954): 18–32.

Jones, Robert E. "The Polish-Lithuanian Monarchy in European Context, 1500–1795." *International History Review* 24, no. 3 (2002): 634–36.

Jordan, William. "'The Damnable Dilemma': African-American Accommodation and Protest During World War I." *Journal of American History* 81, no. 4 (1995): 1562–83.

Jorgensen, Henrik, and Henrik Breitenbauch. "What if We Give Up Conscription?" Danish Institute for Military Studies, University of Copenhagen, 2009.

Jurdjevic, Mark. *A Great and Wretched City: Promise and Failure in Machiavelli's Florentine Political Thought*. Chicago: University of Chicago Press, 2014.

Kaegi, Walter. *Muslim Expansion and Byzantine Collapse in North Africa*. New York: Cambridge University Press, 2010.

Kagan, Donald. *The Peloponnesian War*. New York: Viking Press, 2003.

Kahn, Michael. "Shattering the Myth About President Eisenhower's Supreme Court Appointments." *Presidential Studies Quarterly* 22, no. 1 (1992): 47–56.

Kamen, Henry. "The Mediterranean and the Expulsion of Spanish Jews in 1492." *Past & Present* 119, no. 1 (1988): 3–55.

Kaminski, Andrzej. "Neo-Serfdom in Poland-Lithuania." *Slavic Review* 34, no. 2 (1975): 253–68.

Kant, Immanuel. *Perpetual Peace* (1795). Translated by M. Campbell Smith. London: George Allen and Unwin, 1917.

Kapelle, William. "Domesday Book: F. W. Maitland and His Successors." *Speculum* 64, no. 3 (1989): 620–40.

Kaplan, Arthur. "Religious Dictators of the Roman Republic." *Classical World* 67, no. 3 (1973): 172–75.

Katz, Solomon. "The Gracchi: An Essay in Interpretation." *Classical Journal* 38, no. 2 (1940): 65–82.

Katznelson, Ira. *Fear Itself: The New Deal and the Origins of Our Time*. New York: W. W. Norton, 2013.

Kaufman, Victor. "Trouble in the Golden Triangle: The United States, Taiwan and the 93rd Nationalist Division." *China Quarterly* 166 (2001): 440–56.

Keller, Robert. "Supply-Side Economic Policies during the Coolidge-Mellon Era." *Journal of Economic Issues* 16, no. 3 (1982): 773–90.

Kelsey, Francis. "Cicero as a Wit." *Classical Journal* 3, no. 1 (1907): 3–10.

Kennedy, Ellen. *Constitutional Failure: Carl Schmitt in Weimar*. Durham, NC: Duke University Press, 2004.

———. Introduction to Carl Schmitt's *Crisis of Parliamentary Democracy*. Cambridge, MA: MIT Press, 1988.

Kennedy, Paul. *The Rise and Fall of the Great Powers: Economic Change and Military Conflict from 1500 to 2000*. New York: Random House, 1987.

Kent, Clement B. R. *The English Radicals: A Historical Sketch*. London: Longmans Green, 1899.

Kent, Dale. "The Florentine Reggimento in the Fifteenth Century." *Renaissance Quarterly* 28, no. 4 (1975): 575–638.

Kershaw, Ian. "'Improvised Genocide?' The Emergence of the 'Final Solution' in the 'Wargenthau.'" *Transactions of the Royal Historical Society* 2 (1992): 51–78.

Kersten, Andrew. "African Americans and World War II." *OAH Magazine of History* 16, no. 3 (2002): 13–17.

Keyssar, Alexander. *The Right to Vote: The Contested History of Democracy in the United States.* New York: Basic Books, 2000.

———. "Peculiar Institution." *Boston Globe.* October 17, 2004.

Kiernan, V. G. "Foreign Mercenaries and Absolute Monarchy." *Past & Present* 11, no. 1 (1957): 66–86.

Kim, Song Bak. "The Impact of Class Relations and Warfare in the American Revolution: The New York Experience." *Journal of American History* 69, no. 2 (1982): 326–46.

Kindleberger, Charles. "The Economic Crisis of 1619 to 1623." *Journal of Economic History* 51, no. 1 (1991): 149–75.

———. *The World in Depression, 1929–1939.* Berkeley: University of California Press, 1973.

King, Desmond, and Rogers Smith. *Still a House Divided: Race and Politics in Obama's America.* Princeton: Princeton University Press, 2011.

King, Peter. "The Episcopate during the Civil Wars, 1642–1649." *English Historical Review* 83, no. 328 (1968): 523–37.

Kingston-Mann, Esther. "Lenin and the Challenge of Peasant Militance: From Bloody Sunday, 1905 to the Dissolution of the First Duma." *Russian Review* 38, no. 4 (1979): 434–55.

Kinzl, Konrad, ed. *A Companion to the Classical Greek World.* Oxford: Blackwell, 2006.

Kiser, Edgar, and April Linton. "Determinants of the Growth of the State: War and Taxation in Early Modern France and England." *Social Forces* 80, no. 2 (2001): 411–48.

Kiser, Edgar, and Joachim Schneider. "Bureaucracy and Efficiency: An Analysis of Taxation in Early Modern Prussia." *American Sociological Review* 59, no. 2 (1994): 187–204.

Kishlansky, Mark. "Consensus Politics and the Structure of Debate at Putney" *Journal of British Studies* 20, no. 2 (1981): 50–69.

———. *The Rise of the New Model Army.* New York: Cambridge University Press, 1979.

———. "What Happened at Ware?" *Historical Journal* 25, no. 4 (1982): 827–39.

Kissinger, Henry. *A World Restored: Metternich, Castlereagh and Problems of Peace.* Boston: Houghton Mifflin, 1957.

Klarman, Michael. *From Jim Crow to Civil Rights: The Supreme Court and the Struggle for Racial Equality.* New York: Oxford University Press, 2004.

———. *Unfinished Business: Racial Equality in American History.* New York: Oxford University Press, 2007.

Kleinschmidt, Harald. "Using the Gun: Manual Drill and the Proliferation of Portable Firearms." *Journal of Military History* 63, no. 3 (1999): 601–30.

Klinkner, Philip A., and Rogers M. Smith. *The Unsteady March: The Rise and Decline of Racial Equality in the United States.* Chicago: University of Chicago, 1999.

Knauer, Christine. *Let Us Fight as Free Men.* Philadelphia: University of Pennsylvania Press, 2014.

Knox, Ronald. "'So Michievous a Beaste'? The Athenian 'Demos' and Its Treatment of Its Politicians." *Greece and Rome* 32, no. 2 (1985): 132–61.

Knudsen, Tim, and Bo Rothstein. "State Building in Scandinavia." *Comparative Politics* 26, no. 2 (1994): 203–20.

Knudsen, Tim, and Uffe Jakobsen. "A Danish Path to Democracy." University of Copenhagen working paper, 2003.

Koenigsberger, H. G. "The Organization of Revolutionary Parties in France and the Netherlands During the Sixteenth Century." *Journal of Modern History* 27, no. 4 (1955): 335–51.

Koenigsberger, H. G., George Mosse, and G. Q. Bowler. *Europe in the Sixteenth Century.* New York: Longman, 1968.

Kohn, Hans. "Arndt and the Character of German Nationalism." *American Historical Review* 54, no. 4 (1949): 787–803.

Kohn, Richard. "The Inside History of the Newburgh Conspiracy: America and the Coup d'Etat." *William and Mary Quarterly* 27, no. 2 (1970): 187–220.

Konig, Wolfgang. "Adolf Hitler vs. Henry Ford: The Volkswagen, the Role of America as a Model, and the Failure of a Nazi Consumer Society." *German Studies Review* 27, no. 2 (2004): 249–68.

Korner, Martin. "Town and Country in Switzerland, 1450–1750." Translated by R. Morris and S. R. Epstein. In S. R. Epstein, ed., *Town and Country in Europe, 1300–1800.* New York: Cambridge University Press, 2001.

Kornweibel, Theodore. Review of *A. Philip Randolph: A Biographical Portrait* by Jervis Anderson. *Journal of Negro History* 58, no. 4 (1973): 471–74.

Kousser, J. M. *Colorblind Injustice: Minority Voting Rights and the undoing of the Second Reconstruction.* Durham: University of North Carolina Press, 2000.

———. *The Shaping of Southern Politics: Suffrage Restriction and the Establishment of the One-Party South, 1880–1910.* New Haven: Yale University Press, 1974.

Kozak, Jerzy. "Mortality Structure of Adult Individuals in Poland in the Feudal Period." *Variability and Evolution* 6 (1997): 81–91.

Kozelsky, Mara. "Casualties of Conflict: Crimean Tatars During the Crimean War." *Slavic Review* 67, no. 4 (2008): 866–91.

Kozuskanich, Nathan. "Pennsylvania, the Militia, and the Second Amendment." *Pennsylvania Magazine of History and Biography* 133, no. 2 (2009): 119–47.

Kraas, Frauke. "The Decline of Ethno-Diversity in High Mountain Regions: The Spatial Development of the Rhaetormansch Minority in Grisons, Switzerland." *Mountain Research and Development* 16, no. 1 (1996): 41–50.

Kraditor, Aileen S. *The Ideas of the Woman Suffrage Movement, 1890–1920.* New York: Columbia University Press, 1965.

Kral, David. "The Czech Republic and the Iraq Crisis—Oscillating between the Two Sides of the Atlantic." Institute for European Policy, 2003.

Kramer, Lloyd. "The Rights of Man: Lafayette and the Polish National Revolution, 1830–1834." *French Historical Studies* 14, no. 4 (1986): 521–46.

Kraus, Christina. "'No Second Troy': Topoi and Refoundation in Livy, Book V." *Transactions of the American Philological Association* 124 (1994): 267–89.

Kryder, Daniel. *Divided Arsenal: Race and the American State During World War II*. New York: Cambridge University Press, 2000.

Kuchta, Mark, Alexandra Newman, and Erkan Topal. "Creating and Implementing a Production Schedule at LKAB's Kiruna Mine." *Interfaces* 34, no. 2 (2004): 124–34.

Kulikowski, Michael. "Barbarians in Gaul, Usurpers in Britain." *Britannia* 31 (2000): 325–45.

Kuznets, Simon. "Proportion of Capital Formation to National Product." *American Economic Review* 42, no. 2 (1952): 522–33.

"Labor's International Action for Peace." *Advocate of Peace* 74, no. 9 (1912): 216–17.

Ladner, Gerhart. "The Holy Roman Empire of the Tenth Century and East Central Europe." *Polish Review* 5, no. 4 (1960): 3–14.

Laitila, Teuvo. "Soldier, Structure, and the Other: Social Relations and Cultural Categorisation in the Memoirs of Finnish Guardsmen Taking Part in the Russo-Turkish Wars, 1877–1878." Dissertation, University of Helsinki, 2001.

Lambert, Nicholas. *Planning Armageddon: British Economic Warfare and the First World War*. Cambridge, MA: Harvard University Press, 2012.

Lambert, Sheila. "The Opening of the Long Parliament." *Historical Journal* 27, no. 2 (1984): 265–87.

Lammers, Donald. "Arno Mayer and the British Decision for War: 1914." *Journal of British Studies* 12, no. 2 (1973): 137–65.

Lamothe, Dan. "Pentagon Chooses Machinery over Manpower in Budget Battle." *Foreign Policy*. March 4, 2014.

Lane, Frederic. "Economic Consequences of Organized Violence." *Journal of Economic History* 18, no. 4 (1958): 401–17.

———. *Venice: A Maritime Republic*. Baltimore: Johns Hopkins University Press, 1973.

Lang, Henry Joseph. "The Fall of the Monarchy of Mieszko II, Lambert." *Speculum* 49, no. 4 (1974): 623–39.

Langmuir, Gavin. "Community and Legal Change in Capetian France." *French Historical Studies* 6, no. 3 (1970): 275–86.

Large, Stephen S. "Nationalist Extremism in Early Shōwa Japan: Inoue Nisshō and the 'Blood-Pledge Corps Incident,' 1932." *Modern Asian Studies* 35, no. 3 (2001): 533–64.

Larsen, Jakob A. O. "The Constitution of the Peloponnesian League." *Classical Philology*, 28, no. 4 (1933): 257–76.

Latimer, Margaret Kinard. "South Carolina—A Protagonist of the War of 1812." *American Historical Review* 61, no. 4 (1956): 914–29.

Lattimore, Owen. "Origins of the Great Wall of China: A Frontier Concept in Theory and Practice." *Geographical Review* 27, no. 4 (1937): 529–49.

Laub, Zachary. "The Taliban in Afghanistan." Council on Foreign Relations, 2014.

Laufer, Robert, M. S. Gallops, and Elley Frey-Wouters. "War Stress and Trauma: The Vietnam Veteran Experience." *Journal of Health and Social Behavior* 25, no. 1 (1984): 65–85.

Lavery, Gerard. "Cicero's 'Philarchia' and Marius." *Greece and Rome* 18, no. 2 (1971): 133–42.

Lawrence, Anthony. *China: The Long March*. Sydney: Murdoch Books, 1986.

Lawrence, Ken. "Thirty Years of Selective Service Racism." A Report Submitted by National Black Draft Counselors to the White House Conference on Youth, 1971.

Lazarus, Simon. *The Genteel Populists*. New York: Holt, Rinehart, and Winston, 1974.

LeBlanc, Steven. *Constant Battles: Why We Fight.* New York: St Martin's Griffin, 2003.

Legon, Ronald P. *Megara: The Political History of a Greek City State to 336 B.C.* Ithaca, NY: Cornell University Press, 1981.

Lehning, James. "Gossiping about Gambetta: Contested Memories in the Early Third Republic." *French Historical Studies* 18, no. 1 (1993): 237–54.

Leland, Anne, and M. J. Oboroceanu. "American War and Military Operations Casualties: Lists and Statistics." Washington, DC: Congressional Research Service, 2010.

Lenin, Vladimir. "Murder of Karl Liebnecht and Rosa Luxemburg." News release, January 19, 1919, in *Pravda*, January 21, 1919.

———. "Opportunism and the Collapse of the Second International" 1915, http://bit .ly/2004013.

———. "Speech at the Opening Session of the Congress," First Congress of the Communist International, March 2, 1919, http://bit.ly/1MNQDiv.

Lentz-Smith, Adriane. *Freedom Struggles: African Americans and World War I.* Cambridge, MA: Harvard University Press, 2009.

Lepper, F. A. "Some Rubrics in the Athenian Quota Lists." *Journal of Hellenic Studies* 82 (1962): 25–55.

Lerner, Craig. "Impeachment, Attainder, and a True Constitutional Crisis: Lessons from the Strafford Trial." *University of Chicago Law Review* 69, no. 4 (2002): 2057–2101.

Levine, Bruce. *The Fall of the House of Dixie: The Civil War and the Social Revolution that Transformed the South.* New York: Random House, 2013.

Levy, Jack. "Preferences, Constraints, and Choices in July 1914." *International Security* 15, no. 3 (1990–91): 151–86.

Levy, Michael. "Freedom, Property and the Levellers: The Case of John Lilburne." *Western Political Quarterly* 36, no. 1 (1983): 116–33.

Lewalski, Kenneth. "Sigismund I of Poland: Renaissance King and Patron." *Studies in the Renaissance* 14 (1967): 49–72.

Lewin, M. "The Immediate Background of Soviet Collectivization." *Soviet Studies* 17, no. 2 (1965): 162–97.

Lewis, David Levering. *W.E.B. Du Bois: A Biography.* New York: Henry Holt, 2009.

Lewis, Gwynn. "The White Terror of 1815 in the Department of the Gard: Counter-Revolution, Continuity and the Individual." *Past & Present* 58, no. 1 (1974): 108–35.

Lewitter, L. R. "Poland, Russia and the Treaty of Vienna of 5 January 1719." *Historical Journal* 13, no. 1 (2009): 3–30.

Libourel, Jan. "Galley Slaves in the Second Punic War." *Classical Philology* 68, no. 2 (1973): 116–19.

Lichnowsky, Karl Max. *My Mission to London, 1912–1914.* New York: Doran, 1918.

Liedman, Sven-Eric, and Mats Persson. "The Visible Hand: Anders Berch and the University of Uppsala Chair in Economics." *Scandinavian Journal of Economics* 94 (1992): S259–S269.

Li Feng. "'Feudalism' and Western Zhou China: A Criticism." *Harvard Journal of Asiatic Studies* 63, no. 1 (2003): 115–44.

Lindsay, Thomas. "Aristotle's Qualified Defense of Democracy through 'Political Mixing.'" *Journal of Politics* 54, no. 1 (1992): 101–19.

Lintott, Andrew. "Aristotle and Democracy." *Classical Quarterly* 42, no. 1 (1992): 114–28.

———. *The Constitution of the Roman Republic.* Oxford: Oxford University Press, 1999.

———. "Electoral Bribery in the Roman Republic." *Journal of Roman Studies* 80 (1990): 1–16.

———. "P. Clodius Pulcher—'Felix Catilina'?" *Greece and Rome* 14, no. 2 (1967): 157–69.

Lipkes, Jeff. *Rehearsals: The German Army in Belgium, August 2014.* Louvain: Leuven University Press, 2007.

Lippmann, Walter. *The Political Scene: An Essay on 1918.* New York: Henry Holt, 1919.

Lipset, Seymour Martin. *Political Man.* Garden City, NY: Doubleday, 1960.

Lipsey, Robert. "U.S. Foreign Trade and the Balance of Payments, 1800–1913." NBER working paper no. 4710, 1994.

Livi-Bacci, Massimo. "On the Human Costs of Collectivization in the Soviet Union." *Population and Development Review* 19, no. 9 (1993): 743–66.

Llavador, Humberto, and Robert Oxoby. "Partisan Competition, Growth and the Franchise." *Quarterly Journal of Economics* 119 (2005): 1155–89.

Lodeman, A. "Victor Hugo in the Estimation of His Countrymen." *Modern Language Notes* 10, no. 4 (1895): 97–104.

Lopez, Robert S. *The Commercial Revolution of the Middle Ages, 950–1350.* New York: Cambridge University Press, 1976.

———. "Hard Times and the Investment in Culture" in Wallace K. Ferguson et al., eds., *The Renaissance: Six Essays.* New York: Harper Torchbooks, 1962.

Lot, Ferdinand. *La Fin du Monde Antique et le Début du Moyen Age.* Paris, 1952.

Lott, John, and L. Kenny. "Did Women's Suffrage Change the Size and Scope of Government?" *Journal of Political Economy* 107, no. 6 (1999): 1163–98.

Lowe, Vaughan. "'Clear and Present Danger': Responses to Terrorism." *International and Comparative Law Quarterly* 54, no. 1 (2005): 185–96.

Luck, J. Murray. *The History of Switzerland.* Stanford, CA: Society for the Promotion of Science and Scholarship, 1985.

Luckham, Robin. "Democracy and the Military: An Epitaph for Frankenstein's Monster?" *Democratization* 3, no. 2 (1996): 1–16.

Ludz, Peter. "Ideology, Intellectuals, and Organization: The Question of Their Interrelation in 19th Century Society." *Social Research* 44, no. 2 (1977): 260–307.

Lukowski, Jerzy. *Liberty's Folly: The Polish-Lithuanian Commonwealth in the Eighteenth Century.* Abingdon, UK: Routledge, 1991.

———. "Recasting Utopia: Montesquieu, Rousseau and the Polish Constitution of 3 May 1791." *Historical Journal* 37, no. 1 (1994): 65–87.

———. "Towards Partition: Polish Magnates and Russian Intervention in Poland During the Early Reign of Stanislaw August Poniatowski." *Historical Journal* 28, no. 3 (1985): 557–74.

Lukowski, Jerzy, and Hubert Zawadzki. *A Concise History of Poland.* New York: Cambridge University Press, 2006.

Lunch, William, and Peter Sperlich. "American Public Opinion and the War in Vietnam." *Western Political Quarterly* 32, no. 1 (1979): 21–24.

Lushkov, Haimson. "Narrative and Notice in Livy's Fourth Decade: The Case of Scipio Africanus." *Classical Antiquity* 33, no. 1 (2014): 102–29.

Lyall, Jason. "Do Democracies Make Inferior Counterinsurgents? Reassessing Democracy's Impact on War Outcomes and Duration." *International Organization* 64, no. 1 (2010): 167–92.

Lyall, Jason, and Isaiah Wilson. "Rage Against the Machines: Explaining Outcomes in Counter-insurgency Wars." *International Organization* 63, no. 1 (2009): 67–106.

Lynch, Lisa. "Truth and Lies at Guantanamo Bay." *Arab Studies Journal* 13/14, nos. 2/1 (2005/2006): 213–18.

Lynn, John. "Recalculating French Army Growth During the Grand Siecle, 1610–1715." *French Historical Studies* 18, no. 4 (1994): 881–906.

———. "States in Conflict." In Geoffrey Parker, ed., *The Cambridge History of Warfare*. New York: Cambridge University Press, 2005.

Maarbjerg, John P. "Sweden, the First Modern State: Tilly's Assertion, 'War Makes States, and Vice Versa.'" *Scandinavian Studies* 76, no. 3 (2004): 385–418.

MacDowall, Simon. *Adrianople AD 378: The Goths Crush Rome's Legions.* Oxford: Osprey, 2001.

MacHardy, Karin. "The Rise of Absolutism and Noble Rebellion in Early Modern Habsburg Austria, 1570 to 1620." *Comparative Studies in Society and History* 34, no. 3 (1992): 407–38.

Machiavelli, Niccolò. *The Discourses* (1531). Edited with an introduction by Bernard Crick using the translation of Leslie Walker with revisions by Brian Richardson. London: Penguin Classics, 1970.

Machinists Monthly Journal 1919, http://bit.ly/235uWlj.

Macpherson, C. B. *The Theory of Possessive Individualism.* London: Oxford University Press, 1964.

Maddicott, John. *The Origins of the English Parliament, 924–1327.* New York: Oxford University Press, 2012.

———. "Sir Thomas Gray, Scalacronica, 1272–1363." *English Historical Review* 121, no. 493 (2006): 1167–68.

Maddox, Graham. "The Economic Causes of the Lex Hortensia." *Latomus* 42, no. 2 (1983): 277–86.

Madison, James. *The Federalist* nos. 10 and 51 (1787–88.)

Magnusson, Lars. "Economics and the Public Interest: The Emergence of Economics as an Academic Subject During the 18th Century." *Scandinavian Journal of Economics* 94 (1992): S249–S257.

Maier, Pauline. *Ratification: The People Debate the Constitution, 1787–1788.* New York: Simon and Schuster, 2010.

Majewski, Wieslaw. "The Polish Art of War in the Sixteenth and Seventeenth Centuries." In J. K. Fedorowizc, ed., *A Republic of Nobles: Studies in Polish History to 1864.* New York: Cambridge University Press, 1982.

Major, Russell. "The French Renaissance Monarchy as Seen through the Estates General." In Henry J. Cohn, ed., *Government in Reformation Europe, 1520–1560.* New York: Harper and Row, 1971.

Malcolm, George. "The Constitution of the Empire of Japan." *Michigan Law Review* 19 no 1 (1920): 62–72.

Mallett, Michael, and Christine Shaw. *The Italian Wars, 1494–1559: War, State and Society in Early Modern Europe.* Harlow: Routledge, 2012.

Maltby, Josephine. "Showing a Strong Front: Corporate Social Reporting and the 'Business Case' In Britain, 1914–1919." *Accounting Historians Journal* 32, no. 2 (2005): 145–71.

Manning, William R. Review of *The Silesian Loan and Frederick the Great* by Ernest Satow. *American Journal of International Law* 10, no. 2 (1916): 457–60.

Mao Tsetung. *The Art of War* (1937). Special Edition. El Paso, TX: El Paso Norte Press, 2011.

Marilley, Suzanne. "Frances Willard and the Feminism of Fear." *Feminist Studies* 19, no. 1 (1993): 123–46.

———. *Woman Suffrage and the Origins of Liberal Feminism in the United States, 1860–1920.* Cambridge, MA: Harvard University Press, 1996.

Markham, C. R. "The Mountain Passes on the Afghan Frontier of British India." *Proceedings of the Royal Geographical Society and Monthly Record of Geography* 1, no. 1 (1879): 38–62.

Marquis, Alice Goldfarb. "Words as Weapons: Propaganda in Britain and Germany During the First World War." *Journal of Contemporary History* 13, no. 3 (1978): 467–98.

Martin, John, and Dennis Romano, eds. *Venice Reconsidered: The History and Civilization of an Italian City-State, 1297–1797.* Baltimore: Johns Hopkins University Press, 2000.

Martines, Lauro. *April Blood: Florence and the Plot Against the Medici.* New York: Oxford University Press, 2003.

———. *Power and Imagination: City-States in Renaissance Italy.* New York: Vintage Books, 1979.

Marx, Karl. *The Eighteenth Brumaire of Louis Bonaparte* (1852), at http://bit.ly/1RXubpp.

Mathieson, Ralph, and Danuta Shanzer, eds. *The Battle of Vouille, 507 C.E.: Where France Began.* Berlin: Walter de Gruyter, 2012.

Matiash, Iryna. "Archives in Russia on the Famine in Ukraine." *Harriman Review* 16, no. 2 (2008): 36–45.

May, Robert E. "Invisible Men: Blacks in the Army in the Mexican War." *Historian* 49, no. 4 (1987): 463–77.

Maybry, William Alexander. "Negro Suffrage and Fusion Rule in North Carolina." *North Carolina Historical Review* 12, no. 2 (1935): 79–102.

Mazower, Mark. *Hitler's Empire: Nazi Rule in Occupied Europe.* London: Allen Lane, 2008.

McCammon, Holly. "Stirring Up Suffrage Sentiment: The Formation of the State Woman Suffrage Organizations, 1866–1914." *Social Forces* 80, no. 2 (2001): 449–80.

McClure, Laura. "Coalition of the Billing—or the Unwilling?" *Salon,* March 31, 2003.

McCoy, W. James. "Thrasybulus and His Trierarchies." *American Journal of Philology* 112, no. 3 (1991): 303–23.

———. "Thrasyllus." *American Journal of Philology* 98, no. 3 (1977): 264–89.

McCreary, Eugene. "Social Welfare and Business: The Krupp Welfare Program, 1860–1914." *Business History Review* 42, no. 1 (1968): 24–49.

M'Crie, Thomas. *History of the Progress and Suppression of the Reformation in Italy in the Sixteenth Century.* Edinburgh: William Blackwood, 1833.

McDaneld, Jen. "White Suffragist Dis/Entitlement: The Revolution and the Rhetoric of Racism." *Legacy* 30, no. 2 (2013): 243–64.

McFarlane, K. B. *The Nobility of Later Medieval Europe.* Oxford: Clarendon Press, 1973.

McGarrah, Jim. Review of *Red Clay On My Boots: Encounters with Khe Sanh, 1968–2005* by Robert J. Topmiller. *Register of the Kentucky Historical Society* 105, no. 4 (2007): 767–69.

McGill, Barry. "Asquith's Predicament, 1914–1918." *Journal of Modern History* 39, no. 3 (1967): 283–303.

McGuire, Danielle. "'It Was like All of Us Had Been Raped': Sexual Violence, Community Mobilization, and the African American Freedom Struggle." *Journal of American History* 91, no. 3 (2004): 906–31.

McGuire, Phillip. "Desegregation of the Armed Forces: Black Leadership, Protest and World War II." *Journal of Negro History* 68, no. 2 (1983): 147–58.

McKenna, Catherine J. M. "The Curious Evolution of the Liberum Veto: Republican Theory and Practice in the Polish Lithuanian Commonwealth (1639–1705)." PhD dissertation, Georgetown University, 2012.

McKinley, Albert Edward. *The Suffrage Franchise in the Thirteen English Colonies in America.* Philadelphia: University of Pennsylvania Press, 1905.

McLean, Paul D., and John Padgett. "Was Florence a Perfect Competitive Market? Transaction Evidence from the Renaissance." *Theory and Society* 26, nos. 2–3 (1997): 209–44.

McNeely, Ian. "Hegel's Württemberg Commentary: Intellectuals and the Construction of Civil Society in Revolutionary-Napoleonic Germany." *Central European History* 37, no. 3 (2004): 345–64.

McNeill, William H. *Venice: The Hinge of Europe, 1081–1797.* Chicago: University of Chicago Press, 1974.

Mears, John. "The Thirty Years' War, the 'General Crisis,' and the Origins of a Standing Professional Army in the Habsburg Monarchy." *Central European History* 21, no. 2 (1988): 122–41.

Mehnert, Ute. "German Weltpolitik and the American Two-Front Dilemma: The Japanese Peril in German-American Relations, 1907–1917." *Journal of American History* 82, no. 4 (1996): 1452–77.

Mehotra, Ajay. "Lawyers, Guns, and Public Moneys: The U.S. Treasury, World War I, and the Administration of the Modern Fiscal State." *Law and History Review* 28, no. 1 (2010): 173–225.

Meinecke, Friedrich. "The Year 1848 in German History: Reflections on a Centenary." *Review of Politics* 10, no. 4 (1948): 475–92.

Meloni, Giulia, and Johan Swinnen. "The Rise and Fall of the World's Largest Wine Exporter (And Its Institutional Legacy)." LICOS Discussion Paper no. 327, 2013.

Menard, Orville. "Lest We Forget: The Lynching of Will Brown, Omaha's 1919 Race Riot." *Nebraska History* 91 (2010): 152–65.

Menchi, Seidel. "Rival Aversions." *Times Literary Supplement* no. 5750 (2013): 14–15.

Mendle, Michael. "The Ship Money Case." *Historical Journal* 32, no. 3 (1989): 513–36.

Mennell, James. "African-Americans and the Selective Service Act of 1917." *Journal of Negro History* 84, no. 3 (1999): 275–87.

Menocal, Maria Rosa. *The Ornament of the World: How Muslims, Jews, and Christians Created a Culture of Tolerance in Medieval Spain.* New York: Little Brown / Back Bay Books, 2002.

Merriman, John. *Massacre: The Life and Death of the Paris Commune.* New York: Basic Books, 2014.

Metcalf, Michael. "Challenges to Economic Orthodoxy and Parliamentary Sovereignty in 18th Century Sweden." *Legislative Studies Quarterly* 7, no. 2 (1982): 251–61.

Mets, James Andrew. *Naval Heroes of Holland.* 1902; reprint New York: Kessinger, 2010.

Meyer, Judith P. "La Rochelle and the Failure of the French Reformation." *Sixteenth Century Journal* 15, no. 2 (1984): 169–83.

Meyer, Kathryn. "Trade and Nationality at Shanghai upon the Outbreak of the First World War, 1914–1915." *International History Review* 10, no. 2 (1988): 238–60.

Miles, Wyndham. "Sir Kenelm Digby, Alchemist, Scholar, Courtier, and Man of Adventure." *Chymia* 2 (1949): 119–28.

Millar, Fergus. *The Crowd in Rome in the Late Republic.* Ann Arbor: University of Michigan Press, 1998.

Miller, Grant. "Women's Suffrage, Political Responsiveness, and Child Survival in American History." *Quarterly Journal of Economics* 123, no. 3 (2008): 1287–1327.

Miller, James. "Foreign Government and Politics: Emergency Legislation in Great Britain." *American Political Science Review* 33, no. 6 (1939): 1073–80.

Minor, Clifford. "Bagaudae or Bacaudae?" *Traditio* 31 (1975): 318–22.

Mitchell, Annie. "A Liberal Republican 'Cato.'" *American Journal of Political Science* 48, no. 3 (2004): 588–603.

Mitchell, L. B. "Background of the Roman Revolution." *Classical Journal* 17, no. 6 (1922): 316–23.

Mitchell, Lynette G., and P. J. Rhodes. "Friends and Enemies in Athenian Politics." *Greece and Rome* 43, no. 1 (1996): 11–30.

Moles, J. L. "Xenophon and Callicratidas," *Journal of Hellenic Studies* 114 (1994): 70–84.

Molho, Anthony. "The Florentine 'Tassa dei Traffichi' of 1451." *Studies in the Renaissance* 17 (1970): 73–118.

———. "A Note on the Albizzi and the Florentine Conquest of Pisa." *Renaissance Quarterly* 20, no. 2 (1967): 185–99.

———. "The State and Public Finance: A Hypothesis Based on the History of Late Medieval Florence." *Journal of Modern History* 67 (1995): S97–S135.

Momigliano, Arnaldo. "Cisalpine Gaul: Social and Economic History from 49 BC to the Death of Trajan." *Journal of Roman Studies* 32, no. 1 (1942): 135–38.

———. "Time in Ancient Historiography." *Quarto contributo alla storia degli studi classici e del mondo antico.* Rome, 1969.

Montefiore, Simon S. *Young Stalin.* New York: Vintage, 2008.

Montesquieu. *The Spirit of the Laws.* New York: Cosimo, 1914.

Moon, David. "Russian Peasant Volunteers at the Beginning of the Crimean War." *Slavic Review* 51, no. 4 (1992): 691–704.

Moore, Barrington. *Social Origins of Dictatorship and Democracy.* Boston: Beacon Press, 1966.

Moore, Frank G. "A Vexed Passage in the Gallic War." *The American Journal of Philology* 37, no. 2 (1916): 206–9.

Moore, John. "Pope Innocent III, Sardinia, and the Papal State." *Speculum* 62, no. 1 (1987): 81–101.

Moore, Michael. *A Sacred Kingdom: Bishops and the Rise of Frankish Kingship, 300–850.* Washington: Catholic University Press, 2011.

Morck, Randall K., and Masao Nakamura. "A Frog in a Well Knows Nothing of the Ocean: A History of Corporate Ownership In Japan." In Randall K. Morck, ed., *A History of*

Corporate Governance around the World: Family Business Groups to Professional Managers. Chicago: University of Chicago Press, 2005.

Morford, Henry. "Better Acquaintance with Switzerland." Aldine 7 (1875): 470–71.

Morgan, Kimberly, and Monica Prasad. "The Origins of Tax Systems: A French-American Comparison." *American Journal of Sociology* 114, no. 5 (2009): 1350–94.

Morris, Ian. "Economic Growth in Ancient Greece." *Journal of Institutional and Theoretical Economics* 160, no. 4 (2004): 709–42.

Morrison, J. S. "Hyperesia in Naval Contexts in the Fifth and Fourth Centuries BC." *Journal of Hellenic Studies* 104 (1984): 48–59.

Morstein-Marx, Robert. *Mass Oratory and Political Power in the Late Roman Republic.* Cambridge, UK: Cambridge University Press, 2004.

Mortimer, Theo, and James J. Loughrey. "James J. Loughrey's Diary of the Wars in the Philippines 1898/1899." *Dublin Historical Record* 56, no. 1 (2003): 78–97.

Moss, Bernard. "Radical Labor Under the French Third Republic." *Science and Society* 58, no. 3 (1994): 333–43.

Mouritsen, Henrik. *Plebs and Politics in the Late Roman Republic.* Cambridge, UK: Cambridge University Press, 2001.

Mowbray, Miranda, and Dieter Gollmann. "Electing the Doge of Venice: Analysis of a 13th Century Protocol." HP Laboratories Bristol Working Paper, 2007, http://bit.ly/1PQwuTm.

Moysey, Robert. "Chares and Athenian Foreign Policy." *Classical Journal* 80, no. 3 (1985): 221–27.

Mueller, John. *War, Presidents and Public Opinion.* New York: John Wiley and Sons, 1973.

Mukerjee, Chandra. "The Great Forestry Survey of 1669–1671: The Use of Archives for Political Reform." *Social Studies of Science* 37, no. 2 (2007): 227–53.

Munro, John H. "The Medieval Origins of the Financial Revolution: Usury, Rentes, and Negotiability." *International History Review* 25, no. 3 (2003): 505–62.

Murphy, William J. "John Adams: The Politics of the Additional Army, 1798–1800." *New England Quarterly* 52, no. 2 (1979): 234–49.

Murray, Bruce. "'Battered and Shattered': Lloyd George and the 1914 Budget Fiasco." *Albion: A Quarterly Journal Concerned with British Studies* 23, no. 3 (1991): 483–507.

———. "The Politics of the 'People's Budget.'" *Historical Journal* 16, no. 3 (1973): 555–70.

Murray, David. "Black Regular Troops in the Spanish-Cuban/American War." In Benjamin Beede, ed., *The War of 1898 and U.S. Interventions 1898–1934: An Encyclopedia.* London: Routledge, 1994.

Murray, John J. "The Peasant Revolt of Engelbrekt Engelbrektsson and the Birth of Modern Sweden." *Journal of Modern History* 19, no. 3 (1947): 193–209.

Murray, Paul. "Blacks and the Draft: A History of Institutional Racism." *Journal of Black Studies* 2, no. 1 (1971): 57–76.

Murray, Robert. "Cicero and the Gracchi." *Transactions and Proceedings of the American Philological Association* 97 (1966): 291–98.

Myers, Andrew H. *Black, White and Olive Drab: Racial Integration at Fort Jackson, South Carolina, and the Civil Rights Movement.* Charlottesville: University of Virginia Press, 2006.

Myerson, Roger. "Political Economics and the Weimar Disaster." *Journal of Institutional and Theoretical Economics* 160 (2004): 187–209.

Najemy, John M. "Civic Humanism and Florentine Politics." In James Hankin, ed., *Renaissance Civic Humanism: Reappraisals and Reflections*. New York: Cambridge University Press, 2000.

————. "Guild Republicanism in Recento Florence: The Successes and Ultimate Failure of Corporate Politics." *American Historical Review* 84, no. 1 (1979): 53–71.

————. *A History of Florence: 1200–1575*. Chichester: John Wiley & Sons, 2006.

————. Review of *In Search of Florentine Civic Humanism: Essays on the Transition from Medieval to Modern Thought* by Hans Baron. *Renaissance Quarterly* 45, no. 2 (1992): 340–50.

Nakategawa, Yoshio. "Isegoria in Herodotus." *Historia* 37, no. 3 (1988): 257–75.

Nalty, Bernard. *Strength for the Fight: A History of Black Americans in the Military*. New York: Free Press, 1986.

Narizny, Kevin. "The Political Economy of Alignment: Great Britain's Commitments to Europe, 1905–39," *International Security* 27, no. 4 (2003): 184–219.

Nash, Alice. "A Review of *The American Revolution in Indian Country: Crisis and Diversity in Native American Communities* by Colin G. Calloway." *American Indian Quarterly* 22, no. 3 (1998): 401–3.

Nason, James, and Shaun Vahey. "The McKenna Rule and UK World War I Finance." *American Economic Review* 97, no. 2 (2007): 290–94.

NATO 2014 http://www.nato.int/cps

Nawid, Senzil. "The State, the Clergy, and British Imperial Policy in Afghanistan During the 19th and Early 20th Centuries." *International Journal of Middle East Studies* 29, no. 4 (1997): 581–605.

"Nazi Outlooks." *World Affairs* 103, no. 3 (1940): 143–47.

Nelsestuen, Grant. "Overseeing Res Publica : The Rector as Vilicus in *De Re Publica* 5." *Classical Antiquity* 33, no. 1 (2014): 130–73.

Nettl, Peter. "The German Social Democratic Party, 1890–1914, as a Political Model." *Past & Present*, no. 30 (1965): 65–95.

Netto, Anil. "Malaysia's Three-Month National Service a Flop?" *Asia Times*, May 4, 2004.

Newman, Richard. "A Review of Peter's War: A New England Slave Boy and the American Revolution by Joyce Lee Malcolm." *New England Quarterly* 82, no. 4 (2009): 730–32.

Nexon, Daniel. *The Struggle for Power in Early Modern Europe*. Princeton: Princeton University Press, 2009.

Nichols, Alice. *Bleeding Kansas*. New York: Oxford University Press, 1954.

Nichols, Johanna. *Linguistic Diversity in Space and Time*. Chicago: University of Chicago Press, 1992.

Nicolet, Claude. *The World of the Citizen in Republican Rome*. Berkeley: University of California Press, 1980.

Nicolle, David. *Poitiers AD 732: Charles Martel Turns the Islamic Tide*. Oxford: Osprey, 2008.

Nippel, Wilfred. *Public Order in Ancient Rome*. Cambridge, UK: Cambridge University Press, 1995.

Nordhaus, William, John Oneal, and Bruce Russett. "The Effects of the International Security Environment on National Military Expenditures: A Multicountry Study." *International Organization* 66, no. 3 (2012): 491–513.

North, Douglass C., and Robert Paul Thomas. "The Rise and Fall of the Manorial System: A Theoretical Model." *Journal of Economic History* 31, no. 4 (1971): 777–803.

North, Douglass C., and Barry R. Weingast. "Constitutions and Commitment: The Evolution of Institutions Governing Public Choice in Seventeenth-Century England." *Journal of Economic History* 49, no. 4 (1989): 803–32.

North, John. "Politics and Aristocracy in the Roman Republic." *Classical Philology* 85, no. 4 (1990): 277–87.

Ober, Josiah. "Defense of the Athenian Land Frontier 404–322 B.C.: A Reply." *Phoenix* 43, no. 4 (1989): 294–301.

———. *Democracy and Knowledge: Innovation and Learning in Classical Athens.* Princeton: Princeton University Press, 2008.

———. " 'I Besieged That Man': Democracy's Revolutionary Start." In Kurt A. Raaflaub, Josiah Ober, and Robert Wallace, eds., *Origins of Democracy in Ancient Greece.* Berkeley: University of California Press, 2007.

———. "Thucydides on Athens' Democratic Advantage in the Archidamian War." In David Pritchard, ed., *War, Democracy and Culture in Classical Athens.* New York: Cambridge University Press, 2010.

Ogg, Frederic A. "The British Representation of the People Act." *American Political Science Review* 12, no. 3 (1918): 498–503.

Ogilvie, Sheilagh. "Institutions and Economic Development in Early Modern Central Europe." *Transactions of the Royal Historical Society* 5 (1995): 221–50.

———. *Institutions and European Trade: Merchant Guilds, 1000–1800.* Cambridge: Cambridge University Press, 2011.

———. "Whatever Is, Is Right? Economic Institutions in Pre-Industrial Europe." *Economic History Review* 60, no. 4 (2007): 649–84.

Ogilvie, Sheilagh, and Jeremy Edwards. "Women and the 'Second Serfdom': Evidence from Early Modern Bohemia." *Journal of Economic History* 60, no. 4 (2000): 961–94.

Ohnacker, Elke. "What If . . . Charlemagne's Other Sons Had Survived?" *Historical Social Research* 34, no. 2 (2009): 184–202.

Ohnuki-Tierney, Emiko. *Kamikaze, Cherry Blossoms, and Nationalisms: The Militarization of Aesthetics in Japanese History.* Chicago: University of Chicago Press, 2002.

Olson, Mancur. "Democracy, Dictatorship, and Development." *The American Political Science Review,*" 87, no. 3 (1993): 567–76.

Oman, Charles. *The Art of War in the Middle Ages.* 1885; reprint Ithaca, NY: Cornell University Press, 1953.

———. *The Sixteenth Century.* London: E. P. Dutton, 1936.

O'Neill, John. "The Exile of Themistocles and Democracy in the Peloponnese." *Classical Quarterly* 31, no. 2 (1981): 335–46.

O'Neill, William. *Interwar U.S. and Japanese National Product and Defense Expenditure.* Alexandria, VA: CNA Corporation, 2003.

Onorato, Massimiliano, Kenneth Scheve, and David Stasavage. "Technology and the Era of the Mass Army." *Journal of Economic History* 74, no. 2 (2014): 449–81.

Oostindie, Gert, and Bert Paasman. "Dutch Attitudes Towards Colonial Empires, Indigenous Cultures, and Slaves." *Eighteenth Century Studies* 31, no. 3 (1998): 349–55.

Orbell, John, and Tomonori Morikawa. "An Evolutionary Account of Suicide Attacks: The Kamikaze Case." *Political Psychology* 32, no. 2 (2011): 297–322.

Oresko, Robert. "The House of Savoy in Search for a Royal Crown in the Seventeenth Century." In Robert Oresko, G. C. Gibbs, and H. M. Scott, eds., *Royal and Republican Sovereignty in Early Modern Europe.* New York: Cambridge University Press, 1997.

Orlove, Benjamin S. "The History of the Andes: A Brief Overview." *Mountain Research and Development* 5, no. 1 (1985): 45–60.

Ormand, W. M. "England in the Middle Ages." In Richard Bonney, ed., *The Rise of the Fiscal State in Europe, 1200–1815.* New York: Oxford University Press, 1999.

Ormisson, Tonis. "Public Opinion and National Defence." Estonian Defence Ministry, 2006, http://bit.ly/1MNTAPT.

Ormrod, W. Mark. "England in the Middle Ages." In Richard Bonney, ed., *The Rise of the Fiscal State in Europe, c. 1200–1815*, 19–52. Oxford: Clarendon, 1999.

———. "The Peasants' Revolt and the Government of England." *Journal of British Studies* 29, no. 1 (1990): 1–30.

Ortalli, Gherardo, and Giovanni Scarabello. *A Short History of Venice.* Pisa: Pacini, 1999.

Osborne, Toby. Review of *The Winter King: Frederick V of the Palatinate and the Coming of the Thirty Years' War* by Brennan Pursell. *International History Review* 27, no. 3 (2005): 589–91.

Ostwald, Martin. *From Popular Sovereignty to the Sovereignty of the Law: Law, Society, and Politics in Fifth Century Athens.* Berkeley: University of California Press, 1986.

Owens, J. B. " 'By My Absolute Authority': Justice and the Castilian Commonwealth at the Beginning of the First Global Age." In James B. Collins and Mack P. Holt, eds., *Changing Perspectives on Early Modern Europe.* Rochester, NY: University of Rochester Press, 2005.

Page, Benjamin, and Richard Brody. "Policy Voting and the Electoral Process: The Vietnam War Issue." *American Political Science Review* 66, no. 3 (1972): 979–95.

Pages, G. *The Thirty Years War, 1618–1648.* London: Adam and Charles Black, 1970.

Palmer, R. R. *The Age of Democratic Revolution.* Princeton: Princeton University Press, 1969.

Papayoanou, Paul A. "Interdependence, Institutions, and the Balance of Power: Britain, Germany, and World War I." *International Security* 20, no. 4 (1996): 42–76.

Paret, Peter. *Clausewitz and the State: The Man, His Theories, and His Times.* Princeton: Princeton University Press, 1985.

Parke, H. W. "The Development of the Second Spartan Empire (405–371 B.C.)." *Journal of Hellenic Studies* 50, Part 1 (1930): 37–79.

Parker, Charles. "To the Attentive, Nonpartisan Reader: The Appeal to History and National Identity in the Religious Disputes of the Seventeenth Century Netherlands." *Sixteenth Century Journal* 28, no. 1 (1997): 57–78.

Parker, Geoffrey. "Dynastic War." In Geoffrey Parker, ed., *The Cambridge History of Warfare.* New York: Cambridge University Press, 2005.

———. *Phillip II.* New York: Little Brown, 1978.

———. *The Thirty Years War.* New York: Routledge, 1984.

Parker, Randall, ed. *The Economics of the Great Depression: A Twenty-First Century Look Back at the Economics of the Interwar Era.* Cheltenham, UK: Edward Elgar, 2007.

Parker, Thornton. "The Evolution of the Colored Soldier." *North American Review* 168, 507 (1899): 223–28.

Parkin-Speer, Diane. "John Lilburne: A Revolutionary Interprets Statutes and Common Law Due Process." *Law and History Review* 1, no. 2 (1983): 276–96.

Parrott, David. *The Business of War: Military Enterprise and Military Revolution in Early Modern Europe.* New York: Cambridge University Press, 2012.

———. *Richelieu's Army: War, Government, and Society in France, 1624–1642.* New York: Cambridge University Press, 2004.

Paterson, Thomas G. "United States Intervention in Cuba 1898: Interpretations of the Spanish-American-Cuban-Filipino War." *History Teacher* 29, no. 3 (1996): 341–61.

Patman, Robert. "Globalisation, the New US Exceptionalism and the War on Terror." *Third World Quarterly* 27, no. 6 (2006): 963–86.

Pauley, Garth. "W.E.B. Du Bois on Woman Suffrage: A Critical Analysis of His Crisis Writings." *Journal of Black Studies* 30, no. 3 (2000): 383–410.

Pavlac, Brian A. Review of *Itinerant Kingship and Royal Monasteries in Early Medieval Germany, c. 936–1075* by John W. Bernhardt. *Speculum* 70, no. 4 (1995): 881–83.

Payne, David. "British Poison Gas Attack: Loos, September 1915." Western Front Association, May 22, 2008, http://bit.ly/1N50R8P.

Payne, Stanley G. "Catalan and Basque Nationalism." *Journal of Contemporary History* 6, no. 1 (1971): 15–33, 35–51.

———. "The Peace Conference." *Political Science Quarterly* 34, no. 3 (1919): 39–68.

Peacey, Jason. "Order and Disorder in Euerope: Parliamentary Agents and Royalist Thugs." *Historical Journal* 40, no. 4 (1997): 953–76.

Peattie, Roderick. "A Study in Mountain Geography." *Geographical Review* 19, no. 2 (1929): 218–33.

Peck, Rosemary. "Athenian Naval Finance in the Classical Period: The Trierarchy, Its Place in Athenian Society, and How Much Did a Trieres Cost?" Dissertation, University of Leicester, March 2001.

Pedersen, Kenneth. Review of *Partier og erhverv: Studier i partiorganisation og byerhvervenes politiske aktivitet 1880–1913* by Vagn Dybdahl." *American Political Science Review* 64, no. 4 (1970): 1337–39.

Pegg, Mark Gregory. Review of *The Southern French Nobility and the Albigensian Crusade* by Elaine Graham-Leigh. *Speculum* 82, no. 3 (2007): 708–10.

Peisakhin, Leonid, and Paul Pinto. "Army as the Forge of Political Loyalty: The Case of Chinese POWs in the Korean War." Yale University manuscript.

Pereira, N. G. O. "Alexander II and the Decision to Emancipate the Russian Serfs, 1855–61." *Canadian Slavonic Papers* 22, no. 1 (1980): 99–115.

Perrie, Maureen. "The Russian Peasant Movement of 1905–1907: Its Social Composition and Revolutionary Significance." *Past & Present* 57, no. 1 (1972): 123–55.

Pesce, Michael. "Private Contracting Gone Wrong?" *Emory Globe,* July 6, 2012.

Pflanze, Otto. "Bismarck and German Nationalism." *American Historical Review* 60, no. 3 (1955): 548–66.

Phillips, Carla Rahn. Review of *Frontiers of Heresy: The Spanish Inquisition from the Basque Lands to Sicily* by William Monter. *Journal of Interdisciplinary History* 22, no. 3 (1992): 509–11.

Phillips, Carla R., and William D. Phillips, Jr. *Spain's Golden Fleece: Wool Production and the Wool Trade from the Middle Ages to the Nineteenth Century*. Baltimore: John Hopkins University Press, 1997.

Pierson, W. W. Review of *The Mesta: A Study in Spanish Economic History, 1273–1836,* by Julius Klein. *Hispanic American Historical Review* 5, no. 2 (1922): 255–57.

Piketty, Thomas. *Capital in the Twenty-First Century*. Cambridge: Harvard University Press, 2014.

Pilbeam, Pamela. "The Economic Crisis of 1827–1832 and the 1830 Revolution in Provincial France." *Historical Journal* 32, no. 2 (1989): 319–38.

———. "The Emergence of Opposition to the Orleanist Monarchy, August 1830–April 1831." *English Historical Review* 85, no. 334 (1970): 12–28.

———. "Popular Violence in Provincial France." *English Historical Review* 91, no. 359 (1976): 278–97.

Pincherle, Marc, and Manton Monroe Marblec. "Vivaldi and the 'Ospitali' of Venice." *Musical Quarterly* 24, no. 3 (1938): 300–12.

Pincus, Steven. *1688: The First Modern Revolution*. New Haven CT: Yale University Press, 2009.

Pinson, Koppel. Review of *Jean Jaurès: A Study of Patriotism in the French Socialist Movement* by Harold R. Weinstein. *American Historical Review* 42, no. 3 (1937): 543–45.

Pirenne, Henri. "The Formation and Constitution of the Burgundian State." *American Historical Review* 14, no. 3 (1909): 477–502.

———. *Mohammed and Charlemagne*. London: George Allen and Unwin, 1954.

Pitkin, Hanna. *The Concept of Representation*. Berkeley: University of California Press, 1967.

Plato. *The Laws*. Translated by Benjamin Jowett. MIT Internet Classics Archive, http://bit.ly/23b2ZFz.

Plutarch. "Solon." In *Greek Lives*. Translated by Robin Waterfield. New York: Oxford University Press 1998

Pocock, J. A. A. *The Machiavellian Moment*. Princeton: Princeton University Press, 1975.

Polišenský, Josef V. *History of Czechoslovakia in Outline*. Bohemia International, 1991.

———. *War and Society in Europe, 1618–1648*. New York: Cambridge University Press, 1978.

Pollard, A. F. "Plenum Parliamentum." *English Historical Review* 30, no. 120 (1915): 660–62.

Pollard, Sidney. *Marginal Europe: The Contribution of Marginal Lands since the Middle Ages*. London: Clarendon Press, 1997.

Polybius. *The Histories*. Oxford: Oxford University Press, 2010.

Pooley, Andrew. "Shooing the Geese: Lincoln and the Army of the Potomac, 1862–1863." *Australasian Journal of American Studies* 21, no. 2 (2002): 86–100.

Porch, Douglas. "The French Army Law of 1832." *Historical Journal* 14, no. 4 (1971): 751–69.

Porritt, Edward. Review of *The Suffrage Franchise in the Thirteen English Colonies in America* by Albert Edward McKinley. *American Historical Review* 11, no. 2 (1906): 403–6.

Posado-Carbo, Eduardo. "Limits of Power: Elections Under the Conservative Hegemony in Colombia, 1886–1930." *Hispanic American Historical Review* 77, no. 2 (1997): 245–79.

Postan, M. M. "Some Social Consequences of the Hundred Years' War." *Economic History Review* 12, no. 1, 2 (1942): 1–12.

Postel, Rainer. "The Hanseatic League and its Decline." Paper read at the Central Connecticut State University, New Britain, CT, 1996, www.hartford-hwp.com/archives/60/039.html.

Pounds, N. J. G. *An Historical Geography of Europe 450 B.C.–A.D. 1330.* Cambridge: Cambridge University Press, 1979.

Prak, Maarten. "Burghers into Citizens: Urban and National Citizenship in the Netherlands During the Revolutionary Era." *Theory and Society* 26, no. 4 (1997): 403–20.

———. "Citizen Radicalism and Democracy in the Dutch Republic: The Patriot Movement of the 1780s." *Theory and Society* 20, no. 1 (1991): 73–102.

Press, Völker. "The Habsburg Court as Center of the Imperial Government." *Journal of Modern History* 58, supp. (1986): S23–S45.

Previte-Orton, Charles. *The Early History of the House of Savoy.* Cambridge, UK: Cambridge University Press, 1912.

Price, R. D. "Ideology and Motivation in the Paris Commune of 1871." *Historical Journal* 15, no. 1 (1972): 75–86.

Price, Roger. *People and Politics in France, 1848–1870.* Cambridge, UK: Cambridge University Press, 2004.

Pritchard, David M. "The Symbiosis Between Democracy and War: The Case of Ancient Athens." In David M. Pritchard, ed., *War, Democracy and Culture in Classical Athens.* New York: Cambridge University Press, 2010.

Proietti, Gerald. *Xenophon's Sparta: An Introduction.* Leiden: E. J. Brill, 1987.

Przeworski, Adam. "Conquered or Granted? A History of Suffrage Extensions." *British Journal of Political Science* 39, no. 2 (2009): 291–321.

Pushkarev, Sergei. "The Russian Peasants' Reaction to the Emancipation of 1861." *Russian Review* 27, no. 2 (1968): 199–214.

Queller, Donald, and Gerald Day. "Some Arguments in Defense of the Venetians on the Fourth Crusade." *American Historical Review* 81, no. 4 (1976): 717–37.

Raaflaub, Kurt. "The Breakthrough of *Dēmokratia* in Mid-Fifth-Century Athens." In Kurt A. Raaflaub, Josiah Ober, and Robert W. Wallace, eds., *Origins of Democracy in Ancient Greece.* Berkeley: University of California Press, 2007.

———. "Politics and Society in Fifth-Century Rome." In M. A. Levi, ed., *Bilancio critica su Roma arcaica fra monarchia e repubblica, in memoria di Ferdinando Castagnoli.* Rome: Accademia Nazionale dei Lincei, 1993.

Raimond, Jean. "Southey's Early Writings and the Revolution." *Yearbook of English Studies* 19 (1989): 181–96.

Rapp, Richard T. "The Unmaking of the Mediterranean Trade Hegemony: International Trade Rivalry and the Commercial Revolution." *Journal of Economic History* 35, no. 3 (1975): 499–525.

Rapport, Mike. *1848: Year of Revolution.* New York: Basic Books, 2008.

Rasler, Karen, and William Thompson. "War Making and State Making: Governmental Expenditures, Tax Revenues, and Global Wars." *American Political Science Review* 79, no. 2 (1985): 491–507.

Raubitschek, A. E. "The Heroes of Phyle." *Hesperia: Journal of the American School of Classical Studies at Athens* 10, no. 3 (1941): 284–95.

Raybould, A. "Fascism in the Tyrol." *Irish Monthly* 54, no. 638 (1926): 407–16.

Rayburn, John. "The Rough Riders in San Antonio, 1898." *Arizona and the West* 3, no. 2 (1961): 113–28.

Reese, Stephen, and Seth Lewis. "Framing the War on Terror: The Internalization of Policy in the U.S. Press." *Journalism* 10, no. 6 (2009): 777–97.

Reich, Simon. "The Ford Motor Company and the Third Reich." *Dimensions: A Journal of Holocaust Studies* 13, no. 2 (1999).

Reich, Steven. "Soldiers of Democracy: Black Texans and the Fight for Citizenship, 1917–1921." *Journal of American History* 82, no. 4 (1996): 1478–504.

Reid, Richard. *Warfare in African History.* New York: Cambridge University Press, 2012.

Reid, Whitney. "Racism, Manhood, and Femininity in the Alabama Suffrage Debate: 1915–1920." *Huntsville Historical Review* 35, no. 2 (2010): 2–33.

Reiter, Dani, and Allan Stam. *Democracies at War.* Princeton: Princeton University Press, 2002.

Renkema, W. E. Review of *The Dutch in the Caribbean and in the Guianas 1680–1791* by Cornelis Goslinga. *Boletín de Estudios Latinoamericanos y del Caribe* 42 (1987): 111–14.

Report of the War Office Committee of Enquiry into "Shell-Shock." London: His Majesty's Stationery Office, 1922.

Reuter, Timothy. "Plunder and Tribute." *Transactions of the Royal Historical Society,* 5th series, 35 (1985): 75–94.

Reuter, Timothy, and Chris Wickham. "The 'Feudal Revolution.'" *Past & Present* 155, no. 1 (1997): 177–208.

Reynolds, Susan. *Fiefs and Vassals: The Medieval Evidence Reconsidered.* Oxford: Clarendon Press, 1994.

Rhill, T. E. "Democracy Denied: Why Ephialtes Attacked the Areiopagus." *Journal of Hellenic Studies* 115 (1995): 87–98.

Rhodes, P. J. *The Athenian Boule.* New York: Oxford University Press, 1972.

———. "The Athenian Code of Laws, 410–399 B.C." *Journal of Hellenic Studies* 111 (1991): 87–100.

———. "Eisaggelia in Athens." *Journal of Hellenic Studies* 99 (1979): 103–14.

———. "The Five Thousand in the Athenian Revolutions of 411 B.C." *Journal of Hellenic Studies"* 92 (1972): 115–27.

———. "Nomothesia in Fourth Century Athens." *Classical Quarterly* 35, no. 1 (1985): 55–60.

———. "Political Activity in Classical Athens." *Journal of Hellenic Studies* 106 (1986): 132–44.

Richards, Judith. "'His Nowe Majestie' and the English Monarchy: The Kingship of Charles I before 1640." *Past & Present,* no. 113 (1986): 70–96.

Richards, Leonard. *Shays's Rebellion.* Philadelphia: University of Pennsylvania Press, 2003.

Riches, Daniel. "Early Modern Military Reform and the Connection Between Sweden and Brandenburg-Prussia." *Scandinavian Studies* 77, no. 3 (2005): 347–64.

Ridley, Ronald. "The Dictator's Mistake: Caesar's Escape from Sulla." *Historia* 49, no. 2 (2000): 211–29.

Riehm, Edith S. "Forging the Civil Rights Frontier: How Truman's Committee Set the Liberal Agenda for Reform 1947–1965." Dissertation, Georgia State University, 2012, http://bit.ly/1RUlKYH.

Riker, William. "Dutch and American Federalism." *Journal of the History of Ideas* 18, no. 4 (1957): 495–521.

Robbins, Frank Egleston. "The Cost to Athens of Her Second Empire." *Classical Philology* 13, no. 4 (1918): 361–88.

Roberts, Jennifer Tolbert. "Arginusae Once Again." *Classical World* 71, no. 2 (1977): 107–11.

Roberts, Matthew. "Popular Conservatism in Britain, 1832–1914." *Parliamentary History* 26, no. 3 (2007): 387–410.

Roberts, Michael. *Essays in Swedish History.* London: Weidenfeld & Nicolson, 1967.

Robertson, Noel. "The Decree of Themistocles in Its Contemporary Setting." *Phoenix* 36, no. 1 (1982): 1–44.

———. "Government and Society at Miletus, 525–442 B.C." 41, no. 4 (1987): 356–98.

———. "Timocreon and Themistocles." *American Journal of Philology* 101, no. 1 (1980): 61–78.

Robertson, Priscilla. "Students on the Barricades: Germany and Austria, 1848." *Political Science Quarterly* 84, no. 2 (1969): 367–79.

Robinson, Arthur. "Cicero's References to His Banishment." *Classical World* 87, no. 6 (1994): 475–80.

Robinson, Eric. *Democracy Beyond Athens: Popular Government in the Greek Classical Age.* New York: Cambridge University Press, 2011.

Robinson, James A. "*States and Power in Africa* by Jeffrey I. Herbst: A Review Essay." *Journal of Economic Literature* 40 (2002): 510–19.

Rodriguez-Picavea, Enrique. "The Armies of the Military Orders in Medieval Iberia." *Mediterranean Studies* 20, no. 1 (2012): 28–58.

Rogers, Clifford. "The Military Revolutions of the Hundred Years' War." *Journal of Military History* 57, no. 2 (1993): 241–78.

Rogow, Arnold. "Relations between the Labour Government and Industry." *Journal of Politics* 16, no. 1 (1954): 3–23.

———. "Taxation and "Fair Shares" under the Labour Government." *Canadian Journal of Economics and Political Science* 21, no. 2 (1955): 204–16.

Roland, Alex. "Once More into the Stirrups." *Technology and Culture* 44, no. 3 (2003): 574–85.

Root, Hilton. "The Redistributive Role of Government: Economic Regulation in Old Regime France and England." *Comparative Studies in Society and History* 33, no. 2 (1991): 338–69.

Rosch, Gerhard. "The Serrata of the Great Council and Venetian Society, 1286–1323." In John Martin and Dennis Romano, eds., *Venice Reconsidered: The History and Civilization of an Italian City State, 1297–1797,* 67–88. Baltimore: Johns Hopkins University Press, 2000.

Rosen, Josef. "Prices and Public Finance in Basle, 1360–1535." *Economic History Review* 25, no. 1 (1972): 1–17.

Rosenberger, Veit. "The Gallic Disaster." *Classical World* 96 (2003): 365–73.

Rosenman, Samuel. *The Public Papers of Franklin D. Roosevelt,* vol. 2, *The Year of Crisis.* New York: Random House, 1938.

Rosenstein, Nathan. "Aristocrats and Agriculture in the Middle and Late Republic." *Journal of Roman Studies* 98 (2008): 1–26.

————. *Rome at War.* Chapel Hill: University of North Carolina Press, 2004.

Rosivach, Vincent J. "The Requirements for the Solonic Classes in Aristotle, AP 7.4," *Hermes* 130, no. 1 (2002): 36–47.

Ross, Jason. "Shaping the Chinese People's Liberation Army's Image: Historical Roots to Modern Trends," Masters thesis, University of Oregon, 2008. http://bit.ly/1PQwBhK.

Rothrock, George A., Jr. "The French Crown and the Estates General of 1614." *French Historical Studies* 1, no. 3 (1960): 295–18.

Rotz, Rhiman. "The Lübeck Uprising of 1408 and the Decline of the Hanseatic League." *Proceedings of the American Philosophical Society* 121, no. 1 (1977): 1–45.

Rousseau, Jean-Jacques. *A Discourse Upon the Origin and the Foundation of the Inequality Among Mankind.* 1755. Project Gutenberg, http://bit.ly/1R1fxGp.

————. *The Government of Poland.* Trans. Willmoore Kendall. Indianapolis: Hackett, 1985.

————. *The Social Contract.* Trans. Jonathan Bennett. Online at http://bit.ly/29RWymp.

Rowland, Robert J., Jr. "C. Gracchus and the Equites." *Transactions and Proceedings of the American Philological Association* 96 (1965): 361–73.

Rowlands, Guy. *The Dynastic State and the Army under Louis XIV: Royal Service and Private Interest: 1661–1701.* New York: Cambridge University Press, 2002.

————. "Louis XIV, Vittorio Amedeo II and French Military Failure in Italy, 1689–96." *English Historical Review* 115, no. 464 (2000): 534–69.

Rubinstein, Nicolai. "The Beginnings of Political Thought in Florence: A Study of Medieval Historiography." *Journal of the Warburg and Courtauld Institutes* 5 (1942): 198–227.

Rudelle, Odile. "The Third French Republic: A Essay using Quantitative Methods to Study Public Opinion." *Historical Science Research / Historische Sozialforschung* 35 (1983): 34–43.

Ruehl, Martin A. "'In This Time without Emperors': The Politics of Ernst Kantorowicz's Kaiser Friedrich der Zweite Reconsidered." *Journal of the Warburg and Courtauld Institutes* 63 (2000): 187–242.

Rueschemeyer, Dietrich, Evelyne Huber, and John Stephens. *Capitalist Development and Democracy.* Chicago: University of Chicago Press, 1992.

Russell, Conrad. "Monarchies, Wars, and Estates in England, France, and Spain, c. 1580–1640." *Legislative Studies Quarterly* 7, no. 2 (1982): 205–20.

Russett, Bruce, and William Antholis. "Do Democracies Fight Each Other? Evidence from the Peloponnesian War." *Journal of Peace Research* 29, no. 4 (1992): 415–34.

Russett, Bruce, and John Oneal. *Triangulating Peace: Democracy, Peace, and International Organizations.* New York: W. W. Norton, 2001.

Rutter, Keith. "Sicily and South Italy: The Background to Thucydides Books 6 and 7." *Greece and Rome* 33, no. 2 (1986): 142–55.

Ruzicka, Stephen. "Epaminondas and the Genesis of the Social War." *Classical Philology* 93, no. 1 (1998): 60–69.

Saab, Ann, John Knapp, and Francoise Knapp. "A Reassessment of French Foreign Policy During the Crimean War Based on the Papers of Adolphe de Bourqueney." *French Historical Studies* 14, no. 4 (1986): 467–96.

Sahlins, Peter. *Boundaries: The Making of France and Spain in the Pyrenees.* Berkeley: University of California Press, 1989.

———. "The Nation in the Village: State-Building and Communal Struggles in the Catalan Borderland During the Eighteenth and Nineteenth Centuries." *Journal of Modern History* 60, no. 2 (1988): 234–63.

Saldin, Robert P. "Strange Bedfellows: War and Minority Rights." *World Affairs* 173, no. 6 (2011): 57–66.

Salisbury, Laurence E. "Personnel and Far Eastern Policy." *Far Eastern Survey* 14, no. 25 (1945): 361–64.

Salmon, Edward T. "The Cause of the Social War." *Phoenix* 16, no. 2 (1962): 107–19.

Salmon, J. H. M. "Peasant Revolt in Vivarais, 1575–1580." *French Historical Studies* 11, no. 1 (1979): 1–28.

———. "Venality of Office and Popular Sedition in Seventeenth-Century France: A Review of a Controversy." *Past & Present*, no. 37 (1967): 21–43.

Salmond, Paul D. "Sympathy for the Devil: Chares and Athenian Politics." *Greece and Rome* 43, no. 1 (1996): 43–53.

Salyer, Lucy. "Baptism by Fire: Race, Military Service, and U.S. Citizenship Policy, 1918–1935." *Journal of American History* 91, no. 3 (2004): 847–76.

Samons, L. J., II. "Democracy, Empire, and the Search for the Athenian Character." *Arion*, 3rd ser., vol. 8, no. 3 (2001): 128–57.

Sandelius, Walter. "Dictatorship and Irresponsible Parliamentarism—A Study in the Government of Sweden." *Political Science Quarterly* 49, no. 3 (1934): 347–71.

Satow, Ernest. *A Diplomat in Japan.* London: Seely, 1921.

Schaefer, Richard. "The Ku Klux Klan: Continuity and Change." *Phylon* 32, no. 2 (1971): 143–57.

Schapiro, J. Salwyn. "How France Is Governed." *American Political Science Review* 8, no. 2 (1914): 318–19.

Schaub, Gary, Kristian Kristensen, and Flemming Pradham-Blach. "Long Time Coming: Developing and Integrating UAVs into the American, British, French, and Danish Armed Forces." Center for Military Studies. Copenhagen: University of Copenhagen, 2014.

Scheidel, Walter. "Human Mobility in Roman Italy, I: The Free Population." *Journal of Roman Studies* 94 (2004): 1–26.

———. "Human Mobility in Roman Italy, II: The Slave Population." *Journal of Roman Studies* 95 (2005): 64–79.

Scheidel, Walter, and Steven Friesen. "The Size of the Economy and the Distribution of Income in the Roman Empire," *Journal of Roman Studies* 91 (2009): 61–99.

Schilling, Heinz. "The Reformation in the Hanseatic Cities." *Sixteenth Century Journal* 14, no. 4 (1983): 443–56.

Schindling, Anton. "The Development of the Eternal Diet in Regensburg." *Journal of Modern History* 58 (1986): 64–75.

Schleifley, William. "An Epic Genius: Paul Adam." *Sewanee Review* 29, no. 1 (1921): 76–89.

Schlesinger, Arthur. *One Thousand Days.* Boston: Houghton Mifflin, 1965.

Schmitt, Carl. *The Crisis of Parliamentary Democracy.* Cambridge, MA: MIT Press, 2000.

———. "The Dictatorship of the Reich President." Reprinted in *Constellations* 18, no. 3 (2011): 299–323.

Schoffer, I. "The Dutch Revolt Atomized." *Comparative Studies in Society and History* 3, no. 4 (1961): 470–77.

———. "The Second Serfdom in Eastern Europe as a Problem of Historical Explanation." *Historical Studies: Australia and New Zealand* 9, no. 33 (1959): 46–61.

Schonhardt-Bailey, Cheryl. "Parties and Interests in the 'Marriage of Iron and Rye.'" *British Journal of Political Science* 28, no. 2 (1998): 291–332.

Schorr, Daniel. "Bush's Path to Reelection Runs Through Iraq." *Christian Science Monitor,* May 21, 2004.

Schortemeier, Frederick. *Rededicating America: The Life and Speeches of Warren G. Harding.* Indianapolis: Bobbs Merrill, 1920.

Schott, Marshall. "Louisiana Sugar and the Cuban Crisis, 1895–1898." *Louisiana History: Journal of the Louisiana Historical Association* 31, no. 3 (1990): 265–72.

Schrader, William. "Careers in the Church and the Extinction of Noble Families in Westphalia." *Catholic Historical Review* 73, no. 3 (1987): 424–29.

Schreiber, E. M. "Anti-War Demonstrations and American Public Opinion on the War in Vietnam." *British Journal of Sociology* 27, no. 2 (1976): 225–36.

Schultz, David A. *The Encyclopedia of American Law.* New York: Facts on File, 2002.

Schulze, Winfried. "Majority Decision in the Imperial Diets of the Sixteenth and Seventeenth Centuries." *Journal of Modern History* 58 (1986): 46–63.

Schumpeter, Joseph A. "The March Into Socialism." *American Economic Review* 40, no. 2 (1950): 446–56.

Scott, James. *The Art of Not Being Governed: An Anarchist History of Upland Southeast Asia.* New Haven, CT: Yale University Press, 2009.

Scott, Rebecca. "Gradual Abolition and the Dynamics of Slave Emancipation in Cuba, 1868–86." *Hispanic American Historical Review* 63, no. 3 (1983): 449–77.

Scott, Tom. *Town, Country, and Regions in Reformation Germany.* Leiden: Brill, 2005.

Scott, Tom, ed. *The Peasantries of Europe from the Fourteenth to the Eighteenth Centuries.* New York: Addison Wesley Longman, 1988.

Scotto, Peter. "Prisoners of the Caucasus: Ideologies of Imperialism in Lermontov's 'Bela.'" *PMLA* 107, no. 2 (1992): 246–60.

Screen, J. E. O. "Marshal Mannerheim: The Years of Preparation." *Slavonic and East European Review* 43, no. 101 (1965): 293–302.

Seaberg, R. B. "The Norman Conquest and the Common Law: The Levellers and the Argument from Continuity." *Historical Journal* 24, no. 4 (1981): 791–806.

Seager, Robin. "Clodius, Pompeius and the Exile of Cicero." *Latomus* 24, no. 3 (1965): 519–31.

———. "Herodotus and the Ath.Pol on the Date of Cleisthenes' Reforms." *American Journal of Philology* 84, no. 3 (1963): 287–89.

———. "Thrasybulus, Conon, and Athenian Imperialism, 396–386 B.C." *Journal of Hellenic Studies* 87 (1967): 95–115.

Sealey, Raphael. "Athens After the Social War." *Journal of Hellenic Studies* 75 (1955): 74–81.

———. "IG II.1609 and the Transformation of the Second Athenian Sea-League." *Phoenix* 11, no. 3 (1957): 95–111.

Sechser, Todd S., and Elizabeth N. Saunders. "The Army You Have: The Determinants of Military Mechanization, 1979–2001," *International Studies Quarterly* 54 (2010): 481–511.

Segal, David. "Diversity in the Military." *Sociological Forum* 14, no. 3 (1999): 531–39.

Seignobos, Charles. *The History of the Roman People.* Translated by William Fairley. New York: Holt, 1904.

Sekunda, N. V. "Athenian Demography and Military Strength 338–322 B.C." *Annual of the British School at Athens* 87 (1992): 311–55.

Seligman, Matthew. *The Royal Navy and the German Threat, 1901–1914: Admiralty Plans to Protect British Trade in a War Against Germany.* New York: Oxford University Press, 2012.

Sella, Barbara. "Milan." In Christopher Kleinhenz, ed., *Medieval Italy, An Encyclopedia,* vol. 2. New York: Routledge, 2004.

Semple, Ellen Churchill. "Geographic Factors in the Ancient Mediterranean Grain Trade." *Annals of the Association of American Geographers* 11 (1921): 47–74.

Seton-Watson, R. W. "Transylvania, II." *Slavonic Review* 1, no. 3 (1923): 533–51.

"Seventeenth Century." *National Magazine* 2, no. 1 (1831): 109–13.

Shand, James D. "Doves among the Eagles: German Pacificists and Their Government during World War I." *Journal of Contemporary History* 10, no. 1 (1975): 95–108.

Sharp, James R. *American Politics in the Early Republic: The New Nation in Crisis.* New Haven: Yale University Press, 1993.

Shaw, Christine. "The French Invasions and the Establishment of the Petrucci Signoria in Siena." In Stella Fletcher and Christine Shaw, eds., *The World of Savonarola: Italian Élites and Perceptions of Crisis, 168–81.* Aldershot, UK: Ashgate, 2000.

———. "Memory and Tradition in Sienese Political Life in the Fifteenth Century." *Transactions of the Royal Historical Society* 9 (1999): 221–31.

Shee, M. E. "Studies Among the Leaves." *Crayon* 6, no. 3 (1859): 94–100.

Sheehan, Colleen. "The Politics of Public Opinion: James Madison's 'Notes on Government.'" *William and Mary Quarterly* 49, no. 4 (1992): 609–27.

Sheehan, James. *German History: 1770–1866.* New York: Oxford University Press, 1989.

———. *German Liberalism in the Nineteenth Century.* Chicago: University of Chicago Press, 1978.

Shepard, Walter J. "The New German Constitution." *American Political Science Review* 14, no. 1 (1920): 34–52.

Sherborne, J. W. "The Hundred Years' War. The English Navy: Shipping and Manpower 1369–1389." *Past & Present* 37 (1967): 163–75.

Sherman, G. W. Review of *The Proud Tower* by Barbara W. Tuchman. *Science and Society* 32, no. 4 (1968): 462–65.

Short, Philip. *Mao: A Life.* London: Hodder and Stoughton, 1991.

Shugart, Matthew, and John Carey. *Presidents and Assemblies.* New York: Cambridge University Press, 1992.

Siddle, D. J. "Migration as a Strategy of Accumulation: Social and Economic Change in Eighteenth-Century." *Economic History Review* 50, no. 1 (1997): 1–20.

Sides, John. "Public Opinion Polling before the Internment of Japanese-Americans." *American Prospect,* January 2, 2012.

Sièyes, Abbé. *What Is the Third Estate?* 1789. Online at http://bit.ly/29PSol1.

Sihler, E. G. "Aristotle's Cricisms of the Spartan Government." *Classical Review* 7, no. 10 (1893): 439–43.

Silva, Milton N. Review of *The Guernica Generation: Basque Refugee Children of the Spanish Civil War* by Dorothy Legarreta. *International Migration Review* 21, no. 4 (1987): 1562–64.

Silvalupus. "Politics and War: Scipio Africanus and the Battle of Zama." *Lego I Lynx Fulminata,* 2012. http://bit.ly/1Xc3HPg.

Silverstein, K. "Ford and the Führer." *Nation* 270, no. 3 (2000): 11–16.

Simmons, Beth. *Who Adjusts? Domestic Sources of Foreign Economic Policy During the Interwar Period.* Princeton: Princeton University Press, 1994.

Simon, Walter. *The Failure of the Prussian Reform Movement, 1807–1819.* Ithaca: Cornell University Press, 1955.

Simpson, Lesley Byrd, Gordon Griffiths, and Woodrow Borah. "Representative Institutions in the Spanish Empire of the Sixteenth Century." *Americas* 12, no. 3 (1956).

Sitkoff, Harvard. "Racial Militancy and Interracial Violence in the Second World War." *Journal of American History* 58, no. 3 (1971): 661–81.

Sklaroff, Lauren Rebecca. "Constructing G.I. Joe Louis: Cultural Solutions to the 'Negro Problem' During World War II." *Journal of American History* 89, no. 3 (2002): 958–83.

Skocpol, Theda.. "Social Revolutions and Mass Military Mobilization." *World Politics* 40, no. 2 (1988): 147–68.

Skrentny, John. "The Effect of the Cold War on African-American Civil Rights: America and the World Audience, 1945–1968." *Theory and Society* 27, no. 2 (1998): 237–85.

Skowronek, Stephen. *Building a New American State: The Expansion of National Administrative Capacities, 1877–1920.* Cambridge: Cambridge University Press, 1982.

Slosson, Edwin. "From the Other Side of the Barricade." *Sigma Xi Quarterly* 5, no. 4 (1917): 110–16.

Sluiter, Engel. "Dutch-Spanish Rivalry in the Caribbean Area, 1594–1609." *Hispanic American Historical Review* 28, no. 2 (1948): 165–96.

Smethurst, S. E. "Cicero and the Senate." *The Classical Journal* 54, no. 2 (1958): 73–78.

———. "Politics and Morality in Cicero." *Phoenix* 9, no. 3 (1955): 111–21.

Smith, Amy C. *Athenian Political Art from the Fifth and Fourth Centuries BCE: Images of Political Personifications.* Stoa Project, 2003.

Smith, Geoffrey. "Isolationism, the Devil, and the Advent of the Second World War: Variations on a Theme." *International History Review* 4, no. 1 (1982): 55–89.

Smith, Jay. "Russia and the Origins of the Finnish Civil War of 1918." *American Slavic and East European Review* 14, no. 4 (1955): 481–502.

Smith, Rogers. "Beyond Tocqueville, Myrdal, and Hartz: The Multiple Traditions in America." *American Political Science Review* 87, no. 3 (1993): 549–66.

Snodgrass, A. M. "The Hoplite Reform and History." *Journal of Hellenic Studies* 86 (1965): 110–22.

Snyder, Jack. *Myths of Empire: Domestic Politics and International Ambition.* Ithaca: Cornell University Press, 1991.

Snyder, Terri. Review of *Forced Founders: Indians, Debtors, Slaves, and the Making of the American Revolution in Virginia* by Woody Holton. *Virginia Magazine of History and Biography* 108, no. 3 (2000): 310–12.

Souyri, Pierre Francois. *The World Turned Upside Down: Medieval Japanese Society.* New York: Columbia University Press, 2001.

Spalding, K. "The Idiom of a Revolution: Berlin 1848." *Modern Language Review* 44, no. 1 (1949): 60–74.

Sparrow, Elizabeth. "The Swiss and Swabian Agencies, 1795–1801." *Historical Journal* 35, no. 4 (1992): 861–84.

Speidel, M. Alexander. "Roman Army Pay Scales." *Journal of Roman Studies* 82 (1992): 87–106.

Spence, I. G. "Pericles and the Defense of Attika During the Peloponnesian War." *Journal of Hellenic Studies* 110 (1990): 91–109.

Sperber, Jonathan. *The Kaiser's Voters: Electors and Elections in Imperial Germany*. Cambridge: Cambridge University Press, 1997.

Springford, John. "Old and New Europeans United: Public Attitudes Towards the Iraq War and US Foreign Policy." Centre for European Reform, December 11, 2003, http://bit.ly/1PQwwL8.

Spruyt, Hendrik. *The Sovereign State and Its Competitors*. Princeton: Princeton University Press, 1994.

Sreenevaan, Govind. "The Social Origins of the Peasants War of 1525 in Upper Swabia." *Past & Present* 171, no. 1 (2001): 30–65.

Stagg, J. C. A. "Soldiers in Peace and War: Comparative Perspectives on the Recruitment of the United States Army, 1802–1815." *William and Mary Quarterly* 57, no. 1 (2000): 79–120.

Stalnaker, John C., and H. J. Ginsburg. "Auf Dem Weg Zu Einer Sozialgeschichtlichen Interpretation Des Deutschen Bauernkrieges 1525–1526." *Geschichte und Gesellschaft. Sonderheft* 1 (1975): 38–60.

Standemann, Hartmut Pogge. "Domestic Origins of Germany's Colonial Expansion under Bismarck." *Past & Present* 42, no. 1 (1969): 140–59.

Staniland, Paul. "States, Insurgents, and Wartime Political Orders." *Perspectives on Politics* 10, no. 2 (2012): 243–64.

Starr, Paul. "War and Liberalism: Why Power Is Not the Enemy of Freedom," *The New Republic,* March 5 and 12, 2007: 21–24.

Stasavage, David. *Public Debt and the Birth of the Democratic State: France and Great Britain, 1688–1789.* New York: Cambridge University Press, 2003.

———. "Transparency, Democratic Accountability, and the Economic Consequences of Monetary Institutions." *American Journal of Political Science* 47, no. 3 (2003): 389–402.

Staveley, E. S. *Greek and Roman Voting and Elections.* Ithaca, NY: Cornell University Press, 1972.

Stearns, Stephen J. "Conscription and English Society in the 1620s." *Journal of British Studies* 11, no. 2 (1972): 1–23.

Stefansson, Jon. *Denmark and Sweden, with Iceland and Finland.* New York: G. P. Putnam's Sons, 1917.

Steinberg, Michael. "The Twelve Tables and Their Origins: An Eighteenth-Century Debate." *Journal of the History of Ideas* 43, no. 3 (1982): 379–96.

Stephens, John D. "Class Formation and Class Consciousness: A Theoretical and Empirical Analysis with Reference to Britain and Sweden." *British Journal of Sociology* 30, no. 4 (1979): 389–44.

Steptoe, Taniya. *Dixie West: Race, Migration, and Color Lines in Jim Crow Houston.* Ph.D. dissertation, University of Wisconsin, Madison, 2008.

Stevens, Jacqueline. "The Reasonableness of John Locke's Majority: Property Rights, Consent, and Resistance in the Second Treatise." *Political Theory* 24, no. 3 (1996): 423–63.

Steyn, Johan. "Guantanamo Bay: The Legal Black Hole." *International and Comparative Law Quarterly* 53, no. 1 (2004): 1–15.

Stow, George B. Review of *Richard II: The Art of Kingship* by Anthony Goodman and James L. Gillespie. *Albion* 32, no. 3 (2000): 476–78.

Strauss, Barry. "Democracy, Kimon, and the Evolution of Athenian Naval Tactics in the Fifth Century B.C." In Pernille Flensted-Jensen, Thomas H. Nielsen, and Lene Rubinstein, eds., *Polis and Politics: Studies in Ancient Greek History.* Copenhagen: Museum Tusculanum Press, 2000.

———. "Memorandum for Workshop on Military Organization and Political Regimes in Classical Greece." Yale University, December 5–6, 2004.

———. "Thrasybulus and Conon: A Rivalry in Athens in the 390s B.C." *American Journal of Philology* 105, no. 1 (1984): 37–48.

Strayer, Joseph R. *Medieval Statecraft and Perspectives of History: Essays by Joseph Strayer.* Princeton: Princeton University Press, 1971.

Streb, Jochen, Joerg Baten, and Shuxi Yin. "Technological and Geographical Knowledge Spillover in the German Empire 1877–1918." *Economic History Review* 59, no. 2 (2006): 347–73.

Streider, Jacob. *Jacob Fugger The Rich: Merchant and Banker of Augsburg, 1459–1525.* New York: Adelphi, 1931.

Strong, Frank. "Fifty Years of 'Clear and Present Danger': From Schenck to Brandenburg and Beyond." *Supreme Court Review* 1969 (1969): 41–80.

Stubbs, H. W. "Spartan Austerity: A Possible Explanation." *Classical Quarterly* 44, no. 1 (1950): 32–37.

Sturdy, D. J. "Tax Evasion, the Faux Nobles, and State Fiscalism: The Example of the Generalite of Caen, 1634–35." *French Historical Studies* 9, no. 4 (1976): 549–72.

Sussman, Nathan. "Debasements, Royal Revenues, and Inflation in France During the Hundred Years' War, 1415–1422." *Journal of Economic History* 53, no. 1 (1993): 44–70.

Sutherland, Daniel. "Guerrilla Warfare, Democracy, and the Fate of the Confederacy." *Journal of Southern History* 68, no. 2 (2002): 259–92.

Sutherland, L. S. Review of *Myth and Reality in Late-Eighteenth Century British Politics and Other Papers* by I. R. Christie. *English Historical Review* 87, no. 344 (1972): 633–34.

Svensson, Palle. "Parliament and Foreign Policy Making in Denmark." *Irish Studies in International Affairs* 2, no. 4 (1988): 19–39.

Swain, George. "Caesar's Strategy in the Gallic War." *Classical Journal* 3, no. 2 (1907): 67–73.

Swank, Duane, and Sven Steinmo. "The New Political Economy of Taxation in Advanced Capitalist Democracies." *American Journal of Political Science* 46, no. 3 (2002): 642–55.

Swiss Coalition Against Arms Trade. "Report on the Exports of Arms from Switzerland." Group for Switzerland Without an Army, 2010.

Symcox, Geoffrey. *Victor Amadeus II: Absolutism in the Savoyard State, 1675–1730.* Berkeley: University of California Press, 1983.

Syme, Ronald. "The Allegiance of Labienus." *Journal of Roman Studies* 28, no. 2 (1938): 113–25.

Tago, Atsushi. "When Are Democratic Friends Unreliable? The Unilateral Withdrawal of

Troops from the 'Coalition of the Willing.'" *Journal of Peace Research* 46, no. 2 (2009): 219–34.

Talbot, Michael. "Vivaldi's Venice." *Musical Times* 119, no. 1622 (1978): 314–17.

Tauger, Mark. "The 1932 Harvest and the Famine of 1933." *Slavic Review* 50, no. 1 (1991): 70–89.

Taylor, Lily Ross. "Forerunners of the Gracchi." *Journal of Roman Studies* 52, nos. 1/ 2 (1962): 19–27.

———. *Roman Voting Assemblies*. Ann Arbor: University of Michigan Press, 1996.

T.C. "The Economic Development of the British Colonial Empire." *Bulletin of International News* 20, no. 4 (1943): 139–45.

Teele, Dawn L. "Ordinary Democratization: The Electoral Strategy That Won British Women the Vote." *Politics & Society* 42, no. 4 (2014): 537–61.

Temin, Peter. *Lessons from the Great Depression*. New York: MIT Press, 1989.

ter Braake, Serge. "Parties and Factions in the Late Middle Ages: The Case of the Hoeken and Kabeljauwen in The Hague (1483–1515)." *Journal of Medieval History* 35 (2009): 97–111.

't Hart, Marjolein. "Cities and Statemaking in the Dutch Republic, 1580–1680." *Theory and Society* 18, no. 5 (1989): 663–87.

Therborn, Göran. "The Rule of Capital and the Rise of Democracy." *New Left Review* 103 (1977): 1–41.

Thompson, David. "Norwegian Military Policy, 1905–1940: A Critical Appraisal and Review of the Literature." *Journal of Military History* 61, no. 3 (1997): 503–20.

Thompson, E. A. *Attila and the Huns*. Oxford: Oxford University Press, 1948.

Thompson, I. A. A. "Money, Money, and Yet More Money! Finance, the Fiscal State and the Military Revolution: Spain 1500–1600." In Clifford Rogers, ed., *The Military Revolution Debate*. Boulder, CO: Westview Press, 1995.

Thompson, James Westfall. "The Crown Lands in Feudal Germany." *Journal of Political Economy* 31, no. 3 (1923): 360–70.

———. "Early Trade Relations between the Germans and the Slavs." *Journal of Political Economy* 30 (1922): 543–58.

———. *Economic and Social History of Europe in the Later Middle Ages (1300–1530)*. London: Ungar, 1960 (first pub. 1928).

———. "German Feudalism." *American Historical Review*, 28, no. 3 (1923): 440–74.

Thompson, Mark. *The White War: Life and Death on the Italian Front, 1915–1919*. New York: Basic Books, 2008.

Thomsett, Michael C. *The German Opposition to Hitler: The Resistance, the Underground, and Assassination Plots, 1938–1945*. Jefferson: McFarland & Company, 1997.

Thorpe, Andrew. "The Industrial Meaning of 'Gradualism': The Labour Party and Industry, 1918–1931." *Journal of British Studies* 35, no. 1 (1969): 84–113.

Thucydides. *History of the Peloponnesian War*. Tranlated by Rex Warner with an introduction and notes by Moses Finley. London: Penguin Books, 1972.

Tilly, Charles. *The Vendee*. Cambridge: Harvard University Press, 1963.

Tilton, Timothy. "Why Don't the Swedish Social Democrats Nationalize Industry." *Scandinavian Studies* 59, no. 2 (1987): 142–66.

The Times Documentary History of the War. 11 vols. London: The Times Publishing Co., 1917–20.

Togami, Cynthia, and Arthur Hansen. Review of *Executive Order 9066: The Internment of 110,000 Japanese Americans* by Elizabeth Shepherd; and *Manzanar: A Selection of Photographs* by Ansel Adams. *Public Historian* 15, no. 1 (1993): 114–17.

Tollebeek, Jo. "Historical Representation and the Nation-State in Romantic Belgium (1830–1850)." *Journal of the History of Ideas* 59, no. 2 (1998): 329–53.

Tomich, Dale. "World Slavery and Caribbean Capitalism: The Cuban Sugar Industry, 1760–1868." *Theory and Society* 20, no. 3 (1991): 297–319.

Tooze, Adam. *The Wages of Destruction: The Making and Breaking of the Nazi Economy.* New York: Penguin Books, 2006.

Totanes, Henry. Review of *Sitting in Darkness: Americans in the Philippines* by David Bain. *Philippine Studies* 34, no. 1 (1986): 111–15.

Toynbee, Arnold. "The Growth of Sparta." *Journal of Hellenic Studies* 33 (1913): 246–75.

"The Transformation of the Racial Views of Harry Truman." *Journal of Blacks in Higher Education* 26 (1999–2000): 28–30.

Treharne, R. F., and I. J. Sanders. *Documents of the Baronial Movement of Reform and Rebellion, 1258–1267.* Oxford: Clarendon Press, 1973.

Trenchard, John, and Walter Moyle. *An Argument Shewing, that a Standing Army is inconsistent with a Free Government, and absolutely destructive to the Constitution of the English Monarchy.* London, 1697, http://bit.ly/1Oov60p.

Trotter, Joseph William. *The African American Experience from Reconstruction.* Boston: Houghton Mifflin, 2001.

Trumpener, Ulrich. "The Road to Ypres: The Beginnings of Gas Warfare in World War I." *Journal of Modern History* 47, no. 3 (1975): 460–80.

Tsang, Carol R. *War and Faith: Ikkō Ikki in Late Muromachi Japan.* Cambridge: Harvard University Asia Center, 2007.

Tuchman, Barbara. *A Distant Mirror.* New York: Alfred A. Knopf, 1978.

Tull, Charles. Review of *The Politics of Normalcy: Governmental Theory and Practice in the Harding-Coolidge Era* by Robert Murray. *Journal of Southern History* 39, no. 4 (1973): 618–20.

Turnbull, Stephen. *The Mongolian Invasions of Japan.* New York: Osprey Books, Random House, 2013.

Turner, Henry Ashby. "The Myth of Chancellor Von Schleicher's Querfront Strategy." *Central European History* 41, no. 4 (2008): 673–81.

Turner, Ralph. "William De Forz, Count of Aumale: An Early Thirteenth-Century English Baron." *Proceedings of the American Philosophical Society* 115, no. 3 (1971): 221–49.

Tyler, J. E. *The Alpine Passes in the Middle Ages, 962–1250.* Oxford: Basil Blackwood, 1930.

"UK Election Statistics: 1918–2012." Research Paper, 12/43, August 7, 2012, House of Commons Library.

Ullman, Harlan, and James Wade. *Shock and Awe: Achieving Rapid Dominance.* Washington, DC: National Defense University, 1996.

Upton, A. F. "The Riksdag of 1680 and the Establishment of Royal Absolutism in Sweden." *English Historical Review* 102, no. 403 (1987): 281–308.

Usher, Abbot Payson. "Interpretations of Recent Economic Progress in Germany." *American Historical Review* 23, no. 4 (1918): 797–815.

Valentin, Veit. "Wallenstein, After Three Centuries." *Slavonic and East European Review* 14, no. 40 (1935): 154–62.

Vallely, Richard. *The Two Reconstructions: The Struggle for Black Enfranchisement.* Chicago: University of Chicago Press, 2004.

Vanhulle, Bert. "Dreaming about the Prison: Édouard Ducpétiaux and Prison Reform in Belgium (1830–1848)." *Crime, Histoire & Sociétés / Crime, History & Societies* 14, no. 2 (2010): 107–30.

Vann, James Allen. *The Making of a State: Württemberg, 1593–1793.* Ithaca, NY: Cornell University Press, 1984.

———. *The Swabian Kreis: Institutional Growth in the Holy Roman Empire 1648–1715.* Brussels: Studies Presented to the International Commission for the History of Representative and Parliamentary Institutions, 1975.

Verbruggen, J. F. *The Art of Warfare in Western Europe During the Middle Ages: From the Eighth Century to 1340.* Martlesham: Boydell & Brewer, 1997.

Viazzo, Pier Paolo. *Upland Communities: Environment, Population, and Social Structure in the Alps since the Sixteenth Century.* New York: Cambridge University Press, 1989.

Vieusseux, Andre. *A History of Switzerland from the First Irruption of the Northern Tribes to the Current Time.* London: Henry Bohn, 1846.

Vile, John. "The Critical Role of Committees at the U.S. Constitutional Convention of 1787." *American Journal of Legal History* 48, no. 2 (2006): 147–76.

Villalon, L. J. A., and Donald J. Kagay. "The Hundred Years War: A Wider Focus (History of Warfare, no. 25)." *American Historical Review* 110, no. 4 (2005): 1302.

Vincent, J. R. "The Parliamentary Dimension of the Crimean War." *Transactions of the Royal Historical Society* 31 (1981): 37–49.

Vink, Markus. "The World's Oldest Trade: Dutch Slavery and Slave Trade in the Indian Ocean in the Seventeenth Century." *Journal of World History* 14, no. 2 (2003): 131–77.

Viroli, Maurizio. *From Politics to Reason of State: The Acquisition and Transformation of the Language of Politics, 1200–1600.* New York: Cambridge University Press, 1992.

Volin, Lazar. "The Russian Peasant and Serfdom." *Agricultural History* 17, no. 1 (1943): 41–61.

Von der Dunk, Hermann. "Conservatism in the Netherlands." *Journal of Contemporary History* 13, no. 4 (1978): 741–63.

Von Laue, Theodore. *Why Lenin? Why Stalin? A Reappraisal of the Russian Revolution, 1900–1930.* Philadelphia: Lippincott Williams & Wilkins, 1971.

Von Reden-Dohna, Armgard. "Problems of Small Estates of the Empire: The Example of the Swabian Imperial Prelates." *Journal of Modern History* 58, supp. (1986): S76–S87.

Waaranperä, Ulrika. "The Finnish Civil War of 1918 Remembered." 2008. Socialistworld.net.

Walbank, F. W. "Polybius on the Roman Constitution." *Classical Quarterly* 37, nos. 3/4 (1943): 73–89.

Walford, Cornelius. "An Outline History of the Hanseatic League, More Particularly in its Bearings upon English Commerce." *Transactions of the Royal Historical Society* 9 (1881): 82–136.

Walker, Francis. "The German Steel Syndicate." *Quarterly Journal of Economics* 20, no. 3 (1906): 353–98.

Wallace, Robert W. *The Areopagus Council.* Johns Hopkins University Press, 1989.

———. "Revolutions and a New Order in Solonian Athens and Archiac Greece." In Kurt A. Raaflaub, Josiah Ober, and Robert Wallace, eds., *Origins of Democracy in Ancient Greece.* Berkeley: University of California Press, 2007.

Wallace, W. P. "Kleomenes, Marathon, the Helots, and Arkadia." *Journal of Hellenic Studies* 74 (1954): 32–35.

Waller, Robert. "Business and the Initiation of the Teapot Dome Investigation." *Business History Review* 36, no. 3 (1962): 334–53.

Walling, William English. "The Wilson-Kerensky Peace Policy." *Proceedings of the Academy of Political Science in the City of New York* 7, no. 2 (1917): 124–30.

Walsh, Kevin. "Risk and Marginality at High Altitudes: New Interpretations from Fieldwork on the Faravel Plateau, Hautes-Alpes." *Antiquity* 79, no. 304 (2005): 289–305.

Walsh, Kevin, Suzi Richer, and J. L. de Beaulieu. "Attitudes to Altitude: Changing Meanings and Perceptions within a 'Marginal' Alpine Landscape: The Integration of Palaeoecological and Archaeological Data in a High-Altitude Landscape in the French Alps." *World Archaeology* 38, no. 3 (2006): 436–54.

Walsh, Martin. "The 'Urner Tellenspiel' of 1512: Strategies of Early Political Drama." *Comparative Drama* 34, no. 2 (2000): 155–73.

Wandycz, Piotr Stefan. *The Lands of Partitioned Poland, 1795–1918.* Seattle: University of Washington Press, 1974.

Watt, Jeffrey. "The Reception of the Reformation in Valangin, Switzerland, 1547–1588." *Sixteenth Century Journal* 210, no. 1 (1989): 89–104.

Weart, Spencer R. "Peace Among Democratic and Oligarchic Republics." *Journal of Peace Research* 31, no. 1 (1994): 299–316.

Weber, Max. "Politics as a Vocation." 1918, http://bit.ly/RjIZkk.

Weerakoon, R. *Solzhenhitsyn: Soldier, Prisoner, Writer.* Colombo, Ceylon: International Publishers, 1972, http://bit.ly/2004J2r.

Weinstein, Jeremy M., and Macartan Humphreys. "Handling and Manhandling Civilians in Civil War." *American Political Science Review* 100, no. 3 (2006): 429–47.

Westheider, James. *The Vietnam War.* Westport, CT: Greenwood Press, 2007.

Wettergreen, John. "James Harrington's Liberal Republicanism." *Polity* 20, no. 4 (1988): 665–87.

Whaley, Joachim. *Germany and the Holy Roman Empire: Volume I: Maximilian I to the Peace of Westphalia, 1493–1648.* Oxford History of Early Modern Europe. Oxford: Oxford University Press, 2012.

White, Stephen. "The 'Feudal Revolution': Comment." *Past & Present* 152, no. 1 (1996): 205–23.

White, Eugene N. "From Privatized to Government-Administered Tax Collection: Tax Farming in Eighteenth-Century France." *Economic History Review* 57, no. 4 (2004): 636–63.

Whittemore, Gilbert. "World War I, Poison Gas Research, and the Ideals of American Chemists." *Social Studies of Science* 5, no. 2 (1975): 135–63.

Whittlesey, C. R. "Excise Taxes as a Substitute for Tariffs." *American Economic Review* 27, no. 4 (1937): 667–79.

Whittlesey, Derwent. "Andorra's Autonomy." *Journal of Modern History* 6, no. 2 (1934): 147–55.

Wickham, Christopher. *Early Medieval Italy: Central Power and Local Society, 400–1000.* Ann Arbor: University of Michigan Press, 1981.

———. *The Mountains and the City: The Tuscan Apennines in the Early Middle Ages.* New York: Oxford University Press, 1988.

———. "Problems of Comparing Rural Societies in Early Medieval Europe." *Transactions of the Royal Historical Society.* 6th ser., vol. 2 (1992): 221–46.

Williams, F. W. "The Manchu Conquest of China." *Journal of Race Development* 4, no. 2 (1913): 152–67.

Williams, Henry S. *The Historians' History of the World: Poland, the Balkans, Turkey, Minor Eastern States, China, Japan.* New York: Outlook Company, 1904.

Williams, Rachel Marie-Crane. "A War in Black and White: The Cartoons of Norman Ethre Jennett and the North Carolina Election of 1898." *Southern Cultures* 19, no. 2 (2013): 7–31.

Willoughby, William Franklin. "Labor Legislation in France Under the Third Republic." *Quarterly Journal of Economics* 15, no. 3 (1901): 390–415.

Wilson, Charles. "The Massacre of St. Bartholomew and the European Conflict, 1559–1572." *Historical Journal* 16, no. 3 (1973): 635–37.

Wilson, Peter. "The Origins of Prussian Militarism." *History Today* 51, no. 5 (2001).

———. *The Thirty Years War.* Cambridge, MA: Harvard University Press, 2009.

Wilson, Trevor. "Lord Bryce's Investigation into Alleged German Atrocities in Belgium, 1914–15." *Journal of Contemporary History* 14, no. 3 (1979): 369–83.

Wimmer, Andreas, Lars-Erik Cederman, and Brian Min. "Ethnic Politics and Armed Conflict: A Configurational Analysis of a New Global Data Set." *American Sociological Review* 74 (2009): 316–37.

Wines, Roger. "The Imperial Circles, Princely Diplomacy and Imperial Reform 1681–1714." *Journal of Modern History* 39, no. 1 (1967): 1–29.

Wingate, George. "The Truth in Regard to the War of 1812 and the Necessity of Our Knowing It." *North American Review* 189, no. 643 (1909): 831–43.

Winkler, Heinrich. "German Society, Hitler and the Illusion of Restoration 1930–33." *Journal of Contemporary History* 11, no. 4 (1976): 1–16.

Winnacker, R. A. "The Third French Republic, 1870–1914." *Journal of Modern History* 10, no. 3 (1938): 372–409.

Winter, J. M. "Arthur Henderson, the Russian Revolution, and the Reconstruction of the Labour Party." *Historical Journal* 15, no. 4 (1972): 753–73.

Winter, Yves. "Plebeian Politics: Machiavelli and the Ciompi Uprising." *Political Theory* 40, no. 6 (2012): 736–66.

Witte, John F. *The Politics and Development of the Federal Income Tax.* Madison: University of Wisconsin Press, 1985.

Wittfogel, Karl. "Chinese Society: An Historical Survey." *Journal of Asian Studies* 16, no. 3 (1957): 343–64.

Wolfe, Martin. "Jean Bodin on Taxes: The Sovereignty–Taxes Paradox." *Political Science Quarterly* 83, no. 2 (1968): 268–84.

Wolff, Larry. *The Idea of Galicia: History and Fantasy in Habsburg Political Culture.* Stanford, CA: Stanford University Press, 2010.

Wolfson, Arthur M. "The Ballot and Other Forms of Voting in the Italian Communes." *American Historical Review* 5, no. 1 (1899): 1–21.

Womack, Brantly. "Mao before Maoism." *China Journal,* no. 46 (2001): 95–117.

Wood, Gordon. *The Creation of the American Republic, 1776–1787.* New York: W. W. Norton, 1969.

Wood, Jacob, and Ken Harbaugh. "The Limits of Armchair Warfare." *New York Times,* May 20, 2014.

Woodward, C. Vann. *The Battle for Leyte Gulf: The Incredible Story of World War II's Largest Naval Battle.* New York: Macmillan, 1947.

Woolrych, A. H. "The Good Old Cause and the Fall of the Protectorate." *Cambridge Historical Journal* 13, no. 2 (1957): 133–61.

———. "The Calling of Barebone's Parliament." *The English Historical Review* 80, no. 316 (1965): 492–513.

Worden, Blair. "The Bill for a New Representative: The Dissolution of the Long Parliament, April 1653." *English Historical Review* 86, no. 340 (1971): 473–96.

World Affairs Institute. "Crimean War: Loss of Life." *Advocate of Peace* 1, no. 7 (1869): 106–7.

Worthington, David. *Scots in Habsburg Service, 1618–1648.* Leiden: E. J. Brill, 2004.

Worthington, Ian. "The Earlier Career of Leosthenes." *Historia: Zeitschrift für Alte Geschichte* 36, no. 4 (1987): 489–91.

Wright, Barry. "Migration, Radicalism, and State Security: Legislative Initiatives in the Canadas and the United States, c.1794–1804." *Studies in American Political Development* 16 (2002): 48–60.

Wright, David. "Public Opinion and Conscription in France, 1866–70." *Journal of Modern History* 14, no. 1 (1942): 26–45.

Wright, L. P. "The Military Orders in Sixteenth and Seventeenth Century Spanish Society. The Institutional Embodiment of a Historical Tradition." *Past & Present* 43, no. 1 (1969): 34–70.

Wuarin, Louis. "Recent Political Experiments in the Swiss Democracy." *Annals of the American Academy of Political and Social Science* 6 (1895): 1–20.

Wylie, James Aitken. *The History of Protestantism* (1878). 3 vols. London: Cassell, 1899.

Wylie, Turrell V. "The First Mongol Conquest of Tibet Reinterpreted." *Harvard Journal of Asiatic Studies* 37, no. 1 (1977): 103–33.

Wyntjes, Sherrin Marshall. "Family Allegiance and Religious Persuasion: The Lesser Nobility and the Revolt of the Netherlands." *Sixteenth Century Journal* 12, no. 2 (1981): 43–60.

Young, Crawford. "Deciphering Disorder in Africa: Is Identity the Key?" *World Politics* 54, no. 4 (2002): 532–57.

Young, L. H. *The Historical Cabinet: Containing Authentic Accounts of Many Remarkable and Interesting Events Which Have Taken Place in Modern Times.* New Haven: L. H. Young in the Clerk's Office of the District Court of Connecticut, 1895.

Zakheim, Dov. *A Vulcan's Tale: How the Bush Administration Mismanaged the Reconstruction of Afghanistan*. Washington, DC: Brookings Institution, 2011.

Zaller, Robert. "Kingship and Crown Finance." *Albion: A Quarterly Journal Concerned with British Studies* 36, no. 1 (2004): 121–24.

Zaret, David. "Petitions and the 'Invention' of Public Opinion." *American Journal of Sociology* 101, no. 6 (1996): 1497–555.

Zelizer, Julian. "The Forgotten Legacy of the New Deal: Fiscal Conservatism and the Roosevelt Administration, 1933–1938." *Presidential Studies Quarterly* 30, no. 2 (2000): 331–58.

Zenkovsky, Serge. "The Emancipation of the Serfs in Retrospect." *Russian Review* 20, no. 4 (1961): 280–93.

Zhang, Hongxing. "Studies in Late Qing Dynasty Battle Paintings." *Artibus Asiae* 60, no. 2 (2000): 265–96.

Zhang, Shuguang. *Mao's Military Romanticism: China and the Korean War, 1950–1953*. Lawrence: University Press of Kansas, 1995.

Zhmodikov, Alexander. "Roman Republican Heavy Infantrymen in Battle (IV–II Centuries B.C.)." *Historia* 49, no. 1 (2000): 67–78.

Zschokke, Heinrich, and Emil Zschokke. *A History of Switzerland, for the People of Switzerland*. Translated by Francis George Shaw. New York: C. S. Francis, 1855.

Zuckerman, Larry. *The Rape of Belgium*. New York: NYU Press, 2004.

ILLUSTRATION CREDITS

Page 5:   *Anacyclosis: Polybius' cyclical theory of constitutional forms.* Supplied by the authors.

Page 6:   *A hierarchy of constitutions by military capacity.* Supplied by the authors.

Page 15:   *The United States spends more on defense* . . . . Adapted from Peter G. Peterson Foundation.

Page 27:   *Naval battles in the Peloponnesian War.* Adapted from "Map of the Peloponnesian War" via Wikimedia Commons.

Page 33:   *Battle of Marathon.* "They Crashed into the Persian Army with Tremendous Force," illustration from *The Story of Greece* by Mary Macgregor, 1st edition, 1913 (colour print), Crane, Walter (1845–1915) / Private Collection / The Stapleton Collection / Bridgeman Images.

Page 35:   *The Long Walls.* Adapted from "Peloponnesian War—Walls Protecting the City and Port 431 B.C." by U.S. Army Cartographer via Wikimedia Commons.

Page 54:   *Expansion of the Roman Republic.* Adapted from "The Expansion of the Roman Empire to AD 117" by Undevicesimus.

Page 65:   Cicero Denouncing Catiline in the Senate, *by Cesare Maccari, 1889.* Scala / Art Resource, NY.

Page 70:   *Battle of Adrianople.* Adapted from "Battle of Adrianople" map by North Park University, Chicago.

Page 71:   The Dying Gaul . . . . V Korostyshevskiy / Fotolia.

Page 73:   *Invasions of the Roman Empire, 100–500 CE.* Adapted from "Invasions of the Roman Empire 1" by MapMaster, via Wikimedia Commons.

Page 75:   *The Frankish Kingdom in 741,* . . . Adapted from "le royaume franc a la mort de Pepin le Bref" by Jeux-historiques.com.

Page 77:   *The Empire of Charlemagne in the ninth century.* Adapted from "Charlemagne" by Microsoft® Encarta® 97 Encyclopedia.

Page 80:   Defeat of the Jacquerie, *as described in Froissart's* Chronicles, *fourteenth century.* © Michael Nicholson / Corbis.

Page 82:   *An English infantry shield wall* . . . . jorisvo / Fotolia.

Page 85:   *Warring States and Qin Conquest, 278–221 BC*. Adapted from "The Qin Dynasty, 350–249 BCE" by Infobase Publishing and "Ch'in Dynasty 221–206 BC" by Minneapolis Institute of Arts.

Page 87:   *The unification of Japan, 1560–1600*. Adapted from "The Unification of Japan under Oda Nobunaga and Toyotomu Hideyoshi" by F.W. Seals, The Samurai Archives.

Page 94:   *Cathars being expelled from Carcassonne*. Cott Nero E II pt2 f.20v The expulsion of the Albigensians from Carcassonne: Catharist heretics of the 12th and 13th centuries, from *The Chronicles of France, from Priam King of Troy until the crowning of Charles VI*, 15th century, Boucicaut Master, (fl.1390–1430) (and workshop) / British Library, London, UK / © British Library Board. All Rights Reserved / Bridgeman Images.

Page 96:   *The strongest monarchies emerged in France and Spain, . . .* Supplied by the authors.

Page 102:   *The "Reconquest" of Spain, 722–1492*. Adapted from "The Reconquista (AD 722–1492)" by Undevicesimus.

Page 108:   *Magna Carta*. © World History Archive / Alamy Stock Photo.

Page 115:   *English Civil War, 1642–45*. Adapted from "English civil war map 1642 to 1645" via Wikimedia Commons.

Page 116:   *The 1647 Putney Debates*. © Chronicle / Alamy Stock Photo.

Page 121:   *Dutch East India Company . . . .* Adapted from "Dutch East India Company: Trade Routes and Areas of Dutch Control" by Mapping Specialists, Limited.

Page 123:   *Changes in territorial control during the Dutch Revolt, 1576–98*. Adapted from "Dutch Revolt" by Alexander Ganse, 2001.

Page 125:   The Corpses of the Brothers de Witt, *attributed to Jan de Baen in 1672–75*. Attributed to Jan de Baen, Rijksmuseum, Amsterdam, via Wikimedia.

Page 132:   *Renaissance Italy, 1494*. Adapted from "Italy 1494" by Shadowxfox and derivative work by Enokvia via Wikimedia Commons.

Page 134:   Dante and His Poem, *by Domenico di Michelino, 1465*. Scala / Art Resource, NY.

Page 137:   *Michele di Lando*. Private Collection © Look and Learn / Bridgeman Images.

Page 138:   Cosimo de' Medici, *by Agnolo Bronzino, before 1572*. Scala / Art Resource, NY.

Page 140:   Girolamo Savonarola, *by Alessandro Bonvicino*. Alfredo Dagli Orti / The Art Archive at Art Resource, NY.

Page 141:   The Siege of Florence, *by Giorgio Vasari, c. 1560*. Scala / Art Resource, NY.

Page 145:   *Venice and the Lagoon*. Adapted from "Leguna Veneta" by Norman Einstein via Wikimedia Commons.

Page 146:   *Procedure for electing the doge of Venice*. Supplied by the authors.

Page 147:   *The interior of the Sala Maggior Consiglio*. The Great Council of Venice, *by Joseph Heintz der Jüngere, before 1678*. Bonhams.

Page 153:   *The Holy Roman Empire, circa 1000 AD*. Adapted from "Holy Roman Empire 1000 map" by Sémhur and derivative work by Owen Blacker via Wikimedia Commons.

Page 155:   *The Hanseatic League in 1328*. Adapted from "Kaart Hanzesteden en handelsroutes" by Doc Brown via Wikimedia Commons.

Page 158:   *Free Imperial Cities.* . . . Adapted from "Holy Roman Empire 1648 Imperial Cities" via Wikimedia Commons.

Page 160:   *Partition of the Kingdom of Hungary in 1526.* . . . Adapted from "Partition of Hungary" by Esoltas via Wikimedia Commons.

Page 161:   The 1618 Defenestration of Prague, *by Václav Brožík, 1889. The Defenestration 1618* (oil on canvas), Brozik, Vaclav (Wenzel von) (1851–1901) / National Gallery of Victoria, Melbourne, Australia / Bridgeman Images.

Page 162:   *Wallenstein surveying a scene of devastation in the Thirty Years' War, . . . Wallenstein: A Scene of the Thirty Years War* (oil on canvas), Crofts, Ernest (1847–1911) / Leeds Museums and Galleries (Leeds Art Gallery) U.K. / Bridgeman Images.

Page 167:   *Prussian military success and expansion* . . . . Adapted from "Acprussiamap2" via Wikimedia Commons.

Page 169:   *The Holy Roman Empire in 1789.* Adapted from "HRR 1789 EN" by Robert Alfers, kgberger, via Wikimedia Commons.

Page 173:   *Poland's gridlocked republic of nobles* . . . . Adapted from "Territorial changes of Poland 1699, 1772, 1793 and 1795" by Esemono via Wikimedia Commons.

Page 174:   *Kościuszko rallies his men, holding scythes, against the Russians at Raclawice on April 4, 1794.* © Hemis / Alamy Stock Photo.

Page 181:   *A commemorative postcard depicting Swiss mountain men* . . . . © INTERFOTO / Alamy Stock Photo.

Page 182:   *The gradual expansion of the Swiss Confederation* . . . . Adapted from "Territorial-development-Swiss Confederacy" by Marco Zanoli (Sidonius) via Wikimedia Commons.

Page 184:   *Sixteenth-century engraving of Swiss pikemen by Hans Holbein the Younger.* De Agostini Picture Library / Getty Images.

Page 186:   *This topographical map of today's Switzerland* . . . . Adapted from "Karte-ch" by Erstellt von Srml. via Wikimedia Commons.

Page 190:   *A shrine of the Sacred Heart movement in Tyrol.* Hermann Hammer via Wikimedia Commons.

Page 191:   Napoleon at Great St Bernard Pass *by Edouard Castres. Napoleon at the Great St Bernard Pass*, Scarpelli, Tancredi (1866–1937) / Private Collection / © Look and Learn / Bridgeman Images.

Page 194:   *Young Rommel in Isonzo, 1917.* © Sueddeutsche Zeitung Photo / Alamy Stock Photo.

Page 196:   *The ruins of a fort at Lordat.* Jean-Pierre Pomies, photosariege.com.

Page 206:   The Battle of Valmy, *by Horace Vernet, 1826.* . . . © National Gallery, London / Art Resource, NY.

Page 214:   Fighting at the Hôtel de Ville, July 28, 1830, *by Jean-Victor Schnetz, 1833.* Erich Lessing / Art Resource, NY.

Page 215:   Portrait of Gilbert Motier, the Marquis de Lafayette, as a Lieutenant General, 1791, *by Joseph-Désiré Court, 1834.* © RMN-Grand Palais / Art Resource, NY.

Page 217:   Barricade on the Rue Soufflot, *by Horace Vernet, 1848.* bpk, Berlin / Deutsches Historiches Museum / Arne Psille / Art Resource, NY.

Page 218:   *Troops firing into barricades at Alexanderplatz, Berlin, 1848.* bpk, Berlin / Kunst-bibliothek, Staatliche Museen / Knud Petersen / Art Resource, NY.

Page 219:   Frankfurt Assembly in Paulskirche, 1848, *by Leo von Elliott.* akg-images / Newscom.

Page 223:   The Peterloo Massacre of 1819, *published by Richard Carlile in 1819.* iStock.com / HultonArchive / Photo by Rischgitz/Getty Images.

Page 226:   *Britain and France took the side of the Ottomans . . . .* Adapted from *The Cambridge Modern History Atlas,* Cambridge University Press; London. 1912. University of Texas Libraries.

Page 234:   *Britain's version of "Uncle Sam" was Herbert Kitchener, secretary of state for war.* World History Archive / Newscom.

Page 240:   The Harvest of Battle, *by Christopher Nevinson, 1919.* © Crown Copyright. IWM (Art.IWM ART 1921).

Page 242:   *Lenin speaks . . . . Lenin speaks at the Second Congress of the Communist International, Petrograd, 19 July 1920* (b/w photo), Russian Photographer (20th century) / Private Collection / © Look and Learn / Elgar Collection / Bridgeman Images.

Page 246:   *Norwegian soldiers mobilized at the border with Sweden in 1905.* Narve Skarpmoen / National Library of Norway.

Page 249:   *1918* New York Times *front page . . . .* © John Frost Newspapers / Alamy Stock Photo.

Page 251:   *Hitler and Ernst Röhm . . . .* akg-images/Newscom.

Page 255:   *A 1940 postcard showing the 10,000 kilometers of track of Japan's South Manchuria Railway Company.* South Manchuria Railway Company Ltd.

Page 257:   *Japanese Kamikaze pilots . . . .* bpk, Berlin/Art Resource, NY.

Page 261:   *Captured Chinese soldiers . . . .* National Archives ID# 541956. War and Conflict Number 1496. The U.S. National Archives and Records Administration at College Park.

Page 265:   *A topographical map of the Ardennes . . . .* Adapted from "US Army in World War II—The Ardennes: The Battle of the Bulge," US Government document via Wikimedia Commons.

Page 276:   *A bus station in Durham, North Carolina. . . .* Library of Congress, Prints & Photographs Division, FSA / OWI Collection, [LC-DIG-fsa-00199].

Page 285:   *A memo from Jean L. A. Linard, . . .* Linard, Louis Albert. Concerning black American troops, August 7, 1918. W. E. B. Du Bois Papers (MS 312). Special Collections and University Archives, University of Massachusetts Amherst Libraries.

Page 286:   *The white women's procession in New York, 1917.* The New York Times Photo Archives.

Page 291:   *A Philip Randolph with Eleanor Roosevelt, 1946.* © Bettmann / CORBIS.

Page 300:   *The Reverend Martin Luther King Jr. makes a speech at a church in Selma, Alabama, March 27, 1965.* Joseph Klipple / Getty Images.

Page 301:   *President Lyndon Johnson speaking to Senator Richard Russell, . . .* The U.S. National Archives and Records Administration ID# 192493 by Yoichi R. Okamoto. White House Photo Office Collection, Johnson White House Photographs, 11/22/1963–1/20/1969.

Page 307:   *Terrain, technology, and resources* . . . . Supplied by the authors.

Page 308:   *Dimensions of democracy.* Supplied by the authors.

Page 310:   *Historical junctures in state-types.* Supplied by the authors.

Page 312:   *The military capacity of constitutional forms.* Supplied by the authors.

INDEX

Note: Page numbers in italics refer to figures or accompanying captions.

ABOUT THE AUTHORS

John Ferejohn is the Samuel Tilden Professor of Law at New York University. His primary areas of scholarly interest are political theory and the study of political institutions and behavior. His current research focuses on the American Congress, judicial institutions, law and legislation, constitutional adjudication in the United States and Europe and the developing world, separation of powers, political campaigns and elections, and the philosophy of social science. Before joining the NYU faculty, he had been a professor of social sciences at the California Institute of Technology (1972–83), a professor of political science at Stanford University, and a senior fellow of the Hoover Institution (1983–2009).

Ferejohn earned his PhD at Stanford University (1972), received an honorary doctorate from Yale University (2007), and has held fellowships with the Brookings Institution, the Guggenheim Foundation, the Center for Advanced Study at the University of Illinois, and the Center for the Advanced Study of the Behavioral Sciences at Stanford. He is a member of the American Academy of Arts and Sciences and of the National Academy of Sciences. He is the author of *Pork Barrel Politics* (Stanford University Press, 1974) and a coauthor of *The Personal Vote* (Harvard University Press, 1987), and of *A Republic of Statutes* (Yale University Press, 2010). He has written scores of scholarly articles on political science, economics, and philosophy, and he coedited *Information and Democratic Processes* (University of Illinois Press, 1990), *Constitutional Culture and Democratic Rule* (Cambridge University Press, 2001), and *The New Federalism: Can the States Be Trusted?*

(Hoover Institution Press, 1997). He also serves on the board of trustees of the Russell Sage Foundation and the Brennan Center for Justice and on the editorial boards of several scholarly journals.

Frances McCall Rosenbluth is the Damon Wells Professor of Political Science at Yale University, where she has taught since 1994. Her research focuses on the politics of gender, Japanese politics and diplomacy, and comparative political economy.

Rosenbluth received a PhD from Columbia University (1989) and taught at the University of Virginia (1989–90), the University of California, San Diego (1990–93), and UCLA (1993–94) prior to joining the political science faculty at Yale. Her research has been supported by the National Science Foundation, the Fulbright Foundation, the Japan Foundation, the Social Science Research Council, the John Simon Guggenheim Foundation, the Abe Foundation, and the Council on Foreign Relations. She has been a member of the American Academy of Arts and Sciences since 2007. Her previous books include *Financial Politics in Contemporary Japan* (Cornell University Press, 1989), *Japan's Political Marketplace* (with Mark Ramseyer; Harvard University Press, 1993), *The Politics of Oligarchy* (with Mark Ramseyer; Cambridge University Press, 1995), *Women, Work, and Politics* (with Torben Iversen; Yale University Press, 2010), and *Japan Transformed* (with Michael Thies; Princeton University Press, 2010).